Mastering Serverless Computing with AWS Lambda

Unlock Scalability, Optimize Costs, and Drive Innovation with AWS Lambda Serverless Solutions for Modern Cloud Transformation

Eidivandi Omid

www.orangeava.com

First Published: November 2024

Published By: Orange Education Pvt Ltd, AVA®

Address: 9, Daryaganj, Delhi, 110002, India

275 New North Road Islington Suite 1314 London,
N1 7AA, United Kingdom

ISBN (PBK): 978-93-48107-24-4
ISBN (E-BOOK): 978-93-48107-86-2

Scan the QR code to explore our entire catalogue

www.orangeava.com

Dedicated To

My beloved Wife and Son:

Ghazaleh and Adrien

My First and Beloved Motivation

About the Author

Eidivandi Omid brings over 25 years of experience in the software industry, having worked in key roles such as Developer, Lead Developer, Technical Leader, Software Architect, and Solution Architect. With a Bachelor of Science in Software Engineering, Omid has established himself as a leader in cloud computing, specializing in serverless technologies and event-driven architectures.

Omid holds several prestigious certifications, such as Microsoft Professional Certified Developer, Microsoft Azure Certified Architect, AWS Certified Developer, and AWS Certified Architect. His expertise spans across Azure and AWS platforms, with a strong focus on serverless computing and event-driven design over the past eight years.

Beyond his technical achievements, Omid is deeply committed to leadership and mentorship. He firmly believes that fostering strong leadership and providing the right mentorship are essential for shaping future engineers. He emphasizes the importance of guiding engineers not just in technical knowledge, but also in critical thinking, decision-making, and problem-solving – skills that are crucial for tackling the complexities of modern software development. Omid's mentorship philosophy centers on empowering engineers to become self-reliant and innovative, preparing them to lead the future of technology.

Omid is an active blogger, speaker, and tech community member, sharing insights to help others in their professional journeys. He contributes through blog posts, presentations, and online interactions, focusing on problem-solving and knowledge-sharing for engineers globally. As an international speaker, he frequently discusses Serverless Computing, Distributed System Design, and Event-Driven Architecture. He is also a member of tech communities, including AWS Community Builders, where he advocates for serverless computing and promotes collaboration and continuous learning.

Omid is passionate about music and art, enjoying guitar, singing, and dancing as creative outlets that recharge him. Family is central to his life, providing both inspiration and a strong foundation in everything he does. While he loves coding, he values family above all. Omid's commitment to leadership, mentorship, and community, along with his creative and family-oriented spirit, shapes both his personal and professional life.

About the Technical Reviewer

Chayan Datta is a versatile Software Engineer with nearly 5 years of experience across healthcare, Ed-tech, FinTech, and scientific computing. As a full-stack developer, he excels in creating robust applications, blending technologies such as Python, Django, Vue.js, JavaScript, Julia, and Go. His leadership is evident in his past roles, contributing significantly to the success of various platforms.

Chayan is deeply involved in DevOps, system design, and scalability. His expertise lies not only in building robust applications but also in orchestrating seamless integration between development and operations. With a keen eye for system design, Chayan envisions and implements architectures that prioritize efficiency, reliability, and scalability. His practices ensure smooth collaboration between development and IT operations, fostering a streamlined and agile development pipeline. His commitment to scalability extends beyond individual projects, encompassing a holistic approach to designing systems that can adapt and grow with evolving business needs.

Adhering to coding practices, he ensures project longevity. Understanding front-end and back-end synergy, he crafts user-friendly applications. He understands the crucial interplay between front-end design and back-end functionality, ensuring that the user interface is not only visually engaging but also seamlessly integrated with the underlying system architecture. His holistic approach to software development encompasses a keen awareness of the end-user experience, resulting in applications that not only meet technical requirements but also delight users with their usability and design aesthetics.

Besides work, Chayan contributes to open-source projects and maintains a technical blog, showcasing his commitment to knowledge-sharing and community engagement. He brings a well-rounded perspective to his work, fueled by his avid reading habits and a constant desire to stay updated on the latest industry trends and technologies.

Acknowledgements

This book has been a rewarding journey, and it would not have been possible without the support, insights, and encouragement of many individuals.

First and foremost, I want to thank my family for their unwavering support and patience. Their encouragement during late nights and long weekends provided the energy I needed to keep pushing forward.

A special thanks to the serverless community–the developers, engineers, architects, and enthusiasts–whose collective wisdom and shared experiences have shaped the serverless ecosystem. Their passion and dedication continue to push the boundaries of what is possible in the cloud, and this book is, in many ways, a reflection of their contributions.

I am incredibly grateful to the technical reviewers and colleagues who provided invaluable feedback throughout the writing process. Their thoughtful critiques ensured that the concepts presented here are both clear and technically sound.

Finally, I want to thank you, the reader. Whether you are just beginning your journey with serverless computing or are an experienced professional, I hope this book serves as a useful guide and inspires you to continue exploring and building with AWS Lambda.

Preface

The world of cloud computing has evolved rapidly in recent years, and one of the most transformative innovations has been the emergence of serverless computing. This paradigm shift allows developers and organizations to build and deploy applications without the need to manage servers, enabling a focus on core functionality and business value. At the forefront of this change is AWS Lambda, Amazon's serverless compute service that has redefined how modern cloud applications are built and scaled.

This book, *Mastering Serverless Computing with* AWS *Lambda*, is designed to be a comprehensive guide for anyone looking to understand and leverage AWS Lambda to its fullest potential. Whether you are a cloud architect, developer, or system administrator, this book will help you navigate the complexities and opportunities of serverless architectures, with a specific focus on AWS Lambda.

Each chapter takes you step by step through key concepts and real-world applications, from the foundational principles of serverless computing to advanced topics like scaling, security, and event-driven design. The goal of this book is to provide not only the theoretical background but also practical guidance and patterns to help you make informed decisions when architecting serverless applications.

Here's what you can expect to learn:

Chapter 1. Introduction to Serverless Computing: This chapter introduces the core concepts of serverless architecture, comparing it to traditional cloud models, and exploring its unique benefits and challenges. You will gain an understanding of high-performance computing in serverless environments and key concerns such as vendor lock-in and portability.

Chapter 2. AWS Lambda Basics: This chapter covers everything you need to get started with AWS Lambda, from basic configurations to integrating Lambda functions with other AWS services. It provides a solid foundation on function lifecycle, Firecracker micro-VMs, logging, metrics, and the limits of AWS Lambda.

Chapter 3. Invocation Models and Service Integration: This chapter dives deep into the various invocation models Lambda supports—synchronous, asynchronous, and poll-based—and how they integrate with services like Amazon SQS, SNS, EventBridge, and API Gateway.

Chapter 4. Event-Driven Design with Lambda: This chapter explores how to design event-driven architectures using AWS Lambda. You will learn how asynchronous designs solve synchronous design problems, and how event-driven architectures (EDA) scale while standardizing message-driven systems.

Chapter 5. Hyper-Scaling with Lambda: This chapter focuses on the scalability of Lambda, discussing concurrency bottlenecks, cold starts, and the strategies needed to scale Lambda efficiently. You will learn how to overcome Lambda's scaling limitations and tune performance for hyper-scale applications.

Chapter 6. Instrumenting Lambda: This chapter provides a deep dive into how Lambda instrumentation works, covering versioning, tracing, extensions, and the Lambda Telemetry API. This chapter helps you optimize the observability and performance of your serverless applications.

Chapter 7. Resiliency and Design for Failure: This chapter explains how to build resilient serverless applications, handling failures through retries, dead letter queues, and Lambda Destinations. You will also learn to measure and improve resiliency with appropriate metrics.

Chapter 8. Lambda-Less Design: This chapter challenges the notion that Lambda is always necessary, focusing on direct service integration using API Gateway, Step Functions, and EventBridge Pipes. This chapter shows how to minimize unnecessary complexity by avoiding Lambda when possible.

Chapter 9. Edge Computing: This chapter introduces the concept of edge computing, explaining how Lambda@Edge extends serverless computing to the edge for improved performance and latency. You will also explore the challenges and solutions in designing applications for the edge.

Chapter 10. Patterns and Practices: This chapter concludes the book with essential design patterns and best practices for building scalable, high-performance serverless applications. You will explore advanced use cases like interactive distributed communication, generative AI with serverless, and governance in serverless environments.

Throughout this book, practical insights have been emphasized that will help you navigate the complexities of serverless computing while maximizing the benefits that AWS Lambda offers. From architectural patterns to operational challenges, this book aims to provide a holistic understanding of how to design, build, and scale modern applications using serverless technologies.

Whether you are just getting started with serverless computing or looking to refine your expertise, we hope this book becomes a valuable resource in your journey toward mastering AWS Lambda. We look forward to seeing the innovative solutions you will build as you embrace the future of cloud architecture.

Get a Free eBook

We hope you are enjoying your recently purchased book! Your feedback is incredibly valuable to us, and to all other readers looking for great books.

If you found this book helpful or enjoyable, we would truly appreciate it, if you could take a moment to leave a short review with a 5 star rating on Amazon. It helps us grow, and lets other readers discover our books.

As a thank you, we would love to send you a free digital copy of this book, and a **30%** discount code on your next cart value on our official websites:

www.orangeava.com

www.orangeava.in (For Indian Subcontinent)

☑ **Here's how:**

Leave a review for the book on Amazon.

Take a screenshot of your review, and send an email to **info@orangeava.com** (it can be just the confirmation screen).

Once, we receive your screenshot, we will send you the digital file, within 24 hours.

Thank you so much for your support – it means a lot to us!

Downloading the code bundles and colored images

Please follow the links or scan the QR codes to download the
Code Bundles and Images of the book:

https://github.com/OrangeAVA/Mastering-Serverless-Computing-with-AWS-Lambda

The code bundles and images of the book are also hosted on
https://rebrand.ly/7b3f7b

In case there's an update to the code, it will be updated on the existing GitHub repository.

Errata

We take immense pride in our work at **Orange Education Pvt Ltd,** and follow best practices to ensure the accuracy of our content to provide an indulging reading experience to our subscribers. Our readers are our mirrors, and we use their inputs to reflect and improve upon human errors, if any, that may have occurred during the publishing processes involved. To let us maintain the quality and help us reach out to any readers who might be having difficulties due to any unforeseen errors, please write to us at :

errata@orangeava.com

Your support, suggestions, and feedback are highly appreciated.

DID YOU KNOW

Did you know that Orange Education Pvt Ltd offers eBook versions of every book published, with PDF and ePub files available? You can upgrade to the eBook version at **www.orangeava.com** and as a print book customer, you are entitled to a discount on the eBook copy. Get in touch with us at: **info@orangeava.com** for more details.

At **www.orangeava.com**, you can also read a collection of free technical articles, sign up for a range of free newsletters, and receive exclusive discounts and offers on AVA® Books and eBooks.

PIRACY

If you come across any illegal copies of our works in any form on the internet, we would be grateful if you would provide us with the location address or website name. Please contact us at **info@orangeava.com** with a link to the material.

ARE YOU INTERESTED IN AUTHORING WITH US?

If there is a topic that you have expertise in, and you are interested in either writing or contributing to a book, please write to us at **business@orangeava.com**. We are on a journey to help developers and tech professionals to gain insights on the present technological advancements and innovations happening across the globe and build a community that believes Knowledge is best acquired by sharing and learning with others. Please reach out to us to learn what our audience demands and how you can be part of this educational reform. We also welcome ideas from tech experts and help them build learning and development content for their domains.

REVIEWS

Please leave a review. Once you have read and used this book, why not leave a review on the site that you purchased it from? Potential readers can then see and use your unbiased opinion to make purchase decisions. We at Orange Education would love to know what you think about our products, and our authors can learn from your feedback. Thank you!

For more information about Orange Education, please visit **www.orangeava.com**.

Table of Contents

CHAPTER 1
Introduction to Serverless Computing

Introduction

This chapter provides a detailed overview of serverless computing, computing needs, the applicable designs in different cases and the advantages of each. The chapter delves into the traditional distributed cloud computing and deep dive into some challenges brought by those solutions, briefing how serverless computing overcomes those challenges, including scaling, infrastructure management, performance bottlenecks, and cost optimization.

The Vendor Lock-in concept will be explored to see how and when a cloud provider can be considered as a lock during transformation and afterward. Finally, the chapter puts a fair focus on challenges and complexities of serverless design, despite its well-suited characteristics.

Structure

In this chapter, we will discuss the following topics:

- Serverless at a Glance
- High-Performance and High-Throughput Computing
- Serverless versus Traditional Cloud
- Serverless Computing
- Vendor Lock-In
- Portability in Serverless
- Challenges and Complexities when Designing Serverless

Serverless at a Glance

Defining Serverless computing is an interesting exercise due to the multitude of definitions and varied perspectives surrounding the concept. Different organizations and thought leaders have their own interpretations and nuances of what Serverless means. However, it can be confidently stated that serverless is an economic model primarily focused on minimizing costs associated with ownership and maintenance of technology.

Discussions about Serverless often revolve around its scalability, its cost-effectiveness, and its ability to reduce time-to-market in comparison to self-hosted or managed solutions, even with modern cloud platforms.

To better describe its differentiation, let us examine how Serverless addresses the following challenges:

- Infrastructure Management Overhead
- Scalability
- Development Velocity
- Cost

Infrastructure Management Overhead

Establishing a new infrastructure or foundation for digital platforms can be a lengthy process involving definition, evaluation, and strategic decision-making, particularly in large organizations. Assembling a team of experts and ensuring they are aligned in terms of vision is not a straightforward task. Maintaining and evolving these foundations also require time and effort.

Serverless can alleviate some of these overheads by offering solutions (or delaying some decisions) for some of these initial tasks, albeit sometimes with an opinionated approach.

Moreover, Serverless architectures reduce management overhead by abstracting away the need for server provisioning, scaling, and reduced maintenance.

Scalability

Traditional hosting on managed cloud services or on-premise servers may require teams to provision, manage, and scale servers, storage, and network resources in a more involved approach, leading to a more complex management process. Furthermore, it often requires upfront capacity planning, which involves predicting future demand to provision adequate resources and can lead to over-provisioning (provisioning more than workload requires) or under-provisioning (provisioning less than workload requires) if predictions are off.

In contrast, serverless offerings are specifically designed with scalability as a core feature. They automatically adjust resources based on demand, ensuring that applications can handle varying levels of traffic efficiently. This is often achieved without the need for upfront planning, allowing for a more responsive infrastructure.

As a result, serverless architectures are better equipped to provide a seamless scaling solution for modern applications.

Development Velocity

Traditional managed infrastructure entails responsibilities such as selecting server sizes, managing operating systems, and ensuring security, which can slow down development and deployment as teams need to focus more on infrastructure.

In contrast, serverless computing enables faster development cycles as developers can focus on writing code without worrying about infrastructure management. This leads to a more efficient development process and a shortened feedback loop.

Generally, serverless offerings often provide integration with other services and tools, further accelerating the development process.

Cost

Cost is a very important dimension for organizations when they need to scale. They mostly would like to pay for what brings value to their business. These organizations rely a lot on Return on Investment (ROI) and Total Cost of Ownership (TCO). Companies like to pay for what they consume.

Serverless can help reduce costs by eliminating the need for provisioning and maintaining physical servers, as the cloud providers automatically manage the scaling of resources based on demand. This pay-as-you-go model allows organizations to pay only for the actual computing time and resources used, optimizing expenses and minimizing waste.

Serverless on AWS

In this book, we will delve into the concept of serverless computing, specifically focusing on its implementation within the context of Amazon Web Services (AWS), with a particular emphasis on the AWS Lambda service. We will demonstrate how it can be utilized to build scalable and efficient applications.

We often associate serverless with AWS Lambda, but it is important to note that Lambda is just one, albeit iconic, among numerous serverless solutions offered by AWS.

For example, Amazon Simple Queue Service (SQS) is a serverless message queuing service that enables the decoupling and scaling of microservices. Amazon Simple Storage Service (S3) is another serverless service that provides object storage with a simple API, allowing you to store and retrieve any amount of data at any time. AWS App Runner, AWS Step Functions, and Amazon API Gateway are other examples of serverless services that help you build, deploy, and manage applications without the need to provision or manage servers.

By grounding our discussion in the AWS ecosystem, we aim to provide readers with practical insights and hands-on experience with serverless technologies on one of the leading cloud platforms.

High-Performance and High-Throughput Computing

Serverless solves a wide variety of computational challenges, primarily using Lambda service. However, not all computing needs can be managed by a single service like Lambda. Like all other services, Lambda has its pitfalls and limits. To solve different computing needs, there are other serverless services that can be used to solve these challenges collaboratively with lambda service.

To better understand the computational needs and delve further into this book to see how serverless helps to achieve different computational requirements, it is essential to understand how High-Performance Computing (HPC) and High-Throughput Computing (HTC) systems operate.

Overview

The HPC and HTC models are two design approaches to tackle computational problems. Both of these designs are valuable in their own place and can live alone or coexist as complementary to each other.

Computing is the core of any digital design, but choosing the right design is all about trade-offs and needs to be considered based on the priorities over the design principle pillars, such as performance, scalability, reliability, cost, and operational requirements at the core.

High-Performance Computing

High-performance computing describes systems with a higher need for computing power, such as Data processing or Simulations. In HPC design, we mostly rely on compute processors and nodes as the power of computation, and resource sharing and division as the power of parallelization. The HPC systems need mastery of computation and an understanding of how the process behaves. These are highly attached to a programming model, and not a programming language, but differ from traditional computing systems. In HPC, the parallel processes share some information while computing, introducing a tight coupling that is essential for the success of the process.

In modern HPC, based on needs and coupling, the process relies on distributed communication over the network. So, for a successful and reliable process, a high-speed and reliable network is necessary. While the network can be reliable, the doubt around its reliability brings overhead and needs good supervision and maintenance effort.

HPC Systems Characteristics

Here are some of the characteristics of HPC systems:

- **Speed**: The HPC systems can perform computational treatments at a high speed due to their utilization of resources such as Processes and Tasks.
- **Parallelism**: In HPC systems, parallel models are highly used to accelerate and achieve result accuracy at a higher rate by resource sharing at processor scope.
- **Throughput**: HPC scales well at the computational level with its sole consideration on how to achieve consistent and accurate results at the workload level. However, HPC cannot scale well with high throughput with a precise time metric.

Figure 1.1 illustrates a typical HPC system on AWS:

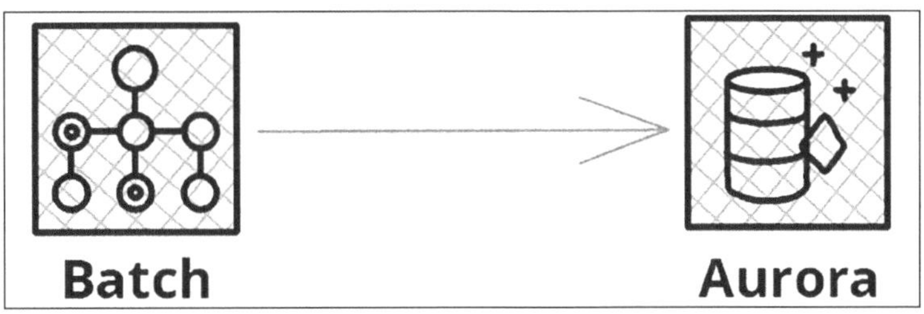

Figure 1.1: *Typical HPC system on AWS*

High-Throughput Computing

High-Throughput computing describes systems that can treat too many tasks in parallel with a high rate of throughput at a given time. In HTC, scaling can be achieved well by using an arrangement of distributed nodes shaping a cluster. HTC systems have the capacity to be easily adopted and bring a higher level of flexibility in contrast to HPC systems. In HTC, the processes are decoupled and act independently; any process can use a different runtime.

HTC Systems Characteristics

Here are some of the characteristics of HTC systems:

- **Throughput**: HTC systems, due to their core design, can handle many demands at a given time. They benefit from computational nodes in a distributed way to better handle the high rate of demands.
- **Parallelism**: HTC helps to obtain parallel processing using a collection of computing nodes shaping a cluster. These clusters allow the system to go beyond normal needs and treat demands in a stateless and distributed manner.
- **Reliability**: HTC runs small tasks in a distributed way, so the overall system has a high level of reliability due to the separation of running tasks, ensuring that no single task will affect the overall process reliability.

Figure 1.2 shows a typical HTC system on AWS:

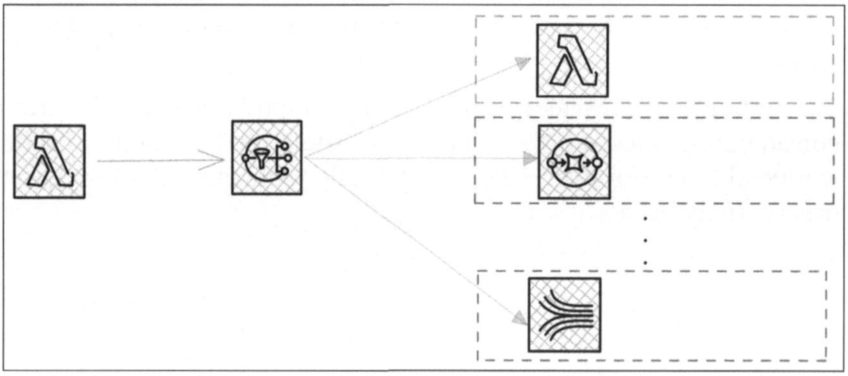

Figure 1.2: *Typical HTC system on AWS*

Serverless versus Traditional Cloud

A growing number of organizations are embracing the cloud or are in the process of transitioning their workloads into the cloud. This shift is driven by the cloud's operational model and its ability to accelerate innovation and growth. Transitioning to the cloud allows organizations to eliminate the challenges associated with managing data centers, resources, and costs.

When it comes to adopting serverless computing, there are often debates comparing on-premises hosting versus serverless. However, we believe that this isn't the most effective way to assess the advantages of serverless adoption.

A better and more simplified approach for a meaningful evaluation involves comparing:

- On-premises hosting versus Traditional cloud hosting
- Traditional cloud hosting versus Serverless

By following this approach, we can gain a more comprehensive and insightful perspective as we navigate the evaluation process.

Advantages of Cloud Hosting Compared to On-Premises Hosting

Here are some of the advantages of Cloud Hosting in comparison to On-premises Hosting:

- **Operational versus Capital Expense**: Moving from Capital Expenses (CapEx) toward Operational Expense (OpEx) means you no longer need to pay in advance for any underlying infrastructure; instead, you pay based on operational activities.
- **Elasticity**: You can reduce the effort spent on estimating your application's capacity requirements upfront. Instead, you can easily implement horizontal scaling with simplified capacity planning and system configuration activities. Resources will then be dynamically allocated, scaling in and out based on your runtime requirements.
- **Global infrastructure**: You can go globally from one geographical location (region) to another and all just within a short period.
- **TTM**: Reducing TTM (Time-to-Market) by focusing more on application and business constraints than infrastructure.
- **Economy at scale**: By using the cloud and benefiting from its shared infrastructure design, you move closer to Pay-per-Consumption billing mode as the infrastructure is highly shared between customers with high-security considerations.
- **Innovation**: The cloud fosters innovation by offering faster access to computing resources and services compared to traditional on-premises hosting environments, enabling businesses to quickly scale and experiment without the limitations of physical hardware. The cloud's agility enables quicker deployment and testing of new applications and services, accelerating development cycles and enabling companies to rapidly iterate and innovate.

Advantages of Serverless Compared to Traditional Cloud

Here are some of the advantages of Serverless in comparison to Traditional Cloud:

- **Adaptive Scaling**: Many serverless solutions automatically scale according to demand, ranging from zero to peak demand and inversely based on your runtime needs. As a result, capacity planning activities are even less involved compared to traditional cloud.

- **Pay-per-consumption**: Serverless computing offers an attractive billing model, where you typically pay for your actual consumption. This cost-effectiveness benefits businesses and increases motivation for adopting serverless. Sometimes, a recurrent fee may apply, but it still proves advantageous compared to the management overhead associated with traditional infrastructure.
- **Software Quality**: With serverless, we can expect improved software quality because the focus shifts from configuring infrastructure to building applications. This shift allows development teams to concentrate more on writing high-quality code and implementing features, resulting in more robust and efficient applications that better serve the end users.
- **Even more Improved TTM**: Serverless computing improves even more TTM (Time to market) by eliminating operational overhead, allowing for more agility through iterative releases, and tightening the feedback loop.

Moving to the Cloud

In the previous section, we have seen that Cloud hosting offers numerous advantages over on-premises hosting. However, this can be just the beginning of a migration journey toward the Cloud. By choosing a more comprehensive strategy, we can further optimize our cloud migration with the 6 R's of the cloud migration framework:

- Re-host
- Re-platform
- Re-purchase
- Re-factor
- Retain
- Retire

The decision to migrate to the cloud or retain a solution on-premises is a significant one, and we won't delve deeper into it in this book. However, it's crucial to ensure that your decision brings long-term value to the enterprise.

Agronomy of Traditional Computational Cloud Solutions

Let us create a visual representation to make it more comprehensive for anyone.

Here, we are exploring four application deployments in a single region of cloud providers.

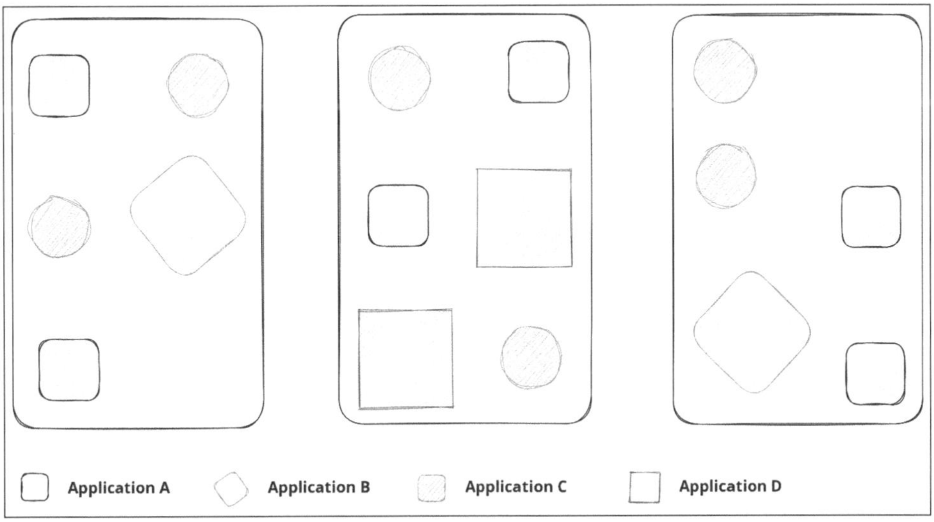

Figure 1.3: *Traditional cloud computing solutions*

Let us suppose these four applications use the EC2 compute platform along with autoscaling groups and for some multi-AZ deployment:

- **Application #A, #C**: Both are deployed in three availability zones with autoscaling configured for a minimum desired capacity of three. Whenever their peak load grows or a failure occurs, there will be other nodes going up to respond to the application need.
- **Application #B**: It is deployed in a large instance configured in two availability zones with a minimum desired capacity of one. Whenever the peak raises or a failure happens in the first instance, a second instance will be initiated in a secondary availability zone.
- **Application #D**: It is deployed in a single availability zone with a minimum desired capacity of two instances. In case of growth or failure, another instance will be initiated in the same availability zone.

Note: *An availability zone (AZ) is a physically isolated data center within a cloud provider's geographic region, designed to enhance redundancy and high availability by ensuring that if one zone experiences an outage, services can failover to another.*

Issues to addresse

This design could certainly be improved, as it has some issues, including:

- **Fault tolerance**: When it comes to autoscaling and high availability, it is crucial to ensure that any critical workload is prepared for any type of failure. This includes software failures, resource failures, and availability zone failures.

In our example, Application D has two nodes in a single availability zone that impacts the fault tolerance pillar of his solution.

- **Provisioning**: Determining the required software resources can be challenging, and over-provisioning presents its own set of problems for Applications B and D.

There are no one-size-fits-all best practices for provisioning resources, as it depends on the workload running on the node. While you can optimize your resource provisioning, doing so requires analyzing workload metrics, which means you need initial provisioning and subsequent monitoring of the metrics, or automating the metric analysis.

There are services on AWS, like AWS Compute Optimizer, that help you in this analysis and provide recommendations for optimizing your workloads.

In our example, whether all four applications are highly available or not, achieving a design based on well-architected pillars requires continuous refinement. It is essential to monitor any solution in real-time, anticipate new behaviors, and always be prepared to reassess the scaling, performance, and cost requirements to better align with the business needs.

Agronomy of Serverless Computing Solutions

Let us now have a look at a serverless deployment using AWS Lambda:

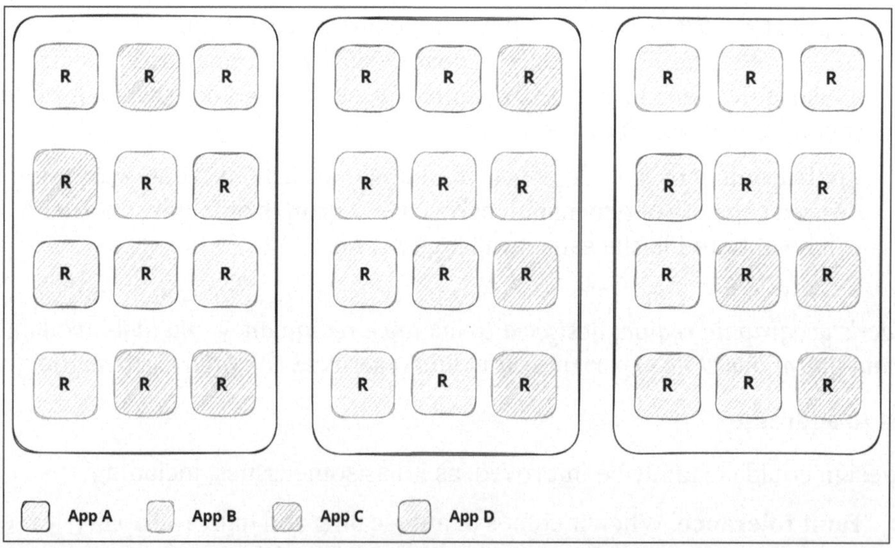

Figure 1.4: *Serverless computing solutions*

Each request is executed in a micro container with its own runtime environment and execution context. After fulfilling a request, the container is *'frozen'* to preserve the same context, and '*thawed*' again when the same context experiences a new request. If no request is happening for a certain period of time, the micro container will be shut down and cleaned, freeing up resources for other customer needs.

All the aspects related to AZ, Networking, Scaling, and more, are handled under the hood. Customers are not involved in these under-the-hood decisions.

AWS Lambda naturally facilitates the sharing of underlying infrastructure, which is how it helps reduce unnecessary resource consumption. The reason some folks consider serverless a great candidate for sustainability is its attractive economic model.

Design Comparability

Let us start by examining two simple design diagrams to better understand two distinct designs. Later, we will discuss the differences between them based on important design pillars.

Figure 1.5 shows the traditional design of a three-tier application:

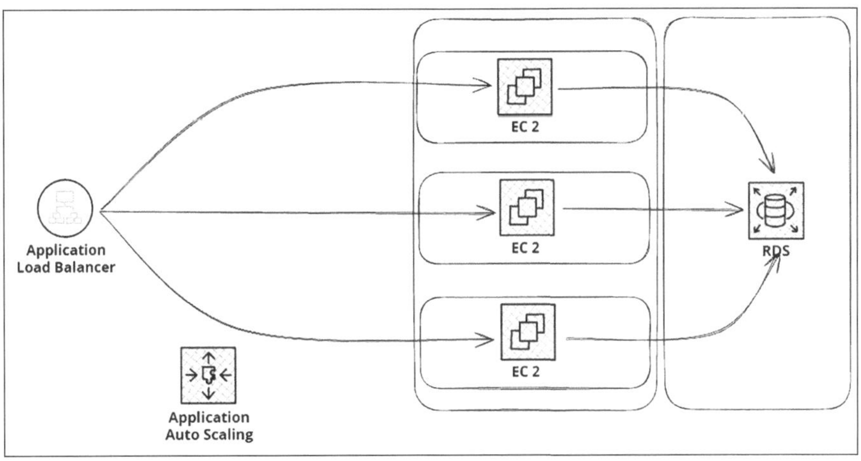

Figure 1.5: *Traditional design of a three-tier application*

Figure 1.6 shows the Serverless design for a three-tier application:

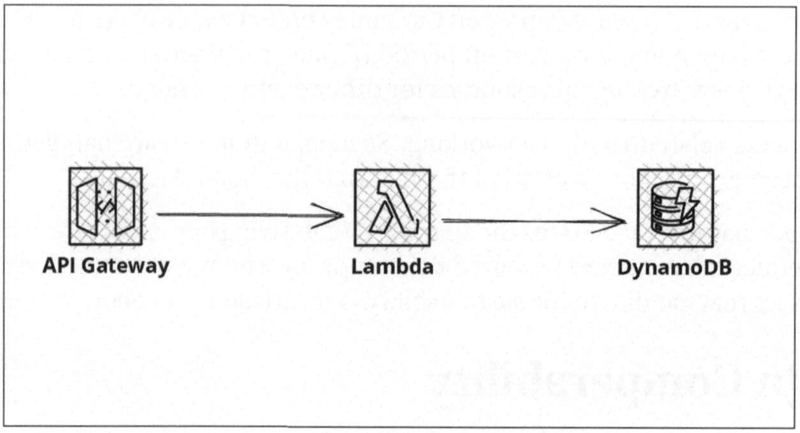

***Figure 1.6**: Serverless design for a three-tier application*

- **High Availability**: Both Serverless and Traditional cloud designs can achieve high availability, but there are some key distinctions to highlight.

  In the traditional cloud design, high availability can be attained through configurations such as multi-AZ setups. However, even when the workload has zero or very low demand, you still pay for some level of resource usage.

  This is where serverless becomes compelling due to its '*Scale to 0*' capability. When designing serverless solutions, you rarely have to consider the High Availability pillar, and in many scenarios, there is no need to configure high availability for your solutions.

  Serverless services are inherently designed with high availability in mind and managed by the service provider, so you can trust the service guidelines and your design remains highly available without extra effort.

- **Fault Tolerance**: Another crucial aspect of design is fault tolerance. A system's design must respond gracefully to failures without impacting the workload or causing degradation in other parts of the system. This can be achieved with both serverless and classic designs, but there are some significant differences in how it is implemented.

  The traditional design uses health checks and load balancing to achieve fault tolerance. You need to define deployment across multiple Availability Zones (AZ's) and have a load balancer that distributes the load across all the instances with health checks configured.

  The serverless design achieves the same fault tolerance with a different conceptual model. In the serverless model, each single request is handled by a single container, called a Micro-VM. The queue of requests does not occur at the instance or container level but rather within the AWS Lambda service, which is highly available and fault-tolerant.

A failure at the container level will impact only one request, and the Lambda service will replace that container if any inconsistent situation is detected. This means that you only need to set up your application code, and all fault tolerance aspects are managed by AWS.

- **Cost**: Cost is also an important design pillar. In traditional design, it is necessary to study the workload and identify the pricing model that best fits that workload. This means there is always a trade-off between performance and cost, and you need to reassess your decisions if any changes occur. To achieve a fair balance between performance and cost, you need to estimate upfront or perform reserved instance calculations to overcome high expenses.

  In traditional design, there is often a waste of money since your workload does not have a 24/7 demand. To combat this and optimize costs, it is essential to first examine the total cost of ownership (TCO). This includes evaluating costs such as workload costs, operational costs, monitoring costs, time costs, maintenance costs, and more. In serverless architectures, we benefit from a "*Pay as you go*" billing model and a "*Scale to 0*" approach, where costs are generally reduced to zero when there is no demand.

- **Scaling**: Scalability is one crucial aspect of design these days, which means your design needs to respond to any change in terms of load.

  In traditional design, we use auto-scaling that can be configured per some metrics such as CPU consumption. Let's say, we consider the need for a new instance when the instance CPU consumption reaches 75% of the available CPU, this means that during high load or any unpredictable peak, we go beyond actual capacity and will be able to handle that load. However, what if we set the threshold to 95%? Can our workload be consistent between 75 and 95? How do we detect which part of the software consumes extra resources? Is it because of higher throughput, or is it because of database latency?

  The responses to all of these questions are based on workload and how the workload behaves in different situations.

In summary, with the traditional design, we easily reach a stale state where provisioning and configurations no longer respond to our needs. This needs a continuous observability system and resource monitoring.

In serverless design, managed services are auto-scaled, so there is no need to estimate the needs of resource consumption based on different situations or states of load. Simply, in serverless, the load of the system relies on the concurrency level. The number of demands will be presented as the number of concurrent executions, and the concurrency limits are set per second. So, if your container executes faster, the chance of more treatment per seconds will be better.

Serverless Computing Operational

Serverless computing relies on a network of distributed stateless containers that are isolated and ephemeral. A container is responsible for handling a single request at a given time, indicating no concurrent execution at the container level. This behavior has implications for the underlying infrastructure. Serverless containers are fast at the initialization phase, and the execution phase performance depends on the code that runs inside that container and its level of optimization.

Figure 1.7 demonstrates how a serverless container responds to a single request:

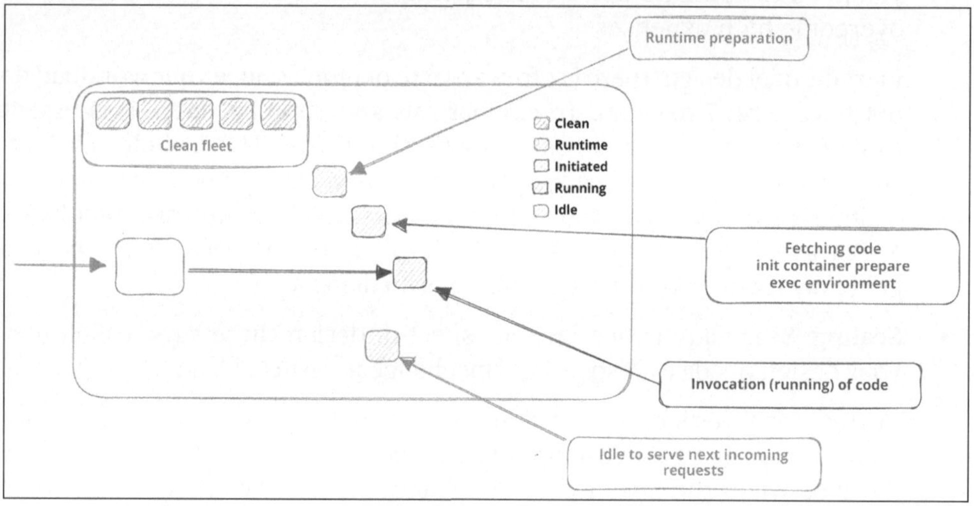

Figure 1.7: *Response of a serverless container to a single request*

Serverless introduces a pay-per-consumption, but it also works well in a design that allows running for consumption. This means you can simply avoid running unnecessary workloads to verify or detect any pending data and treat them. Instead, this relies on an integration concept where any compute container will be initiated and executed when something happens, with a configured trigger to treat that fact.

Figure 1.8 shows how serverless computing can be configured to respond to demand in real-time:

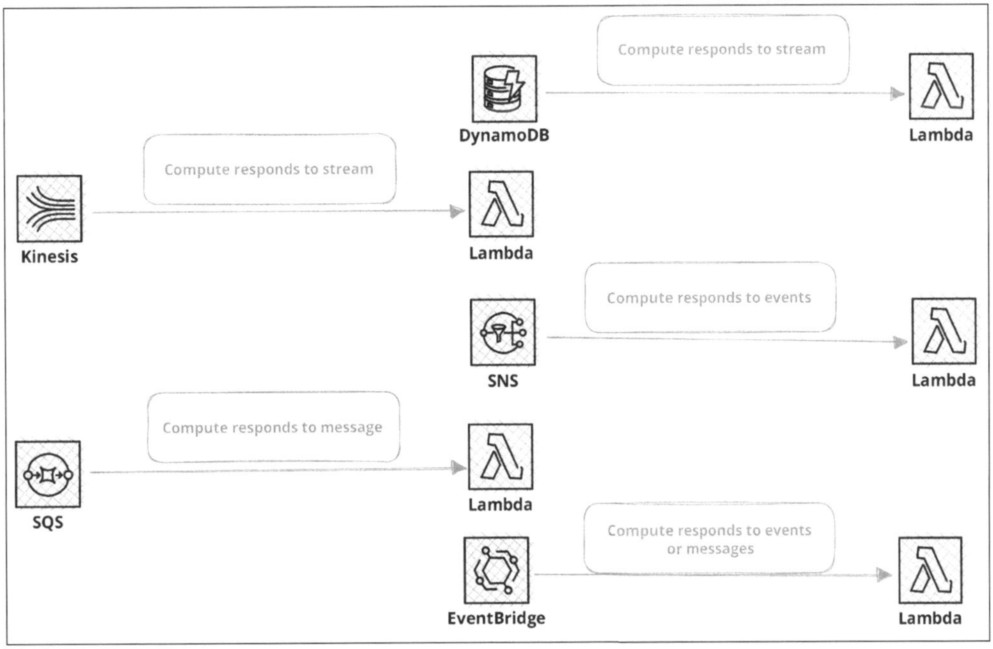

Figure 1.8: *Configuring serverless computing to respond to real-time demand*

Scalability of serverless computing can go beyond software needs, and we can achieve hyper scaling with serverless functions easily by respecting some simple guidelines. In contrast to responding to many demands, serverless can scale down to zero when there is no demand.

The scalability of serverless functions is based on the concurrency level, which is a metric over time axis, the time represents "*at a given time*" dimension and simultaneous operations. To achieve higher scalability, we need to optimize our application code and configuration to make that part of the system better performing. On the other side of the concurrency level, another limitation that applies to scalability is throughput.

To better understand the scalability of serverless functions, we first need to understand the concurrency and throughput.

Throughput: It is the limit of allowed executions per second, which means the requests per second (RPS).

Figure 1.9: *Throughput metric overview*

Concurrency: It is the number of demands running simultaneously at a given time. The concurrency level varies based on how the running functions behave.

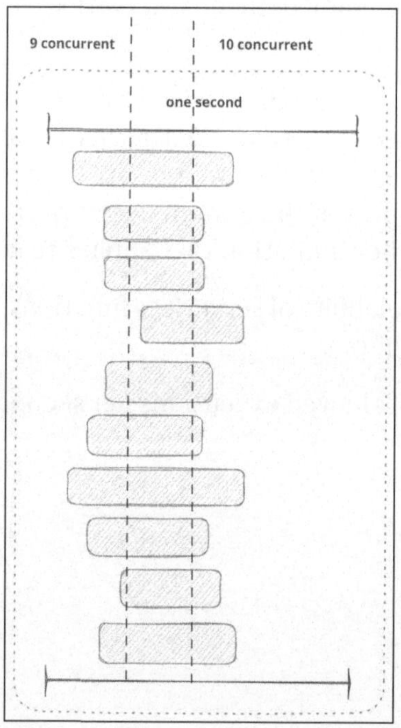

Figure 1.10: *Concurrency metric overview*

The best approach to achieve better scalability is to optimize the throughput by increasing the number of treatments by concurrency level during the limit of the throughput time unit. As an example, if you have a concurrency limit of 10 and a throughput of 10 RPS, this means that the function execution duration is about 1 second. By optimizing the function, you can obtain more executions per second, leading to a higher level of throughput. We will cover more about concurrency optimization in *Chapter 5, Hyper-Scaling with Lambda.*

Vendor Lock-In

Vendor lock-in is a well-known concern when adopting serverless, with many people fearing that moving to serverless ties them to a specific vendor's ecosystem. The question arises: is this a good, bad, or unsubstantiated argument?

Before making any concrete decision, some questions should be answered to clarify our direction.

- Can moving to other solutions keep you safe and out of the vendor ecosystem?
- Is adopting "*cloud agnostic*" deployment like using containers a better strategy?
- What is the effort of not to be locked versus get out of lock?

We firmly believe that serverless can address most use cases, and the level of vendor lock-in can be mitigated with smart design choices and development practices.

Let us look at container service at a high level:

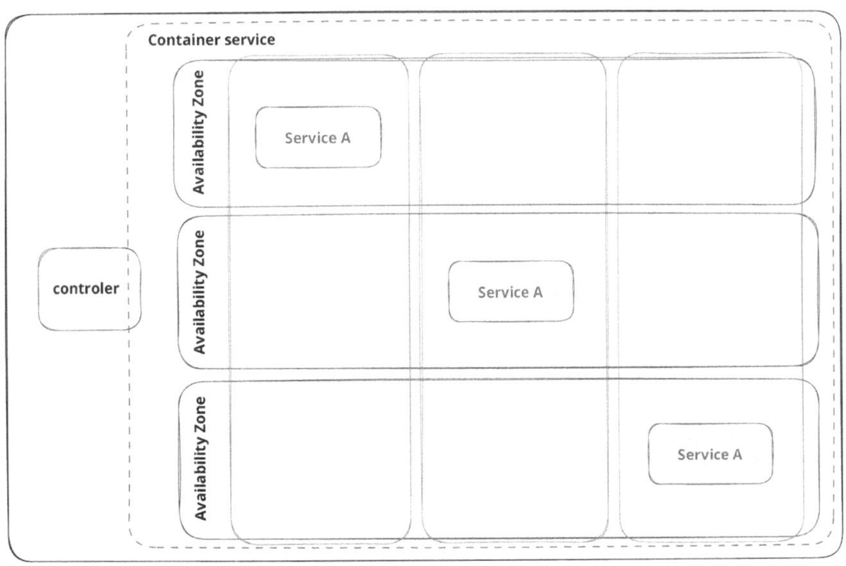

Figure 1.11: *Containers operational overview*

Here, let us look at AWS lambda service:

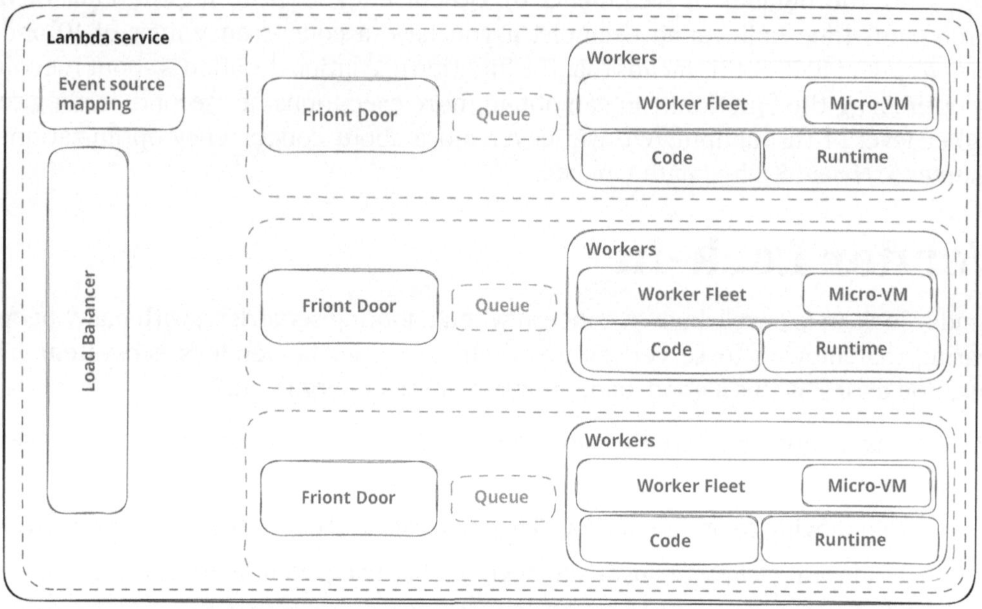

Figure 1.12: *Lambda operational overview*

Comparing the two approaches when using containers, you need to consider all the details depicted in the schema, with the exception of the controller (coordinator). In contrast, the AWS Lambda service provides an abstraction that simplifies the complexity associated with containers. It is essential to be fair during the design phase and choose a container design when it is best suited for a specific use case. However, in this discussion, we are focusing on exploring what AWS Lambda offers and how this abstraction can lead to cost savings during the design and development phase.

The Exact Meaning of Vendor Lock-In

Lock-in refers to a situation where a business ecosystem is tightly bound to a vendor ecosystem, making it difficult or costly to transition from one vendor to another.

What about containers or VM-level design?

For more than a decade, major cloud providers such as Microsoft, Amazon Web Services, and Google Cloud have been offering cloud platforms with a variety of services covering Computing, Orchestration, AI/ML, Data, and integration needs. While the solutions provided by these vendors are not exactly the same, they do offer similar features. Their engineering teams strive to provide the best solutions based on their internal integration practices, which is a common approach across platforms.

The Locked-In Time

Lock-in is not just an ecosystem matter; it's also a mental one. As engineering leaders, when making decisions about technologies, we weigh our decisions based on different axes. Ideally, we should separate the base axis from the trade-offs. A trade-off may not be a strong argument, as it evolves based on the situation and timing. An argument around trade-offs may no longer be relevant in the future.

Any solution based on any technology can be designed in a way that can be easily moved from one vendor to another or from one technology decision to another. What truly matters is the business process, not the technology.

Technology's Unlocking Power

Every technology is based on scientific research and important pillars that the tech giants try to optimize or achieve. This means adopting serverless or any kind of technology will never be an obstacle against your autonomy, and the Serverless approach is not an exception.

You only get locked-in in the case a technology is not equally provided by known and economic vendors. Today serverless is one of the major ecosystems provided and maintained around the same philosophy by AWS, Microsoft, and GCP (among others). Thus, moving from one vendor to another vendor is not a fair argument for abandoning the serverless adoption.

Portability in Serverless

Referring back to the *Serverless versus Traditional Cloud* section where we discussed some of the *modern software advantages*, we mentioned portability as '*A component must not be dependent on underlying infrastructure configuration or standards.*' But what exactly does this mean in practice?

Let's examine a typical serverless solution where the design includes various serverless services as well as Lambda functions.

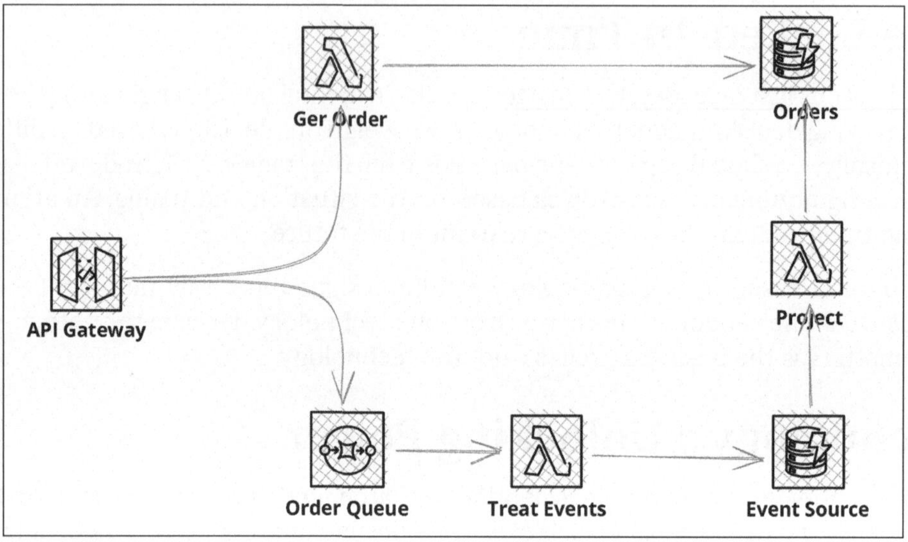

Figure 1.13: *Typical serverless solution*

In this design, the microservice accepts an order and listens to all commands related to an order. Upon receiving a command, it is processed by a Lambda function. The Lambda function checks the most recent event state of the order and registers the event and event state in a DynamoDB table (Event write source). The DynamoDB stream captures this change and updates the Orders table (Read source) with the result.

Let us ask ourselves some questions:

- Which part of this design is the core of the solution?
- Where is the business logic implemented?
- What are these arrows and boxes (service icons)?

There is no one-size-fits-all approach, you need to evaluate your design segments and parts, think about the priorities behind each part, and define the core elements based on the higher scores that you give.

In our example:

- Process events handle state validation and verification, so it's a core functionality.
- The projection feeds the orders table.
- Event ordering is important, so we need a queue with FIFO characteristics.
- Ideally, we prefer an event store with a change data capture (CDC) feature.
- We need an API Gateway with a Rest feature set.

Now that we have a list of critical elements of our design, let's first move it to a container-based solution.

Moving to a container system like Elastic Container Service (ECS) is the simplest part as we can continue integrating with the same database, queuing, and API management services.

The only challenging part is changing the bundles per lambda code into a code building and packaging.

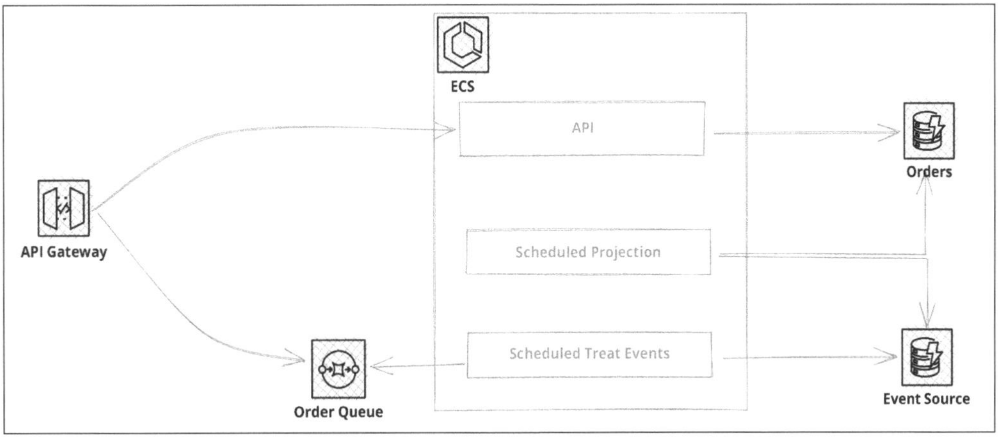

Figure 1.14: *Container-based solution*

Here, we simply moved our principal design into a container-based solution.

How could we easily move Lambda Function code into an ECS Task?

One solution is to build the system by following the Clean principles at design and coding level:

- Critical and core features should be implemented in a core layer and should not be coupled with Lambda handlers and Storage.
- The core of the application should not be aware of the underlying infrastructure or Database Engine.
- Changes need to be defined in driving adapters, and the core should be designed based on ports for communicating with the infrastructure layer.

By following some design best practices, portability is not the hardest aspect to achieve; it simply requires adhering to established principles and some practical conventions.

Challenges and Complexities when Designing Serverless

Serverless is a significant advancement in application architectures, but it also brings its own complexities and challenges that need to be mitigated. Even though Serverless architectures shift the responsibility model of digital solutions by transferring all the infrastructure complexities to the cloud provider, some aspects related to the deployment of serverless workloads need to be addressed properly.

Figure 1.15 illustrates a simple software that handles computing, storage, messaging, and networking in a single node:

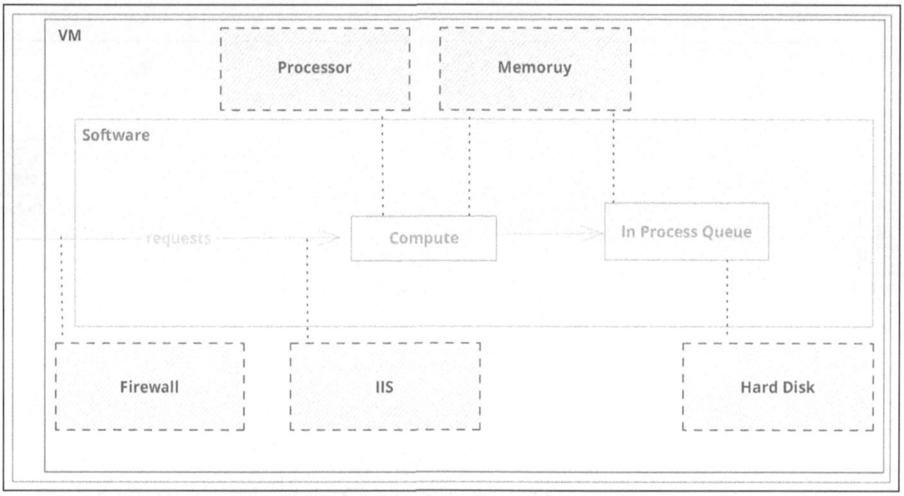

Figure 1.15: *Overview of a software handling computing, storage, messaging, and networking in a single node*

This diagram gives an idea of how a software co-hosts side by side of kernel and core server components.

Let's see what we consider as problems:

- A single node manages all the underlying parts such as firewall, HDD, reverse proxy, and more.
- Scalability becomes a real pitfall, hard and impossible.
- Any category-level failure impacts the whole node.
- The software lifecycle is attached to underlying infrastructure and core services.
- The node acts as a front door and this becomes really hard to keep failures transparent for consumers.

How Services Decomposition Works

The previous figure can be decoupled, as illustrated in *Figure* 1.16, using multiple services in a distributed manner.

AWS offers a higher number of services in a variety of service categories. We can use SQS for messaging, Lambda for computing, API Gateway for the front door, and WAF (web application firewall) for security.

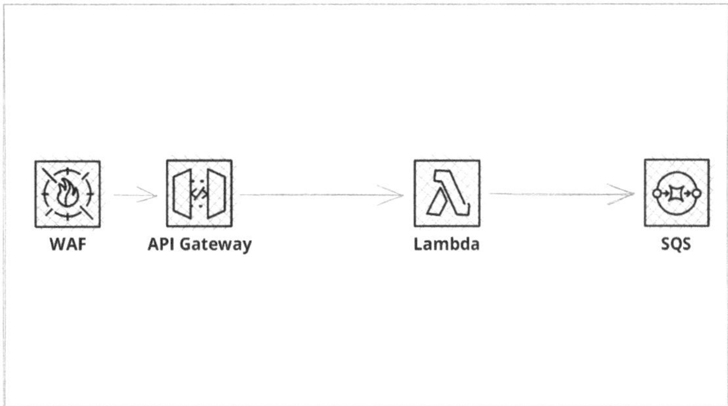

Figure 1.16: AWS *service categories*

- The security checks are separate from the application Core, providing a dedicated layer of protection to the design.
- The API Gateway reduces the attack surface.
- The Lambda service provides the necessary computing resources for the software code to run.
- SQS ensures a highly available queue with a retention-based durability assurance of up to 14 days.

How Serverless Adds Complexity

The preceding example of decomposing a single node breaks down software into a simple serverless design. While its simplicity is a plus, it also introduces a learning curve.

Here are some challenges of serverless:

- **Choosing the Right Service**: The number of serverless services offered is quite extensive. When constructing a serverless architecture, we often encounter multiple services that appear to solve the same problem. However, upon closer inspection, we uncover specific details that aid in selecting the most suitable service. In the realm of AWS, when considering serverless computing, our two main options are AWS Lambda and Fargate.
- **Learning Curve**: Given the diverse range of services in the serverless ecosystem, this also becomes a lengthy journey of learning and educating our teams about the various services. Fortunately, there are numerous learning resources available today, and AWS and the AWS community are strongly focused on accelerating the learning phase for customers. They provide online platforms such as Skill Builder, Virtual Workshops, Serverless Land (https://serverlessland.com), and numerous YouTube channels like Serverless Hours, This is My Architecture, and more.

- **Integration Complexity**: As mentioned, the serverless ecosystem consists of a large number of fine-grained, autonomous, and highly available services. However, placing all these services side by side introduces the challenge of integration. In the simplest terms, integration refers to the ability to establish a connection between two services. The complexity arises from the fact that not all services are integrated in the same manner due to their technical designs, which can make adopting new services challenging at first.
- **Limitations**: Most serverless services have quotas and limits that are generally high enough to cover a variety of business use cases. However, these limits can become a bottleneck when your business requirements exceed what AWS offers. In such situations, we often re-evaluate the business requirements or consider how to redesign the solution to better fit the serverless model. These limitations are usually quite high, depending on the service. For example, AWS SQS allows up to 120,000 messages in flight, which is a significant number, and SQS offers an unlimited number of messages per queue. This means you can send an unlimited number of messages but can only process a maximum of 120,000 messages at any given time. Meanwhile, services like AWS Lambda have per-account/region limits. The Lambda service allows up to 1,000 concurrent executions in a single region/account, but this is a soft limit that can be increased.
- **Pricing versus Cost**: The Serverless pricing model is attractive, but it can become challenging if you lose control over your costs. For example, if you run a serverless solution based on AWS Lambda that is under heavy load 24/7 with 1,000 requests per second (RPS), this can become a real problem in terms of cost. In such cases, we need to ask two questions: Is the chosen computing service the best choice for our needs? Should we allow all this load to reach our solution, or can we manage it more effectively?

The first step is to explore alternative solutions and weigh the trade-off between budget and maintenance costs. For our example, Fargate on AWS ECS could be a good fit, but it does introduce a slightly increased maintenance burden.

Conclusion

In this chapter, we aimed to achieve a better understanding of serverless and the challenges that can be addressed through this tactical decision. We explored how the serverless ecosystem can overcome the traditional designs and improve some important pillars of a well-architected design.

In the upcoming chapter, we will delve into the AWS serverless ecosystem and how a wide range of services can be integrated with AWS Lambda service. We will also explore some race conditions that can arise from different integration types and focus on effective strategies for their better care and management.

CHAPTER 2
AWS Lambda Basics

Introduction

This chapter helps us understand the initial building blocks for creating AWS Lambda functions and how the function execution environment behaves at runtime. We explore the AWS Lambda service, types of Function as a service provided in the AWS ecosystem and a bit about Lambda service internal composition. We discover the details about Lambda configurations and how to configure a simple function using AWS CDK. Additionally, we explore the available information at runtime during function execution. As a must have, we explore how to set up a new project using SAM CLI or manually, and how to prepare and use code bundling as part of the development and integration phase.

The chapter also delves into the function and execution lifecycle and how firecracker works behind the scenes. It provides a high-level overview of these details to help readers have a better understanding of the Lambda service and benefits that this serverless computing service provides.

Structure

In this chapter, we will discuss the following topics:

- AWS Lambda Service
- Obligatory Hello World Handler
- Local Development
- Configuring Functions
- Logs and Metrics
- An Overview to Firecracker
- Execution Environment Lifecycle
- AWS Lambda Limits

Understanding AWS Lambda Service

Lambda is a **Function-as-a-Service (FaaS)** serverless offering by Amazon Web Services, released in 2014. The initial goal of this service was to relieve developers of the burden of server maintenance and configuration, enabling development teams to focus on building applications rather than dealing with infrastructure. Lambda functions were initially designed to respond to event-based integrations with other AWS services like DynamoDB and S3. However, today, Lambda has a much broader scope of usage, including IoT, backend services, frontend components (micro frontends), event streaming, and event-driven services.

AWS Lambda is exceptionally well-suited for systems with sporadic or unpredictable workloads, as well as for event-driven architectures. AWS Lambda offers support for a range of runtimes and introduces the concept of custom runtimes, allowing you to use runtimes not yet natively supported by AWS.

Types of Functions

Lambda service offers actually three type of functions, including:

- Lambda Function
- Lambda Edge
- CloudFront Function

Lambda Function

This is the fundamental category of AWS Lambda, widely used for both regional and multi-region solutions. Lambda functions execute customer-defined code through synchronous or asynchronous invocations and support multiple runtimes, including high-level languages such as Node.js, Java, C#, and more. These Lambda functions are executed under the `` `lambda.amazonaws.com` `` service.

Lambda Edge

`Lambda@Edge` functions are a specific type of functions with a limited runtime, supporting only Node.js and Python. These functions are executed at edge-optimized locations within the AWS global infrastructure. They are primarily designed for executing workloads at the edge, but can be also used for request or response validation and transformation. **`Lambda@Edge`** functions come with a more constrained configuration compared to standard Lambda functions and are executed under the edgelambda.amazonaws.com service.

CloudFront Functions

AWS has enhanced edge-optimized computing by introducing CloudFront Functions, which streamline lightweight edge-level processing. However, this service does come with specific limitations, such as restricted access to the request body and support for only a low-level JavaScript runtime.

Runtimes

AWS Lambda provides support for multiple programming languages through the runtime environments. A runtime serves as an execution stage for a specific programming language ensuring that the function code meets the minimum language-specific requirements to obtain the processing purpose. However, it's important to note that runtimes do not include external dependencies required for a particular use case, these dependencies must be supplied alongside the code bundle. As an example, the `moment` package for Node.js is not provided by runtime, so that must be provided as part of the bundle.

At the time of writing, the AWS Lambda service supports following runtimes:

- Nodejs (nodejs18, nodejs20)
- C# (dotnet6, dotnet8)
- Python (python3.9, python3.10, python3.11, python3.12)
- Ruby (ruby3.2, (ruby3.3)
- Java (java8, java11, java17, java21)

Deprecation Phase

AWS Lambda has two deprecation phases: Phase 1 and Phase 2. A deprecation means end of support of that runtime so there will be no possibility of creating new functions with that runtime by the end of Phase 1 and no more updates of existing functions or creating new ones by the end of Phase 2. This is how it's introduced in AWS lambda runtime documentation.

Runtime Updates

AWS Lambda has the possibility to upgrade automatically to patch and minor version updates. This is an option of configuration for any individual function. For the major version updates, you need to upgrade it by your own and validate all possible breaking changes and the correct operation of your function code. We will discover more in the *Configuring Lambda* Section.

Custom Runtime

A custom runtime helps to run the code for an unsupported runtime like Java 21 at the moment (20 October 2023). The custom runtime brings the possibility to deliver a runtime alongside of function code, as it interacts with AWS Lambda Runtime Interface (API) behind the scenes.

The custom runtime is initiated and prepared in the bootstrapping phase of the execution environment where the Lambda initiates a new runtime, prepares the execution environment and loads the function code into the container.

Memory

AWS Lambda, like any computing service, requires memory and CPU resources. The amount of memory you configure for your Lambda function determines the corresponding virtual CPU (vCPU) resources it receives. For instance, if you allocate 1,769 MB of RAM to your function, it is equivalent to having one vCPU available. We will delve deeper into this topic in the *Configuring Lambda* section.

Storage

Lambda functions are provided with a **`/tmp`** directory which is a writable directory that you can use to store temporary files during the execution of your function. It provides up to 10Gb of storage with fast I/O throughput that can be used for various purposes, such as downloading large files, creating temporary files, or processing data that doesn't fit into memory. The **`/tmp`** directory can also serve as a temporary cache for data shared between invocations on the same Lambda execution container.

Network

Lambda functions already run in isolated and secure environments on a multi-AZ configuration and on a dedicated account for the Lambda service. However, the customers must take care of their security as well for private and public layers of the network they are designed internally. The Lambda Function can be attached to multiple subnets on a customer-owned VPC.

Security

Like almost every AWS service, Lambda integrates seamlessly with the AWS Identity and Access Management (IAM) service. Each function must have an IAM role attached. You can create a dedicated role for your function that grants only the necessary permissions required for the code to execute.

Lambda Service Under the Hood

The Lambda service is a collection of well-defined services that collaborate together to give the best collaborative results in terms of security, performance and operations.

Referring back to the *Vendor Lock-In* section in the previous chapter we looked briefly at how lambda is designed under the hood.

The lambda service is generally designed in two parts:

- **Data plane**: This plane is responsible for runtime needs of AWS lambda like invocations, environment preparation, concurrency limit check, and more.
- **Control plane**: The control plane is responsible for management tasks like creating, updating, publishing new versions, and more.

To find more about Data and Control planes, refer to AWS docs: https://docs.aws.amazon.com/whitepapers/latest/security-overview-aws-lambda/lambda-executions.html

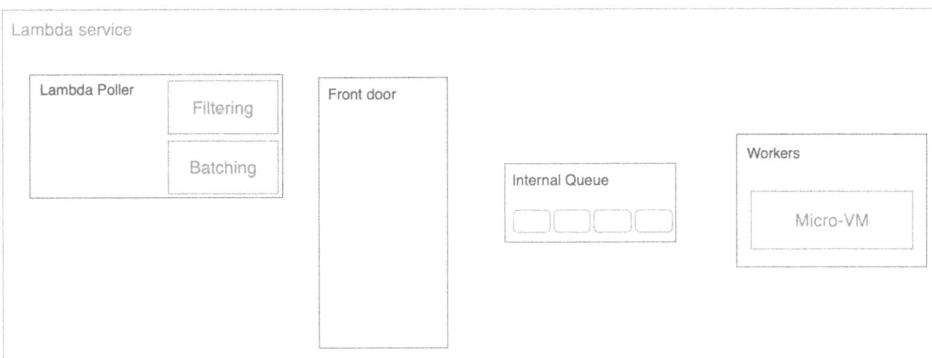

Figure 2.1: *Lambda service components*

As demonstrated, the Lambda service consists of different under the hood services, such as:

- Function Workers
- Lambda Front Door
- Lambda Poller
- Lambda Service Queue

Function Workers

The Worker component operates under the control of the Worker Manager, which assists in providing the optimal container based on the function's requirements.

Initially, containers are selected with the aid of Firecracker, an open-source lightweight virtualization system that facilitates the rapid execution of micro-VMs in just a fraction of the time.

Lambda Front Door

The Lambda Front Door is responsible for receiving invocation requests and forwarding them to the underlying Lambda service's internal processes. The Front Door is also responsible for validating customer requests and making decisions regarding throttling limits, among other responsibilities.

Lambda Poller

The Lambda Poller is a component of the Lambda service that handles a category of services supporting Event Source Mapping (ESM). The poller processes filtering and batching if configured, and then passes the event through the Front Door to the Lambda function worker.

Some of these services are SQS, DynamoDb Streams, and Kinesis.

Lambda Service Queue

The Queue is used for all Async communication with lambda workers. It is used by services that integrate with lambda asynchronously and again via Lambda Front Door. Some of these services are Event Bridge, SNS, and S3.

Lambda Invocation

Lambda integrates effectively with AWS services that are event-driven, such as SQS, SNS, EventBridge, DynamoDB Streams, and Kinesis. However, there are use cases where the need is to respond to internet-facing requirements, such as request/response REST, WebSocket, or GraphQL APIs. These use cases can be achieved using an Application Load Balancer, API Gateway, or direct calls with Lambda Function URLs.

Lambda integrates well with a large number of AWS services using event-based mechanisms: **Amazon SQS, SNS, EventBridge, Kinesis, DynamoDB, Cognito, MQ, MSK, S3, CloudFront, Api Gateway, CloudWatch Logs, AWS Step Functions, Config, Secret Manager,** and **Application Load Balancer.**

We will discover more in *Chapter 3, Invocation Models and Service Integrations.*

Throughout this chapter and the subsequent ones, the examples provided will be written in Node.js, TypeScript, and the AWS Cloud Development Kit (CDK).

The Obligatory Hello World Handler

As mentioned previously, each Lambda function has its own execution environment and runtime, but all of these would not be operational without customer-defined code. The Lambda service fetches the function code (package) upon function initialization, that happens after runtime and extensions initialization phase in an orderly manner. A deployment package can be provided in several ways.

There are two types of deployment packages: Zip file and Container images. These can be delivered in three ways: uploaded zip to function, S3 bucket or container image.

The responsibility of preparing the bundle and zipping the package code is on the customer side.

Handler

A Handler represents the entry point of a lambda function and is a method in code that serves for execution. The handler will be executed upon receiving an invocation request. The function's execution continues until the code returns a response, throws an error, times out, or exits without a response.

The handler takes two arguments: the Event and the Context.

Event

Event is the representation of a demand in handler method, containing both the request information and metadata in JSON format. The event information varies based on the source of the event. For instance, if the function is triggered by a batch of Amazon SQS messages, the event object will contain details about the SQS event that triggered the function alongside records representing the messages. Here's an example of an SQS event:


```
{
 "Records": [
   {
     "messageId": "6f0bae1e-3855-4f1d-91cf-d2f44017e1f9",
     "receiptHandle": "LEhzZ2RqRFNKaGRnamgS0pRWEhGS0pESEZLRA-
     oKUURGTEtES...",
     "body": "{\"Title\": \"Serverless computing with AWS
     Lambda\"}",
     "attributes": {
       "ApproximateReceiveCount": "1",
       "SentTimestamp": "1697963088",
       "SenderId": "AIDAIENQZJOLO23YVJ4VO",
       "ApproximateFirstReceiveTimestamp": "1545082650649"
```

```
      },
      "messageAttributes": {},
      "eventSource": "aws:sqs",
      "eventSourceARN": "arn:aws:sqs:eu-west-1:607050363559:books-
       queue",
      "awsRegion": "eu-west-1"
    }
  ]
}
```


Context

Context object gives information about the invocation, function and execution environment, providing methods and properties that give details about the invocation and the runtime environment. Here are some common methods provided by the Context object in AWS Lambda that can be used to get extra information:

- **`memoryLimitInMB`**
- **`invokedFunctionArn`**
- **`functionName`**
- **`FunctionVersion`**
- **`getRemainingTimeInMillis`**

Handler Code

Handler method is a custom code provided by customer's software that receives an event from a service like SQS and processes that event.

The handler execution terminates by:

- Returning a response
- Throwing a custom error
- A runtime exception like timeout

```
import { SQSEvent, Context } from "aws-lambda";

export async function handler(
 event: SQSEvent,
 context: Context
): Promise<void> {

 const body = JSON.parse(event.Records[0].body);

 try {
   // ... Your code goes here
```

```
    if (
      "Serverless Computing with AWS Lambda".localeCompare(
        body.Title,
        undefined,
        { sensitivity: "accent" }
      ) === 0
    ) {
      console.log("Title is correct");
    }
    console.log(
      "Cotext Remaining time in MS: ", context.getRemainingTime
       InMillis());

  } catch (err) {
    throw new Error("something went wrong");
  }
}
```

The `**aws-lambda**` library provides all strongly typed interfaces for all AWS services that integrate with AWS lambda, such as SQS, SNS, DynamoDB, and so on. The package brings dedicated interfaces for different integration types of a single service (if supported). An example can be **ApiGateway** Event interfaces, including `**APIGatewayAuthorizerEvent**`, `**APIGatewayProxyEvent**` and `**APIGatewayProxyEventV2**`.

The function handler can also use arrow function notation:

```
export const handler = async (
 event: SQSEvent,
 context: Context
): Promise<string> => {};
```

We can also use a class-based notation to define our handler function. This can be particularly useful for encapsulating initialization logic or to leverage the use of decorators on your lambda class handler method:

```
import { Tracer } from '@aws-lambda-powertools/tracer';
import { LambdaInterface } from '@aws-lambda-powertools/commons';

const tracer = new Tracer({ serviceName: 'MyAwesomeService' });

class MyAwesomeLambda implements LambdaInterface {
 @tracer.captureLambdaHandler()
 public async handler(event, context): Promise<void> {
   ...
 }
}
```

```
const lambda = new MyAwesomeLambda();
export const handler = lambda.handler.bind(lambda);
```

In the preceding example, the Lambda function uses the Lambda Powertools tracing utility and captures lambda invocation by using the **`@tracer.captureLambdaHandler()`** function decorator. We then export the **`handler`** method after instantiating the **`MyAwesomeLambda`** class.

In the subsequent chapters, we will explore more about Lambda Powertools.

Class-based notation can also prove useful if you want to leverage Inversion of Control (IoC) containers and dependency injection via constructors.

Execution Role

Lambda function relies on AWS Identity and Access Management service to access underlying services like CloudWatch. A function at runtime needs to get temporary credentials to access other services. Achieving credentials proceed via assuming a role with required permissions. The Role must be created with all required permissions required at runtime.

Here is an example of a policy statements:

```
{
   "Version": "2012-10-17",
   "Statement": [
       {
           "Effect": "Allow",
           "Action": [
               "logs:CreateLogGroup",
               "logs:CreateLogStream",
               "logs:PutLogEvents"
           ],
           "Resource": "*"
       }
   ]
}`
```

As the Lambda Function is invoked, it will achieve temporary credentials by assuming the role. The function needs to have the **`sts:assumerole`** permissions. This permission will be attached to the function role as a **`trust policy`**.

Example of a Role using CDK (Cloud Development Kit):

```
const role = new Role(this, 'function-role', {
   assumedBy: new ServicePrincipal('lambda.amazonaws.com'),
   managedPolicies: [
     ManagedPolicy.fromAwsManagedPolicyName(
```

```
      'service-role/AWSLambdaBasicExecutionRole')
         ]
      });
```

In this example, the service principal indicates the lambda service as a trust policy, letting the lambda service assume that role. The Managed policy is provided by AWS and has all base permissions for lambda function at runtime, as demonstrated above.

For custom needs, the Role construct also provides the `inlinePolicies` that help adding custom policies based on needs.

```
const role = new Role(this, 'enrich-function-role', {
    assumedBy: new ServicePrincipal('lambda.amazonaws.com'),
    managedPolicies: [
      ManagedPolicy.fromAwsManagedPolicyName(
            'service-role/AWSLambdaBasicExecutionRole')
    ],
    inlinePolicies: {
      'dynamodb-access': new PolicyDocument({
        statements: [
          new PolicyStatement({
            effect: Effect.ALLOW,
            actions: [
              'dynamodb:Query',
              'dynamodb:GetItem',
              'dynamodb:PutItem',
            ],
            resources: [
              table.tableArn
            ],
          })
        ]
      })
    }
  });
```

The least privilege principle, or Keeping permissions restrictive and granting only the required actions for lambda execution is a really important point when working with functions.

For more details, you can refer to AWS documentation: https://docs.aws.amazon.com/IAM/latest/UserGuide/best-practices.html#grant-least-privilege

Local Development

Before writing code, we need to prepare the development environment by creating the project and install the necessary dependencies.

You need to install nodejs18 from (https://nodejs.org/en/download).

We can create a lambda project manually or by using SAM (Serverless Application Model) Command line interface, we will discover both of them here.

Setup Manually

Manual project setup is not complicated but is not as straightforward as the other methods.

Creating a project folder and initializing a Node.js project inside is a straightforward process.

```
mkdir firstlambdahandler && cd firstlambdahandler
npm init
```

Follow the **init** instructions to initialize a new project in your current directory.

Next, we need to install the required dependencies, `**aws-lambda**` is a typescript npm library with all required typings, allowing developers to write code with ease and faster.

```
npm i -D aws-lambda @types/aws-lambda @types/node typescript ts-node
```

This command installs `**aws-lambda**` and `**@types/aws-lambda**` as a **dev** dependency and as node requirements.

To create the first function, use the following snippet.

```
mkdir handlers && cd handlers
cat > firsthandler.ts
```

The handler will have the following code snippet:

```
import { ApiGatewayProxyEvent } from 'aws-lambda'

export const handler = async ( event: ApiGatewayProxyEvent) => {
 return {
   statusCode: 200,
   body: JSON.stringify({ message: "successfully done."})
 }
}
```

Setup Using SAM

The Serverless Application Model (SAM) is an abstraction around serverless computing offered by AWS.SAM helps and removes a lot of burden around developer challenges when designing serverless solutions using lambda and managed services like SQS, Eventbridge, ApiGateway, and so on.

First, install the AWS SAM CLI by following the AWS documentation instructions: https://docs.aws.amazon.com/serverless-application-model/latest/developerguide/install-sam-cli.html

Be sure to have installed the docker on your machine, this is required by SAM for local invocations.

use **sam cli** to initiate a **sam** project

```
> sam init
```

Follow the instructions :

```
Which template source would you like to use?
        1 - AWS Quick Start Templates
        2 - Custom Template Location
Choice:
```

Choose the 1st option, then select the corresponding template for your project:

```
Choose an AWS Quick Start application template
        ...
        7 - Serverless API
        ...
Template:
```

Choose the 7th option `Serverless Api` and then choose **nodejs18:**

```
Which runtime would you like to use?
         1 - dotnet6
         2 - nodejs20.x
         3 - nodejs18.x
         4 - nodejs16.x
         5 - nodejs14.x
Runtime: 2
```

Next, select if you would like to activate X-Ray tracing or not:

```
Would you like to enable X-Ray tracing on the function(s) in your
application?  [y/N]:
```

Choose your preference for activating CloudWatch insights for your functions::

```
Would you like to enable monitoring using CloudWatch Application In-
sights?
[y/N]:
```

Select an appropriate name for your project:

```
Project name [sam-app]: sam-example
```

SAM Bundling

SAM allows you to set up bundling in the SAM template using the Metadata section. The Metadata needs the basic configuration as demonstrated here:

```
MySimpleFunction:
 Type: AWS::Serverless::Function
 Properties:
   CodeUri: my-simple-function/
   Runtime: nodejs20.x
   Handler: index.handler
  Metadata:
   BuildMethod: esbuild
   BuildProperties:
     Target: es2023
     Minify: true
     EntryPoints:
       - index.ts
```

The metadata section is based on **esbuild** and covers a set of required **esbuild** parameters. To discover more, refer to AWS documentation: ::https://docs.aws.amazon.com/serverless-application-model/latest/developerguide/serverless-sam-cli-using-build-typescript.html

CDK Bundling

The AWS CDK also supports bundling part of function configuration. To use this bundling feature, the `**NodejsFunction**` construct provides a well-defined interface to pass the bundling parameters. The requirement to have this functionality operational is to install the **esbuild** library part of **cdk** project dependencies.

```
npm intall -D esbuild
```

The CDK `**NodejsFunction**` provides a bundling interface as part of the construct properties. The bundling supports image-based bundling and **esbuild** bundling (discover more at: https://docs.aws.amazon.com/cdk/api/v2/docs/aws-cdk-lib.aws_lambda_nodejs.BundlingOptions.html)

A simple bundling config for a lambda function will be as follows:

```
const function =  new NodejsFunction(this, 'MySimpleFunction', {
   entry: functionPath,
   functionName: `my-simple-function`,
   memorySize: 128,
   runtime: Runtime.NODEJS_20_X,
   timeout: Duration.seconds(5),
   handler: 'handler',
```

```
      bundling:{
        externalModules:[ "aws-sdk" ],
        target: 'es2023',
        minify: true,
        sourceMap: true
      }
    })
```

The bundle results will be provided by `synth` step so running `cdk synth` in the terminal will generate the results.

Manual Bundling

To make this code executable in a lambda environment, we need to **`transpile`** that to a **`nodejs`** compatible code. We will use the **`esbuild`** and typescript to **`transpile`** and bundle the handler.

We will create a **`tsconfig.json`** in our project root:

```
cat > tsconfig.json
```

The **`tsconfig`** file should resemble the following:

```
{
   "compilerOptions": {
       "alwaysStrict": true,
       "module": "commonjs",
       "noImplicitAny": true,
       "target": "esNext",
       "types": [
           "node"
       ],
       "baseUrl": "./",
       "outDir": "dist",
       "skipLibCheck": true,
       "experimentalDecorators": true,
       "emitDecoratorMetadata": true,
       "forceConsistentCasingInFileNames": true,
       "moduleResolution": "node",
       "esModuleInterop": true,
       "resolveJsonModule": true,
       "noUnusedLocals": true,
       "noUnusedParameters": true
   },
   "require": [
       "ts-node/register/transpile-only"
   ],
   "exclude": [
```

```
            "esbuild.config.js",
            "node_modules"
        ]
    }
```

To bundle, we first install the dev dependencies for **esbuild**.

```
npm i -D esbuild esbuild-plugin-tsc glob
 cat > esbuild.config.js
```

Use the following content for your **esbuild** config:

```
const path = require('path')
const esbuild = require('esbuild')
const {  globSync }  = require("glob");

const entryPoints = globSync("./handlers/**/*.ts", { ignore:
"node_modules/**"})
 const outDir = `dist`

 require('esbuild').build({
     entryPoints: entryPoints,
     entryNames: '[dir]/[name]',
     outbase:'.',
     bundle: true,
     minify: true,
     sourcemap: true,
     outdir: path.join(__dirname, outDir),
     platform: 'node',
     mainFields: ["module", "main"],
     write: true
 }).catch(() => process.exit());
```

To manually bundle the typescript files, simply running the previously explored `` `esbuild.config.js` `` can result in bundled assets.

```
 > node esbuild.config.js
```

Local Testing

The essential part of any software development project is local development. Local development consists of having a comfortable IDE, runtime and possibility to test or run the code locally. Serverless, as explained previously, has some challenges and complexities, and part of them is the developer experience (DEX) that is still present these days.

The Serverless community does a good job, and in recent years, a bunch of interesting tools have been released.

Requirements

Before starting to run the function code locally and deep dive how easy the debugging can be, the following requirements have to be concerned:

- Installing Docker desktop from [docker desktop official site] (https://www.docker.com/products/docker-desktop/)
- Installing SAM CLI following [AWS SAM documentation] (https://docs.aws.amazon.com/cli/latest/userguide/getting-started-install.html)
- Installing VSCode from [Visual studio official website] (https://code.visualstudio.com/)

All examples and practices in this book will be based on Visual Code community edition.

Manual Debugging

The manual setup and debugging process simply executes the function code based on an invoke configuration configured in VS Code.

VS Code provides `**launch configuration**` where we can set up our different configurations and easily trigger the code using the Debug extension provided by the default part of VS Code.

Before setting up the debug configuration manually, the function code must be bundled and transpiled to `**nodejs**`, as explored in the `**Manual Bundling**` part of this section.

When using VS Code, you can setup a debug launch config as follows:

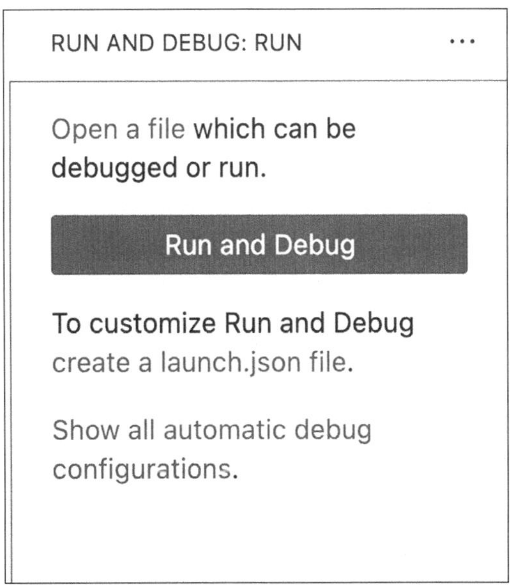

Figure 2.2: *VS-code debug extension window*

Choosing the `**Create a launch.config file**` will open and create a `**launch.config**` file in the `**.vscode**` folder.

Use the following configuration to set up the local function invoke.

```
{
  "configurations": [
    {
      "type": "aws-sam",
      "request": "direct-invoke",
      "name": "Invoke first lambda",
      "aws": {
        "credentials": "profile:my-profile"
      },
      "invokeTarget":{
        "architecture": "x86_64",
        "target": "code",
        "projectRoot": "Path-to-handler",
        "lambdaHandler": "index.handler"
      },
      "lambda": {
        "runtime": "nodejs20.x",
        "payload": {
          "path": "path-to-test-events/myevent.json"
        }
      }
    }
  ]
}
```

projectRoot: The `**projectRoot**` must be configured based on the project folder hierarchy.

payload: The `**lambda.payload**` has to be pointed to the event provided as a JSON file.

Selecting the `**Invoke first lambda**` from the debug menu and choosing the **Run Debug** button will start debugging preparation.

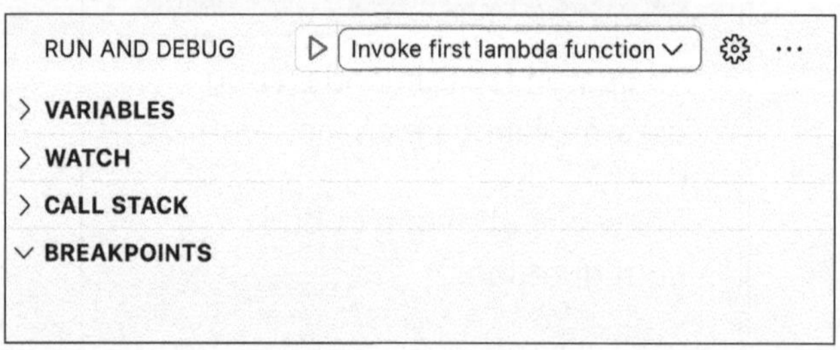

***Figure 2.3:** running function handler from debug extension*

The execution environment preparation proceed as follows:

- Pulling the corresponding **sam** image from docker hub
- Mounting the bundled file into the running container
- Hitting the function entry

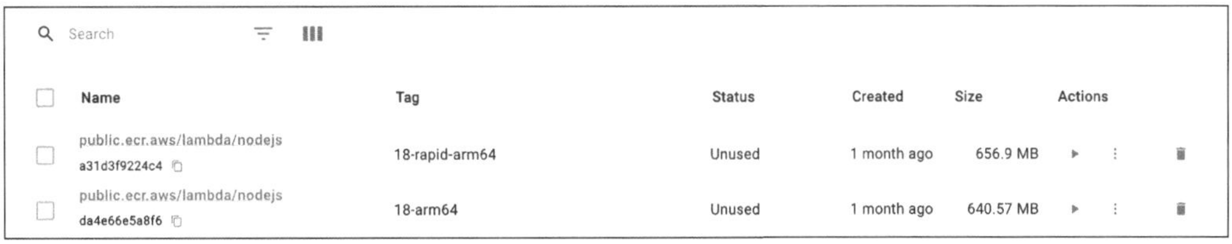

Figure 2.4: *Docker desktop SAM image*

The preceding config can be used with all SAM, CDK and manual bundling. The only requirement is that bundling must be done before invocation.

SAM Debugging

Using **SAM cli**, invoking the function is as simple as running a command:

```
> sam local invoke myFirstFunction --event events/event-test.json
```

Also, if the serverless **api** is chosen when creating project using SAM, the following command can execute a local **api**:

```
> sam local start-api
```

The **start-api** provides a localhost **api** that you can invoke using Postman, curl, or your preferred tool.

As mentioned previously, the SAM build generates artifacts in the `**.aws-sam**` folder, considering this path the Manual debug configuration can be used for SAM projects just by changing the **projectRoot**.

CDK Debugging

At the time of this writing, there is no official local testing process provided by AWS CDK, but following the bundling using CDK, the CDK generates two artifacts behind the `**cdk synth**`, the `**cloudformation template**` as json and the `**nodejs**` bundle file.

Using **SAM Cli**,

```
> sam local invoke myFirstFunction --no-event -t ./cdk.out/my-
FirstFunction.template.json
```

Using Launch configuration, find the asset path of function looking at generated template:

```
"Metadata": {
 "aws:cdk:path": "my-first-function-stack/my-first-function/Resource",
 "aws:asset:path": "asset.52f6453f04b7613947fba3089869b8fd68495f02eee343a6045bf01c6289fae6",
```

Figure 2.5: CDK *generated asset path*

The value of the `**aws:asset:path**` key must be used for launch configuration as `**projectRoot**` and run the debugger by running the debug config from the Debug panel.

```
{
 ...
 "invokeTarget":{
   "architecture": "x86_64",
   "target": "code",
   "projectRoot": "cdk.out/asset.52f6453f04b7613947fba3089869b8f
    d68495f02eee343a6045bf01c6289fae6",
   "lambdaHandler": "index.handler"
 }
}
```

Debugging Tests

During the development phase, we find highly the need of running and debugging the local tests written in Typescript. You can easily run your tests but the importance is how to debug using breakpoints and follow the steps included in a process.

Here an example of Launch configuration letting debug locally using Jest.

```
{
     "name": "Debug Jest Tests",
     "type": "node",
     "request": "launch",
     "runtimeArgs": [
       "--inspect-brk",
       "src/node_modules/jest/bin/jest.js",
       "--runInBand",
       "-c",
       "src/jest.config.js"
     ],
     "console": "integratedTerminal",
     "internalConsoleOptions": "neverOpen",
     "port": 9229
  }
```

Configuring Functions

This section explores the essential parts of AWS Lambda functions configuration. Understanding function configuration drives optimal performance, effective monitoring, and robust security.

Function Configuration

Memory Allocation: Allocate memory judiciously, as it directly impacts your function's performance, CPU power, and network bandwidth.

Memory allocation ranges from 128MB to 10,240MB. This choice significantly influences your function's capabilities, with higher memory providing more CPU power and bandwidth. However, it also increases costs. Align memory allocation with your function's requirements.

Based on AWS documentation at 1769 MB of memory the function has 1 vCpu available. A function gets 6 vCpu at 10 GB of memory that is equivalent to Ceiling (10240 % 1760). You can increase the Lambda memory by 1MB increment. (https://docs.aws.amazon.com/lambda/latest/dg/configuration-function-common.html#configuration-memory-console)

When configuring the function memory, evaluating the processing and memory needs alongside the particular runtime capabilities plays the role as a successor. Always consider keeping the memory close to the runtime consumption needs as more memory costs more. Choosing the most appropriate configuration helps balance the performance and costs aligned. *Chapter 5, Hyper-Scaling with Lambda*, covers more about cost and memory adjustments and lambda optimization.

A function by default has two cores based on benchmarks using following nodejs **`handler`**

```
exports.handler = async function (event, context) {
   const os = require("os");
   console.log("cpu: ", os.cpus());
   console.log("platform: ",os.platform());
   console.log("architecture: ",os.arch());
   console.log("paralelism available :", os.available
   Parallelism());
   console.log("total memory : ", os.totalmem());
   console.log("machine : ", os.machine());
}
```

Simply use `` `os.cpus()` `` in your Lambda to print out an array of CPUs. The result will be as follows for a Lambda function with Arm64 architecture and 128MB of memory.

```
cpu:  [{
   model: 'Neoverse-N1',
   speed: 0,
   times: { user: 3140, nice: 0, sys: 300, idle: 235530, irq: 0 }
 },{
   model: 'Neoverse-N1',
   speed: 0,
   times: { user: 310, nice: 0, sys: 3500, idle: 235300, irq: 0 }
}]
platform:  linux
architecture:  arm64
paralelism available : 2
total memory :  200273920
machine :  aarch64
```

Benchmarking multiple memory configurations, 1024 MB and 3008 MB of memory give the same results for CPU and number of cores does not evolve per memory configuration.

While **os.cpus()** might report multiple CPUs available in your Lambda function, it's important to understand that these are virtual CPUs (vCPUs) provided by AWS Lambda's Micro-VMs. The actual amount of memory available may also be higher than what you've configured, and this can be used by the guest operating system (Guest OS) for its needs. For more details, please refer to: (https://nodejs.org/en/docs/guides/event-loop-timers-and-nexttick).

For multi-thread tasks like filesystem read, the function code does not use the second core. There is a possibility to go beyond one core using workers, but this is not commonly used in most software development scenarios.

Lambda gives one-credit per second that theoretically bursts the vCPU power and makes the function execution faster than expected in some scenarios. These credits affect only the second core, so for runtimes like Node.js, they may not have a significant impact.

You can set your memory size when creating a Lambda function. Here is an example using AWS CDK:

```
const myFunction = new lambda.Function(this, 'MyFunction', {
   runtime: lambda.Runtime.NODEJS_20_X,
   handler: 'index.handler',
   code: lambda.Code.fromAsset('function-code'),
   memorySize: 256
});
```

Always profile your function to determine its memory requirements, balance cost, and performance effectively.

Runtime: As highlighted earlier, Lambda runtimes and supported runtimes are essential for Lambda functions. Each function has a configured runtime that lets the Lambda to provision a worker using the appropriate runtime.

A runtime environment is a black box inside the worker that lets the code on the worker run correctly providing all language specific instructions. A runtime is an immutable configuration at version level (we will discuss versioning in a later chapter). This means you cannot modify the runtime attached to a function version, but you can create new versions with new runtimes. However, the runtime changes are possible for the latest version of the function at all times, as the latest version is the only mutable instance of a function at any given time.

You can have functions that evolve over time and can move from .NET6runtime to Nodejs18 or inversely.

Ephemeral Storage: Lambda gives the possibility to associate a temporary storage of up to 10GB to the function. This can be helpful if your function needs some sort of storage during the process, the storage will be found under `/tmp` folder.

By default, when creating new functions, Lambda associates a minimum of 512 MB to your function at no additional cost. However, increasing this memory can lead to extra costs based on the pricing model.

An important point about the `/tmp` folder is that Lambda service does not clean up that storage, and it passes the responsibility to the function owner. Taking care of cleanup is crucial if the sensitive data is registered, as not cleaning can lead to exposing this data to another execution of the same function. As a best practice, if possible for storage needs, use S3 or if using the ephemeral storage, keep the data lifecycle attached to the execution. This can be a good place if you need some local cache that cannot be put on Memory.

Timeout Duration: Lambda provides a timeout configuration between 1 second and 15 minutes that allows you to control how long your function can run before termination. Set timeouts slightly higher than your function's typical execution time, ensuring tasks completion without incurring unnecessary costs.

As a best practice, when coding Lambda functions, take care of your http or Database timeout and retries. Keep track of the worst-case scenario to avoid reaching function timeout. A typical error when working with developers and applying best practices in microservice design is using code-level retries with exponential backoff when calling other services. However, the configuration must be realistic based on function configuration. If we are calling a service with 5 retries and a backoff rate of 1.5, and a timeout of 5 seconds, the result of your single call in the worst case (when the service reaches the timeout on all retries in addition to the initial call) will be more than 10 seconds. Imagine the function timeout set to 5 seconds. If you reach the function timeout in the middle of execution, you will get a timeout error from Lambda service.

While this may not be a real problem, it can lead you to the difficulties around service observability and automation.

A better approach will be to set the retries at function level. This way, the Lambda service will take care of retries with Asynchronous invocations or communicating with Caller service using poll-based invocations like SQS.

Here an example of AWS CDK Code demonstrating creation of a lambda function with timeout:

```
const function = new Function(this, 'SampleFunction', {
   runtime: lambda.Runtime.NODEJS_20_X,
   handler: 'index.handler',
   code: lambda.Code.fromAsset('function-code'),
   timeout: cdk.Duration.seconds(5), // Set timeout duration in
   seconds
});
```

For timeout as well as a best practice, observe and profile your function's runtime behavior for accurate timeout settings.

Function URLs

Lambda function URLs provide a simplified way of exposing a function via an HTTP URL. This feature provides two response types called invoke modes: **`BUFFERED`** that is the default one and **`RESPONSE_STREAM`** that allows sending response continuously and partially to the client.

Response streaming is an option when dealing with large response payloads. Besides the responsiveness that it brings to the client, it allows you to bypass the **`BUFFERED`** response payload size limit. The limitations will be explored in the ***Lambda Limitation*** section in this chapter.

Example of creating a lambda function with Function URL:

```
const role = new Role(this, 'Role', {
 assumedBy: new iam.ServicePrincipal('lambda.amazonaws.com'),
});

const function = new Function(this, 'SampleFunction', {
   runtime: lambda.Runtime.NODEJS_20_X,
   handler: 'index.handler',
   code: lambda.Code.fromAsset('function-code')
});

const url = function.addFunctionUrl({
   authType: FunctionUrlAuthType.NONE,
```

```
    invokeMode: InvokeMode.RESPONSE_STREAM,
});

url.grantInvokeUrl(role);
```

Monitoring and Logging Configuration

CloudWatch Logs: Effective Observability is essential in any distributed design and to have an effective observable system, setting up monitoring is an important pillar. Logs help find the anomalies faster and better observe the design in different circumstances. Stream logs to Amazon CloudWatch for in-depth insights into your function's behavior and performance. Adequate log retention is crucial for troubleshooting and optimization purposes. A significant log retention period can help lower costs and ensure effective logging. By default, when creating a Lambda function a default log group will be created having the exact name of the Lambda function prefixed by `aws/lambda/`. The default log group has an unlimited retention period and keeps the logs forever, which can lead to increased costs.

Changing a function's default log group to a custom log group with a retention policy can be a bit tricky. You must create a log group with the same name as the Lambda function, but you will get an error in **cloudformation** saying the resource already exists. A workaround is to remove the existing log group before creating the new one. However, if your workloads are under heavy traffic, there is a 99% chance that the default log group will be recreated after deletion and before creation of the new one.

If you face this situation, remove the `logs:*` permissions from Lambda role and remove the default log group. This way, the Lambda function will continue working without any error, but without creating the log group or putting logs to log group. Then, create your new log group and set the permissions back to Lambda execution role.

Creating a custom log group using AWS CDK Code:

```
import * as logs from '@aws-cdk/aws-logs';
const { RetentionDays } = logs;

const role = new Role(this, 'Role', {
 assumedBy: new iam.ServicePrincipal('lambda.amazonaws.com'),
});

const myFunction = new lambda.Function(this, 'MyFunction', {
 runtime: lambda.Runtime.NODEJS_20_X,
 handler: 'index.handler',
 code: lambda.Code.fromAsset('function-code'),
 role
```

```
});

role.addManagedPolicy(
 iam.ManagedPolicy.fromAwsManagedPolicyName(
   "service-role/AWSLambdaBasicExecutionRole"));

const logGroup = new logs.LogGroup(this, 'MyFunctionLogGroup', {
 retention: logs.RetentionDays.THREE_MONTHS,
});

myFunction.addLogGroup(logGroup);
```

Custom Metrics: Custom metrics enhance your understanding of function behavior and resource usage. You can create custom metrics tailored to your specific performance indicators. Utilize these metrics for informed decisions and optimizations. You can create custom metrics to observe and raise alerts based on business-critical situations or to monitor function anomalies and raise alerts. When creating metrics, think about your aggregation function and dimensions. For example, if you need to monitor the number of orders getting into your e-commerce system distinguished by **`orderId`** and product. In this case, you need two dimensions: **`OrderId`** and **`ProductId`**. Think well about your metrics, as they are not free of charge and just take in consideration what matters per use case.

Creating custom metric using AWS CDK:

```
const customMetric = new cloudwatch.Metric({
 namespace: 'Custom/LambdaMetrics',
 metricName: 'MyCustomMetric'
});

customMetric.createAlarm(this, 'CustomMetricAlarm', {
 threshold: 10,
 evaluationPeriods: 1,
});
```

Security Configuration

IAM Role: Lambda service is fully integrated with IAM. You can use IAM roles and permissions as gatekeepers in design. Grant only necessary permissions to ensure the principle of least privilege. This protects your design against any extra cost in case of vulnerabilities. This can be caused by a suspicious dependency package, for example. However, giving your function the minimum and just required permissions protects you by reducing your surface attack.

IAM roles define what AWS resources your Lambda functions can access.

AWS CDK Code:

```
const lambdaRole = new iam.Role(this, 'LambdaRole', {
 assumedBy: new iam.ServicePrincipal('lambda.amazonaws.com'),
});

lambdaRole.addManagedPolicy(iam.ManagedPolicy.fromAwsManagedPoli-
cyName('service-role/AWSLambda_FullAccess'));
```

Encryption: Security is paramount. Enable encryption for your function's environment variables and data at rest. Encryption safeguards sensitive information from unauthorized access. It is recommended to use the secret manager as a secure repository and fetch the secrets or sensitive keys at runtime from the secret manager. However, this is mostly avoided in software due to the secret manager pricing model, as it becomes too expensive to fetch secrets many times.

AWS Lambda encrypts the function using server-side Key Management Service (KMS). However, in most cases, we need to use the credentials like API Keys within the function to call some third-party or internal services. As a practice, these credentials are often stored as environment variables. You can as well configure your function to use a customer-managed key (CMK) for encryption at rest.

AWS CDK Code:

```
const keyPolicy = new iam.PolicyDocument({
 statements: [new iam.PolicyStatement({
   actions: [
     'kms:Create*',
     'kms:Describe*',
     'kms:Enable*',
     'kms:List*',
     'kms:Put*',
   ],
   principals: [new iam.AccountRootPrincipal()],
   resources: ['*'],
 })],
});
const key = new kms.Key(this, 'CustomerManagedKey', {
 policy: myCustomPolicy,
});

const myFunction = new Function(this, 'MyFunction', {
 runtime: lambda.Runtime.NODEJS_20_X,
 handler: 'index.handler',
 code: lambda.Code.fromAsset('function-code'),
 environment: {
```

```
    DB_PASSWORD: 'db_p@ssword',
  },
  environmentEncryption: key.keyId
});
```

VPC Integration and Subnet Configuration: When your Lambda functions need to access AWS services within a Virtual Private Cloud (VPC), configure relevant subnets and security groups. VPC integration ensures secure communication within a defined network environment and allows traffic to get out of your network. This improves your security level and the latency, as your communications no longer need to go to the public internet and back inside. This also reduces data transfer out of your network.

AWS CDK Code:

```
const vpc = Vpc.fromLookup(this, 'account-regional-vpc', {
    vpcId: props.vpcId
});

myFunction.addToRolePolicy(new iam.PolicyStatement({
 actions: [
   'ec2:CreateNetworkInterface',
   'ec2:DescribeNetworkInterfaces',
   'ec2:DeleteNetworkInterface'
 ],
 resources: ['*'],
}));

const subnets = vpc.selectSubnets({
 subnetType: ec2.SubnetType.PRIVATE_WITH_EGRESS
});

const securityGroups =  new ec2.SecurityGroup(this,
'SecurityGroup', {
 vpc,
 allowAllOutbound: true,
 disableInlineRules: true
});

const function = new Function(this, 'MyFunction', {
 runtime: lambda.Runtime.NODEJS_20_X,
 handler: 'index.handler',
 code: lambda.Code.fromAsset('function-code'),
 vpcSubnets: subnets,
 securityGroups: [ securityGroups ]
});
```

VPC Endpoints: Establish private connections between your VPC and AWS services for enhanced security. VPC endpoints prevent internet exposure, ensuring secure access to AWS services.

AWS CDK Code:

```
const s3Endpoint = new ec2.InterfaceVpcEndpoint(this,
'S3Endpoint', {
 service: ec2.InterfaceVpcEndpointAwsService.S3,
 vpc: myVpc });
```

Concurrency Configuration

Lambda service has Provisioned, Reserved, and Max Concurrency notion when configuring your lambda or an integration with other services. Managing concurrency is vital for optimal function performance. Let us understand Provisioned, Reserved, and Max Concurrency for effective resource utilization.

- **Provisioned Concurrency:** Provisioning helps to maintain a specific number of pre-warmed function instances, ensuring consistent performance during traffic spikes.
- **Reserved Concurrency:** Reserved concurrency limits the maximum concurrent executions, preventing over-provisioning.
- **Max Concurrency:** AWS-defined limits on concurrent function invocations. It is crucial for resource planning and scaling.
- **Relevance to Amazon SQS Integration:** When integrating Lambda with AWS Simple Queue Service (SQS), understanding max concurrency is essential. It determines how many messages from an SQS queue can be processed concurrently by Lambda functions.

AWS CDK Example for Amazon SQS Integration:

Here's an example using AWS CDK to configure an event source mapping for an SQS queue, specifying the batch size and maximum concurrency:

```
const sqsQueue = new sqs.Queue(this, 'MyQueue');

const lambdaFunction = new lambda.Function(this, 'MyFunction', {
 // Lambda function configuration
});

const eventSource = new lambdaEventSources.SqsEventSource(sqs-
Queue, {
 batchSize: 5, // Number of messages per batch
 maxBatchingWindow: cdk.Duration.seconds(10), // Maximum time to
wait for more messages
```

```
  maxConcurrency: 2, // Max concurrency for processing messages
});

lambdaFunction.addEventSource(eventSource);
```

Throttling: Effective concurrency management is crucial for preventing function overloading.

Define strategies for handling concurrency limits and ensure your function gracefully manages concurrent requests beyond its configured limits.

Error Handling Configuration

Dead Letter Queues (DLQs): DLQs are a means to ensure no loss of data in case of interruptions or failures. DLQs are simple queues that are used as a backup mechanism. DLQs also give a chance of reestablishment to the root of failure. DLQs are your safety net for capturing and managing errors.

When integrating lambda with other services, DLQs are supported and for asynchronous invocations, Lambda Destinations help to attach a DLQ and move the events in case of failure for further analysis or processing.

We'll explore how to configure DLQs in *Chapter 6, Instrumenting Lambda.*

Retries and Backoff Strategies: Customizing error handling through retries and backoff strategies enhances reliability.

We'll discuss how to configure retries and backoff strategies within your Lambda function code to ensure robust error recovery.

AWS CDK Code: Implementing custom retry and backoff logic within your Lambda function code is a valuable strategy for handling transient errors effectively.

This comprehensive exploration of AWS Lambda's configuration options empowers you to optimize your serverless functions for peak performance, security, and reliability. The included AWS CDK code snippets and diagrams illustrate how to implement each configuration aspect effectively.

By mastering these configuration options, you'll be well-equipped to build robust and efficient serverless applications in the AWS cloud.

Logs and Monitoring

In the realm of serverless computing and distributed cloud architectures, the systems are formed as a composition of thousands of small services. Managing the system under a well-defined monitoring system allows for better observation, analysis and detection of defects and anomalies. Effective monitoring and logging are your trusty companions on the journey of managing AWS Lambda functions as a single business process composed of multiple functions that result in a value collaboratively. Observability provides valuable insights into how your functions behave, their performance, and even the mysteries behind any errors they may encounter. In this section, let's dive into the fascinating world of monitoring and logging options available for AWS Lambda, armed with AWS Cloud Development Kit (CDK) examples that make the learning process engaging.

Logging

In serverless design on AWS, Lambda functions are the heart of the operation. They operate as distributed, stateless entities, responding to various triggers and events. However, as we venture into this dynamic landscape, we face distinct challenges.

Capturing and preserving logs generated by Lambda functions is a vital piece of the puzzle. Inadequate logging would be like walking in the dark. We require the capability to detect and resolve issues, comprehend the behavior of our functions, and uncover the root causes and reasons behind system inconvenient behaviors.

CloudWatch Logs acts as the central hub for monitoring and serves as the treasure by collecting, storing, and granting access to the log data that our Lambda functions produce. Logs help for better monitoring, troubleshooting, and even auditing the journeys of our Lambda functions.

What CloudWatch Logs brings to the table:

- **Centralization**: It provides a centralized platform for log management, simplifying the complexity of tracking logs across a distributed landscape.
- **Metrics Integration**: Seamlessly integrates with CloudWatch Metrics, adding an extra layer of insight into the behavior of our functions.
- **Effortless Accessibility**: CloudWatch provides a simplified way for accessing logs and metrics, making analysis and exploration a breeze.
- **Retention and Archiving**: It empowers setting retention and archiving rules, ensuring the preservation of valuable log data, avoiding storage of unnecessary or ephemeral logs.
- **A Word of Caution**: In our journey, we must be mindful of the costs that may arise from high log volumes. Additionally, the effectiveness of CloudWatch Logs depends on the wisdom of its configuration. `cloudwatch` raises a significant cost for ingestion, which should be carefully considered. The `cloudwatch` logs costs are divided into ingestion and storage costs.

  When configuring Lambda functions, think about what is the required LogLevel and the rate of ingesting logs that the function produces. This can help to optimize the costs in an early stage.

Creating a function with Logs retention using AWS CDK

```
import * as logs from '@aws-cdk/aws-logs';
const { RetentionDays } = logs;

const myFunction = new lambda.Function(stack, 'MyFunction', {
   runtime: lambda.Runtime.NODEJS_20_X,
   handler: 'index.handler',
   code: lambda.Code.fromAsset('function-code'),
   logRetention: logs.RetentionDays.ONE_MONTH
});
```

As discussed, the CloudWatch is a central monitoring system that is integrated well with AWS service and can act as a source for streaming the generated logs to some of the services mentioned below.

Actually, AWS CloudWatch log group can be integrated with:

- Kinesis Data Streams
- Kinesis Firehose
- Lambda Function
- Amazon OpenSearch

Understanding how Lambda integrates with CloudWatch logs and sends logs to CloudWatch is important as it helps to better instrument lambda functions. Let us first look at an example of Typescript handler that uses logging:

```
export const handler = async (event: ApiGatexayProxyEvent) => {
 // apigateway request body
 // { "name": "Serverles Computing" }
 const name =  JSON.parse(event.body).name;
 console.log("Event :", name);
}
```

The preceding snippet logs the event in CloudWatch. The log will be presented as:

```
2023-10-27T21:51:41.761Z  0e0ebe28-2766-4317-b897-c30378094078
INFO  Event
{
     "name": "Serverles Computing"
}
```

As we talked about logs, it's time to explore more how logs are distributed behind Lambda.

Each Lambda function has a single log group attached that is named exactly the same as the function name. This is how Lambda and CloudWatch are correlated at runtime, a log group is a collection around function logs.

When a Micro-VM or worker is initiated, the Lambda function streams the logs and flush them to CloudWatch. Each execution environment has a single LogStream during its lifecycle. This log stream is related to all invocations in a single Micro-VM.

The lambda service has three types of logs: `**platform**`, `**function**`, and `**extension**`.

Platform: These are logs gathered by Lambda service and are kind of reports managed by Lambda to improve the observability of functions. In platform logs, there are Logs indicating beginning of a request, the end of a request and an execution report log. But when Lambda service initializes a new worker, there is also a log around the start of Initialization.

Here's an example of the preceding example of lambda log:

```
INIT_START Runtime Version: nodejs:18.v15 Runtime Version
ARN: arn:aws:lambda:eu-west-1::runtime:aeac50a783a9decf6cb-
be903303b13414f001986dcfb239990eea232debf8cc2

REPORT RequestId: 2bc336d1-c5dc-4059-a416-509d21728b85  Dura-
tion: 43.95 ms  Billed Duration: 44 ms  Memory Size: 128 MB Max
Memory Used: 66 MB  Init Duration: 171.66 ms
```

Function: The Function category relates to all logs sent to `**stderr**` or `**stdout**`. For example, `**console.log**` in Node.js environment is a type of function log. Additionally, in case of unhandled exceptions, the Lambda service writes a log to `**stderr**`, which is also considered a function log. All function logs are like platform logs sent to the CloudWatch log group and you can find them in the corresponding log stream of the function execution.

In software development, there is often a need of looking at logs as they come in. This can be valuable for production debugging or observation. In development environments, you can simply find the latest **logstream** and look at the logs. But when it comes to production and high traffic environments, it can be challenging to find the corresponding log stream.

CloudWatch logs offer a `**Tailing**` feature that allows you to view the logs for all your invocations and log streams in a single interface, making it easier to find problems or anomalies. The **Tailing** interface as well as a **Filtering** option helps you tail just a single or a portion of logs.

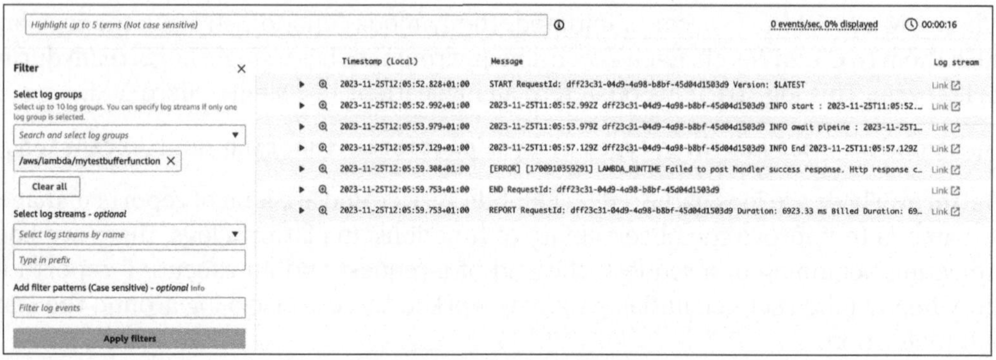

Figure 2.6: *CloudWatch tails*

You can also apply multiple filtering patterns in the filter section.

Metrics

In the ever-evolving landscape of serverless and distributed cloud designs, monitoring the performance and behavior of AWS Lambda functions is a necessity. While CloudWatch Logs serve as our storyteller, CloudWatch Metrics are our vigilant guardians, keeping an eye on the health and well-being of our functions.

As Lambda functions work with events, triggers, and various invocations, understanding their performance and resource utilization becomes complex. We require metrics that offer insights and trends, helping us make informed decisions.

CloudWatch Metrics gather and provide a wealth of data about the operational aspects of our Lambda functions. These metrics enable us to monitor and analyze performance, troubleshoot issues, and optimize resource usage.

- **Performance Insights**: They offer a detailed view of how our functions are behaving, including execution duration, invocation count, and error rates.
- **Resource Usage**: These offer insights about system usage like CPU, Disk, Memory and Network. You need to activate these metrics on your function, by default those are deactivated.
- **Alarming Capabilities**: We can set alarms on specific metrics to receive notifications when predefined thresholds are breached.
- **Custom Metrics**: Tailor metrics to suit your specific needs, allowing you to monitor application-specific attributes.

A Word of Caution: While metrics are powerful, they should be used judiciously. Too many metrics can lead to complexity and increased costs.

Lambda Functions have CloudWatch Metrics in three categories: `**Invocations**`, `**Performance**`, and `**Async Invocations**`.

Here's a CDK example to guide you:

```
const myFunction = new lambda.Function(stack, 'MyFunction', {
 runtime: lambda.Runtime.NODEJS_20_X,
 handler: 'index.handler',
 code: lambda.Code.fromAsset('function-code'),
});

const invocationCountMetric = new myFunction.Metric
('Invocations');

invocationCountMetric.createAlarm(stack, 'InvocationAlarm', {
 threshold: 100,
 evaluationPeriods: 1,
 alarmDescription: 'Too many invocations!',
 metric: invocationCountMetric
});
```

If there is a need to look at function metrics occasionally for better understanding or detection of root cause to a problem, the Lambda function console offers a monitoring section letting to have an overview of all applied metrics.

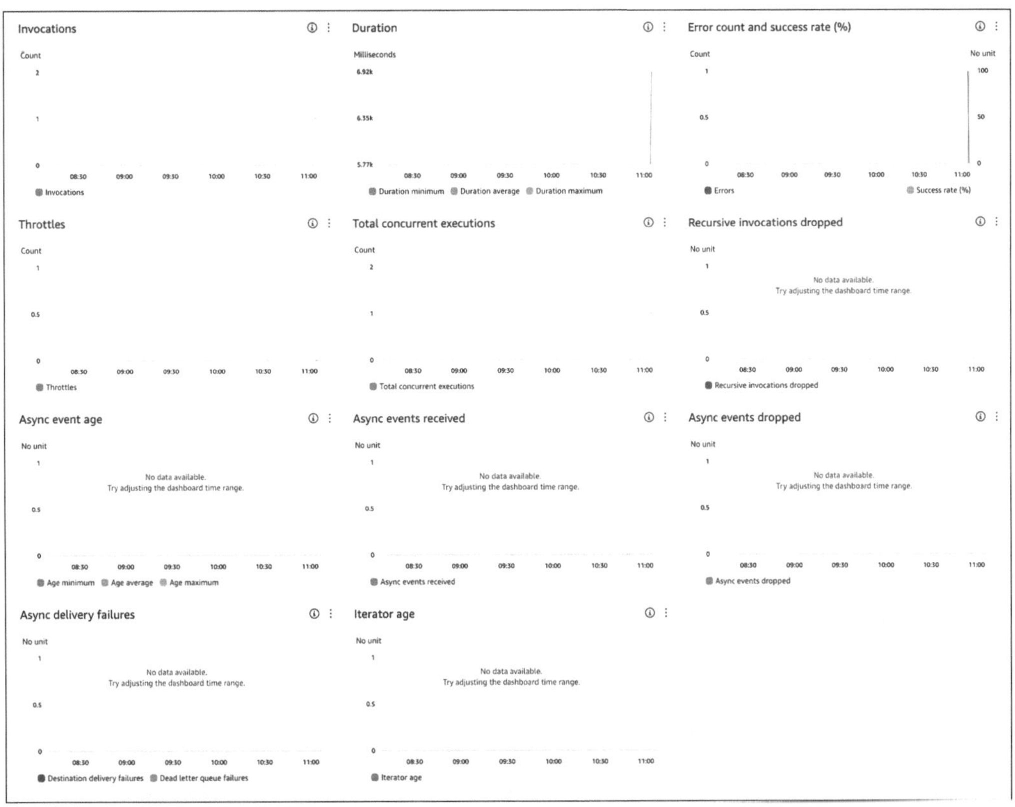

Figure 2.7: *Function metrics dashboard*

AWS X-Ray

AWS X-Ray is a service offered for distributed tracing and help to improve observability in complex and distributed systems. As we traverse the intricate world of serverless and distributed design, gaining insights into the behavior of our AWS Lambda functions becomes paramount. AWS X-Ray is the guiding light that illuminates our path, providing an in-depth look at how our functions interact and perform.

In the dynamic collaboration of Lambda functions with events and triggers, it's often challenging to follow the journey of requests through various services and functions.

AWS X-Ray is a trusted guide. It enables us to trace requests as they traverse our Lambda functions, offering detailed insights into performance bottlenecks and interactions with other AWS services.

Using AWS X-Ray offers:

- **Request Tracing**: It provides an end-to-end view of requests, helping identify performance bottlenecks.
- **Service Map**: Visualize the interactions between various components of your application, making it easier to understand complex workflows.
- **Segmentation**: Break down the execution of your functions into segments, gaining granular insights.
- **A Word of Caution**: While AWS X-Ray is a powerful tool, it should be used when advanced tracing and deep insights are needed due to its associated costs.

Here's a CDK example to guide you:

```
const myFunction = new lambda.Function(stack, 'MyFunction', {
 runtime: lambda.Runtime.NODEJS_14_X,
 handler: 'index.handler',
 code: lambda.Code.fromAsset('function-code'),
 tracing: Tracing.ACTIVE
});
```

When you activate the tracing, the Lambda service sends tracing data to the X-Ray service. X-Ray service provides a meaningful service map as demonstrated here:

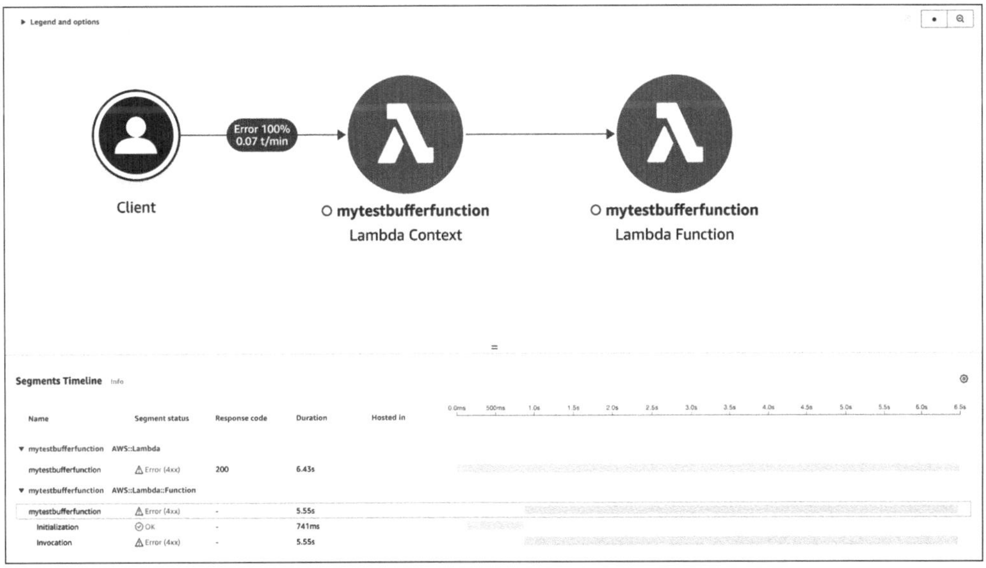

Figure 2.8: *Function tracing in x-ray*

Lambda function tracing activated alone will not bring enough advantage in complex serverless communication, except if you activate the tracing on both the upstream and downstream sides.

Here, we integrate an API Gateway with Lambda function, configuring both with active tracing.

```
const api = new RestApi(this, 'MyApi', {
 deployOptions
:{
   tracingEnabled: true
 }
});

const myFunction = new lambda.Function(stack, 'MyFunction', {
 runtime: lambda.Runtime.NODEJS_20_X,
 handler: 'index.handler',
 code: lambda.Code.fromAsset('function-code'),
 tracing: Tracing.ACTIVE
});

const lambdaProxyIntegration = new LambdaIntegration(myFunction);
   const lambdaApiResource = this.Api.root.addResource
   ('myfunction');
   lambdaApiResource.addMethod(
        'POST',
        lambdaProxyIntegration);
```

The API Gateway samples requests and for each sampled request, adds some headers. These headers lead Lambda to check if it should send a trace to X-ray or not. On the other side, we have managed services like SQS, SNS and Step Functions that also support tracing. By activating the tracing on an SQS or SNS as an upstream, we will have an end-to-end tracing perspective.

Simply, you need to capture that trace data using following example and the rest will be managed automatically:

```
const sns = AWSXRay.captureAWSv3Client(new SNSClient({}));
```

The Lambda service integrates an X-Ray Daemon in the Lambda execution environment, letting traces be sent to X-ray. The daemon runs in a separate process with some allocated memory up to 16MB. If the function experiences memory starvation, the Lambda service free up the daemon memory to give the function a better chance of success.

Logs and Telemetry APIs

Lambda service provides Logs and Telemetry APIs as part of the internal design. These APIs are not discoverable from your local post or over the internet, but you can access them using Lambda Extensions via API interfaces.

Logs API provides a way to subscribe and receive all generated logs by Lambda. After subscribing, all logs will be streamed to the subscribed endpoint, allowing you to feed them into an external or custom monitoring system.

Telemetry API also provides an API interface that allows you to subscribe and listen to all telemetry data compatible with OpenTelemetry (OTel). The telemetry API sends trace data and logs to the subscribed listener, allowing it to feed any observability system.

We will discover more about Logs and Telemetry APIs in *Chapter 6, Instrumenting Lambda.*

Understanding Firecracker

Firecracker is a minimalist virtualization system using Linux kernel-based virtual machines written in Rust. It allows only secure and lightweight VMs to be run. Firecracker helps setting up the VMs in a fraction of seconds. It is a lightweight virtualization model used for transient or short-lived workloads. AWS Lambda and Fargate benefit from Firecracker. Firecracker has a low memory usage of around 5MB. The Firecracker lightweight model allows running thousands of VMs easily and rapidly on the same host in isolation.

Firecracker Container extends the Containerd (a container runtime) by adding the capability of managing MicroVMs. The AWS Lambda model was built on top of Virtual Machines, an isolated computing model, for a significant period. The challenges of traditional VMs put some computational overhead on top of the service. By introducing Firecracker and using it as a model for AWS Lambda workers, the AWS Lambda could scale faster, and some challenging features were released, such as reserved concurrency, which was basically hard or impossible with the traditional VMs model.

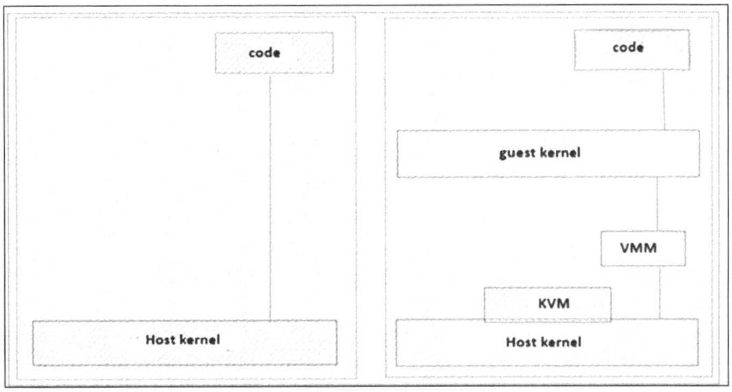

Figure 2.9: *Firecracker KVM model*

VMM (Firecracker) is lightweight as it lacks device-based hardware features like Displays, Sound and USB, unlike traditional VMs that support a variety of device-based features.

In serverless computing, due to the particular computing and economic model, one of the crucial needs is rapid environment provisioning and the ability to destroy those environments safely and in isolation.

Firecracker offers a seamless performant, secure, and rapid mechanism based on MicroVm principle. This allows AWS Lambda to cover a large variety of Scalability needs and security concerns in serverless landscape.

Execution Environment Lifecycle

Lambda Execution Environment Lifecycle relies on the Lambda service's internal state and capacity at any given time. As a customer, there is no need to worry about these states but knowing them let us better optimize and improve the functions during serverless journey on AWS.

The Lambda service generally has three states which are related to a worker's state:

- Init
- Invoke
- Shutdown

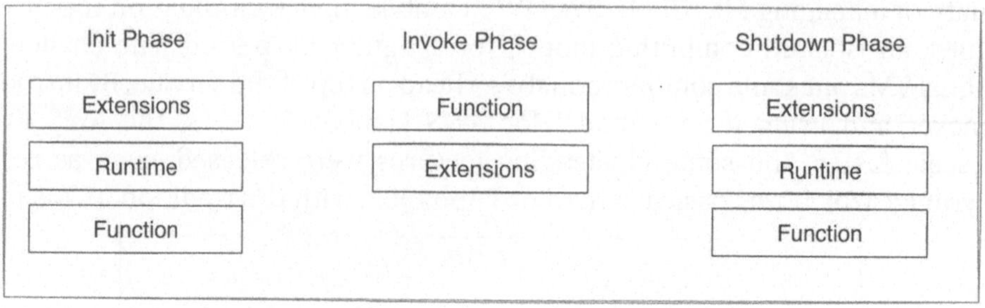

Figure 2.10: *Execution environment lifecycle*

Init

The **`init`** phase happens when the function needs a new worker to be set up and configured for running the function code.

In Init phase, the Lambda service setup evolves in three phases: `` `Runtime Init` ``, `` `Function Init` ``, and `` `Extensions Init` ``. An execution environment gets ready when all phases are passed successfully within a 10-second timeout managed by the Lambda service.

The Execution environment has two APIs: `` `Runtime API` `` and `` `Extensions API` ``. The runtime API takes care of initializing the Runtime and Function, while the Extension API is responsible for Initializing Extensions.

In case of any failure in one of the phases, the Lambda service retries the **`init`** phase before the function invocation, with the timeout configured at the function level.

The Init phase is one of the challenging parts of Lambda service discussions, but the chance of it happening is really small compared to all invocations of Lambda functions. The Init phase happens when a Function has the concurrency needs and there is no warm worker available yet, or in case of peak load on the system and Lambda service face a scale-up situation.

As mentioned above, the **`init`** phase of lambda **`consts`** of:

- Runtime initialization
- Extensions Initialization
- Function Initialization

The following figure shows how the function participates in initialization phase:

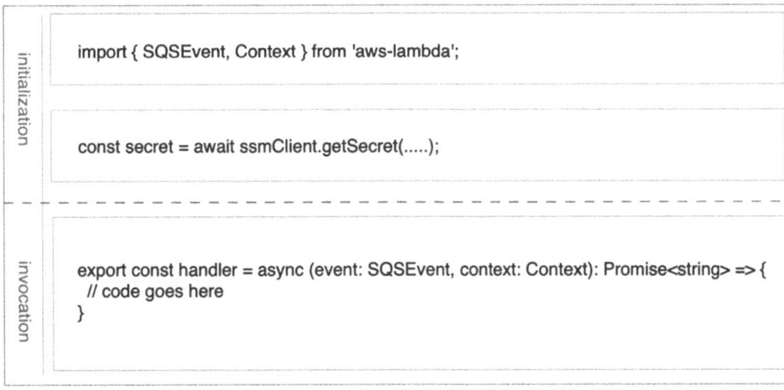

Figure 2.11: *Function handler phase*

The Lambda service sends an **`init`** request, which will run the part of Lambda function code outside the handler method as part of Init phase. This is also called Static code (the code outside handler method).

The Init phase for extensions and runtime takes place as follows:

- Ask for runtime bootstrapping
- Ask for Extensions to start

At any step the concerned task will send back a success task result by sending a `**Next**` signal. This communication between the Process and Runtime or extension APIs happens on a local http call `**127.0.0.1:9009**`, which is available under the `**AWS_LAMBDA_RUNTIME_API**` environment variable.

Here is an example of how you can signal the next step to approve a success:

```
const extensionPath = `http://${process.env.AWS_LAMBDA_RUNTIME_
API}/2020-01-01/extension`
await fetch(`${extensionPath}/event/next`, {
 headers: {
   'Lambda-Extension-Identifier': extensionId
 }
});
```

Invoke

The Invocation phase is the only phase that happens most of the time. This is when actually lambda service has most of the effort to put on. In the Invocation phase, the Lambda service begins the process by involving the `**Runtime API**` and `**Extension API**`. When this phase happens, the Lambda service executes the handler function. However, this phase happens after receiving a `**Next**` response from Init phase, and Lambda sends an invoke request to the runtime and all extensions. Calling the handler method is done by the runtime part of the runtime invoke API call.

The Invocation phase duration consists of the duration of Runtime response and extensions and it must be succeeded before the configured function timeout reaches.

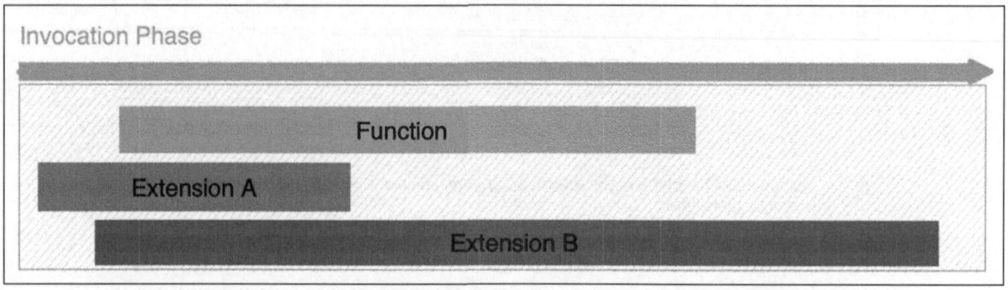

Figure 2.12: *Invocation phase*

After invocation, the runtime and all extensions must send back a signal using `Next` API call as demonstrated above.

Shutdown

The use of execution environments is a way toward more scalability and performance optimization. But the Lambda service for optimizing the resource usage and costs will keep any execution environment for some time. This is actually a variable time and there is no documentation around to rely on.

After the Invocation phase ends, an execution environment will be in an `Idle` state where any new invocation request can reuse that execution environment. If no request is reached for that particular function, the Lambda service sends a `SHUTDOWN` request to the runtime and all extensions, hoping they will do all necessary cleanup. If during shutdown, an exception happens or the shutdown request takes more than 2 seconds the Lambda service will request a termination via a `SIGKILL` to immediately terminate the process. The SIGKILL is a Unix/Linux-based signal used to kill processes.

Lifecycle Exceptional Behaviors

We explored how the three phases of the lifecycle occur and how these are chained one after another. However, there are some exceptional situations that Lambda service handles exceptionally and here we are going to discover a bit about the Invocation phase.

Invoke Phase when Errors Happen

During the invocation process and while in progress, the Runtime API keeps track of the execution process. In some cases, the invocation can encounter unhandled exceptions. In this case, the Lambda service requests the Runtime a `RESET` followed by a `Shutdown` request to all extensions.

After the encountered situation and reset and shutdown requests are done, the Lambda service will give a chance to the worker to process an invocation. In this case, the invocation phase will have the Init of Runtime and extensions part of the invocation phase.

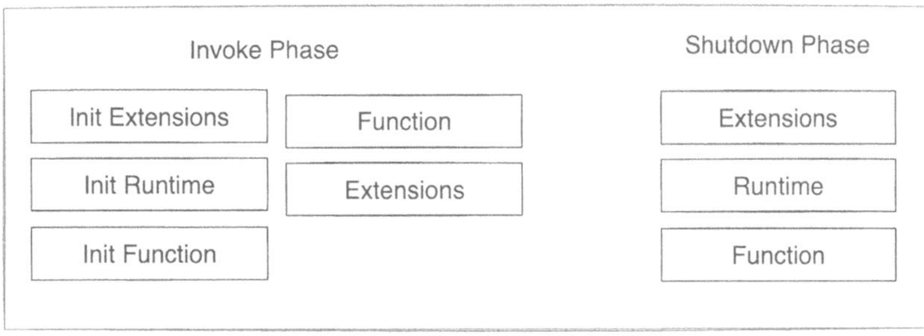

Figure 2.13: *Invoke phase after failures including init*

Execution Lifecycle for Scaling

The mentioned three phases of the Execution environment are the principal points in a function lifecycle, but now let's dive deep a bit more to explore how those phases of collaboration bring improvements in the process.

Lambda service keeps track of the state of workers. This is achieved by a collaboration of two internal components of AWS lambda service: **`Worker manager`** and **`Placement service`**. These communicate to choose the best decision for a worker request and improve the chance of reusability of already **`Idle`** workers.

Using `Idle` workers improves the need for rapidity at scale and when the peak of function is significant. However, at a higher peak, it can happen that the Lambda service needs to scale up (initiating new workers). In this situation, the placement service lets the worker manager know about where the worker is located and can be initiated. If you have an unpredictable load and your workload faces a high peak, the function will go to the Init phase for a large number of workers, which can bring latency and performance issues.

The lambda service, for on-demand functions, occasionally sent **init** requests for the functions to give them more chance of not facing an **`Init`** phase.

Lambda Limits

Lambda service as a computing service with all its powers and scaling capacity, also has some limitations that can become a blocking point when designing highly scalable systems. It is better to understand the Lambda limitation and consider those limits in the early phase of design.

Limits on AWS can be soft or hard, the hard limits can be blocked as there is no way to increase that limit but the soft limits can be increased by a support ticket and a brief explanation of the situation and why that increase is required.

Memory

The Lambda memory max limit is actually 10GB, this means if the function process needs more than this limit, the Lambda function will not be the available choice in serverless ecosystem as the memory limit is a hard limit. As per the memory for this maximum limit of 10GB, the Lambda gets 6 vCPU (Round (10240 % 1769)), so for a process needing more vCPU than this limit, the Lambda again is not the available choice of service.

GPU Based

At the time of writing this book, the AWS Lambda offers no GPU based possibility. This is certainly due to the AWS Lambda infrastructure and the underlying instances behind the scene. So, AWS lambda will not be a choice for GPU based processes.

Timeout

The Lambda Max execution timeout is limited to 15 minutes (900 seconds), which leads to Lambda not being a choice for long running processing. For use cases with a higher need, there are other alternatives in AWS serverless ecosystem that we will explore in this book. The timeout also is a hard limit and cannot be exceeded.

Response-Streaming

This feature has some limits as follows:

- Support for Node.js Runtime only, other runtimes can be managed using custom runtime.
- Operates only via Function URLs, CLI and AWS SDK.
- The Max response payload size for any single part cannot exceed 20MB.
- Bandwidth limit of 2MBPS beyond 6MB of response payload size

Runtime

Lambda service supports a limited set of runtimes that were explored previously in this chapter. To overcome this limitation, Lambda service introduces custom runtime that can be used as a custom image respecting the Lambda service runtime API interface. The Lambda behind the scene takes care of initializing and running the custom runtime.

Payload

Lambda service introduces payload limit. The payload represents an envelope of event data, headers, and so on. The payload limit is valid for the request as well the response.

Note: The payload limit is a hard limit and cannot be exceeded.

Synchronous

The payload limit differs based on the invocation model. For `RequestResponse` as a synchronous invocation the payload is limited to 6MB.

Type of Synchronous invocation is integration lambda function with an `ApiGateway` or Application Load Balancer.

When using an API Gateway that has a 10MB limit for request and response, consider the limit of 6MB behind the scenes on the Lambda service side. On the other hand, when integrating Lambda with an Application Load Balancer, consider that contrary to the 6MB of Lambda limit, the Target Group limit when integrating with lambda service is up to 1MB.

Asynchronous

Asynchronous invocations are limited to 256KB. This is the case when integrating the lambda function with services like Simple Notification Service (SNS) or Simple Storage Service (S3). This limit can be a blocking point for some use cases with a larger payload. In this case, we can adopt some patterns like Claim pattern to overcome this limit.

The Claim pattern uses externalizing the large payload from the event and sending the necessary info to let the consumer fetch the payload behind getting notified. A simple design on AWS would be using S3 as a source for externalizing the payload and sending the object key as a notification via SNS, letting the Lambda to fetch that object for processing.

Response Streaming

The Limit for Response streaming is up to 20MB for each streamed response. That means returning a large payload of 75MB will be achievable in 4 streaming responses (3 X 20MB and 1 X 15MB). This limit actually is a soft limit and can be increased by support request.

Package

As mentioned previously in this chapter, the package can be provided as a Zip File or custom image. Regardless of the format, the Zip cannot exceed 50MB, and the unzipped package must be less than 250MB. This is valid also for layers and custom runtimes.

Note: *The package size limit is a hard limit and cannot be exceeded.*

Storage

The `tmp` storage has a limit of 10GB, which is convenient for most use cases. However, it can be a blocking point for some other scenarios. To overcome this limit, you can use S3 as storage instead of `tmp`.

Note: *The `tmp` storage size limit is a hard limit and cannot be exceeded.*

Layers

Layers are a means of augmenting the power of Lambda functions or standardizing some tasks at enterprise level. Layers also come with a limit of 5 layers per function. Additionally, when using layers, consider their size impact on the function package size limit.

Note: *This limit is a hard limit and cannot be exceeded.*

Elastic Network Interface

Each function associated with a subnet will achieve an ENI that will be dedicated to the ENI Hyperplane. This limit of the number of ENIs are not related to Lambda service but to Virtual Private Cloud (VPC). Consider this limit when you use the functions in a VPC. The association of ENI proceeds during the function creation phase and will not impact the runtime execution.

Concurrency

The Lambda service manages concurrency per region and account. This means the concurrency limit affects all functions of an account within any single region. The Lambda service comes with a default limit of 1000 concurrent executions per account and region. This limit is a soft limit and can be increased.

Conclusion

In this chapter, we delved into the realism of setting up a lambda function and explored the fine details of how an execution context works as a mandatory step to better understand how to set up the functions.

The exploratory of this chapter is a starting point for delving deeper into lambda invocation models and how it integrates with different services in the AWS ecosystem. Understanding how the monitoring part of AWS Lambda works as part of the system is really useful for debugging and troubleshooting the system, as it can save time.

In the next chapter, we will discover the different integration models and how lambda integrates with different services in each category.

CHAPTER 3
Invocation Models and Service Integrations

Introduction

In this chapter, we will focus on practical examples to better discover the AWS Lambda integrations and how the invocation models work and help in a design. The Synchronous, Asynchronous, and Poll-Based Invocation models will be described with the corresponding integration examples.

We will also delve into the design principles of any integration model by exploring the inconveniences that a chosen integration may bring at runtime. The focus will rely on scalability, concurrency, and back pressure that may be faced in any integration.

The result of any integration example helps us discover details about that kind of integration and provides advice on avoiding the resulting pitfalls in a design.

Structure

In this chapter, we will discuss the following topics:

- Invocation Models and Integrations
- Poll-Based Invocation Model
- Asynchronous Invocation Model
- Synchronous Invocation Model
- Integration with Amazon SQS
- Integration with Data Streams
- Integration with Amazon SNS

- Integration with EventBridge Bus
- Integration with Amazon API Gateway

Invocation Models and Integrations

In the preceding chapter, AWS *Lambda Basics*, we delved into the diverse spectrum of AWS services that seamlessly interface with AWS Lambda. A fundamental aspect of comprehending serverless design lies in grasping the intricacies of integration, which is pivotal for having the runtime interactions among different services within a design. Beyond the significance of choosing services appropriately, it is equally crucial to gain insight into the operational dynamics of these interconnections.

When incorporating a Lambda function into a system alongside other services, it is crucial to consider the following four aspects:

- **Transitioning Information**: Data in transition within the AWS ecosystem commonly adopts JSON format, ensuring both machine readability and human comprehensibility. When handling such data, it becomes imperative to address factors like data integrity, compliance, security, and governance.
- **Handling Failures**: Dealing with failures in the communication between services is an inherent challenge. To tackle this, it is essential to systematically assess the following potential failure points:
  - Does the failure stem from a network issue occurring at the initiation, midpoint, or conclusion of communication?
  - Is it a scenario where the response to a dispatched request is interrupted?
  - Could the failure be attributed to the upstream experiencing an excessive load?
  - Is it a consequence of the target service's incapacity to process the request?
  - Are the consumers at risk of not being idempotent?
  - And so more ...
- **Scaling Collaboratively**: Enabling effective scaling for both upstream and downstream sides is crucial in distributed communication. This necessitates making design choices capable of unexpected scaling requirements. Such an approach not only facilitates scalability but also guards against constraints coming from the other ends of communication.
- **Ensuring Operational Requirements**: In a serverless distributed design, the performance of individual components holds significance. Nevertheless, the ultimate gauge of success is the combined behavior of the entire system. If a design choice enhances the efficiency of one component but adversely affects downstream components under scalability pressure, it necessitates a

thorough review. This refined version preserves the essential content while enhancing scalability and coherence.

AWS Lambda Invocation Models

This section serves as an exploration into the nuanced realm of AWS Lambda's invocation models, an integral facet of serverless computing within the AWS serverless ecosystem. As we navigate through the dynamic interoperability between Lambda functions and diverse AWS services, a holistic comprehension will unfold the notion of Lambda invocation demands and the details in diverse scenarios. The principal points of this chapter encompass three primary invocation models:

- **Synchronous Invocation**

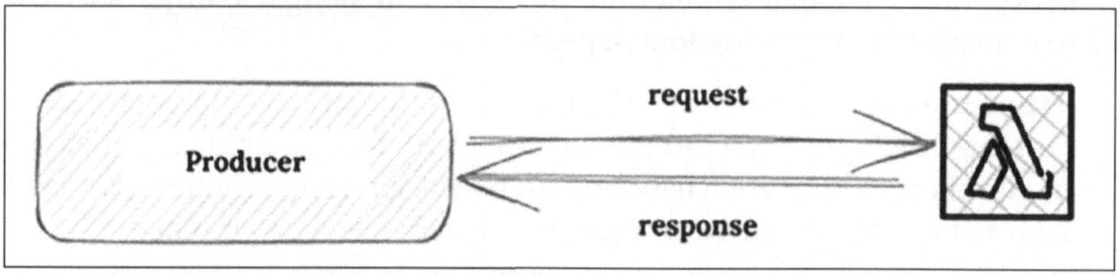

Figure 3.1: *Synchronous invocation flow*

- **Asynchronous Invocation**

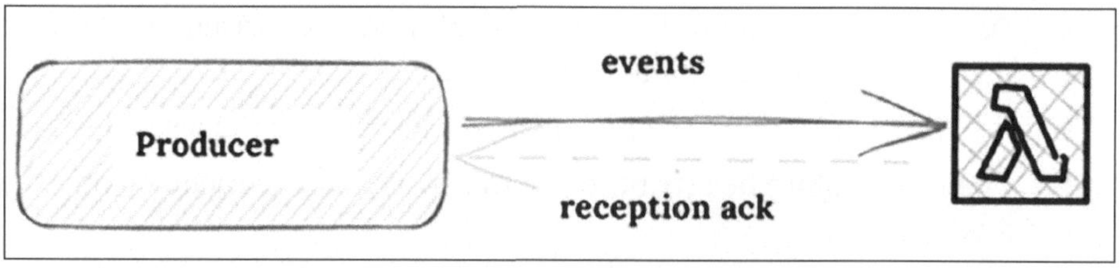

Figure 3.2: *Asynchronous invocation flow*

- **Poll-Based Invocation**

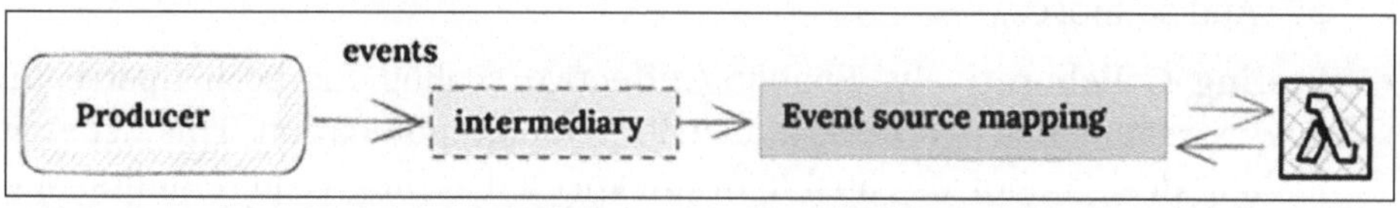

Figure 3.3: *Poll-based invocation flow*

Offering insights and practical examples, this chapter illuminates the distinctive characteristics and applications inherent in each model.

Poll-Based Invocation

Within the Poll-Based Invocation model, the Lambda service routinely checks source services, including Amazon SQS, Amazon Kinesis, or DynamoDB Streams, to initiate their execution. Unlike the prompt push-based invocation, Lambda service independently polls for fresh messages, processing them at specified intervals.

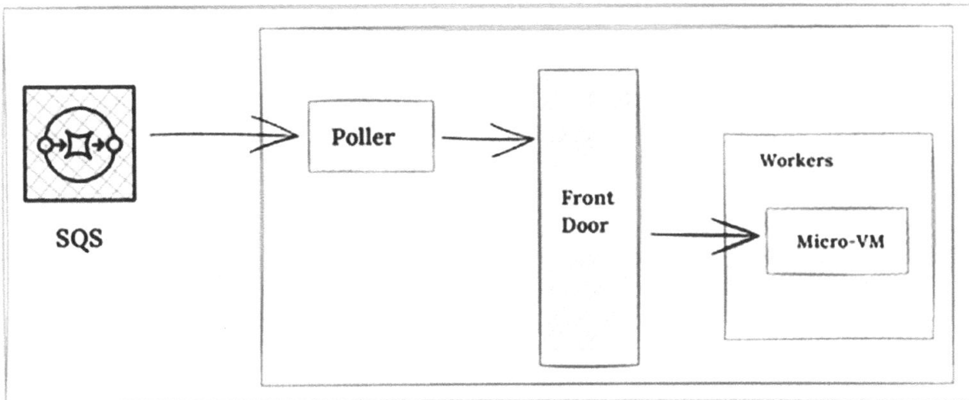

Figure 3.4: *Lambda service Poll-based invocation*

The communication method employed by the Lambda service to interact with services compatible with the Poll-Based Invocation model is done through Event Source Mapping. Event source mapping (ESM) is an internal service of Lambda that does the heavy lifting in terms of message polling, batching, scaling and some aspects of error handling. To set up an Event Source Mapping for Lambda, we establish an **`EventSourceMapping`** resource by specifying parameters such as (https://docs.aws.amazon.com/AWSCloudFormation/latest/UserGuide/aws-resource-lambda-eventsourcemapping.html):

- **`BatchSize`**
- **`EventSourceArn`**
- **`MaximumBatchingWindowInSeconds`**
- **`MaximumRecordAgeInSeconds`**
- **`MaximumRetryAttempts`**
- **`ParallelizationFactor`**
- **`FunctionName`**
- **`FilterCriteria`**
- **`BisectBatchOnFunctionError`**
- **`ScalingConfig`**

The configuration differs depending on the internal technical design of the source service. Specifically, Kinesis and DynamoDB Streams follow a Shard-based technical design, while SQS adopts a simpler Queue-based technical design. Lambda uses the

State Manager and Stream Tracker to keep the service integration operational and event-based.

This model is particularly prevalent in services such as:

- **Amazon SQS (Simple Queue Service)**: An option for enabling decoupled communication and offloading processes between components on AWS involves the use of the SQS service. Lambda service frequently polls, via ESM, the events to retrieve and process messages from SQS queues by invoking the function synchronously.

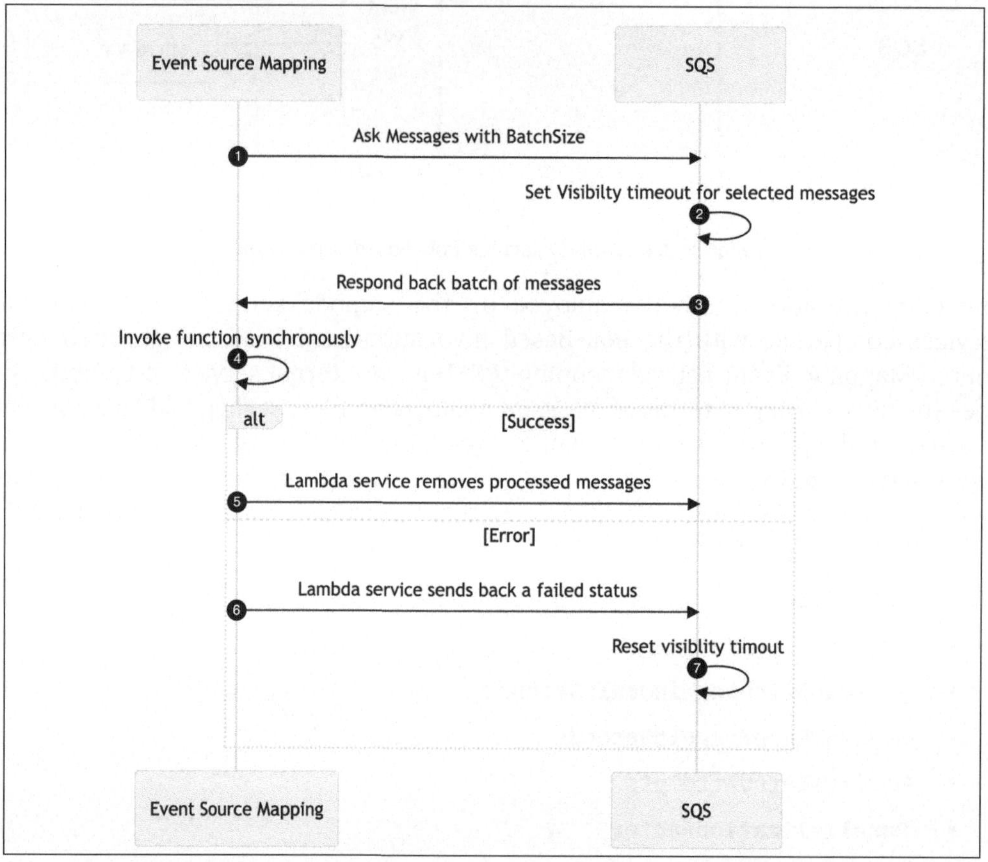

Figure 3.5: *Amazon SQS and Lambda Integration Sequence diagram*

- **Amazon Kinesis or Dynamodb Streams**: In scenarios requiring real-time data processing, design choice often involves the use of Data Streams. The Lambda service uses a polling model by regularly polling data streams, facilitating the receipt of streaming data. The polling mechanism for shards operates somewhat differently, as the configuration pertains to each individual shard (partition in DynamoDB). In other words, when defining an event source mapping for data streams, the configuration specified will function on a per-key basis, which is utilized to partition the data across distinct isolated data nodes. By default, the Lambda service associates a single execution environment with each shard, but this can be altered using the `ParallelizationFactor` property in the event source mapping configuration. The Lambda service initiates the process by checking the data streams to identify the shards, followed by querying the `Iterator` for any single shard. Subsequently, Lambda requests records from that shard. This entire process can be illustrated as a sequence diagram, as depicted in *Figure 3.6*.

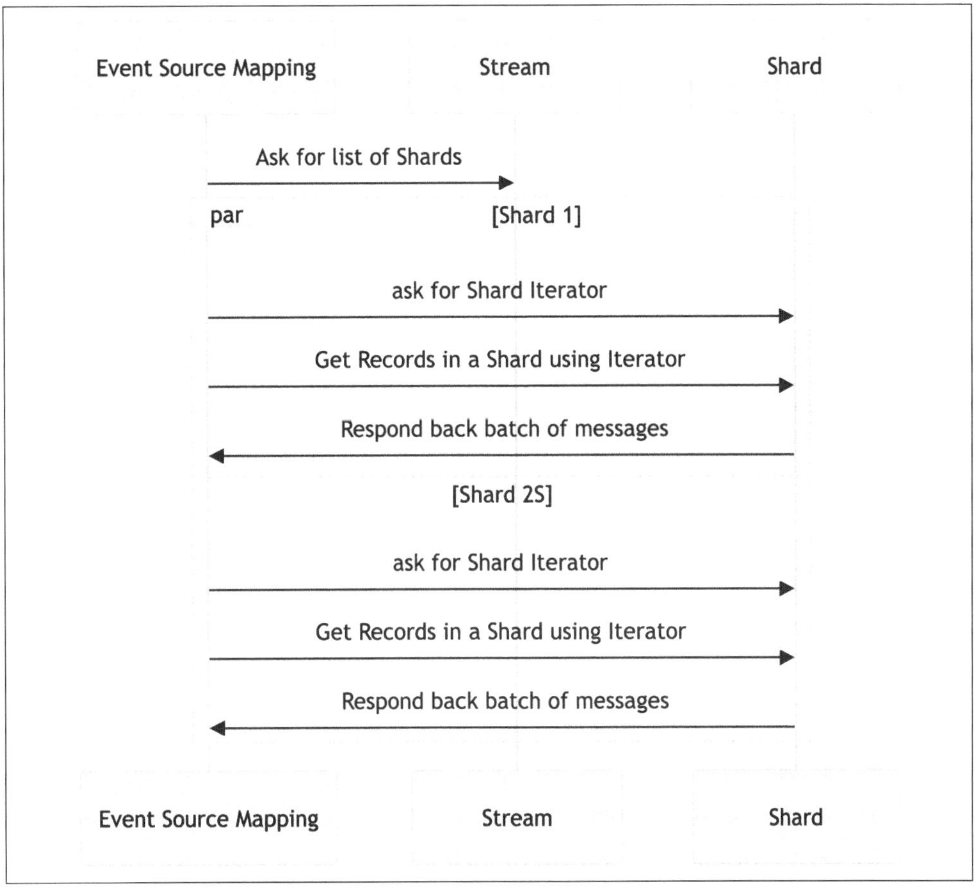

Figure 3.6: *Data Stream and Lambda Integration Sequence diagram*

AWS Event source mapping allows configuring the integration for partial failures. With partial failures, the integration will manage if some messages in a batch were not successfully processed and will mark the successful messages as successful, avoiding the retry of the whole batch of messages in case of a single point of failure. We will discover more in *Chapter 5, Hyper-Scaling with Lambda*.

Example: Poll-Based Invocation

Here's an example of an Event source mapping configuration demonstrated using AWS CDK:

```
import * as cdk from "aws-cdk-lib";
import * as sqs from "aws-cdk-lib/aws-sqs";
import * as lambda from "aws-cdk-lib/aws-lambda";
import * as lambdaEventSources from "aws-cdk-lib/aws-lambda-event-sources";

const app = new cdk.App();
const stack = new cdk.Stack(app, "PollBasedInvocationExampleStack");

const queue = new sqs.Queue(stack, "queue", {
 queueName: 'pollebased-example-queue',
 visibilityTimeout: cdk.Duration.seconds(300),
});

const pollBasedLambda = new lambda.Function(stack, "PollBasedLambda", {
 runtime: lambda.Runtime.NODEJS_20_X,
 handler: "index.handler",
 code: lambda.Code.fromAsset("lambda"),
});

pollBasedLambda.addEventSource(
 new lambdaEventSources.SqsEventSource(queue, {
   batchSize: 5,
 })
);
```

Here, we are creating two components: a Lambda Function and an SQS Queue. The integration is achieved through event source mapping with a batch size set to 5. In this context, the Lambda function is triggered by the Event Source Mapping (ESM) for a batch of five items, which it subsequently processed.

Lambda Function handler (TypeScript)

```
import { SQSEvent, Handler, SQSRecord } from "aws-lambda";

export const handler: Handler = async (event: SQSEvent) => {
 await Promise.all(event.Records.map( (record: SQSRecord) => {
   const message = JSON.parse(record.body);
   console.log(`Processing message: ${message.Id}`);
 }));
};
```

Testing becomes straightforward by sending a batch of 10 messages to the queue. Given that the event source mapping is set with a batch size of 5, your function will be invoked multiple times, with the potential of having up to five messages in each invocation.

As the following test uses the AWS CLI, it needs a batch of messages to be provided as a JSON file:

Name the file as `pollbased-example-batch-source.json`

```
[
 {
   "Id": "pollbased-example-1",
   "DelaySeconds": 20,
   "MessageBody": "{\"Id\":\"1\"}"
 },
 {
   "Id": "pollbased-example-2",
   "DelaySeconds": 20,
   "MessageBody": "{\"Id\":\"2\"}"
 },
 {
   "Id": "pollbased-example-3",
   "DelaySeconds": 20,
   "MessageBody": "{\"Id\":\"3\"}"
 },
 //...
 {
   "Id": "pollbased-example-10",
   "DelaySeconds": 20,
   "MessageBody": "{\"Id\":\"10\"}"
 }
]
```

Running the following command will send the whole batch of messages from JSON file to the queue:

Replace the `REGION` and `ACCOUNT_NUMBER` placeholders with your own account ID and region.

```
aws sqs send-message-batch
--queue-url https://sqs.{REGION}.amazonaws.com/{ACCOUNT_NUMBER}/polle-
based-example-queue
--entries file://pollbased-example-batch-source.json
```

Providing the given input, dispatching a batch of messages will entail sending 10 messages to SQS with a 20-second delay, resulting in the unavailability of messages during this timeframe. Upon examining the Lambda function metrics, we observe a total of five invocations, as indicated by the invocation metric.

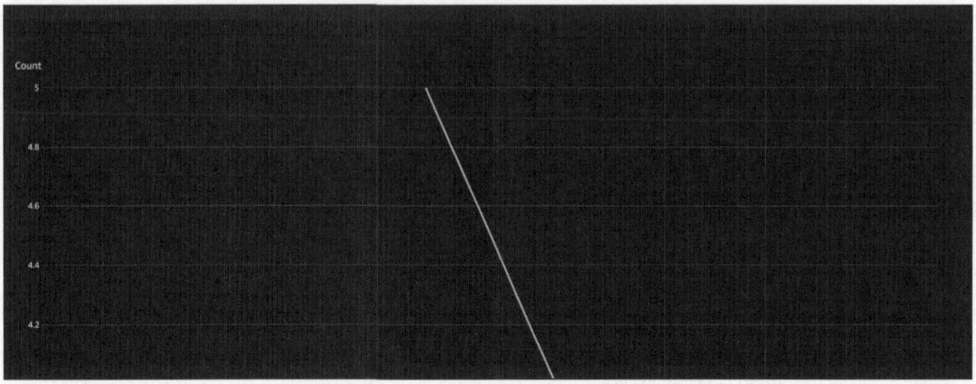

Figure 3.7: *SQS received message metric*

Well-aligned with the invocation metric, we also find five log streams added to the CloudWatch log group of our function, as shown in *Figure* 3.8. Each execution environment represents a dedicated log stream.

Figure 3.8: *Lambda invocation log streams*

Looking each log stream, we find a different number of lines of log from the function:

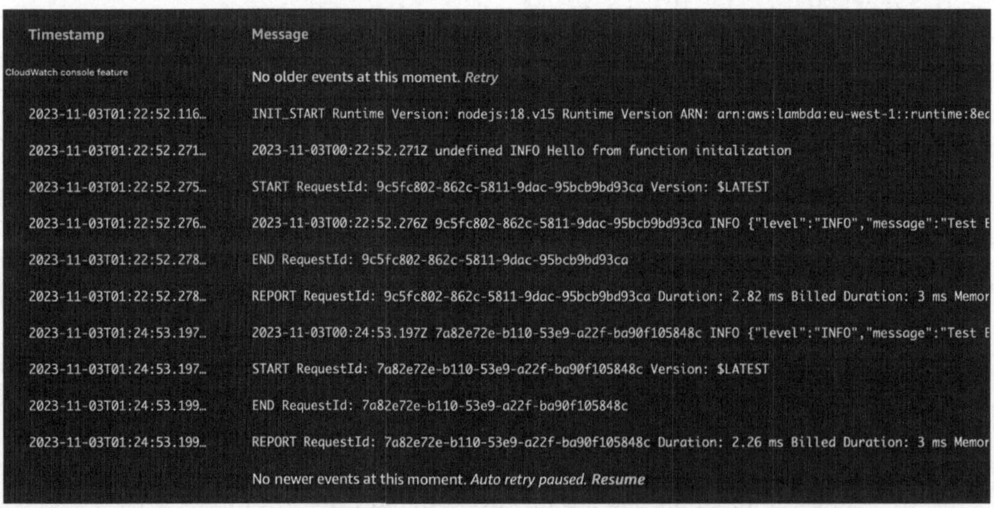

Figure 3.9: *Lambda Log Stream logs*

The expected result in theory was to have a single invocation for each batch of five messages, resulting in two invocations and two log streams consequently (one per invocation). Batching will be explored deeply in the batching section of *Chapter 5, Hyper-Scaling with Lambda*, to achieve the expected results.

Asynchronous Invocation

AWS Lambda's Asynchronous invocation provides an immediate and non-blocking triggering mechanism. In this approach, the calling service doesn't need to await an immediate response from the function to determine the success or failure of processing. Asynchronous invocation supports parallel processing, making it well-suited for scenarios that demand rapid and non-blocking interactions.

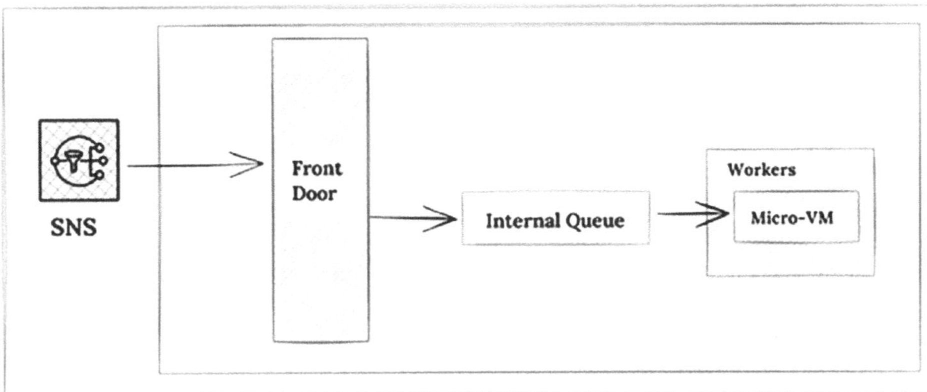

Figure 3.10: *Lambda service Asynchronous invocation*

Within the asynchronous invocation model, the caller initiates a Lambda invocation request. Once the request passes through the entry point and undergoes validation, it is directed to an internal queue on the Lambda service side. At this juncture, the caller receives confirmation of the request's reception, and a worker will be asynchronously associated with the request for processing. In asynchronous communication, the trigger communication takes the form of a subscription or trigger configuration. In this setup, the Lambda service instructs the service to dispatch a request to the Lambda service when an event becomes available on the service side. Examples include a new published message in SNS, new events in the EventBridge bus, or the creation of a new object event in the S3 service.

Upon receiving a message from the internal queue, the Lambda service assesses the concurrency level, a situation that may result in throttling errors. In the event of a failed invocation due to throttling or service errors (5XX), Lambda autonomously retries the invocation. These unsuccessful invocations are placed back in the queue for subsequent retry attempts within a timeframe of up to 6 hours. In the case of function errors, the Lambda service executes up to three retry attempts.

We will discover more about retry and failures in *Chapter 7*, *Resiliency and Design for Failure*.

This model finds its application in services such as:

- **Amazon SNS (Simple Notification Service)**: SNS provides the functionality to broadcast messages to consumers that are subscribed, effectively breaking the temporal coupling between the sender and receiver. When establishing integration with the SNS service, the Lambda service is required to send a subscription request to the SNS, along with providing a filter policy if applicable. Subsequently, the SNS service distributes any published messages within the topic to the Lambda service by issuing an invocation request.
- **Amazon S3 (Simple Storage Service)**: Lambda functions are triggered when new objects are either created or modified within an S3 bucket, enabling the asynchronous processing of files and data.
- **AWS Step Functions**: Step Functions enable the orchestration of multiple AWS services into serverless workflows. With Lambda functions, Step Functions can invoke Lambda in two ways: asynchronously or synchronously. The state machine can invoke Lambda synchronously, ensuring precise control and orchestration flow handling by using the processing response as part of the orchestration state, or asynchronously just by requesting an invocation without waiting for an immediate response.

Example: Asynchronous Invocation

Let's see this example:

Infrastructure as Code with AWS CDK:

```
const bucket = new Bucket(stack, 'ImageBucket');

const asyncLambda = new Function(stack, 'AsyncLambda', {
 runtime: Runtime.NODEJS_20_X,
 handler: 'index.handler',
 code: Code.fromAsset('lambda'),
});

bucket.addEventNotification(EventType.OBJECT_CREATED, new Lambda
Destination(asyncLambda));
```

Lambda Function Handler (TypeScript):

```
import { S3Event, S3Handler } from 'aws-lambda';

export const handler: S3Handler = async (event: S3Event) => {
 event.Records.forEach(record => {
```

```
    const bucketName = record.s3.bucket.name;
    const objectKey = record.s3.object.key;
    console.log(`Processing image ${objectKey} in bucket ${bucketName}`);
  })
};
```

To manually trigger a Lambda function using asynchronous invocation via the AWS CLI with Amazon S3 payload, use the following command:

```
aws lambda invoke \
  --function-name AsyncLambda \
  --invocation-type Event \
  --payload '{\"Records\": [{\"eventVersion\": \"2.1\",\"eventSource\":
\"aws:s3\",\"eventName\": \"ObjectCreated\",\"s3\": {\"s3SchemaV-
ersion\": \"1.0\",\"bucket\": {\"name\": \"ImageBucket\",\"arn\":
\"arn:aws:s3:::ImageBucket\"},\"object\": {\"key\": \"example-image.
jpg\"}}}]}' \
  response.json
```

This command triggers the **`AsyncLambda`** function using an S3 event simulation, demonstrating asynchronous invocation.

Another example of invoking a Lambda function asynchronously using Step Function is illustrated as follows:

```
const asyncLambda = new Function(stack, 'AsyncLambda', {
  runtime: Runtime.NODEJS_20_X,
  handler: 'index.handler',
  code: Code.fromAsset('lambda'),
});

new StateMachine(stack, 'state-machine', {
  definitionBody: DefinitionBody.fromChainable(
    new LambdaInvoke(this, 'invoke-function', {
      lambdaFunction: asyncLambda,
      invocationType: LambdaInvocationType.EVENT,
      payload: TaskInput.fromJsonPathAt('$.Payload'),
  }))
})
```

As mentioned above, to invoke the Lambda using the async model when dealing with state machines, the `**invocationType**` parameter needs to be set as `**Invocationtye.Event**`, and the Step Function calls the `**Event Frontend service**` of the Lambda service, passing the event payload.

Synchronous Invocation

The AWS Lambda synchronous invocation enables the instantaneous and real-time initiation of Lambda functions, where the invoking service actively awaits a synchronous response. This method is particularly relevant when a calling service necessitates an immediate response from the Lambda function.

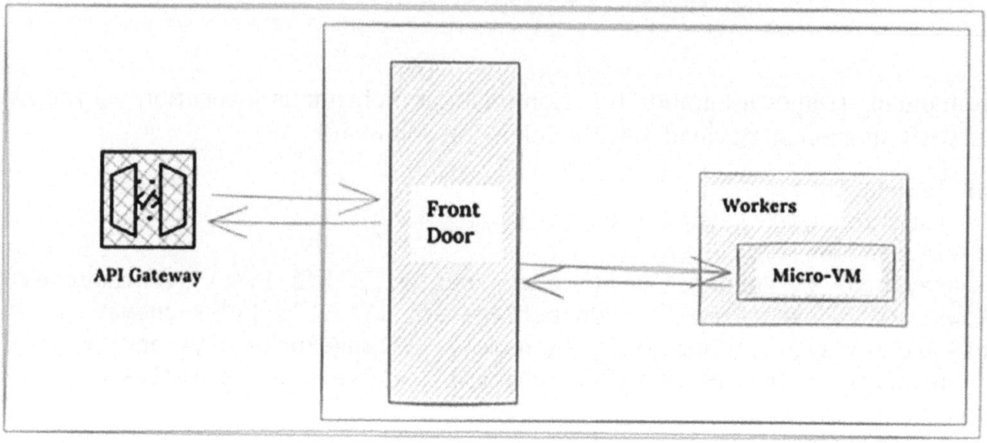

Figure 3.11: *Lambda service Synchronous invocation*

This model finds its application in services such as:

- **Amazon API Gateway**: Lambda functions are commonly used as backends for RESTful APIs hosted on Amazon API Gateway. When clients send HTTP requests, the API Gateway activates Lambda functions, expecting a synchronous response.
- **AWS Step Functions**: As mentioned earlier in the *Asynchronous Invocation* section of this chapter, the state machine can invoke the Lambda synchronously or asynchronously. To ensure precise control and orchestration flow handling by using the processing response as part of the orchestration state, Step Functions can invoke the Lambda synchronously, awaiting an immediate response.

Example: Synchronous Invocation

Infrastructure as Code with AWS CDK:

```
const app = new cdk.App();
const stack = new cdk.Stack(app, 'SynchronousInvocationStack');

const syncLambda = new lambda.Function(stack, 'SyncLambda', {
 runtime: lambda.Runtime.NODEJS_20_X,
 handler: 'index.handler',
 code: lambda.Code.fromAsset('lambda'),
});

const api = new apigateway.RestApi(stack, 'ExampleApi');
```

```
const resource = api.root.addResource('example');
const method = resource.addMethod('GET', new apigateway.LambdaIntegra-
tion(syncLambda));

app.synth();
```

Lambda Function Handler (TypeScript):

```
import { APIGatewayProxyResult } from 'aws-lambda';

export async function handler(): Promise<APIGatewayProxyResult> {
 return {
   statusCode: 200,
   body: JSON.stringify({ message: "Synchronous Lambda Invocation
Example" }),
 };
}
```

To manually trigger a Lambda function using synchronous invocation via the AWS CLI with Amazon API Gateway, use the following command:

```
aws lambda invoke \
  --function-name SyncLambda \
  --invocation-type RequestResponse \
  --payload '{\"httpMethod\": \"GET\", \"path\": \"/example\",
\"headers\": {\"Content-Type\": \"application/json\"},
\"body\": \"\"}' \
  response.json
```

This command sends an HTTP GET request to the SyncLambda function, which is configured as a RESTful API backend, demonstrating synchronous invocation.

Integration with Amazon SQS

Amazon Simple Queue Service (SQS) is an Amazon-provided messaging queue solution designed to facilitate the delegation of tasks among distributed services. AWS Lambda seamlessly integrates with SQS, allowing it to handle messages in an asynchronous manner. As highlighted earlier, the integration between Amazon SQS and AWS Lambda employs a Poll-based invocation model. This integration operates in a synchronous fashion, enabling Lambda to acknowledge SQS through the worker process's success or failure status. This synchronous communication ensures that Amazon SQS can effectively consider the outcomes and manage the associated messages accordingly.

Amazon SQS Message Lifecycle

When message producers dispatch messages to a queue, the messages are made available for AWS Lambda as a consumer to retrieve at an appropriate rate. Once the

Lambda poller retrieves a message, the message will be made invisible to all subsequent retrieval requests, and the message reappears and becomes available only if the Lambda service acknowledges a failure. Conversely, upon a successful acknowledgment, the message poller triggers a request for the removal of the message from the queue. The ensuing diagram illustrates the message visibility cycle.

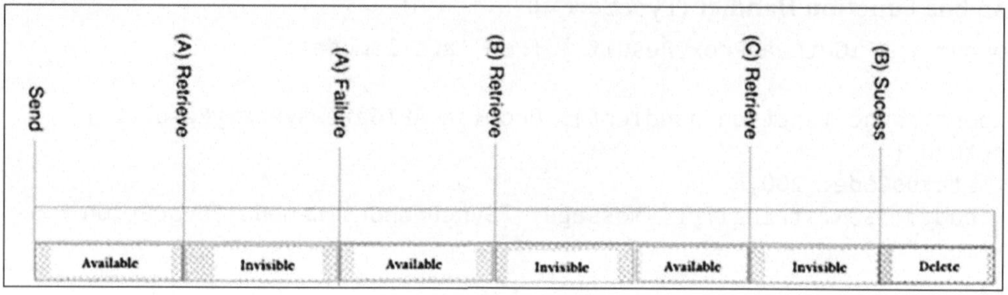

Figure 3.12: *Message Visibility cycle*

To mitigate the occurrence of receiving a message multiple times, it's crucial to strike a balance between the visibility timeout and the function duration or function timeout. For instance, if a queue has a default visibility timeout of 30 seconds and a consumer takes approximately 40 seconds to process a message, the message will remain invisible for the initial 30 seconds of the consumer's processing time. However, before the consumer completes its processing and requests message removal, another consumer may receive the message as it reaches the visibility timeout limit. This situation can result in undesirable behaviors on the consumer side.

To avoid such scenarios, consumers must be designed to be idempotent, capable of handling multiple retrievals of the same message without adversely affecting the software's behavior. This ensures that even if a message is processed multiple times, the end result remains consistent and as intended.

Short and Long Polling

AWS Lambda employs periodic polling to retrieve messages from SQS. By default, when utilizing SQS Queues, the system utilizes "*short polling*." In short polling, the SQS service checks a subset of distributed nodes in response to a `ReceiveMessage` call. However, this approach can result in additional API calls and potentially trigger false empty responses, indicating no available messages even when they exist in other nodes.

In systems with lower throughput, or to minimize the occurrence of empty responses, "*long polling*" proves beneficial. Long polling allows the SQS service to inspect all distributed nodes, increasing the likelihood of identifying messages. This approach helps reduce the number of false empty responses, optimizing the efficiency of message retrieval.

In the context of AWS Lambda, when Long Polling is in use, the `ReceiveMessageWaitTimeSeconds` attribute of the queue is configured with a value above 0, whereas for Short Polling, the default value is 0. The permissible range for **ReceiveMessageWaitTimeSeconds** is between 0 and 20 seconds.

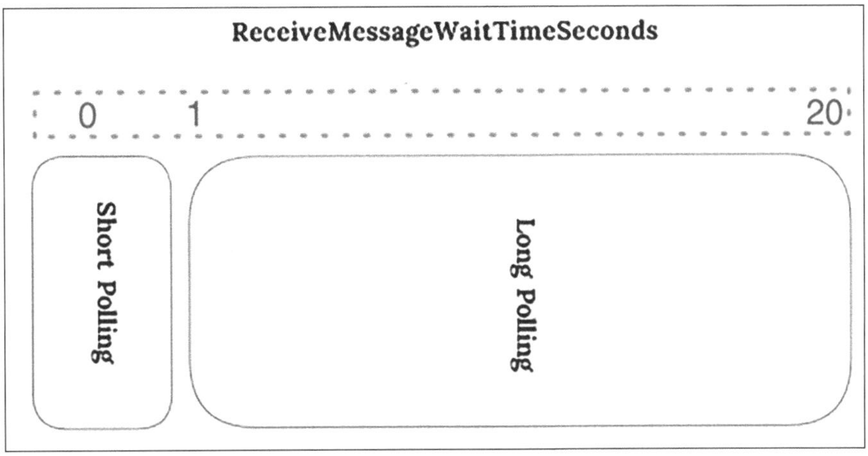

Figure 3.13: *Short and long polling*

This behavior can impact the Lambda service, particularly introducing latencies when the queue experiences insufficient regular throughput. Monitoring this behavior can be achieved through the `NumberOfEmptyReceives` queue metric. Additionally, the `ApproximateAgeOfOldestMessage` metric provides insight into the age of the oldest message present in the queue but not processed yet. It's important to note that this metric can indicate a message that has undergone multiple retrieval attempts without successful processing. In the event of unsuccessful processing multiple times, the unprocessed message is returned to the end of the message backlog.

Back Pressure while Integrating with SQS

Amazon SQS and AWS Lambda stand as two managed, distributed, and highly available services. Amazon SQS boasts unlimited scalability, offering near-unlimited throughput and accommodating up to 120,000 messages in flight simultaneously. When integrating with AWS Lambda, it's crucial to acknowledge SQS's scalability, as AWS Lambda, while featuring adaptive scaling, is constrained by a concurrency limit.

Concurrency will be highlighted in detail in *Chapter* 5, *Hyper-Scaling with Lambda*. It refers to the number of running executions at any given time. Issues may arise if the volume of messages sent to SQS surpasses Lambda's concurrency limits or if Lambda cannot process at the same rate as SQS accepts messages. In such cases, the message backlog gradually increases.

To manage concurrency effectively, a refined mechanism can be implemented at the integration or function level. Lambda defaults to an on-demand concurrency model, scaling the function until it reaches the account/region concurrency limit (a soft limit). This emphasizes the need to carefully consider and regulate concurrency to maintain optimal performance and prevent potential backlogs.

SQS Integration

To better explore the Lambda and SQS integration, exploring based on an example is the simplest and an exploratory way.

Scenario: The following diagram (*Figure* 3.14) demonstrates a subsystem of an e-commerce system where customers submit articles in various formats. The system's software is responsible for validating, enriching, and publishing these articles online. The rate of incoming requests exhibits variations throughout the day, with demands gradually increasing from the morning and reaching its peak in the afternoon.

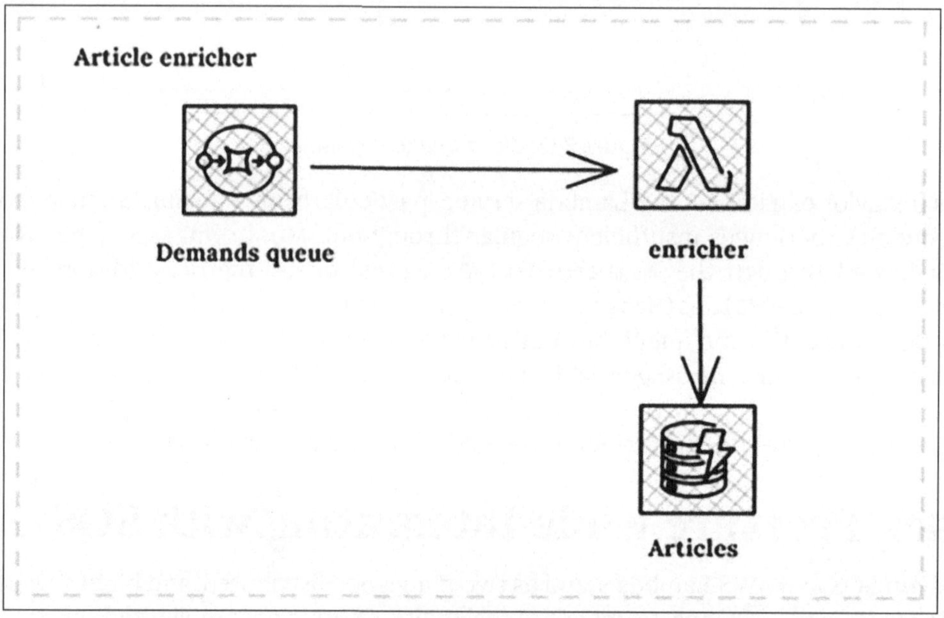

***Figure* 3.14:** *E-Commerce Article enricher using SQS integration example*

Using AWS CDK, the Queue and function integration can be done as follows:

```
const role = new Role(this, 'enrich-function-role', {
 // ...
});
const articlesQueue = new Queue(this, 'articles-queue', {
 // ...
});

articlesQueue.grantConsumeMessages(role);
```

```
const enrichFunction = new NodejsFunction(this, 'enrich-function', {
 // ...
});

enrichFunction.addEventSource(new SqsEventSource(articlesQueue));
```

The Queue grants Consumption rights to execution roles, and the event source mapping will be created by a single line: `**enrichFunction.addEventSource(new SqsEventSource(articlesQueue));**`.

As emphasized earlier, it is considered a best practice to configure the AWS Lambda function timeout in a manner that is well-balanced with the visibility timeout. This alignment helps ensure smooth and consistent processing of messages in a distributed system. Alternatively, implementing specific functions to manage idempotency is also a recommended practice.

For example, the enrich function needs 10 seconds to process and enrich any article and save them to the DynamoDB table. So, to avoid the message becoming available before the end of function processing, the queue visibility timeout is set to 20 seconds.

AWS documentation recommends setting it six times more than the execution time https://docs.aws.amazon.com/AWSSimpleQueueService/latest/SQSDeveloperGuide/sqs-configure lambda-function-trigger.html. In reality, this operates well without configuring six times the function timeout when treating a single item. We will discover more about batching in *Chapter 5, Hyper-Scaling with Lambda.*

The following snippet shows how to configure the visibility timeout and function timeout using AWS CDK:

```
const articlesQueue = new Queue(this, 'articles-queue', {
 queueName: 'articles-queue',
 visibilityTimeout: Duration.seconds(20),
});

const enrichFunction = new NodejsFunction(this, 'enrich-function', {
 entry: resolve(`${SqsIntegrationStack.handlersPath}/enrich/index.ts`),
 functionName: `enrich-function`,
 runtime: Runtime.NODEJS_20_X,
 timeout: Duration.seconds(10),
 handler: 'handler',
 // ...
});
```

To better explore how the misconfiguration of function timeout and the visibility timeout can impact processing, change the function timeout and Queue visibility timeout to 10 seconds for both. Also, add a wait in the handler to decrease the rate of chance for processing the event.

The following snippet of code represents the handler code with a wait of 9 seconds:

```
const Wait = () => new Promise(resolve => setTimeout(resolve, 9000));

export const handler = async (event: SQSEvent) => {
 await Promise.all(event.Records.map(async (record: SQSRecord) => {
   const article = JSON.parse(record.body);
   await Wait();
   const putItemCommand = new PutItemCommand({
     // TABLE_NAME should be correctly set as an environment variable
TableName: process.env.TABLE_NAME!,
     Item: marshall({ ...article, date: new Date().toISOString(), id:
nanoid() }),
   });

   await client.send(putItemCommand);
 }));
  return {
   statusCode: 201
 };
}
```

Sending a single article into the SQS Queue, we receive the message duplicated.

CloudWatch Logs show the reception of the event by the handler two times:

Figure 3.15: *Multi invocation of the same message*

Looking at DynamoDB shows the presence of two items for the same event.

Figure 3.16: *Multiple registrations of the same article, impacting system state*

It is important to take into account these kinds of scenarios and design systems and software considering failures and misconfigurations. Idempotency and design for failures will be explored later in this book.

Controlling Message Visibility Dynamically

One of the most challenging parts of SQS and Lambda integration is the visibility of a single message. This can be a requirement when dealing with some dependencies and a simple retry system cannot achieve those needs.

By default, the SQS redrive policy does not support exponential backoff. Exponential backoff is a kind of retry policy where any attempt will be done based on an exponential time duration. This means that if the first attempt deals with a failure, it may be useless to run a second retry as soon as the failure happens, as the underlying dependency is under pressure, and there is a small chance of successful response by retrying. As the SQS redrive policy does not support exponential backoff, it can be implemented at the Lambda function level.

In the preceding scenario, the enrich function needs to call a dependency to fetch additional information, such as customer contracts. However, as communication relies on the network, which can be unreliable, this API call may fail. If the problem is network instability, a retry can be done with a higher chance of success than if the failure is due to the reduced capacity of the contract API. This means a retry will not help to get a response; indeed, those retries can put the contract API in a worse situation.

Refactoring the handler code at the first step can be achieved by a network simulation and a `try-catch` block.

The network latency and network failures are simply illustrated using a random calculation. To increase the chance of failure, the success case covers only 20%. A latency of 2 seconds is added for all API calls:

```
export interface Article {
 id: number;
 title: string;
 content: string;
}
export class EnrichService {
 Enrich= async (article: Article): Promise<Article> => {
   //Simulate network latency
   await new Promise(resolve => setTimeout(resolve, 2000));

   //Simulate random network failure
   const random = Math.random();
   if (random < 0.2) {
```

```
    return article;
  }

  if (random > 0.5) {
    throw new Error("Network Error");
  }
 }
}
```

In the handler method, a `try-catch` assures error handling in case of failure:

```
try {
 // ...
 await enrichService.Enrich(article);
 // ...
} catch (error) {
 throw error;
}
```

For demonstration purposes in the first step, the catch block has a single log statement.

The AWS SDK provides the required functionalities to achieve the goal of dynamically managing the message lifecycle, as illustrated in the following code snippet:

```
import { ChangeMessageVisibilityCommand } from "@aws-sdk/client-sqs";
import { SQSRecord } from "aws-lambda";

const GetDuration = (record: SQSRecord, base: number) => {
 const backoffrate = 2.5;
 return  parseInt(record.attributes.ApproximateReceiveCount) * backof-
frate * base;
}

const changeVisibilityTimeout = async (record: SQSRecord) => {
 const VisibilityTimeout = GetDuration(record, 30);
 console.log(`Changing visibility timeout to ${VisibilityTimeout}`);

 const changeVisibilityTimeoutCommandInput = {
   QueueUrl: process.env.QUEUE_URL!,
   ReceiptHandle: record.receiptHandle,
   VisibilityTimeout: VisibilityTimeout
 };
  await sqsclient.send(new ChangeMessageVisibilityCommand(changeVisibil-
ityTimeoutCommandInput));
 return VisibilityTimeout;
}
```

The preceding example uses AWS SDK and calculates a simple way of exponential backoff based on the number of received counts. We use this implementation in the handler catch block:

```
try {
 // ...
} catch (error) {
   await changeVisibilityTimeout(record);
   await new Promise( _ => setTimeout(async () => { await HandleArticle
(record); }, GetDuration(record, 15)))
}
```

To achieve these results, the original handler must be refactored, as shown in the following snippet:

```
const GetDuration = (record: SQSRecord, baseInSeconds: number) => {
 // … }

const changeVisibilityTimeout = async (record: SQSRecord) => {
 // … }

const HandleArticle = async (record: SQSRecord) => {
      const enrichAndSave = async() => { // … }
      try {
           await enrichAndSave();
      } catch (error) {
            const attempts = parseInt(record.attributes.Approximate
ReceiveCount ?? "0");
            if( attempts >= MaxAttempts ) throw error;
            record.attributes.ApproximateReceiveCount = (attempts +
1).toString();

           await changeVisibilityTimeout(record);
           await new Promise( _ => setTimeout(async () => {
await HandleArticle(record);
           },  GetDuration(record, 15000)));
    }
}

const enrichArticle = async (event: SQSEvent) => {
     await Promise.all(event.Records.map(async (record: SQSRecord) => {
           await HandleArticle(record);
     }));
    return {
         statusCode: 201
    };
```

```
}

export const handler = enrichArticle;
```

Sending the following message into the queue will trigger the handler. With the default visibility timeout, this results in a catch and exponential retry, followed by changing the message visibility timeout:

```
{ "name": "Alexa", "price": 78 }
```

`CloudWatch` illustrates well what is happening when failures happen.

Figure 3.17: *Dynamic exponential backoff using visibility timeout*

As `cloudWatch` logs show, a randomly generated number decides the success or failure situation. Success happens after two exponential backoffs and visibility changes. The logs also show the generated values.

This example is intended solely for demonstration purposes and may not represent the optimal solution for production requirements. The challenge addressed here could be addressed more effectively through alternative design approaches. Throughout this book, we will explore other patterns that are considered production-ready, best practices, and offer better value for the cost of adoption in serverless designs.

Integration with Data Streams

AWS Lambda integrates with both DynamoDB Streams and Kinesis Streams. The Lambda service follows a periodic polling approach to check for new events or records in the respective stream. In the case of Kinesis Streams, the term "*shard*" signifies a sequence of records, while in DynamoDB Streams, each partition corresponds to a specific subset of data. Lambda conducts polling on these shards to retrieve and process items or records.

In both DynamoDB Streams and Kinesis Streams, the use of an iterator is an important part for maintaining the state of processing. The iterator plays a key role in ensuring the order of records within a single shard or partition. Lambda utilizes iterators to keep track of its progress and determine the point from which it left off during the last poll. This iterative approach provides a reliable method for sequentially processing events. While DynamoDB Streams and Kinesis Streams share commonalities in their integration with AWS Lambda, it's essential to recognize their individual roles and use cases. DynamoDB Streams capture changes to items in a DynamoDB table, while Kinesis Streams serve as a scalable and durable platform for streaming data. The choice between them depends on the specific requirements of the use case at hand.

The use of iterators in both services plays a vital role in preserving the chronological order of events within a single shard or partition. This sequential order is significant for applications that depend on the accurate processing of event sequences.

It's important to note that, despite sharing comparable integration patterns with AWS Lambda, DynamoDB Streams and Kinesis Streams fulfill distinct roles. DynamoDB Streams capture modifications to items within a DynamoDB table, whereas Kinesis Streams offer a resilient and scalable framework for streaming data. The selection between these services hinges on the specific needs and criteria of the given use case.

Ordering and Concurrency

As mentioned previously, Lambda periodically polls for records in streams while associating, by default, a single function for any given shard. The reason behind this behavior is how shards behave. A shard represents a chronological order of records and responds to Lambda polling requests by sending back a number of older records in a single shard. The streams give the ability to be asked for records based on a specific time; however, regardless of how the request is configured, the records are in order from the oldest record to the newest and are sent sequentially.

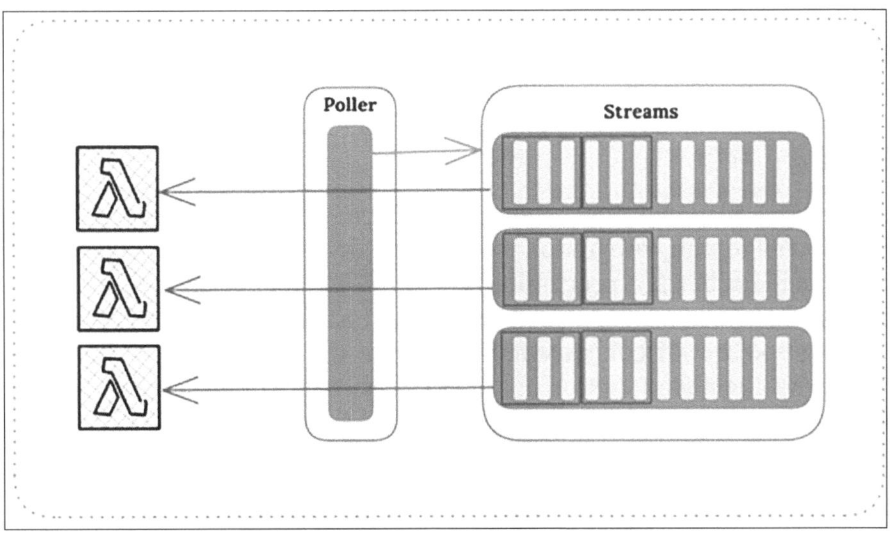

Figure 3.18: *Shard chronological polling*

As shown in *Figure* 3.18, the Lambda Poller requests streams, receives records from shards, and sends the batch of records to a Lambda function. Each shard keeps a single concurrency at the Lambda side by default. For subsequent poller requests, the next patch of records will be chosen from any single shard, considering the previous processing state. To guarantee the ordering of records, the related records can be sent to the same shard.

For DynamoDB Streams, AWS Lambda polls four times per second, while for kinesis, the polling is one time per second.

Back Pressure while Integrating with Data Streams

The concept of back pressure has been explored previously. However, while integrating Lambda with different services, the problem can exist, leading to throttling or errors and preventing the design from scaling up. While Data Streams are not a bottleneck by design, they can lead to pitfalls of scaling when integrating with Lambda due to misconfiguration.

The event source mapping, by default, has a single invocation per shard at a given time. The next batch of records will be sent to Lambda if the previous invocation had a successful result. This can result in latency when the rate of data records entering the shard increases, and as a consequence, this will introduce an increase in the `` `IteratorAge` `` metric of the stream. To solve this situation, the event source mapping can be configured to increase the number of concurrent processing of records using `` `ParallelizationFactor` `` up to 10. Another way of increasing the processing capacity is to evenly distribute data into multiple shards, resulting in more concurrent executions by the Lambda service.

While these solutions seem a help toward scalability, if used without care, they can result in an increase in Lambda concurrency level and result in throttling errors by the Lambda service.

When using the aforementioned techniques, consider thinking about the Lambda service and refine the integration based on your business requirements. If the requirements indicate a fast processing, a solution could be adapting the concurrency limit of Lambda by requesting an increase or setting up reserved concurrency at the function level. Reserved concurrency limits the maximum number of concurrent invocations for a lambda function and can result in function throttling and helps to keep the other lambda functions in the same AWS account/region safe.

Kinesis Data Streams Integration

The following diagram (*Figure* 3.19) illustrates the integration of the Lambda service with Kinesis data streams for log ingestion to an observability system. The solution receives logs of all applications and sends them to an observable system after transforming and normalizing the log data. The data comes from different applications, each application sends logs to CloudWatch at its proper rate and can log any level of log based on its needs.

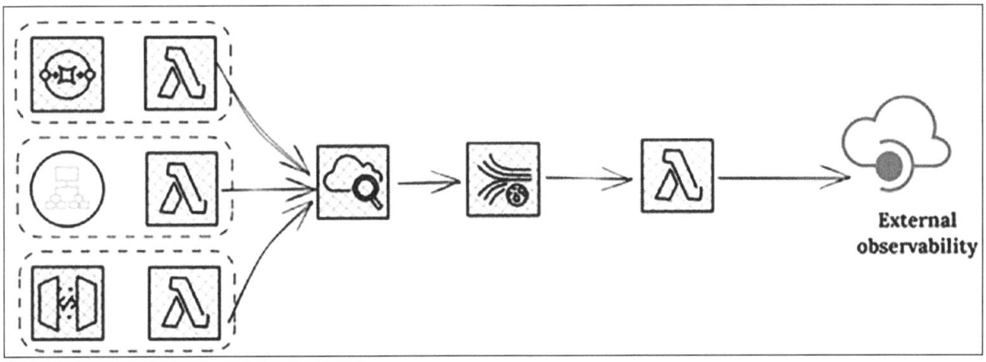

Figure 3.19: *Stream Integration for logs delivery to external services*

Using AWS CDK to integrate the Kinesis and Lambda function using event source mapping:

```
const role = new Role(this, 'send-logs-function-role', {
  //...
});

const kinesisDataStream = new Stream(this, 'logs-stream', {
  //...
});

kinesisDataStream.grantRead(role);

const enrichFunction = new NodejsFunction(this, 'send-logs--function',
{
  //...
});

enrichFunction.addEventSource(new KinesisEventSource(kinesisDataStream,
{
  startingPosition: StartingPosition.LATEST,
  enabled: true,
  retryAttempts: 3
}));
```

The event source mapping is configured to receive only the latest records and retry attempts of three. If any failure happens after three retry attempts at the Lambda service side, the record will be sent to a DLQ if configured (not configured here) or acknowledged to the data stream by the failure.

Here is the handler code in TypeScript:

```
const logService = new LogService();

const transformAndSendLogs = async (event: KinesisStreamEvent) => {
 // The actual configuration has a batch size of 1 so records array
contains 1 item
 await Promise.all(event.Records.map(async (record: KinesisStreamRecord)
=> {
   const log = JSON.parse(record.kinesis.data);
   await logService.Send(log);
 }));
  return {
   statusCode: 201
 };
}

export const handler = transformAndSendLogs;
```

The handler accepts a `**KinesisDataStreamEvent**` containing an array of records (actually a single record) of type `**KinesisStreamRecord**`. The record log data can be accessed in `**kinesis: { data: "..." }**` from `**KinesisStreamRecord**`.

In this example, the Lambda poller periodically polls records. The Kinesis `**GetRecords**` metrics show that Lambda pools periodically.

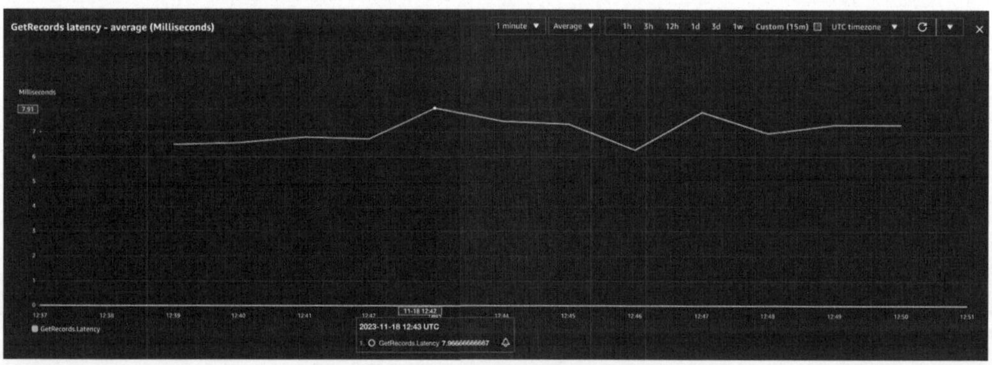

Figure 3.20: *Stream GetRecords metric*

Using the AWS CLI, a record will be sent to Kinesis:

```
aws kinesis put-record --stream-name 'logs-stream' --cli-binary-for-
mat raw-in-base64-out --partition-key "shardId-000000000000" --data
"{\"id\":\"id-0001\",\"message\":\"a simple message\",\"timestamp\":\"20
23-11-18T12:00:00.000z\"}"
```

Now, Data Streams returns the records in response to the Lambda Poller request, and the Lambda Poller triggers a function invocation.

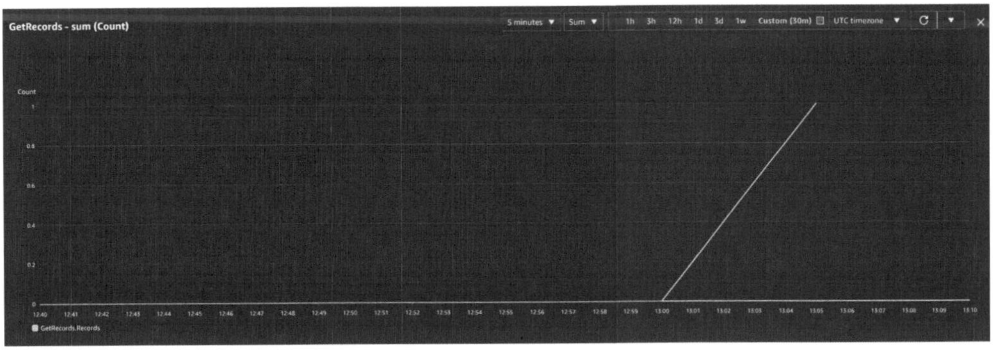

Figure 3.21: *Stream GetRecords evaluation point*

Behind polling of records from the data stream, the Lambda service invokes the function synchronously and applies the event source mapping configuration before invoking the function. While receiving the response, as shown in the following figure, the Lambda invocation metric shows occurrence of four invocations due to simulated network failure in function code.

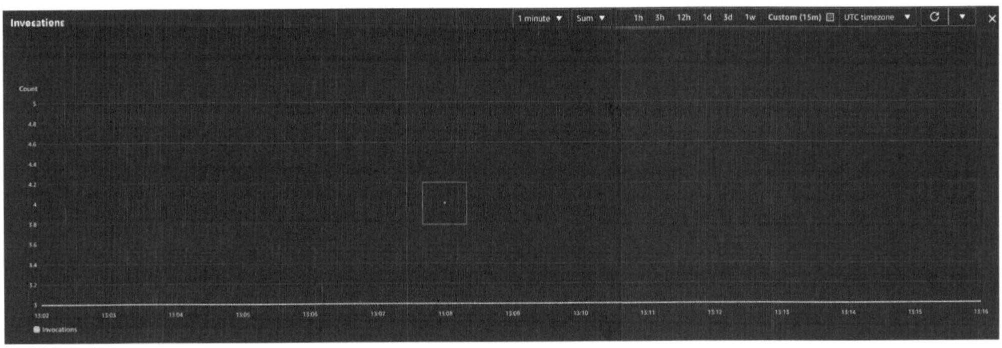

Figure 3.22: *Stream Polling Lambda invocation*

The Kinesis record's schema received by Lambda is as follows:

```
{
 kinesis: {
   kinesisSchemaVersion: '1.0',
   partitionKey: 'shardId-000000000000',
   sequenceNumber: '49646548549898327383415508351993872570125657009408704514',
   data: 'eyJpZCI6ImlkLTAwMDEiLCJtZXNzYWdlIjoiYSBzaW1wbGUgbWVzc2FnZSIsInRpbWVzdGFtcCI6IjIwMjMtMTEtMThUMTI6MDA6MDAuMDAweiJ9',
   approximateArrivalTimestamp: 1700314819.218
 },
 eventSource: 'aws:kinesis',
```

```
 eventVersion: '1.0',
 eventID: 'shar-
dId-000000000000:49646548549898327383415508351993872570125657009408704514',
 eventName: 'aws:kinesis:record',
 invokeIdentityArn: 'arn:aws:iam::607050363559:role/StreamIntegrationStack-sendlogsfunctionrole4AE60A07-gGFn6uJeA5E7',
 awsRegion: 'eu-west-1',
 eventSourceARN: 'arn:aws:kinesis:eu-west-1:607050363559:stream/logs-stream'
}
```

As presented, the data format is a base64 and needs to be considered in the handler before use. The way to transform the base64 in Node.js can be done using the following syntax:

```
   const log = JSON.parse(Buffer.from(record.kinesis.data, 'base64').toString());
```

As the event source mapping is configured for three retry attempts, if any error happens in the function handler, the initial invocation will be followed by three additional attempts. However, if all attempts fail, the poller will no longer fetch that record, resulting in an inconsistent behavior in the system.

By simulating the failures as before, used in the SQS integration part, all four attempts failed due to simulation. After all attempts, the poller no longer received that record.

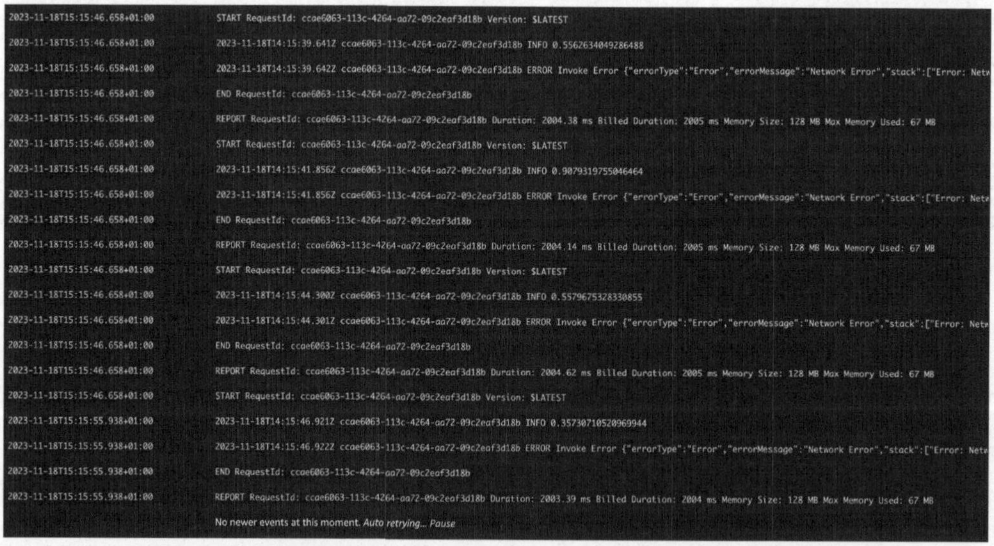

Figure 3.23: *Stream Integration Simulated Errors*

The event source mapping lets configuring a Dead Letter Queue (DLQ) at the integration level and helps prevent data loss in case of failures or any inconsistent behavior while interacting with downstream systems.

Adding a Queue and serving that as a **`DeadLetterQueue`** is an ideal way of designing resilient solutions. The following snippet shows how to add a DLQ at the ESM integration level:

```
const deadletterqueue = new Queue(this, 'dead-letter-queue', {
  queueName: 'dead-letter-queue'
});
 deadletterqueue.grantSendMessages(role);

enrichFunction.addEventSource(new KinesisEventSource(kinesisDataStream,
{
  startingPosition: StartingPosition.TRIM_HORIZON,
  enabled: true,
  onFailure: new SqsDlq(deadletterqueue),
  retryAttempts: 3
}));
```

After deploying the new configurations, the full failed attempts will result in the presence of a record in the dead letter queue that can be served for analysis and re-triggering the Lambda function.

A new invocation with four failed attempts now sends the record in DLQ.

Name	Type	Created	Messages available	Messages in flight	Encryption
dead-letter-queue	Standard	2023-11-18T15:37+01:00	1	0	Amazon SQS key (SSE-SQS)

Figure 3.24: *Event source mapping configured DLQ*

It's important to note that DLQ does not receive the actual record payload. Instead, a reference to the record is stored in the DLQ. The responsibility falls on the application to fetch the record payload for further investigation and error recovery.

Integration with Amazon SNS

Amazon SNS is an AWS offering and a managed service for Pub/Sub communication patterns and broadcasting scenarios when a single message must be delivered to all or a subset of subscribers. SNS can be integrated to distribute the published messages to a wide range of destinations such as Amazon SQS, AWS Lambda, Amazon Kinesis Data Firehose, and SMS. Additionally, Amazon SNS can send messages to HTTPS, Email, or Native mobile push platforms. Amazon SNS introduces "*Topic*" as a communication channel.

Amazon SNS integrates with AWS Lambda using the Asynchronous Invocation Model (refer to *Invocation Models* in this chapter). This means the rate of Lambda function invocation will be managed by AWS Lambda service in an asynchronous way. However, the rate of calling the Lambda service API will be per topic and dependent on the scalability level of the SNS service. Amazon SNS calls the destinations per message without the ability to batch or group the messages.

SNS Message Ordering

Amazon SNS standard topics guarantee at least one delivery, so destinations can receive a message twice or more. To avoid duplication, consumers must consider idempotency as part of their design. Additionally, Amazon SNS standard topics don't provide an ordering guarantee. When message ordering is an important design attribute, SNS FIFO topics can be used. FIFO topics support strict ordering and exactly once-delivery.

SNS Integration

To integrate AWS Lambda with SNS topics, Lambda subscribes to SNS topics and gives the invoke permissions to the topic, allowing the SNS service to trigger the Lambda function.

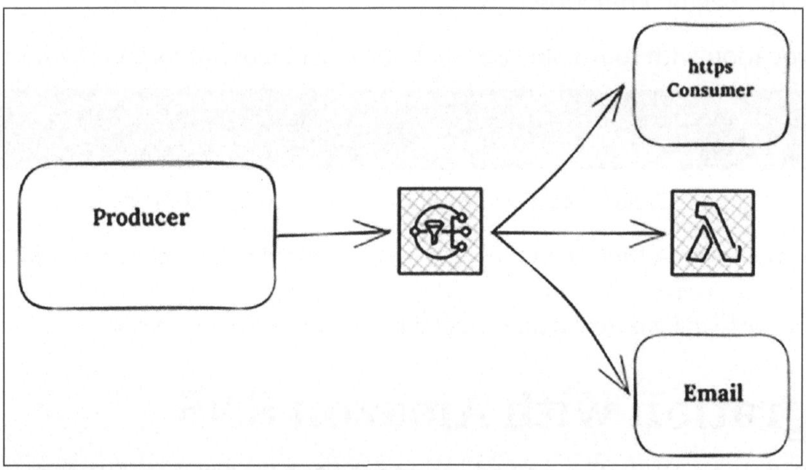

Figure 3.25: SNS *integration*

Using AWS CDK to integrate the SNS topic and Lambda function:

```
const role = new Role(this, 'listener-function-role', {
  //..
});

const listenerFunction = new NodejsFunction(this, 'listener-function', {
  //..
});

const snsTopic = new Topic(this, 'topic', { topicName: 'topic' });
```

```
 const subscriptionDeadLetterQueue = new Queue(this, 'subscription
-dead-letter-queue', { queueName: 'subscription-dead-letter-queue' });
 subscriptionDeadLetterQueue.addToResourcePolicy(new PolicyStatement({
   //..
 }))

 snsTopic.addSubscription(new LambdaSubscription(listenerFunction, {
   deadLetterQueue: subscriptionDeadLetterQueue
 }))
```

The preceding integration uses a `**Dead letter queue**` to add more resiliency and avoid data loss. This DLQ will be used just by the SNS service at the integration level when the message cannot be delivered to the destination and does not consider the function invocation errors. Amazon SNS will not be acknowledged of any failures on the Lambda service side as it integrates with the Lambda service asynchronously.

The Lambda needs to add a dead letter queue at the function level to act behind the failures at the function level. If no dead letter queue is configured for the Lambda function, the Lambda service retries the failed invocation three times by default. In case of a function error, the retries will be intervalled as one minute between the first two attempts and two minutes between the second and third attempts. In case of service errors, such as throttling, the events will be kept up to 6 hours in the queue and will be retried exponentially from 1 second to a maximum of 5 minutes intervals (refer to AWS documentation: https://docs.aws.amazon.com/lambda/latest/dg/invocation-async.html#:~:text=the%20command%20output.-,Lambda,-manages%20the%20function%27s).

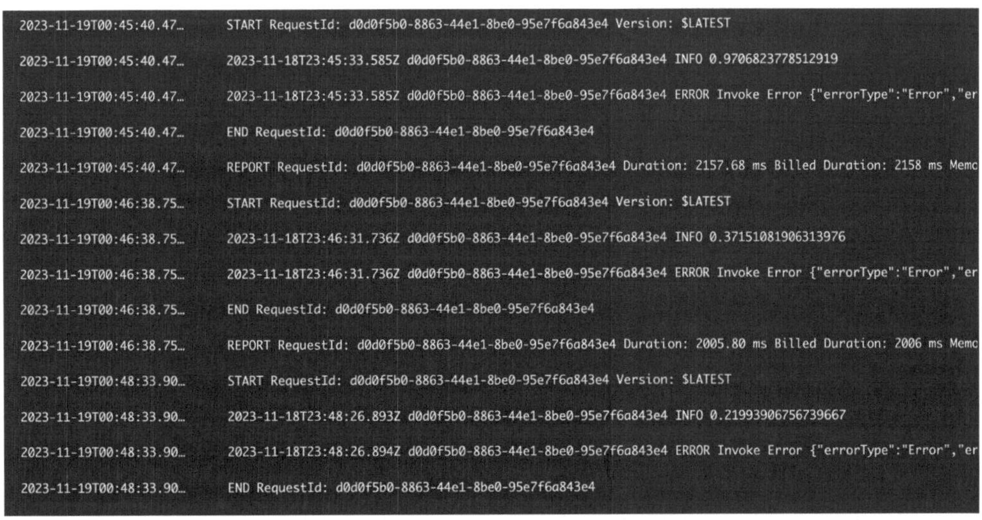

***Figure 3.26:** Lambda async retry trigger without DLQ*

This behavior is just for asynchronous invocation models, and the Lambda function, by default, creates this configuration for any function but considers it just for asynchronous invocations.

***Figure 3.27:** Async Invocation configuration*

While this seems nice as errors can be resolved in the following invocations, if all invocations fail, the message will be ignored and lost. To avoid the loss of messages, Lambda provides multiple ways of handling errors.

- **DeadLetterQueue**: A dead letter queue can be an SQS queue or an SNS Topic and will be served just for async invocation models.

Using AWS CDK, the configuration will be as follows:

```
const listenerDeadletterqueue = new Queue(this, 'listener-dead-letter
-queue', { queueName: 'listener-dead-letter-queue' });
listenerDeadletterqueue.grantSendMessages(role);

const listenerFunction = new NodejsFunction(this, 'listener-function', {
 //..
 deadLetterQueue: listenerDeadletterqueue
});
```

After deploying the new DLQ configuration and after three attempts for a failed message, the message will appear in **`DeadLetterQueue`**.

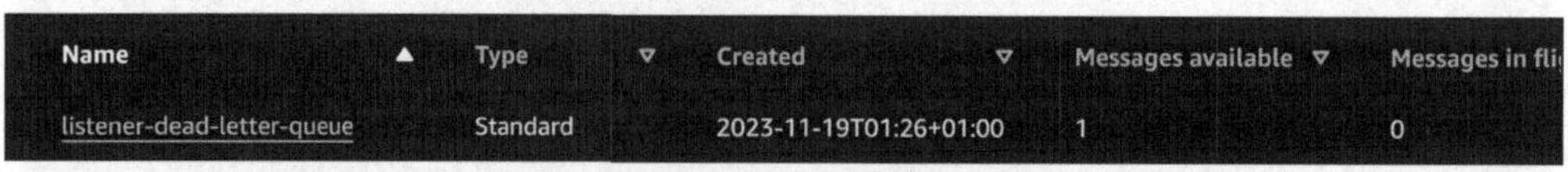

***Figure 3.28:** Async Invocation DLQ*

Integration with EventBridge

Amazon EventBridge is an AWS offering of a serverless and managed Event Bus. It is an ideal solution to centralize the event-driven design and inter-component communications. EventBridge covers both Point-to-Point (P2P) and Broadcasting (pub/sub) patterns. It provides some categories of services: Pipe service (`**`pipes.amazonaws.com`**`), events service (`**`events.amazonaws.com`**`), and scheduler (`**`scheduler.amazonaws.com`**`). Pipes are ideal for service-level integration, such as integrating with DynamoDB streams and P2P communication, while EventBus is the best choice for publish/subscribe patterns. The scheduler provides some ways of scheduling tasks or compute services and running them based on time or cron.

Event Ordering

The EventBridge bus (**`Events service (`events.amazonaws.com`)`**) provides event routing functionality and does not provide any guarantee of event ordering. The Events service provides the possibility to distribute events to multiple destinations. The EventBridge archive and replay feature is an enhanced feature of the EventBridge, allowing the replay of events in case of failures. As the replay functionality is a multi-threaded process, it does not guarantee the ordering of events as their original order.

EventBridge pipes (**`Pipes service (`pipes.amazonaws.com`)`**) provides an ordering guarantee based on the source, meaning that if the source guarantees the ordering, EventBridge will provide the same ordering at the best effort by controlling concurrency limits of the source service to achieve the same order of events.

EventBridge Bus Integration with Lambda

The following example (*Figure* 3.29) illustrates how the integration of Lambda with EventBridge can be done. The design represents a routing mechanism using events service:

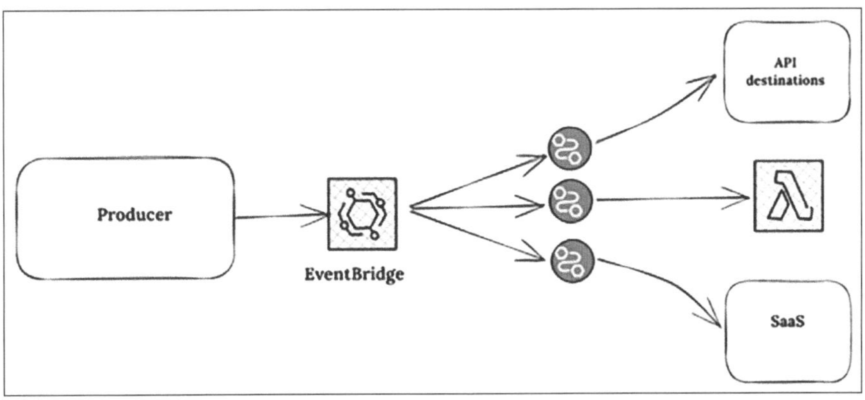

***Figure 3.29**: EventBridge integration*

The following snippet shows how Lambda can integrate with an EventBridge bus using AWS CDK:

```
const role = new Role(this, 'listener-function-role', {
  //..
});

const eventBus =  new EventBus(this, 'event-bus', { eventBusName:
'event-bus' })
```

```
 const listenerdeadletterqueue = new Queue(this, 'listener-dead-letter
-queue', { queueName: 'listener-dead-letter-queue' });
 listenerdeadletterqueue.grantSendMessages(role);

 const listenerFunction = new NodejsFunction(this, 'listener-function',
{
   //..
 });

 new Rule(this, 'event-bus-lambda-integration', {
   ruleName: 'event-bus-lambda-integration',
   eventPattern: {
     source: ['com.company.myservice']
   },
   eventBus,
 }).addTarget(new LambdaFunction(listenerFunction));
```

In this example, the Lambda receives all events with a source of `**com.company.myservice**`. This is the source sent by the `**myservice**` app as an event producer. EventBridge integrates with the Lambda service asynchronously, so failure handling must be considered in two parts: integration and execution. On the integration side, error handling is under EventBridge service responsibility, and EventBridge will retry server-side failures up to 24 hours and 185 times. However, this behavior cannot be the best fit for a variety of scenarios as it can produce unnecessary pressure on the target side. This behavior can be changed at the rule level.

Here's an example of overriding EventBridge default behavior:

```
const targetDeadletterqueue = new Queue(this, 'target-dead-letter-
queue', { queueName: 'target-dead-letter-queue' });

 new Rule(this, 'event-bus-lambda-integration', {
   ruleName: 'event-bus-lambda-integration',
   eventPattern: {
     source: ['*']
   },
   eventBus,
 }).addTarget(new LambdaFunction(listenerFunction, {
   deadLetterQueue: targetDeadletterqueue,
   maxEventAge: Duration.hours(1), // Default 24 hours
   retryAttempts: 3 // Default 185 times
 }));
```

The other side of failure handling, as mentioned, is at the function level. As the EventBridge integration is asynchronous, the default asynchronous invocation configuration will produce the same behaviors that were explored earlier in the `SNS

Integration` section. To overcome this default behavior, the configuration can be overridden:

```
const listenerFunction = new NodejsFunction(this, 'listener-function', {
     // ...
     retryAttempts: 2, // Default 2 ( Max Limit)
     maxEventAge: Duration.hours(1)
   });
```

An important note to consider is that the `**retryAttempts**` max limit is two retries and cannot be configured beyond this limit. To overcome this limitation, the `Lambda Destination` can be used, which will be covered in *Chapter 7, Resiliency and Design for Failure*.

Integration with API Gateway

API Gateway is an API management service that simplifies creating, documenting, and securing REST, HTTP, and WebSocket APIs. API Gateway integrates well with AWS services via proxy or direct integration. API Gateway integrates with AWS Lambda via both proxy and direct integration, offering a low-latency communication between front and backend tiers.

The API Gateway runs under `**apigateway.amazonaws.com**` service and is covered by IAM service, allowing simplified access management. For external access management, API Gateway integrates well with Amazon Cognito to enable authentication and authorization processes.

Proxy Gateway

API Gateway behaves as a proxy to augment the capabilities of an API. API Gateway can be used to manage some API management aspects, such as security, rate limiting, and throttling, as well as request and response mapping.

API Gateway effectively addresses RESTful APIs requirements by enabling the creation of resources that seamlessly integrate with Lambda functions. This allows the execution of business requirements in isolation, alleviating the need to manage cross-cutting concerns.

Back Pressure

By design, API Gateway covers synchronous request-response design needs. API Gateway has a hard limit of a 30-second max timeout, and this must be considered for scenarios that overlap this limit.

When integrating with Lambda, API Gateway proxies all accepted requests to the Lambda service using a synchronous invocation model and waits for the response.

The Lambda service receives the API Gateway request and uses a worker to run and process the request. By synchronous invocation use, the concurrency of Lambda can be passed by the limits.

To avoid back pressure situations, API Gateway has a throttling limit per API and can be extended by configuring usage plans. The default limit is 10,000 RPS per account and per region. However, this limit is higher than the default concurrency level of the Lambda service and must be considered. API Gateway offers a concept of usage plan that can be used to set the limits per client, per API, or per stage.

Error Handling

When using API Gateway, the responsibility of handling failures and retrying will be at the client side. The client must be aware of any constraints and errors that can happen at runtime. For example, if a client sends lots of requests with rate limiting in place, API Gateway will start throttling the requests and send back a 429 HTTP code, indicating `Too Many Requests`. In this case, the client must consider balancing the request rate as per the communicated rate limiting.

API Gateway Integration with Lambda

The following example (*Figure* 3.30) shows how API Gateway can integrate with the Lambda service using a synchronous invocation model:

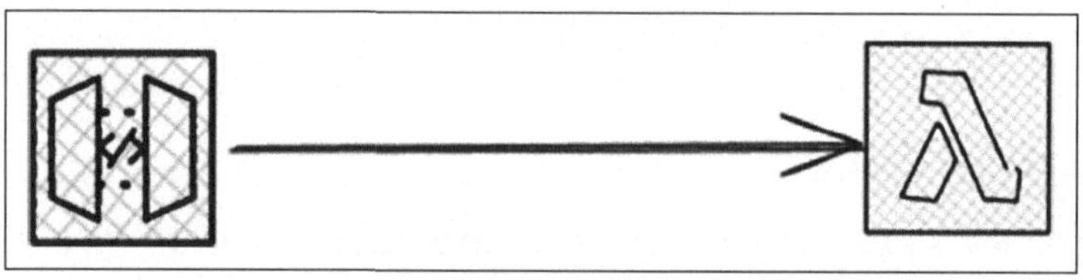

***Figure* 3.30:** *API Gateway integration with the Lambda service using a synchronous invocation model*

This simple design can be created using AWS CDK, as demonstrated in the following code snippet:

```
const role = new Role(this, 'listener-function-role', { // ... });

const agw = new RestApi( this, RestApi.name, {
     restApiName: `apigateway-rest-api`,
     endpointTypes: [EndpointType.REGIONAL],
     deployOptions: {
       stageName: 'live'
     }
});
```

```
const proxiedFunction = new NodejsFunction(this, 'listener-function', {
     timeout: Duration.seconds(10)
// ... });

const lambdaProxyIntegration = new LambdaIntegration(proxiedFunction, {
     timeout: Duration.seconds(15)
});
const lambdaApiResource = agw.root.addResource('lambda');
   lambdaApiResource.addMethod(
       'POST',
       lambdaProxyIntegration);
}
```

In this example, API Gateway integrates with the Lambda function using a simple proxy integration. The timeout of API Gateway is conferred as 15 seconds (overriding the 30-second default value). The Lambda function timeout is kept slightly lower than 15 seconds for an added layer of safety to overcome situations where the integration latency between API Gateway and Lambda service can increase and to avoid race conditions (actually this is near 0% in occurrence).

The Lambda handler is a simple handler function receiving an **`ApiGatewayProxyEvent`** and fetching the body for processing:

```
const listenerService = new ListenerService();
export const handler = async (event: APIGatewayProxyEvent) => {
 const message = JSON.parse(event.body);
 await listenerService.Send(message);

 return {
   statusCode: 201
 };
}
```

Conclusion

In this chapter, we discovered how AWS Lambda integrates with the AWS serverless ecosystem and explored how those integrations can behave at runtime in terms of latency, failures, and invocations.

Understanding the different integration levels is a vital part of design, and by ensuring the reader's understanding level, we will move forward into event-driven design in the next chapter. This will allow us to discover a wide range of patterns and event-based designs that lead to achieving better-performing solutions in terms of scalability, resiliency, and latency.

CHAPTER 4

Event-Driven Design with Lambda

Introduction

In this chapter, we will focus on some real scenarios to better discover the tradeoffs when designing and deciding to adopt a design. Different communication patterns like Messaging, Streaming, Bidirectional and how to adopt the best design will be covered.

We will also delve into the scalability and standardization of event driven systems by exploring the different aspects of governance, such as catalogs, schema registry, incompatibility checks, versioning and real time change triggers.

Structure

In this chapter, we will discuss the following topics:

- Distributed Systems
- Synchronous Design
- Asynchronous Design Overcomes Synchronous Design Problems
- Circumstances and Design Decisions
- Event-Driven Design
- Messaging
- Event Streaming
- Bidirectional Communication
- Event Bus
- Scalability with EDA
- Standardization

Distributed Systems

In the traditional computing landscape, tasks were accomplished by executing software code on a single node, where a node represented a physical boundary of resources, ensuring the isolation of software execution. However, with the evolution of software requirements, the need for nodes with more power and resources became apparent. This transition allowed for the achievement of parallelism, where resources could be shared, and the required amounts of resources allocated to different sub-tasks, marking a significant jump in software development. The advent of multiple virtual CPUs simplified parallel execution of background tasks, leading to nodes running continuously and periodically persisting states for potential recovery in the event of a node crash.

While this approach enhanced computational capabilities, it also introduced a higher level of software complexity. The software, initially focused on business-centric processes, now had to consider the edge cases and race conditions related to underlying nodes and infrastructure.

The challenges of single-node computing extended beyond software intricacies to encompass runtime issues, scalability, and fault tolerance. Addressing a surge in workload proved cumbersome, and determining the requisite resources became a time-consuming and frustrating verification process. Moreover, a crash in a single node had a cascading impact on the entire system, intensifying the need for efficient recovery mechanisms.

In contrast, a distributed system comprises a network of collaborative and independent computing nodes. These nodes work together to accomplish a shared objective, relying on decentralization and autonomous components that communicate over a network through information transfer and coordinated activities.

Key Characteristics of Distributed Systems:

- **Decentralization**: Unlike centralized systems where a single entity controls all resources, distributed systems distribute tasks across multiple nodes, fostering collaboration and shared responsibility.
- **Concurrency**: Distributed systems embrace concurrent execution, enabling parallel processing and enhancing overall system performance.
- **Communication**: Nodes communicate over a network, facilitating the sharing of information, coordination of activities, and maintenance of system-wide consistency.
- **Scalability**: Distributed systems can scale horizontally by adding nodes to handle increased workloads, providing a flexible solution to growing demands.
- **Fault Tolerance:** Resilience to individual node failures is a hallmark of distributed systems, ensuring continued operation with minimal disruption.

Distributed systems find applications in diverse domains, including cloud computing, peer-to-peer networks, web applications, and large-scale data processing. Their advantages, such as scalability and fault tolerance, make them well-suited for addressing the demands of modern computing.

Designing and managing distributed systems involves navigating challenges related to coordination, consistency, fault tolerance, and communication. A profound understanding of distributed system principles is essential for professionals and students in computer science and related fields as they navigate the intricacies of contemporary computing environments.

Synchronous Design

In response to the escalating complexities and challenges faced by software and systems, adopting a distributed design emerged as an initial solution to the question of how components inter-communicate. The early days of distributed systems witnessed a revolutionary approach employing synchronous communication through a network of components. This method relied on a request/response pattern for interactions, where services communicated with each other synchronously. In this design, the upstream service initiated communication with downstream services by sending a request and awaiting a response, introducing a level of coupling in terms of both process and infrastructure.

In a synchronous design, a service, beyond understanding its own design and process requirements, must also be cognizant of related service designs and processes. This awareness is crucial for making optimal runtime decisions in various scenarios. However, as the number of related downstream services increases, this heightened awareness contributes to escalating software complexity.

Consider the example illustrated in *Figure 4.1*, where various challenges associated with synchronous design are explored.

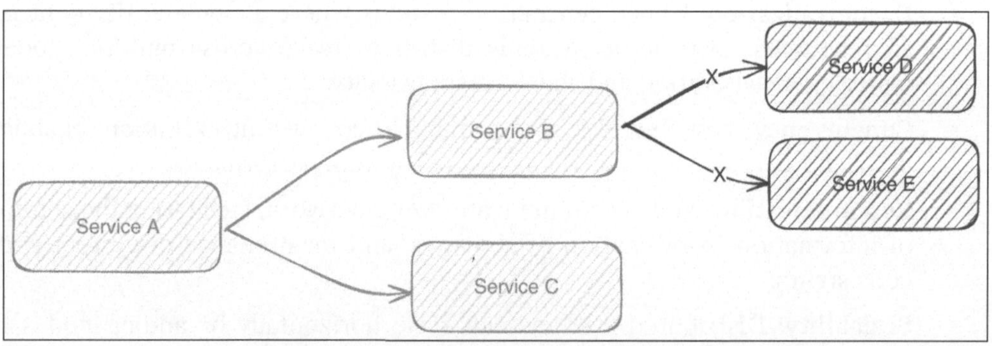

Figure 4.1: *Distributed system sync behavior*

The diagram depicts the communication complexity involved in accomplishing a single operational task. Service A, in this scenario, calls Services B and C to obtain information. While this design may seem unproblematic initially, a single node's degradation can have a cascading impact on all consumers of Service A.

- **Performance**: Latency introduced by Services D and E will be propagated to Service A, impacting its consumers and, consequently, the overall system performance.
- **Fault Tolerance**: The red lines denoted by X represent potential sources of failures. Any degradation or downtime in Service D will simultaneously affect Services B and A. Additionally, network latency or database overloads in Services D or E can result in timeouts or temporal errors affecting Services B and A.
- **Scalability**: Despite Service A's ability to scale efficiently, the design coupling may lead to backpressure and vulnerability to poor scalability in underlying downstream services, such as Service E or Buck head problem.
- **Coordination**: Services B and A must orchestrate the operational workflow, introducing further software complexity. This may involve managing orchestration node states or grappling with the two-phase commit problem.

While synchronous design addresses scalability and fault tolerance challenges as an initial advantage of decentralization in distributed systems, the coupling among components in an operation introduces the aforementioned challenges.

Synchronous design introduces the following challenges :

- Latency
- Reliability
- Software Complexity
- Dependencies
- Atomicity

Overcoming Synchronous Design Problems Using Asynchronous Design

Recognizing the operational significance of addressing the challenges inherent in synchronous design, the transition to asynchronous design emerged as a strategic step towards reducing coupling, minimizing latency, and fostering greater operational cohesiveness. This shift aligned seamlessly with the decentralization goals of distributed design.

In the realm of asynchronous design, a departure from the blocking request/response pattern is evident, as upstream and downstream components embrace a non-blocking request/reply (request/callback) pattern. Here, the upstream component initiates a process asynchronously, receiving acknowledgment from the downstream side, which subsequently replies with the processed results. While this pattern efficiently handles numerous simple distributed tasks, it introduces design and operational complexities in more sophisticated scenarios.

The accompanying diagram (*Figure* 4.2) delves into the intricacies of the asynchronous communication pattern.

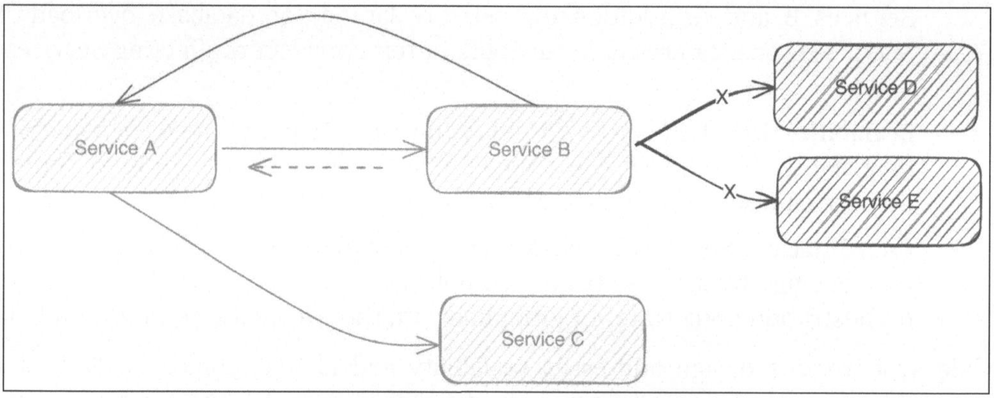

Figure 4.2: *Asynchronous communication*

As illustrated, the processing complexity is effectively decoupled between Service A and Service B. Notably, latencies and temporal failures in Service B no longer impact Service A. Service B communicates the processing results only when the task is completed and finalized. This design not only aids in reducing latencies and decoupling upstream and downstream processing details but also ensures a consistent and reliable process result.

The asynchronous approach, while introducing complexities in handling sophisticated tasks, brings forth a paradigm shift that enhances system resilience and responsiveness. By allowing components to autonomously achieve processing results, asynchronous design aligns with the core principles of decentralization, offering a more robust foundation for distributed systems.

While asynchronous communication stands out as a cornerstone for well-architected distributed systems, it simultaneously introduces challenges, especially in the context of sophisticated and orchestrated processing. Orchestrated communication involves the upstream entity making orchestration decisions based on the outcomes of underlying downstream processes. To maintain distributed consistency and prevent the system from entering any stale states, orchestrators must implement intricate design patterns like Saga or Compensating transactions.

The challenges associated with asynchronous design can be encapsulated as follows:

- **Communication Complexity**: Asynchronous communication can introduce intricacies in coordinating communication flows between upstream and downstream components. Managing the flow of messages and ensuring timely responses become critical aspects of system design.
- **Orchestration**: Orchestrating processes in an asynchronous environment requires careful consideration. The upstream component must make decisions based on the asynchronous responses from downstream processes, demanding robust orchestration mechanisms to maintain coherence and order in complex workflows.
- **Delay**: The inherent nature of asynchronous communication introduces delays in processing, as upstream components may proceed without waiting for immediate responses. While this can enhance overall system responsiveness, it necessitates strategies to handle and mitigate potential delays.
- **Discoverability**: Asynchronous systems may face challenges in discovering and coordinating with dynamically changing components. Ensuring that components can efficiently discover each other and adapt to changes in the system landscape becomes crucial for seamless communication.
- **Reverse Dependencies**: In scenarios where upstream decisions depend on downstream results, managing reverse dependencies becomes a critical concern. The asynchronous nature may lead to complexities in handling dependencies and ensuring that the system responds appropriately to changes in downstream states.

In navigating these challenges, the goal is to strike a balance between the advantages of asynchronous communication, such as improved system responsiveness and decentralization, and the complexities introduced in managing sophisticated, orchestrated processes. Thoughtful consideration of design patterns and careful system architecture can help overcome these challenges, fostering the development of robust and resilient distributed systems.

Circumstances and Design Decisions

Circumstances of using synchronous design reflect as follows:

- **Predictable Processing Flows**: Synchronous design finds its strength in scenarios where the processing flow is predictable and well-defined. When each step depends on the immediate completion of the preceding one, synchronous communication ensures a linear and deterministic execution path.

- **Simple Workflows**: In cases where the operational workflow is straightforward and lacks intricate dependencies, synchronous design offers simplicity. It aligns well with scenarios where tasks can be executed in a sequential manner without the need for complex coordination.
- **Immediate Response Requirements**: Situations demanding immediate responses benefit from synchronous communication. Real-time interactions, where timely feedback is crucial, find synchronous design fitting due to its inherent request/response pattern.

Relying on preceding challenges when designing distributed systems, some design decision considerations can be explored as follows:

- **Tight Coupling**: Synchronous design inherently involves a tight coupling between the upstream and downstream components. This design decision can be advantageous in situations where a high degree of coordination is essential.
- **Performance Optimization**: When the primary concern is optimizing performance and minimizing latencies, synchronous design, with its direct and immediate communication, becomes a preferred choice.
- **Simplified Error Handling**: In synchronous communication, error handling is more straightforward as the response is expected promptly. This simplicity can be advantageous in systems where rapid error resolution is critical.

Asynchronous design circumstances when designing distributed systems can be categorized as follows:

- **Complex Workflows**: Asynchronous design excels in scenarios where operational workflows are complex, involve multiple steps, and require non-blocking interactions. It is particularly beneficial when tasks can be executed independently, enhancing system modularity.
- **Decentralized Autonomy**: When emphasizing decentralized autonomy is crucial, asynchronous design allows components to process information independently, reducing dependencies and enabling more granular control over each step.
- **Fault Tolerance and Resilience**: In situations where fault tolerance and resilience are paramount, asynchronous communication provides flexibility. It enables systems to continue processing tasks even if individual components experience delays or failures.

Again, relying on preceding circumstance categorization, the design decisions need to consider following design details:

- **Loose Coupling**: Asynchronous design inherently promotes loose coupling between components, allowing them to operate independently. This design decision fosters flexibility and scalability by reducing dependencies.

- **Orchestrated Processing**: For tasks that require orchestration and decision-making based on the results of multiple asynchronous processes, an orchestrator is introduced. Design decisions involve implementing patterns like Saga or Compensating transactions to ensure distributed consistency.
- **Optimizing for Latency Tolerance**: While asynchronous communication introduces delays, it also provides the opportunity to optimize for latency tolerance. Design decisions involve strategies to handle delays and ensure a responsive and resilient system.

Choosing the Right Approach

There is no one-size-fit-all approach but leveraging the convenient and inconvenient parts of each decision based on tradeoffs needs some guidelines and agreements.

- **Consider Workflow Complexity**: Evaluate the complexity of the operational workflow. For straightforward and linear processes, synchronous design may be more suitable, while complex workflows benefit from the modularity of asynchronous design.
- **Prioritize Responsiveness**: If immediate responses are critical, especially in real-time interactions, synchronous communication is preferred. Asynchronous design is more suitable for scenarios where responsiveness can be balanced with the benefits of decentralization.
- **Assess Fault Tolerance Needs**: If fault tolerance and resilience are top priorities, asynchronous design provides a more resilient framework. Synchronous design may face challenges in handling failures without disrupting the entire system.
- **Plan for Future Scalability**: Consider future scalability needs. Asynchronous design, with its loose coupling, often scales more seamlessly as it accommodates growing workloads by allowing components to operate independently.

In distributed systems, the choice between synchronous and asynchronous design depends heavily on the specific circumstances, workflow characteristics, and the priorities of the system architecture. Striking a balance and making informed design decisions are paramount to building resilient, responsive, and scalable distributed systems.

Event-Driven Design

Event-Driven Design presented as a transformative paradigm, offering a solution to challenges posed by both synchronous and asynchronous designs. By leveraging the concept of events (distinct occurrences or state changes), this approach addresses key issues while providing valuable gains across fundamental pillars of distributed system architecture.

Loose Coupling

Synchronous design often involves tight coupling, leading to interdependencies between components.

Asynchronous design, although promoting loose coupling, can introduce complexities in managing dependencies during orchestrated processing.

Event-Driven Design inherently decouples components through the use of events. Components communicate through events, allowing them to remain independent while responding to relevant changes in the system.

Event-Driven Design employs event bus and queues, where components are loosely coupled by point-to-point paradigm using queues or publish and subscribe using the event bus, promoting a modular and independent architecture. In Event-Driven Design, components act as observers, reacting to events of interest.

Scalability

Synchronous design can encounter scalability issues due to dependencies and the need for immediate responses.

Asynchronous design scales well but may face challenges in orchestrating complex workflows.

Event-Driven Design adopts a publish-subscribe model. Publishers emit events, and subscribers react to specific events, allowing for independent scaling of components.

Event-Driven Design facilitates scalability by enabling components to react to relevant events independently, fostering a more modular and scalable system architecture.

Fault Tolerance

Synchronous design may lead to system-wide failures if a critical component experiences downtime.

Asynchronous design, while resilient, may encounter difficulties in managing failures across distributed components.

Event-Driven Design supports fault isolation. If a component fails, it does not necessarily disrupt the entire system. Other components can continue processing events, enhancing fault tolerance and system resilience.

Event-Driven Design enhances fault tolerance by allowing components to operate independently, ensuring that failures in one component do not propagate throughout the system.

Responsiveness

Synchronous design excels in immediate response scenarios but may struggle with complex workflows.

Asynchronous design allows flexibility but can introduce delays in certain processing scenarios.

Event-Driven Design strikes a balance by allowing immediate responses to specific events while accommodating asynchronous processing for complex workflows. Components react to events in a timely manner, providing a responsive system.

Event-Driven Design ensures responsiveness by allowing components to react promptly to relevant events, combining the benefits of both synchronous and asynchronous approaches.

Event-Driven Challenges

Despite the advantages, Event-Driven Design comes with its own set of challenges, including:

- **Event Loss**: Ensuring events are not lost during processing failures is crucial for maintaining system integrity.
- **Event Bottlenecks**: Overreliance on a single event bus can lead to bottlenecks. Ensuring scalability of the event bus is crucial.
- **Event Order**: Ensuring the correct order of events can be challenging, especially in distributed systems.
- **Chattiness**: When communicating via events the chattiness can be accumulated on the consumer side and can be duplicated for all consumers which is a cause of poor event modeling and lack of consumer first event modeling.

Event-Driven Design serves as a unifying force, offering gains across diverse pillars of distributed system architecture. By embracing loose coupling, scalability, fault tolerance, and responsiveness, this approach harmonizes the challenges of synchronous and asynchronous designs. Through well-defined event communication boundaries, Event-Driven Design empowers distributed systems to achieve a seamless and adaptable architecture, promoting resilience, flexibility, and future-ready systems.

Private and Public Events

Events can be categorized in two layers of visibility: Private and Public. This categorization helps to balance the exigence of event contractualization, less chatty communication and avoiding to distribute events with no interested subscriber.

- **Public Events**: The public events are the contracts and promises between two or multiple bounded contexts. These are the well documented events that need more exigences in the modeling and documentation phases, as these are the long-term promises and contracts. Any changes must be investigated in advance to avoid the inconsistency and stale state in the whole system.

- **Private Events**: Private events are the events that help to connect two processing modules in a single bounded context. Mostly these events are handled by a single team or two teams with a partnership. The private events can be compromised to immediate changes with a minimum effort of communication between teams or members. A private event does not need a contractualized documentation and mostly the private events follow a light technical documentation in contrast to public events.
- **Event Types:** As component's need to communicate elevates, this leverages the need to event distribution and evolution in the event model. While the system is small, this can be achievable by simplicity, but when the system starts to grow and the inter-component communication leads to changes frequently, the need of understanding event types and how to model them grows simultaneously.

Events introduce a fact in the system by introducing enough information to represent a change in the system that will help the consumers or other components do the desired actions behind receiving the event. Looking at the consumer needs when designing events is an important topic leading to simplified and maintainable systems.

Events can be introduced in following categories at modeling level: Integration events, Notification events, and Event-Carried State Transfer events.

- **Integration Events:** In Event-Driven Design, an integration event is a type of event that signifies a state change or an action that occurred within a software system and is intended to be communicated to other parts of the system or external systems for integration purposes. Integration events are a key mechanism for enabling communication and coordination between different microservices or components in a distributed system.

  As the name implies, integration events are commonly employed in scenarios where different services or systems need to communicate with each other. This can include notifying other services about changes in state, triggering business processes, or updating data in other parts of the system. This leads to the requirement of having a minimum of related information to be presented as part of an event letting those components take the desired decisions before interacting. An integration event is an ideal and most used type of event type in distributed systems. Due to this, the importance of well-defined event modeling when defining integration events is an evident requirement. The payload is used by the receiving components to understand the context of the event.

- **Notification Events:** In Event-Driven Design, a notification event is a type of event that serves the purpose of notifying or broadcasting information to interested parties within a system. Unlike integration events that are typically used for cross-system communication and coordination, notification events are more focused on disseminating information within the boundaries helping to achieve integrity and consistency between systems by presenting a particular state change or occurrence.
- **Event-Carried State Transfer Events:** An Event-Carried State Transfer event functions as a singular occurrence, delivering a holistic understanding of changes within the system to consumers. Its intent is to minimize the requirement for prolonged and repetitive communication, streamlining the resolution of dependencies linked to the presented change. This strategy places a premium on prompt assimilation, enabling consumers to quickly apprehend pertinent details and diminishing the need for extended communication to discern dependencies. The design underscores rapid awareness and responsiveness, recognizing a compromise with the immediate consistency prerequisite in favor of a more efficient communication approach.

Event-Driven Design Patterns

In the realm of event driven design, the representation of a single change in the system is prioritized due to the advantages the event based design introduces in a distributed design, such as loose coupling, scalability, and resiliency. This section gives a detailed overview of design patterns and principles and how they help solve any distributed design problem.

- **Messaging:** Another modern software and process requirement is decoupling the business process, letting the different components of a system act autonomously and independently. Decoupling leads to more agility and optimized continuous delivery and improvement processes. This pattern can be implemented using Amazon SQS or Amazon MQ that integrates well with AWS Lambda.
- **Publish Subscribe**: One of the major requirements in an Event-Driven Design is the need of distributing the changes across components in real time and in a reliable way. The AWS ecosystem provides a variety of services that helps achieve the broadcasting needs of multiple consumers in real time. We can use Amazon SNS or EventBridge to design for fanout or change broadcasting. Both services integrate well with lambda service as we explored before in *Chapter* 3, *Invocation Models and Service Integrations.*
- **Event Streaming:** In cases where the software needs to act behind data changes at a given time, it needs the ability to act and consider the latest valuable state of the data and avoid introducing stale state between systems. In this case, a streaming pattern is the best fit. Event Streaming can be applied using Amazon

DynamoDB Streams or Amazon Kinesis Data Streams. These Services both use the same design approach and stream the data isolated by a shard concept, with each shard in a guaranteed order based on change occurrence. Both services integrate well with AWS Lambda using a polling model as explored in *Chapter 3, Invocation Models and Service Integrations*.

- **Event Bus:** In Scenarios when the adoption of event driven design comes to a higher rate at enterprise level, the control and governance of the distributed communication becomes hard. The Event Bus pattern helps to centralize and uniformize the event distribution between those system components. AWS provides EventBridge as a serverless Event Bus that can be handy in some level of enterprises with fast growth.

Messaging

Messaging is a kind of design that helps to offload different parts of a system by adding a higher level of control in any single component. This section provides a detailed understanding of various decoupled messaging patterns, examining the issues each pattern addresses and the inconveniences it introduces into the design. The patterns and examples explored aim to tackle common problems within distributed designs.

For each individual pattern, the fundamental considerations include:

- Operational requirements
- Consistency
- Fault tolerance
- Scalability
- Performance

To better understand the problem-solving aspects of each pattern throughout the rest of this chapter, we will delve into the example of a Client Support software.

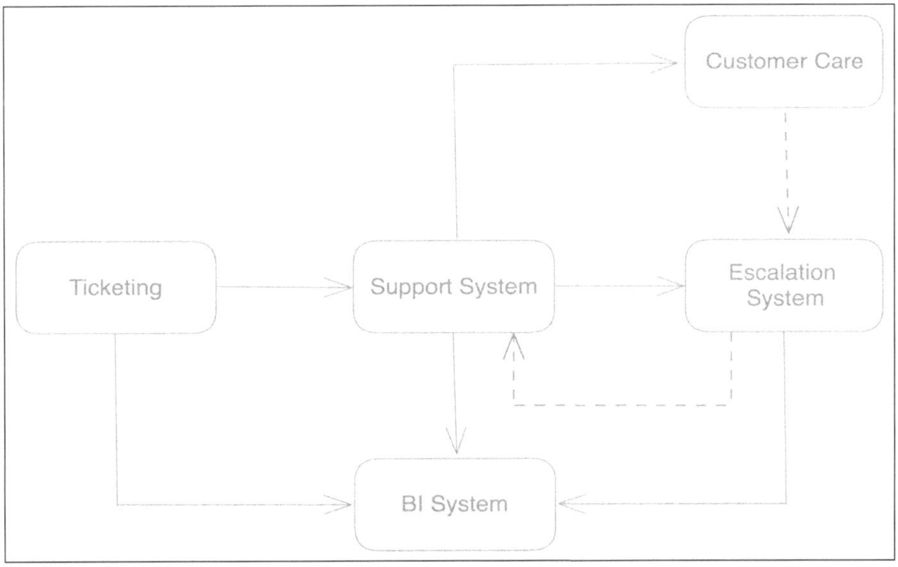

Figure 4.3: *Ticketing system*

The Client Support Software streamlines the handling of incoming tickets by choosing the most suitable individual to address customer tickets. When a customer creates a support ticket detailing the issue, the ticketing system is responsible for internally selecting a qualified person to respond through various available channels. The customer's ticket submission process does not concern itself with the selection of the best person to respond; it simply submits the ticket. The detailed technical design is illustrated in the following diagram.

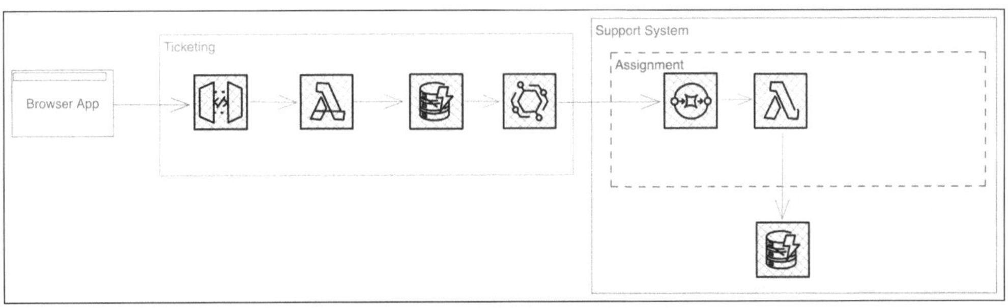

Figure 4.4: *Ticketing / Support system*

The ticketing process will be as:

1. The customer submits a request via the web application.
2. The ticketing service processes the incoming request.
3. The Support system receives the ticket through an SQS queue.

4. A Lambda function is triggered to process messages and generate an unavailability status.
5. The Lambda function selects the most suitable individual for the request, considering their availability and the best match for the ticket category.
6. The Lambda function publishes a message to an SNS topic.
7. The SNS topic disseminates the message to the Escalation System.
8. The SNS sends out a mobile app notification and an SMS to the selected individual.

To address the above considerations, the Selection of services and refined service integration configuration are important.

Point to Point Communication

Starting with ticketing system using AWS CDK (Cloud Development Kit), the code will be as follows, where an API gateway acts as a reception point to allow a Lambda function process the ticket and add it if eligible. The data source is a DynamoDB table with a **HashKey(PartitionKey)** as **TicketId** and some other attributes as category, **creationDate** and message. The system behind registering the ticket will send a message to the assignment system queue. The DynamoDB streams are used and are integrated using EventBridge pipes to send the message to the assignment SQS queue. (Some codes are omitted for brevity; the source code is provided in C04 **Version1** Examples Point 2 Point Design).

Creating API gateway and integrating with Lambda function:

```
const api = new RestApi(this, 'TicketingApi', { ... });
const addTicketFunction = new NodejsFunction(this, 'AddTicketFunction',
{ ... });
const lambdaProxyIntegration = new LambdaIntegration(addTicketFunction);
const lambdaApiResource = api.root.addResource('ticket');
lambdaApiResource.addMethod( 'POST', lambdaProxyIntegration);
```

The **AddTicket** Lambda function provides a small and simple code to register and return the http response to the caller, to avoid having duplication, as a guard the registration to Dynamodb uses a conditional check to assure the first reception ticket persistence.

The following snippet demonstrates the handler function code:

```
  try {
        const { category, message, ticketId } = JSON.parse(event.body);
        await repository.createTicket(category, ticketId, message)
```

```
        return {
          statusCode: 201,
          body: JSON.stringify({...})
        }
    } catch (error: InternalException) {
        if ( error instanceof TicketAlreadyExistException) {
          return { ... A bad request response ... }
    }

        return { ... Internal Server Error ... }
    }
```

To deploy the **`Ticketing`** example, refer to the **Version1** of **`C04/p2p-communication`** and follow the Readme instructions to deploy the CDK application.

The Support Assignment system actively monitors incoming messages, assigning each ticket to the most qualified staff member available and ensuring the identification of suitable staff for ticket resolution. The assignment process is outlined as follows:

1. Locate the earliest accessible staff member.
2. Ensure that the chosen staff member has the longest period of availability since their last assignment.
3. Verify that the staff member is relevant to the ticket category.

To deploy the **`SupportAssignment`** example, refer to the **Version1** in `` `C04/p2p-communication` `` and follow the Readme instructions to deploy the CDK application.

Testing Phase

The AWS CDK deploy command will return back the REST API URL in terminal:

Figure 4.5: *CDK rest api gateway url output*

Send a POST request to the endpoint and append `` `/ticket` `` path to the url, the request body will be:

```
curl --location '<Puth-Your-Url-From-Cdk-Output>/ticket' \
--header 'Content-Type: application/json' \
--data '{
   "category": "HighPriority",
   "ticketId": 927,
   "message": "we are investigating a production problem and need urgent
help from support to re-establish the situation asap."
}'
```

Sending the request, the API will respond with a `**201**` http status code confirming reception of the ticket.

Looking at the Support Assignment DynamoDb Table, we find the records as shown in the following figure.

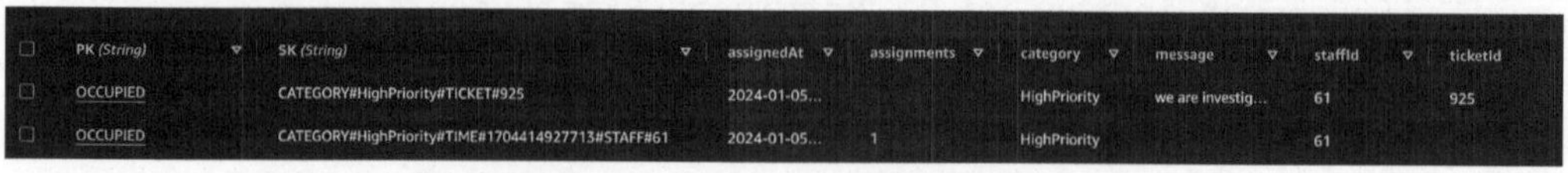

Figure 4.6: *Dynamodb registered assignments*

Each Staff has a single line for assignment with a status PK and a SK including **`Category`**, **`Date`**, and **`StaffId`**, this helps to better find the best match based on criteria mentioned earlier.

Design Consideration and Requirements

In actual design, all incoming tickets are registered and finally are transformed and distributed via DynamoDB streams and Eventbridge pipes. Having a PK as **`TicketId`** helps to isolate treatment of each ticket and provide a better level of parallelism, using SQS helps to decouple the producer and consumer sides and also have a real time messaging communication. As SQS guarantees at least once delivery, we must be prepared for duplications. Additionally, SQS does not guarantee the order of messages as per arrival. In actual design, the EventBridge keeps the ordering per invocation order per shard (PK), which is not useful as we create a new record just a single time and the following request for the same ticket will be rejected.

The requirements and consideration of solution must cover:

- The tickets must be treated in order.
- The ticket must be sent to a single person to avoid disturbing the customers and staff.

Let us look at any single part of our design:

- **Order**: As ordering is important, we need to consider a First-In-First-Out (FIFO) Queue. AWS SQS offers two types of queues: Standard and FIFO.
- **Duplication**: The assignment must be deduplicated, this means we cannot send a single demand to multiple persons suddenly or by accident. To achieve this behavior, Amazon SQS FIFO offers a deduplication mechanism at the group of message or queue level. If the messages have no variable content (like date and time) the FIFO queue also offers **`ContentBasedDeduplication`** that helps to abandon duplicated messages. The deduplication process works in a 5-minute evaluation period.
- **Scalability**: As the number of demands can rise and is not predictable in advance, the support system must be able to handle any peak of demands.

The Amazon SQS is a scalable and managed service and can respond to peak load. At the time of writing, the FIFO queues have a 70K TPS (transactions per second) limit per API Call, that sounds enough for high-traffic scenarios (we will explore later how to increase the throughput and bypass limits in the next chapter). However, this design might encounter the back pressure situations in the lambda side. The lambda service scales well, but to increase the level of assurance in this design, we need to better control the service collaboration at the integration level by refining the Event Source mapping configuration.

The Lambda function behind the SQS FIFO will be triggered, to reduce the rate of lambda invocations, the use of Batch Sizing and Concurrency limit can be a solution.

Improvements

Actual design causes a duplicated assignment by running the request two times, leading to the assignment of the same ticket to two different staff members which means producing inconsistent behavior in the customer support system. To achieve these requirements, we need to consider some changes in our design and integration configurations. To achieve the tickets ordering and guarantee an optimized assignment, first the assignment queue must be changed to a FIFO queue.

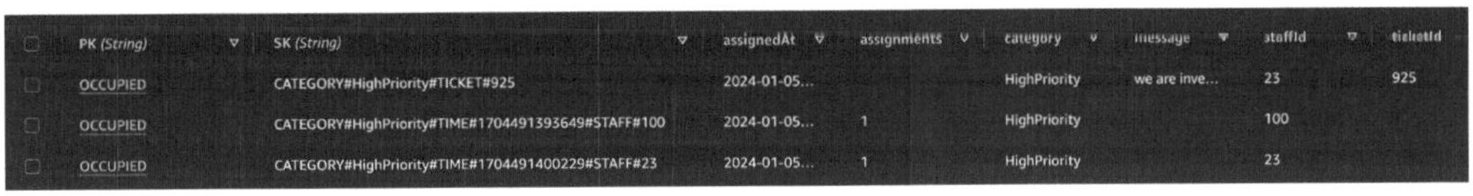

PK (String)	SK (String)	assignedAt	assignments	category	message	staffId	ticketId
OCCUPIED	CATEGORY#HighPriority#TICKET#925	2024-01-05...		HighPriority	we are inve...	23	925
OCCUPIED	CATEGORY#HighPriority#TIME#1704491393649#STAFF#100	2024-01-05...	1	HighPriority		100	
OCCUPIED	CATEGORY#HighPriority#TIME#1704491400229#STAFF#23	2024-01-05...	1	HighPriority		23	

Figure 4.7: *Duplicated assignment*

Moving to FIFO queue will be done simply by changing the CDK code for Queue as follows:

```
import { Queue } from '@aws-cdk/aws-sqs';

const incomingDemandsQueue = new Queue(this, 'AssignmentIncoming
DemandsQueue', {
     queueName: 'assignment-incoming-demands-queue.fifo',
     fifo: true,
     ...
}
```

The `.fifo` must be appended to the **queueName** and the **fifo** parameter needs to be set as `true`. The **DeadLetterQueue** also must be modified as a FIFO queue.

For the deduplication purpose, the SQS FIFO accepts two parameters to configure the deduplication process. SQS Deduplication is based on a 5-minute period, this means for each predefined 5-minutes, the first message will be treated, and the following will be abandoned transparently. If the first message fails or will be discarded by application code, there will be no chance to have the following messages. The 5-minute counter starts by any single **DeduplicationId** as part of request.

FIFO queues provide deduplication at queue level or group level. To achieve grouping of messages, the SQS provides a **MessageGroupId** parameter. The **MessageGroupId** is useful when there is a need for isolation of messages in groups, such as when designing a Fan-In pattern using SQS. Multiple producers send messages, and **MessageGroupId** helps to consider the ordering of messages and treatment in an isolated way.

The assignment system needs a queue level deduplication and based on message Content and can be configured as follows:

```
import * as cdk from '@aws-cdk/core';
import { Queue, DeduplicationScope } from '@aws-cdk/aws-sqs';
const incomingDemandsQueue = new Queue(this, 'AssignmentIncomingDemands-
Queue', {
     queueName: 'assignment-incoming-demands-queue.fifo',
     fifo: true,
     deduplicationScope: DeduplicationScope.QUEUE,
     contentBasedDeduplication: true,
     visibilityTimeout: cdk.Duration.seconds(30),
     retentionPeriod: cdk.Duration.days(10),
     deadLetterQueue: {
       queue: incomingDemandsDeadLetterQueue,
       maxReceiveCount: 3
     }
});
```

To deploy the **SupportAssignment** example, refer to the **Version2** in `` `C04/p2p-communication` `` and follow the Readme instructions to deploy the CDK application.

There are some difficulties to test the new solution as we already have application deduplication enforcement in the ticketing system. To test the deduplication, it will be possible to send a message directly multiple times to the queue. Doing so, the Lambda function will be triggered a single time for a 5-minute duration.

Deduplication and Ordering

Deduplication has different meaning in different cases. In the preceding example, duplication had a real impact on both the internal side and the customer side. Another example of ordering and deduplication in the real world is banking transactions, as duplication can cause an impact on client accounts or, in case of loss of order, a transaction will be validated that actually should not.

In some cases, duplicated requests have no real impact and can be tolerated by the system without a real business impact. Therefore, designing with idempotency in mind can be a solution to decrease the impact level.

There are some constraints in the default deduplication process that are not ideal in real-world examples.

- **Five-minute interval**: Often, the deduplication needs to be treated at a really short period of time.
- Content-based deduplication does not work as there will be dynamic elements like data in the message.
- The failure of the first message can cause a state inconsistency in the system.

To resolve the 5-minute interval, the producer can include a partial range of actual Date (**`Date.now()`**) as part of **`DeduplicationId`**. For example, 2024-01-01T12:30 and 2024-01-01T12:31 for the subsequent messages. This ensures that the deduplication id will be unique just for one minute (you can reduce down to the seconds, **`2024-01-01T12:30:00`**, **`2024-01-01T12:30;30`**).

By default, content-based deduplication relies on the **`DeduplicationId`** just by generating a hash of whole message content. However, if there are the dynamic elements like date, you can simply achieve deduplication by constructing a custom **`MessageDeduplicationId`** using only the desired parts of the message.

For managing deduplication better in case of failures, considering a customized shorter deduplication as explained above can be useful. Additionally, an alerting system is a must to monitor the **`DeadLetterQueue`**.

Priority Queue

The priority queue pattern relies on an ordered treatment based on each message priority. In this pattern, the queue can reorder the messages based on the priority. As Amazon SQS does not support the reordering, the solution is having multiple queues. The Ticketing system can receive tickets with different priority levels as **`LowPriority`**, **`HighPriority`**. The solution must cover the business requirements.

- The **`LowPriority`** tickets tolerate a delayed assignment.
- The **`HighPriority`** tickets must be assigned immediately.

The following figure illustrates the changes adopted in design to achieve the Separation of High and Low Priorities. Actually, the Lambda function does the same job for both priorities, the immediate or delayed reception will be managed by two separate SQS configurations.

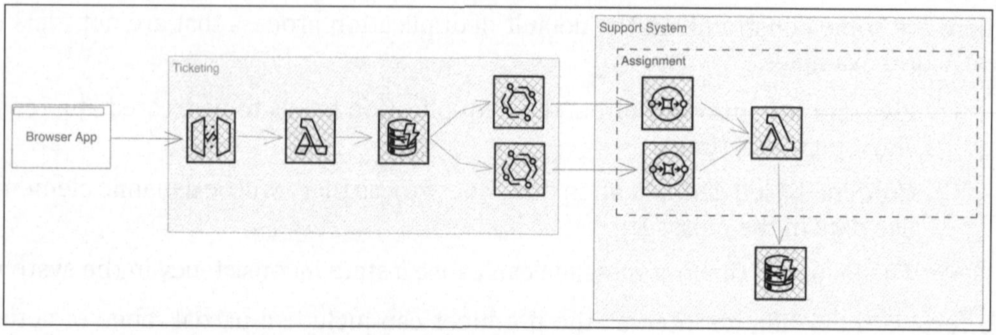

Figure 4.8: *Priority Queue*

Temporal Priority

The temporal processing sets the rapidity level of treatments per priority of messages. The assignment system will add another queue with a delivery delay configuration for low priority tickets, ensuring all high priorities pass at first.

```
import * as cdk from '@aws-cdk/core';
import { Queue } from '@aws-cdk/aws-sqs';

const assignmentLowPriorityQueue = new Queue(this, 'AssignmentIncoming-
DemandsQueue', {
     queueName: 'assignment-low-priority-queue.fifo',
     fifo: true,
     deliveryDelay: cdk.Duration.minutes(15),
     ...
}
```

To deploy the **SupportAssignment** example, refer to the **Version3** in `` `C04/priority-queue/` `` and follow the Readme instructions to deploy the CDK application.

The ticketing system should send each priority to the corresponding queue in the support assignment system. This will be achievable by using filtering at the EventBridge pipe configuration level.

```
new CfnPipe(this, 'LowPriorityPipe', {
     ...
     sourceParameters: {
       dynamoDbStreamParameters: { ... },
       filterCriteria: {
         filters: [{
           pattern: JSON.stringify({
             dynamodb: {
             NewImage: {
                          category: {
                                S: ["LowPriority"]
```

```
                            }
                }
                }
                })
            }]
        }
    },
    ...
});
```

The pipe filters out the **LowPriority** category and sends it to SQS after input transformation.

To deploy the **Ticketing** example, refer to the **Version3** in **C04/priority-queue** and follow the Readme instructions to deploy the CDK application.

Send three requests with low and high priority.

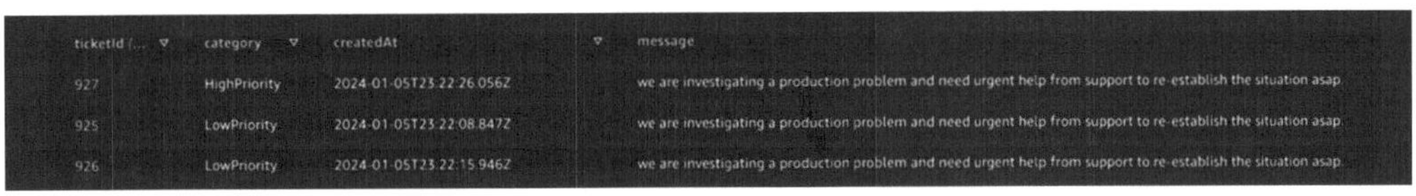

ticketId (...	category	createdAt	message
927	HighPriority	2024-01-05T23:22:26.056Z	we are investigating a production problem and need urgent help from support to re-establish the situation asap.
925	LowPriority	2024-01-05T23:22:08.847Z	we are investigating a production problem and need urgent help from support to re-establish the situation asap.
926	LowPriority	2024-01-05T23:22:15.946Z	we are investigating a production problem and need urgent help from support to re-establish the situation asap.

Figure 4.9: *Low and high priority items*

However, looking at the assignment system, we find only the high priority ticket assigned. Looking at the low priority queue, the queue has no in-flight or available messages. But looking at EventBridge pipe invocations and SQS sent message metrics, these show the success of dissemination of messages to the queue.

PK (String)	SK (String)	assignedAt
OCCUPIED	CATEGORY#HighPriority#TICKET#927	2024-01-05T23:22:27.409Z
OCCUPIED	CATEGORY#HighPriority#TIME#1704496947409#STAFF#7	2024-01-05T23:22:27.409Z

Figure 4.10: *high priority assignment*

Waiting until the end of the delivery delay, the messages will be polled by the Lambda service, and the assignment result will be present in the Assignment Dynamodb table.

Scale Controlled Priority Queue

The Sized processing adapts the capacity of massage treatment based on priority. Amazon SQS, when integrating with Lambda as part of the Event Source Mapping configuration, gives the possibility of setting the `**maxConcurrency**`. This limit leads the Lambda service poller to control the design concurrency configured at function level. This means in the assignment system, the Lambda scales lower for `**LowPriority**` than `**HighPriority**`.

```
// SQS event source for the high priority queue
assignmentFunction.addEventSource(new    SqsEventSource(assignmentHigh-
PriorityQueue, {
    enabled: true,
  }));

//SQS event source for the low priority queue
  assignmentFunction.addEventSource(new SqsEventSource(assignmentLow-
PriorityQueue, {
    maxConcurrency: 1,
    enabled: true,
  }));
```

This solution helps to have a relatively close behavior in normal situations but prioritizes behavior at peak load and high scale.

Event Streaming

In an event-driven distributed system where the events are the facts and the source of communication to keep the overall system transactionally consistent at the highest trustable level, the number of interested actors for any single event increases. This situation leads to adopting a design allowing near real-time communication and bringing more responsiveness into design. However, at the same time, as the number of interested actors grows, it becomes hard and, in some cases, impossible for event producers to keep track of all interested actors and guarantee the reliability of consumption.

In the ticketing example, as the number of interested actors behind Support Assignment system grows, the assignment needs to send events to Customer Care, Escalation, Legacy Backoffice, Emailing and Application Notification services. Additionally, it needs to send SMS to assignee. Managing each consumer separately and correctly becomes a challenging step. In this case, the Support Assignment system provides an Event Broker that lets the consumers handle their needs in a more decoupled and scalable manner.

Data Streaming

The Support Assignment system, after assigning the ticket to any staff member, forwards the corresponding event to a BI system for analytics data preparation. The BI system has a requirement of archiving events in specific format and forwarding records to an OpenSearch collection. Besides the BI system, there are a variety of other consumers as illustrated in the following diagram.

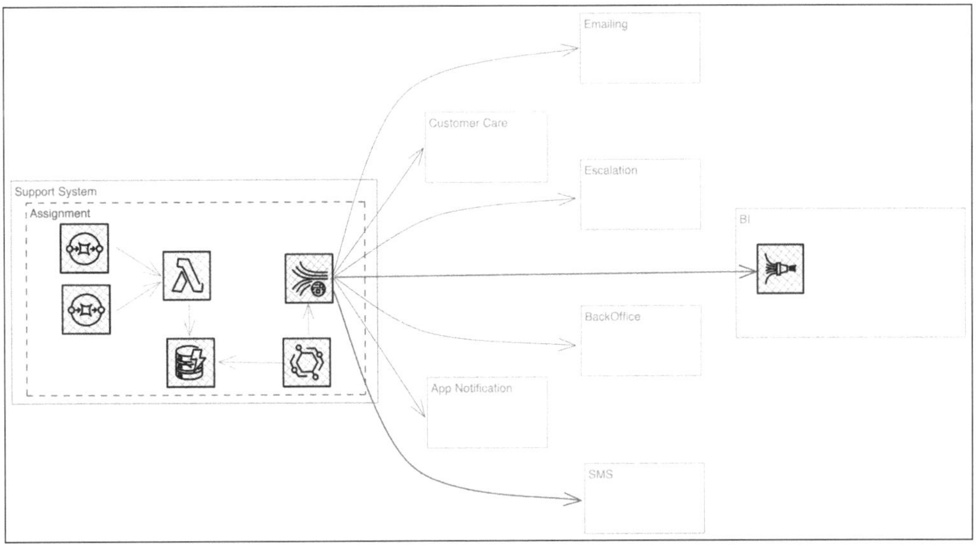

Figure 4.11: *Data Streaming*

In this design, all consumers are polling the records and treating them independently on their side. Each consumer has a dead letter queue attached at Lambda Event Source mapping level that lets retry the failed events in the case of processing failures. The Support system uses EventBridge pipes to put events in Kinesis Data Stream.

The following snippet represents the pipe configuration:

```
import { Table } from 'aws-cdk-lib/aws-dynamodb';
import { KinesisStream } from 'aws-cdk-lib/aws-kinesis';

const table = new Table(this, 'MyTable', {...});
const dataStream = new KinesisStream(this, 'MyKinesisStream', {...});

new CfnPipe(this, 'HighPriorityPipe', {
 ...
 source: table.tableStreamArn!,
 sourceParameters: {
   dynamoDbStreamParameters: {
     startingPosition: 'LATEST',
   },
   filterCriteria: {
     filters: [{
         pattern: `{
           "dynamodb": {
             "NewImage": {
               "ticketId": {
                 "S": [ { "exists": true  } ]
               }
```

```
            }
          }
        }`}]
    }
  },
  target: dataStream.streamArn,
  targetParameters: {
    kinesisStreamParameters: {
      partitionKey: EventField.fromPath('$.dynamodb.NewImage.ticket-
Id.S'),
    },
    inputTemplate: `
      {
      "ticketId": <$.dynamodb.NewImage.ticketId.S>,
      "category": <$.dynamodb.NewImage.category.S>,
      "staffId": <$.dynamodb.NewImage.staffId.S>,
      "assignedAt": <$.dynamodb.NewImage.assignedAt.S>
      }`
  }
});
```

The BI system will be integrated with the assignment data stream. The BI CDK stack will use the `**@aws-cdk/aws-kinesisfirehose-alpha**` and `**@aws-cdk/aws-kinesisfirehose-destinations-alpha**` for the sake of L2 constructs.

```
import { Stream } from 'aws-cdk-lib/aws-kinesis';
import { StringParameter } from 'aws-cdk-lib/aws-ssm';
import { Role, ServicePrincipal } from 'aws-cdk-lib/aws-iam';
import { Bucket } from 'aws-cdk-lib/aws-s3'; import { DeliveryStream,
S3Bucket } from '@aws-cdk/aws-kinesisfirehose-destinations-alpha';

const assignmentStreamArn = StringParameter.valueForStringParame-
ter(this,
      '/assignment/datastream/arn');
const assignmentDataStream = Stream.fromStreamArn(this,
"AssignmentDataStreamArnParameter",
assignmentDataStreamArn);
const deliveryStreamRole = new Role(this, 'DeliveryStreamRole', {
assumedBy: new ServicePrincipal('firehose.amazonaws.com') });
const destinationRole = new Role(this, 'DestinationRole', {
assumedBy: new ServicePrincipal('firehose.amazonaws.com') });
const deliveryBucket = new Bucket(this, "DeliveryBucket");
new DeliveryStream(this, 'BiDeliveryStream', {
destinations: [new S3Bucket(deliveryBucket, { role: destinationRole })],
sourceStream: assignmentDataStream,
role: deliveryStreamRole
```

```
});

assignmentDataStream.grantRead(deliveryStreamRole);
```

Sending a new ticket to the ticketing system will result in a new file registered in Kinesis Firehose delivery bucket.

As per the precedent diagram, we have multiple consumers to consume records from Data Stream. For demonstration purposes and to simulate a wide range of consumers, the escalation system will be replicated. The Escalation is connected to the data stream using Lambda Event Source mapping and treats records by starting a step function execution for any single record. The design is illustrated as follows:

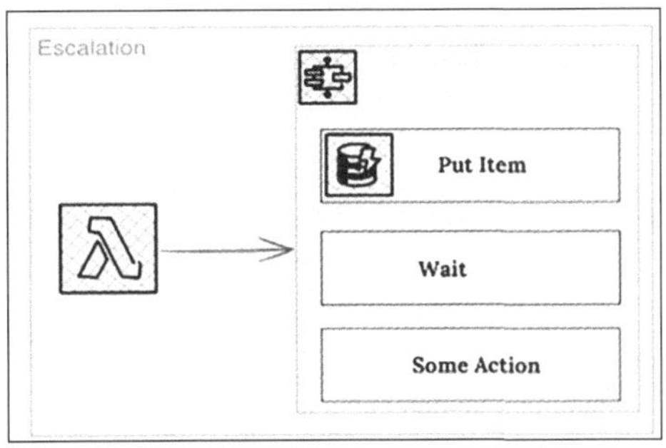

Figure 4.12: *Escalation system*

Any single added ticket by Ticketing system results in a controlled workflow execution. For this example, based on priority, the wait time varies.

To simulate more data stream consumers, the Escalation stack provides a way of deploying new copies using a command line argument. Running the following command, we create 20 copies:

```
for j in {1..20}; do cdk deploy --profile serverless --app "npx ts-node
--prefer-ts-exts cdk/bin/escalation.ts $j" --require-approval never ;
done;
```

* *During deployment, it's possible that the deployment of some stacks can encounter a rate-limiting error. In this case, simply rerun the command after termination.*

Using tools like Postman, there is the possibility to send simultaneous requests. Looking at the Lambda metrics, the **`IteratorAge`** metrics vary per function. This difference approves the latency that Kinesis Data Stream limits can introduce for part of the consumers. Running 1200 requests during 1 minute, leading to 15 requests per second leads to a **`IteratorAge`** metric of between 5s as the lower limit and 55s as the upper limit.

Looking at Kinesis Data Streams **`GetRecords`** Throttling metric, there was a high rate of throttling requests.

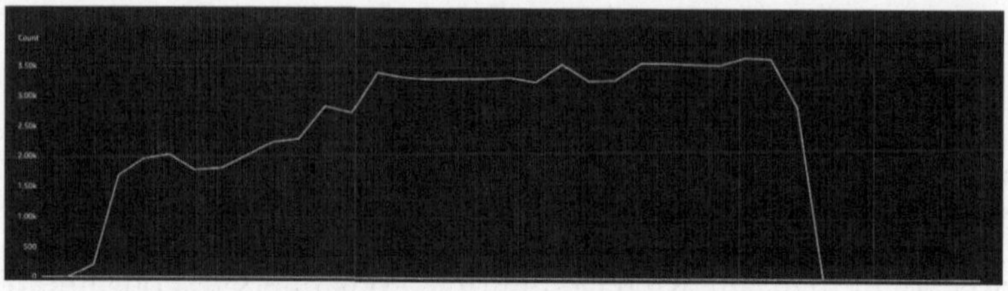

Figure 4.13: *Data stream throttling metric*

Looking at Kinesis firehose metrics, the **`GetRecords`** Throttling metric shows the throttling but **`DescribeStream`** and **`GetShardIterator`** throttling metrics show no throttling evaluation points.

The Firehose was delivered to s3 bucket, but looking at the creation date of the file, there is a 5-minute delay between ticketing request and delivery into s3 bucket.

Destroy Stack

To destroy all simulated stacks at once, use the following command:

```
for j in {1..20}; do cdk destroy --profile serverless --app "npx ts-node
--prefer-ts-exts cdk/bin/escalation.ts $j" --force; done;
```

Publish Subscribe

In previous design, the treatment of records was achieved via kinesis basic consumption. While the design could approve some design problems, it introduced some challenges, such as:

- **Throttling Metric:** The Throttling metric is a metric that helps to identify an inconvenient behavior in a system. However, that design was toward making this metric informative and not as a metric to detect the overall system problem.
- **Latency:** The latency was getting higher as the load increased, this represents a regression at scale and could lead to inconsistent situations in an event driven design if that gets too high.
- **Processing:** In the example, there was no processing on the consumer side, and the consumers were just acting behind the arrival of any single record, except for the BI system that could have some transformation and detailed data preparation specificity.
- **Offloading:** The example provides no offloading practice between producer and consumer. Therefore, the consumers will get impacted and lose treatment capacity with any load increase in producer side. Fortunately, AWS Lambda Event Source Mapping handles this layer of integration well, but this can still get tricky in some cases, such as when dealing with legacy systems.

Bringing all these elements together leads to the adoption of alternative designs. Depending on the requirements of the media assignment, we need to notify multiple consumers behind any assignment with different processing and scaling capabilities. They may need to offload events or process events immediately. The assignment system will be designed as shown in the following diagram to simplify event broadcasting and ensure real-time event broadcasting. Events are no longer subject to one-off processing, but every event must be duplicated or copied by the number of interested actors from a consumption point of view.

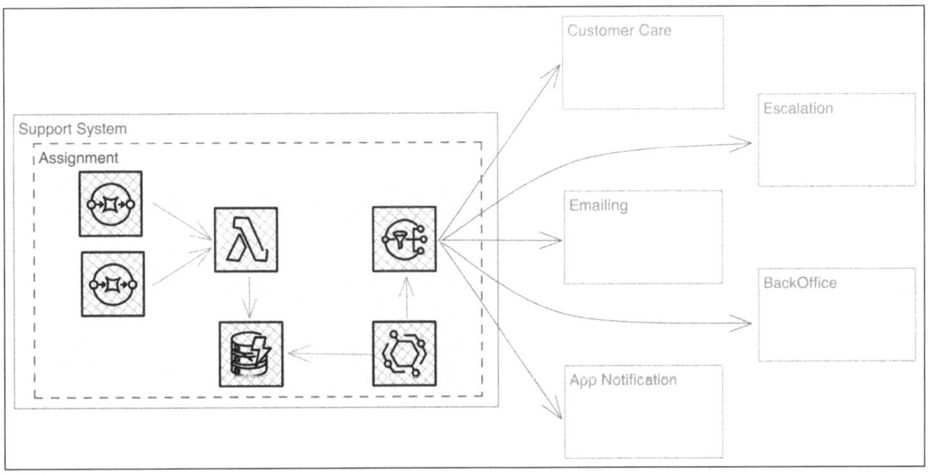

Figure 4.14: *Publish / subscribe*

The assignee events are published to a pub/sub channel and the subscribers will be notified by presence of that assignment in real time. The consumers take care of their own specific considerations like load balancing, error handling and ordering of events and the producer just guarantees the distribution of events.

The Support system keeps the same configuration for pipe configuration, except this time it sends the events in a topic. AWS SNS integrates well with pipes and accepts a large number of subscribers with the filtering option that will be covered in this book.

The Escalation system subscribes to Support Topic using a SQS Subscription with enabled raw message delivery. Any single published message into SNS topic will be delivered to all subscribers except a filter policy excluding that message delivery by individual subscriber.

Again, for the demonstration purpose, the following command deploys 20 times the Escalation stack to simulate the consumers and message delivery in detail.

```
for j in {1..20}; do cdk deploy --profile serverless --app "npx ts-node
--prefer-ts-exts cdk/bin/escalation.ts $j" --require-approval never ;
done;
```

Sending a new ticket request results in a message distribution to all consumers at the exact time. The consumers can subscribe to SNS using SQS as in the example, or using Lambda function subscribed to the topic. The subscription using CDK can be done as follows:

```
assignmentTopic.addSubscription(
 new SqsSubscription(escalationAssignmentQueue, {
   deadLetterQueue: assignmentSubscriptionDLQ,
   rawMessageDelivery: true
 })
);
```

Running a bulk concurrent execution of 1200 requests during 1-minute results in consistent behavior in all SQS consumers. Looking at the message Sent and Received metrics of all SQS, there metrics show the exact behavior

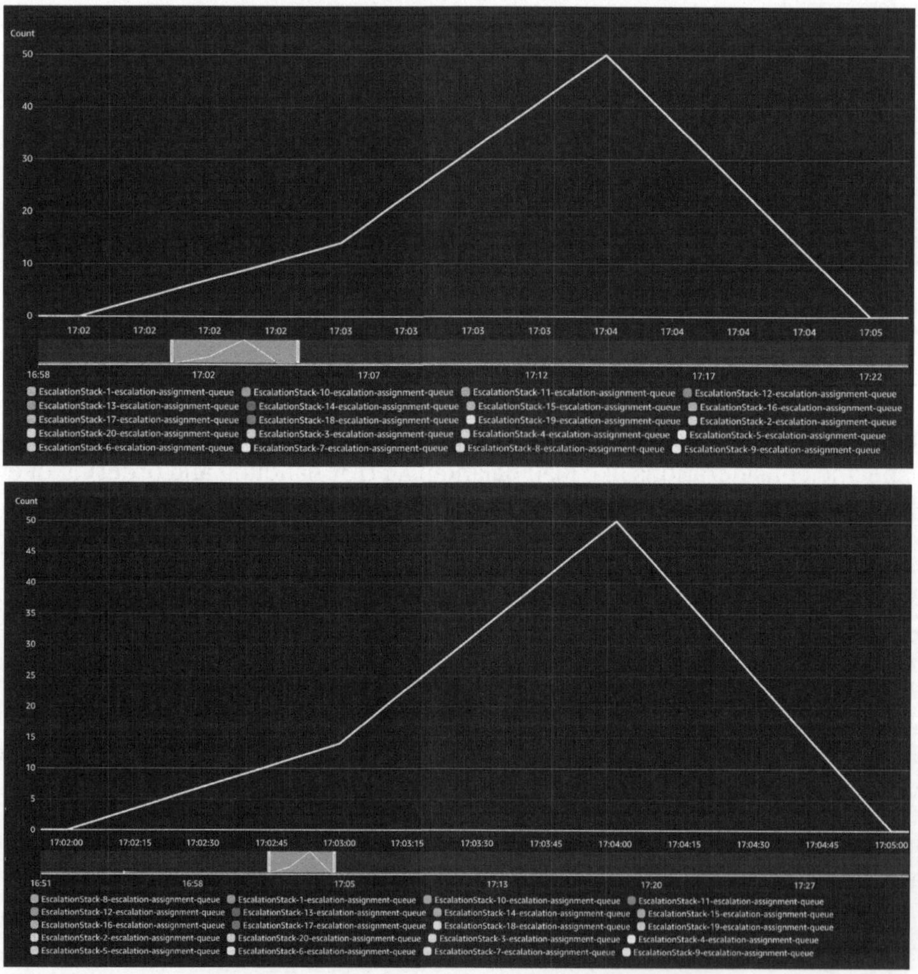

Figure 4.15: SNS/SQS *event receive and send metrics*

Both metrics show approximately the same performance and this is one of the high adoption of Fan Out using SNS/SQS in industry.

Bidirectional Communication

In Scenarios, it can be possible that the producer and consumer need to be aware of each other's process results. This requirement leads to settle a bidirectional communication between both parties of communication.

Async Request-Reply

The Request-Reply helps to decouple two distinct processes but keeping the communication active between the communication parties. The Request/Reply pattern allows the occurrence of a collaborative process, eventually keeping the result and process status consistent in the whole process.

The Request-Reply pattern, as a solution to resolve consistency and state between communication actors, also represent the identical challenges that must be considered before any decision.

- The request and reply must be in two different threads or isolated logical processes.
- It introduces a circular hard dependency on design.
- Keeping the reply dependency lightened can be beneficial.
- Defining the point of lightning depends on the organization boundaries that each party resides in.

In our ticketing example, the Support Assignment system notified the Escalation system to wait for an escalation decision for any new required escalation to be done.

The Escalation process is as follows:

- Receiving an assignment message
- Registering assignment and starting a scheduled survey
- The survey is a dynamic scheduling per assignment
- Sending survey result and alert to escalate staffs

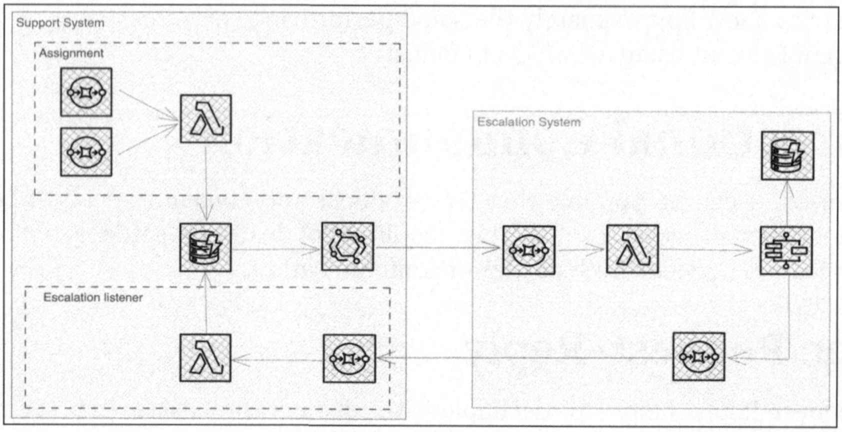

Figure 4.16: *Async request reply*

The Escalation System receives messages via a SQS queue and processes them by calculating the verification time schedule based on priority and starting a Step Functions workflow, giving the schedule time as part of input. The workflow will update the DynamoDB and wait till the defined time and run the verification process.

To deploy the example, refer to the `` `C04/async-request-reply/Version1` `` and follow the Readme instructions to deploy CDK applications.

The Escalation requirements are:

- A Low Priority ticket will be surveyed each 3 hours
- A High Priority ticket will be surveyed each 10 minutes

How the whole communication works:

The Assignment sends the assigned results to escalation, which schedules the verification of customer evaluations and, in case the ticket being in pending state based on priority, will ask the Support system to escalate by reassigning to a new member.

As per *Figure 4.16*, the Support system represents two separate modules running in separate threads. The Escalation listener and Assignment modules share a single DynamoDB database to make the dependency lighter and remove the circular dependency at build and deploy phase. At runtime, the Escalation relies on a variable representing the DynamoDB table identifier. The deployable components follow the following order:

- Assignment Module of Support System
- Ticketing System
- Escalation system
- Escalation Listener Module of Support System

Caution: It is important to note that a bidirectional communication can lead to a circular event triggering. In our example, not being aware of this aspect can lead to resending the changes as a loop. As a workaround, we need to implement in a controlled way this communication on both sides.

Enterprise Event Bus

As the event-based adoption grows at enterprise level, this can lead to a loss of control and a spaghetti or mess of distributed communication with a lack of control, documentation, and governance. One of the solutions to this can be an Enterprise Event bus to remove the coupling and complexity of communication boundaries.

Event Bus

As in our ticketing example, to achieve a well operational result, we need to settle an event-based communication between different systems to achieve a valuable result. As the system grows and the number of producers and consumers rise, it can be unavoidable to keep the overall system under control and governable with less effort and time.

In our example, we can design the system in a way representing the following diagram:

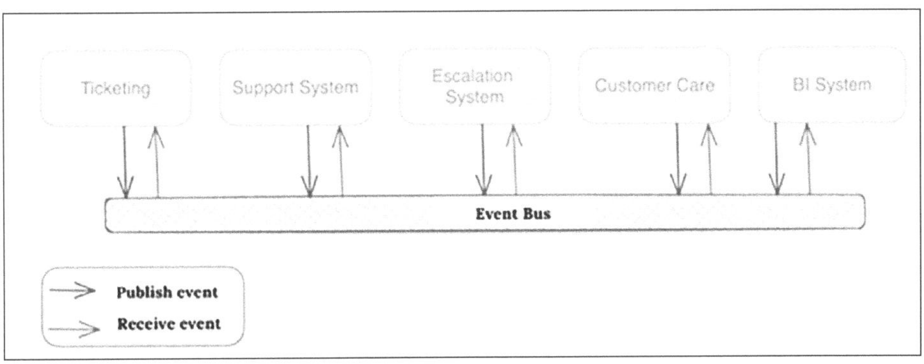

Figure 4.17: *Event bus*

- Any system publish the event in a central event bus
- Any interested system listens to required events

The advantages this design brings include less distributed coupling but a coupling to the enterprise platform. This can be an event bridge or an abstracted event bus.

Event Bridge

Event Bridge is an AWS offering with P2P and broadcasting capabilities. It offers the following extended features:

- Archive/Replay
- Schema discovery
- Rule based subscription
- Multi account communication

In real scenarios, any bounded context can provide a dedicated bus letting contextualized buses. In the ticketing example, we use a single bus as the core of Ticketing context.

- To run this section example, find the `` `C04/event-bus/Version1` `` and deploy stacks, the event bus must be deployed first followed by other stacks in any random order.

Caution: When using centralized event bus patterns, there are some considerations to respect like event modeling, event definition and event documentation to simplify the consumption and avoid any inconsistent event distribution and consumption.

Scalability with EDA

Using the Scalability term is critical as scalability must be considered at both the technical and business levels. The tactical term explains how the system can be adapted to the rise of requirements and load on a system. On the other hand, the business term focuses on rapidity and ease of adoption of new products and changing requirements.

Business Scalability

How the business translates the scalability is all about how new requirements can be adopted.

- New partner onboarding
- New system to achieve new feature based on existing process
- Introducing new contextualized changes for further consumption
- Moving from Pool multi tenancy isolation to Silo or inversely
- Adopting bridge multi-tenancy isolation mode with minimum effort
- Introducing new requirements incrementally and rapidly
- Proof of new ideas with less effort

Tactical Scalability

The tactical scalability relies on the capacity of a system to respond to sudden load and increasing the system capacity without or with minimum effort.

- Ability to increase the system capacity
- Ability to decrease the system capacity
- Avoiding any kind of cascading failures
- Assuring the consumers health behind sudden load
- Ability to control the resource consumption
- Avoiding overwhelming the whole capacity

Lambda Service for Scalability

Lambda service helps in a variety of scenarios and designs having guaranteed scalability. Some of the detailed features of lambda service are:

- Short-lived and ephemeral containers help to adopt and release resources per need without provisioning.
- Event source mapping batching helps to reduce the resource consumption by not reacting to single events but a collection of events or related events.
- Event source mapping Filtering helps avoid unnecessary resource consumption by filtering just the events that any system is interested in.
- Event source mapping time window helps to delay the events collection process by giving more chances to have more events as a batch.
- Event source mapping concurrency limit with SQS helps to control the concurrency level of function invocations without getting throttled or exhausting resource consumption.

Standardization

The standardization is an important concept to settle when designing distributed systems and this is an old existing concept in synchronous distributed systems as well. In traditional distributed systems, different approaches were adopted to achieve standardization and governance of API like Contract Documentation (Swagger, OpenAPI), Versioning, contract modeling, request/response tracking, and so on. However, some other hard-to-achieve concepts were traceable easily like model catalog, request detailed tracking, and backward compatibility checks.

In event-driven design, all these challenges and requirements are valid yet, but the added complexity based on the decoupled distributed nature of eventing makes things harder.

Event Modeling

The events need to follow a model that focuses on business context but at the same time, ease the adoption of event-driven design, simplify the understanding around events and ease of consumption, introducing a standard model envelope is important.

Event envelope represents the whole event data, including metadata and business data representing a detailed change in a domain context. This can be beneficial to adopt a well-defined and well documented model like `` `cloudevents` `` (https://github.com/cloudevents/spec/blob/v1.0.2/cloudevents/spec.md).

Metadata

The event metadata are a collection of context and runtime related information. Here some of the items to explore:

- **`time`**: The event distribution time, which represents the time when the event was distributed and was available for consumption.
- **`id`**: Any single event represents an identifier in the whole system. This can be useful to track and deep dive to achieve more detailed observability.
- **`type`**: An event type represents a single fact in a context and represents what the producer is presenting to other contexts.
- **`source`**: Represents the original source of introduced fact. This is where we avoid having any duplicated event types. Any conjunction of a type and source must be identical to the whole system.
- **`dataSchema`**: The path to the JSON schema related to the event data model.
- **`data`**: Represents the domain related information representing the fact.

Data

The data model represents information about a fact that happened in a domain context. For example, a ticket assigned, in this fact, the data represents the staff Id, ticket number, assignment date, priority, and so on. All of this data helps the consumers have enough information to react without extra effort.

Example

The following example represents an example of assignment model:

```
{
  "id": "<unique_identifier>",
  "source": "ticketing:support",
  "type": "ticket.assigned",
  "time": "2024-01-10T12:54:00.000Z",
  "data_schema": "somepath",
  "data": {
    "assigned_at": "2024-01-10T12:53:58.000Z",
    "staff_id": "S0145468",
```

```
      "ticket_id": "126788654",
      "category": "HighPriority",
      "staff_total_assignments": 1,
      "escalated": false
    }
}
```

Versioning

With the growth of business requirements, the system needs to add, remove, or introduce new models for any single fact. These changes can lead to incompatibility and introduce breaking changes in the consumer side. To avoid any inconvenience processing situation, it is a best practice to think from beginning about versioning, by simply tagging any event with a version. In the preceding example, we can achieve this in two ways.

```
{
  ...
  "source": "ticketing:support",
  "type": "ticket.assigned",
  "data_version": "v1",
  "data": {
    ...
  }
}
```

or this can be achieved in another way as follows:

```
{
  ...
  "source": "ticketing:support",
  "type": "v1.ticket.assigned",
  "data": {
    ...
  }
}
```

Event Documentation

Documenting events can be achieved using any tools but at the core of documentation, we need to have a documentation with following characteristics:

- Based on business lexique or glossary
- Any single event info must have a brief and comprehensible summary
- Represent the model schema and versions
- Can be used to generate code and consumption interfaces easily

- Can introduce the event consumers and command producers
- A lineage feature can be nice to have

There are well suited available tools that can be used to achieve representable documentation and bring ease of use. Some of these tools are:

- Event Catalog (https://www.eventcatalog.dev/)
- Async Api (https://www.asyncapi.com/)
- Backstage (https://backstage.io/)

Each of these tools can help for some of the preceding requirements. However, choosing a tool is all about tradeoffs around ease of use, complexity, maintainability and cost.

Incompatibility Check

The incompatibility check of event models can be done in both the build phase and runtime.

Build Phase

In build phase, using Async-api specification, the `diff` package can be used to check any incompatibility comparing two specifications.

Using the `diff` package is simple and straightforward.

```
npm install @asyncapi/diff
```

The diff can be achieved by parsing the both specs and using the diff method as follows:

```
const output = diff(firstDocument, secondDocument);
output.breaking(); // breaking changes
output.nonBreaking(); // non-breaking changes
output.unclassified(); // unclassified changes
```

Runtime Phase

The event bridge offers the schema discovery feature that can be useful in our case. The following diagram designs a schema discovery using the EventBridge:

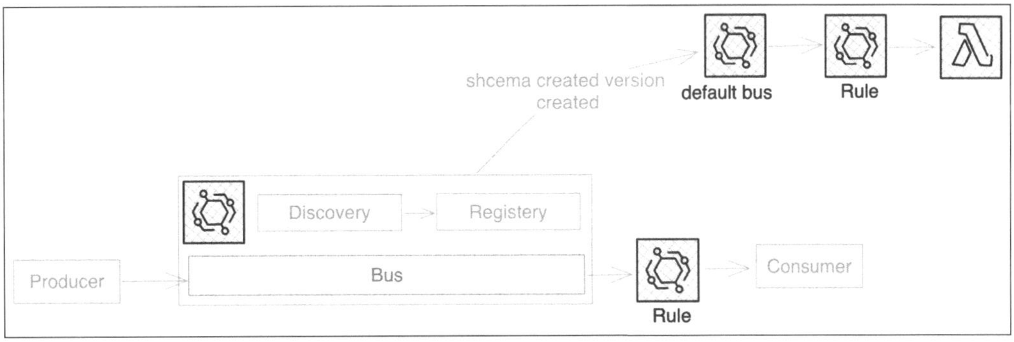

Figure 4.18: *Event schema discovery*

The CDK code will be as follows:

```
const eventBus = new EventBus(this, 'TicketingEventBus');
new CfnDiscoverer(this, 'TicketingSchemaDiscoverer', {
   sourceArn: eventBus.eventBusArn,
   ...
});

const defaultBus = EventBus.fromEventBusName(this, 'TicketingEventBus',
'default');
new Rule(this, 'TicketingSchemaRule', {
 ...
 eventPattern: {
   source: ["aws.schemas"],
   detailType: ["Schema Created"]
 }
});
```

The preceding example can target the default bus rule to a Lambda function. The Lambda received event will be as follows:


```
{
    "version": "0",
    "id": "fad60e28-c83f-f20d-2d09-6b2b9c94b273",
    "detail-type": "Schema Version Created",
    "source": "aws.schemas",
    "account": "607050363559",
    "time": "2024-01-28T01:27:00Z",
    "region": "eu-west-1",
    "resources": [
        "arn:aws:schemas:eu-west-1:607050363559:schema/discovered-schemas/ticketing@V1.ticket.created"
    ],
    "detail": {
        "SchemaName": "ticketing@V1.ticket.created",
        "SchemaType": "OpenApi3",
        "RegistryName": "discovered-schemas",
        "CreationDate": "2024-01-28T01:26:55Z",
        "Version": "3"
    }
}
```


Figure 4.19: *Schema Created event*

The Lambda can also verify the catalog and process industrialization of schema. In *Figure* 4.19, the event type `` `v1.ticket.created` `` has a schema version creation event for **version 3,** the Lambda can behave in this situation by verifying the match between `detail.schemaName` and `detail.version` and send alerts or raise any further automated processing.

Conclusion

This chapter was a deep dive illustration of serverless services mostly used in event driven architectures on AWS. In this chapter, the walkthrough was based on real scenarios and introduced some tactical patterns that help the reader make the best decision per tradeoffs and detailed requirements.

Some concepts like scalability, concurrency control, decoupling, operability, and performance were focused to help the reader achieve more visibility and master some detailed configuration when dealing with different services.

The final takeaway in this chapter is how to design a well architected solution based on tradeoffs with a scalable and governable perspective. This can be beneficial at high scale when the rate of changes and requirements raise and need a more flexible and adaptable solution to tackle the fast growing business.

The next chapter will delve into the Lambda scaling and how by applying some practices and fine-tuning Lambda, you can achieve the highest level of scaling.

CHAPTER 5
Hyper-Scaling with Lambda

Introduction

This chapter delves into Scalability and explores how lambda behaves in the AWS serverless ecosystem. Some lambda optimizations to improve scalability will be covered as well as details when integration with other services will be deep-dived.

The reader will achieve a detailed understanding of how software should behave and scale and will also learn how lambda behaves at runtime and how it scales. The chapter covers lambda power tuning and how to use it to find the best balance between cost and performance.

Structure

In this chapter, we will discuss the following topics:

- Lambda Scalability
- Concurrency Bottlenecks
- Concurrency at Integration Level
- Lambda Cold Start
- The Overhead of Scaling
- Power Tuning
- Choosing the Right Runtime

Lambda Scalability

AWS Lambda scalability has several key concepts that contribute to the efficient and automatic scaling of serverless functions, such as concurrency, invocation sources, cold start, quota, error handling, and statelessness.

Concurrency

In *Chapter 1, Introduction to Serverless Computing*, the throughput and concurrency were briefly explained. In this chapter, the concurrency will be explored in more detail.

In the software industry, the capacity to respond to the actual demand is measured traditionally by throughput per second (TPS) or request per second (RPS). In modern software design, the requirement often is the ability to respond to an increase in the demand without service interruption at any given time; this requirement cannot be measured by a specific measure of time. The term concurrency is the measure of capacity to respond to requirements at any given time.

Throughput

Throughput or TPS is a measure used to define a system's capacity per unit of time. Each system defines the unit of time differently based on the requirements involved. For example, an e-commerce website will be defined more precisely and thinner than an internal back office.

Concurrency and Throughput Ratio

Concurrency is a measure of the capacity of a system to respond to more demands at any given time. As per this definition, Concurrency cannot be measured by a unit of time but is related to the nature of system consumption.

In theory, if the Throughput can be measured with a really small unit of time, the result will be close to the concurrency level. The ratio between Throughput and Concurrency can be calculated with the following formula:

Throughput = Maximum Concurrency/Latency

Problem with Concurrency

Concurrency is a meaningful term in the technical world; however, when considering software products, it loses its significance, as the requirements have two axes: Count and Time. This is why the need to define throughput becomes important.

Before calculating a throughput, we need to achieve Maximum concurrency. To achieve the maximum concurrency, AWS Lambda indicates the scalability and maximum concurrency that can be achieved during a peak load for any single function.

Lambda Concurrency Allocation

AWS Lambda, by default, shares account-level concurrency between all functions in an account. The lambda service for any initial burst scales up to 3000 execution environments per minute, followed by 500 execution environments per minute. It adds up to 1000 new execution environments every 10 seconds for any single function (at the time of writing). This means any single function can achieve 1000 concurrent executions with a 10-second execution latency. *Figure* 5.1 illustrates how the allocation is achieved for a single function:

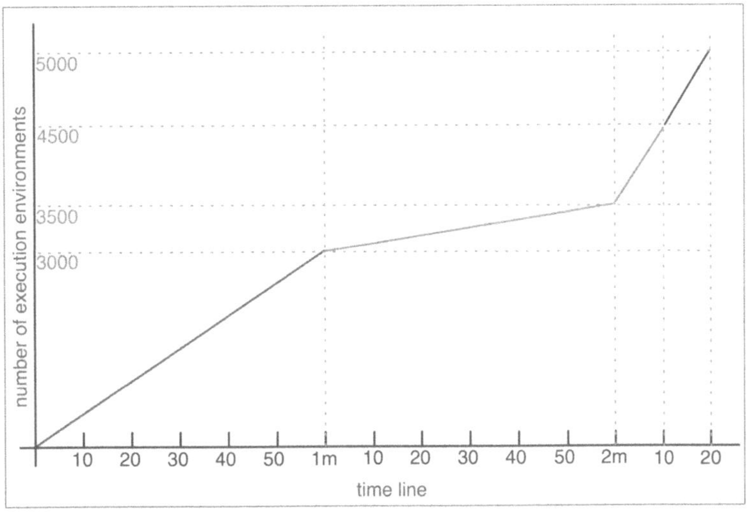

Figure 5.1: *Lambda Scaling timeline*

The lambda scales till it reaches the account limit, and after that, the function invocations will be throttled.

Software Throughput and Concurrency

The measurement cannot be only based on the lambda service, as there is always a collaboration of different services that constitute a software component. The measurement must care when at least one of the following conditions, due to lack of scalability control, will be true for the software underlying layer:

- Impacts synchronously the user experience.
- Impacts the business process and distribution layer.
- Impacts the business contractualization of software products.

Figure 5.2 represents a synchronous software component that is worth measuring the scalability of the component:

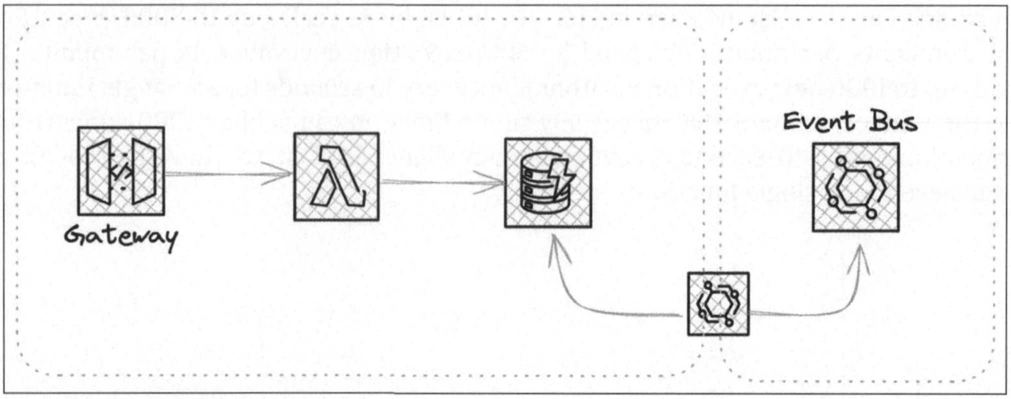

Figure 5.2: *Layered software components*

The Component represents two layers of software. The first layer consists of ApiGateway, Lambda function, and DynamoDB, while the second layer consists of EventBridge Pipe and EventBridge Bus.

The first layer scalability and request rate depend on service consumers and can vary. To measure the concurrency and the capacity of scaling, the first layer will be implemented by a simple lightweight Node.js function adding an item in DynamoDB.

Using Artillery or Postman, we can load test the first layer to see how that behaves. Here is how we use Postman to run a spike test:

Running a spike test of around 5000 invocations shows that the lambda concurrency rose to 58 concurrent executions at the top, with a MAX duration of 400 ms and an average of less than 50 ms. By adding a sleep of 1 second in the lambda function, the concurrency will be increased four times.

The following lambda metrics show the health of the test on the lambda side:

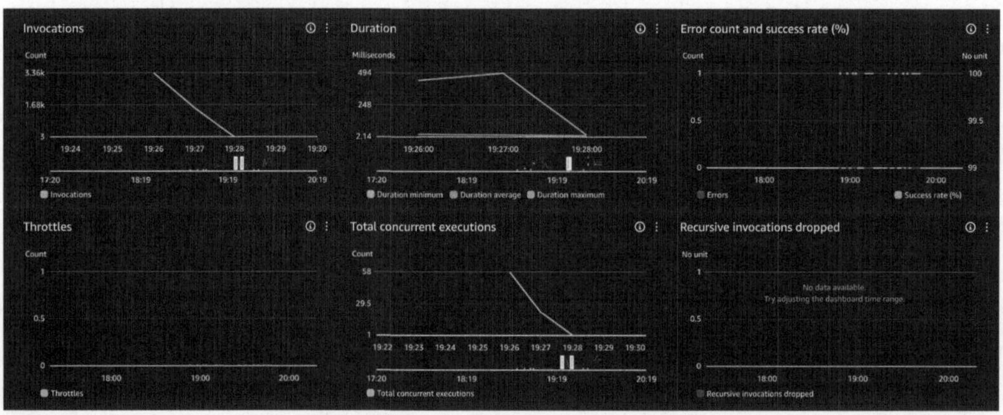

Figure 5.3: *Lambda load test metrics*

In this example, the software concurrency must also consider the API Gateway's max RPS. The **Apigateway** has a per account/region RPS of 10000 and 500 burst, so it's important to consider all services in a single layer. API Gateway offers throttling limit per usage plan to control the consumer limits.

The second layer of the example consists of DynamoDB Stream, EventBridge Pipe, and Event Bus; this layer can be controlled. To better control the resource usage and allocation, filtering, batching, and parallelization factor can be used to avoid backpressure and downstream.

Throughput Indicator

After measuring the Max required Concurrency, the throughput can be as follows:

```
TPS = Concurrency/(latency by second)
```

Based on the preceding tests, the latency was observed around 400 ms at cold and less than 50 ms at the warm stage. The lambda offers 900 concurrent executions for any single function under account limits. So keeping these numbers as base, the TPS will be 20000.

```
TPS = 1000/0.05 = 20000
```

The Overhead of Scaling

Serverless computing on AWS, including services like AWS Lambda, is designed to scale automatically in response to incoming request volume. While the scaling process is efficient and rapid, there is still some overhead associated with it. Here are some factors to consider:

- **Cold Starts:** One of the primary concerns with serverless computing is the concept of "*cold starts*". When a function is invoked, and there is no existing container (an environment where the function runs), AWS Lambda must create one. This process introduces some latency, known as a cold start, as it involves setting up the runtime environment and loading the function code into memory.
- **Scaling Time:** While AWS Lambda can scale quickly, there is still a certain amount of time required for additional instances of a function to be created and become operational. This scaling time is generally short but can be a consideration for workloads with extremely low latency requirements.
- **Concurrency Limits:** AWS Lambda imposes concurrency limits, which determine the maximum number of invocations that can be processed simultaneously for a given function. When these limits are reached, additional invocations are queued until resources become available. Managing concurrency effectively is crucial for optimizing performance.

- **Resource Provisioning:** AWS Lambda dynamically provisions resources based on demand. This means that, in the absence of recent invocations, resources may be scaled down to reduce costs. However, scaling up again when needed can introduce a delay. Understanding and configuring provisioned concurrency can help mitigate this.
- **Network Overhead:** As AWS Lambda scales, there is network overhead associated with coordinating the execution of functions across multiple instances. This overhead is generally low and managed by the AWS infrastructure.
- **Granularity of Scaling:** AWS Lambda scales in response to the number of incoming requests. If the workload experiences rapid fluctuations, the service might scale up or down more frequently, leading to potential overhead.
- **Warm-up Strategies:** To mitigate cold start latency, you can implement warm-up strategies. These involve periodically invoking the function to keep instances warm, reducing the likelihood of cold starts during actual invocations.

It's important to note that while there is some overhead associated with scaling in a serverless environment, the benefits, such as automatic scaling, cost efficiency, and reduced operational management, often outweigh these concerns. Additionally, AWS continues to enhance its services, and improvements are made to reduce cold start times and enhance overall performance. Understanding your application's specific requirements and optimizing configurations can help minimize any perceived overhead.

Concurrency Bottlenecks

To identify the concurrency bottlenecks, first, we need to clarify the execution environment of a function and its life cycle. A function life cycle has three phases, namely `Init`, `Invoke`, and `Shutdown`, as any single MicroVM can be frozen and then thawed for further invocations. The invoke phase is the principal phase that includes all invocations, whereas the `init` and `shutdown` are the one-time occurrence phases for any single execution environment. *Figure* 5.4 illustrates the execution environment lifecycle:

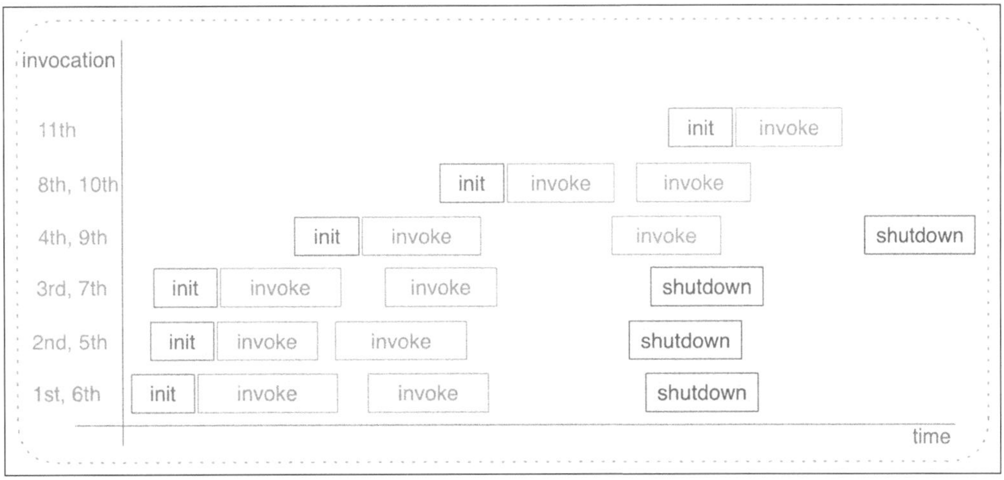

Figure 5.4: *Function execution lifecycle*

- **`INIT` Phase**: The Init phase happens for the preparation of any single execution environment. During this phase, the lambda service hints the extensions, runtime, and static code in order to let the environment prepare. The **`init`** phase has a 10-second timeout, except the use of provisioned concurrency or SnapStart. If the function times out, the first invocation will experience the **`init`** phase during the invocation phase and under the function's configured timeout.

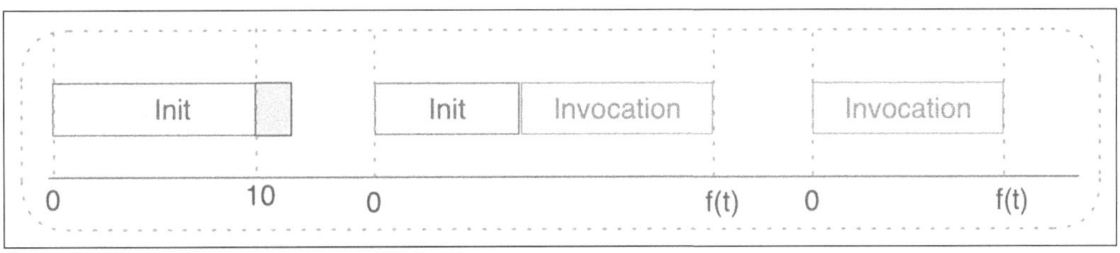

Figure 5.5: *Init phase timeout*

During **`Init`** phase, the runtime, extensions, and static code **`init`** are coupled, and any error can cause the whole **`init`** phase failure. This is important to keep the **`init`** process light and avoid any extra process in this phase when developing lambda extensions or custom runtimes.

- **`INVOKE` Phase**: Invocation of a function consists of extensions and runtime hints after the function's Next request. During the invocation phase, the lambda service provides an isolated process for any single extension. By this design, a failure in the extension invocation phase will not interrupt the function invocation phase. The invocation of function and all extensions are under the function timeout and memory configuration.

If any error happens during function invocation, the runtime gets a **RESET**, and all extensions have a **SHUTDOWN** hint. In this situation, the next invocation will include the whole **INIT** phase before invocation.

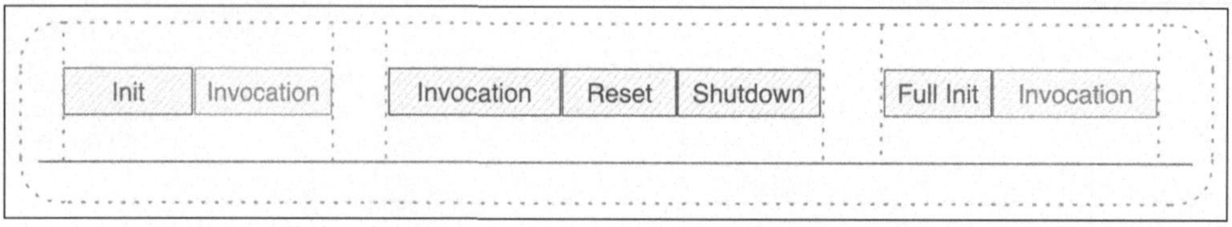

Figure 5.6: *Invoke phase failure*

- **SHUTDOWN Phase**: This phase can happen if the execution environment has no use for some time or the invocation experiences a failure. During this phase, the lambda service shutdowns the runtime, sends the Shutdown request to all extensions, and waits for 2000 ms to get a response. If runtime or any extension does not send a response during this time, the lambda service sends a force kill (**SIGKILL**) signal.

Impact of Execution Environment on Concurrency

As per the preceding details, the execution latency can be raised based on the whole execution environment config, including function code, runtime, and all extensions. The relation between duration, memory, and vCPU is linear in lambda functions, as vCpu will be allocated based on the memory configured. The allocated vCpu will impact the duration and latency of processing. As per the earlier explanation, failures and exceptional behaviors can also affect the duration. Also, the package bundle size can be important, as it can impact the overall **init** phase in terms of duration.

Keeping in account the lightweight extensions, well-configured functions and optimized code bundling can be a measure of better control and define concurrency capacity.

Concurrency at Integration Level

As explained in *Chapter 3, Invocation Models and Service Integrations*, lambda integrates well with a wide range of other services, and when it comes to scalability, it is important to refine those lines of integration. It's evident that designing on top of lambda service can lead to experiencing some scalability limitations if the design just relies on lambda as the only serverless service. However, actually, no software is designed just on lambda service.

Scalability Control at Integration Level

When integrating with other services, lambda integration often scales, and the system appears healthy. However, this works when suddenly something happens that leads to an incapacity of treatment of request. When integrating lambda with other services, it is important to consider the invocation source services and how the lambda integration works.

Integration with Other Services

If the lambda is triggered by a synchronous invocation like API Gateway, it's important to keep the function responsibility at the lowest level if possible. *Figure* 5.7 illustrates an API Gateway integration with a function doing some interaction with DynamoDB and sending the processing result to another service.

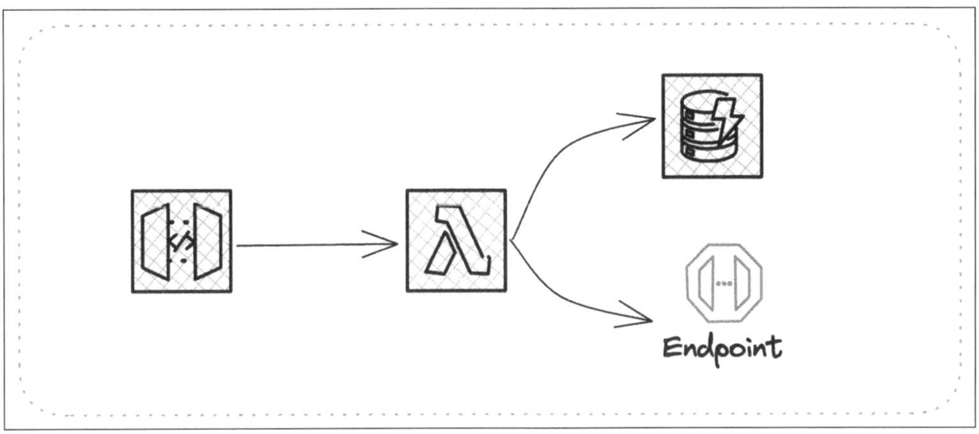

Figure 5.7: *Sync invocation integration concurrency*

Looking at this design, multiple integration details need to be considered:

- API Gateway timeout has a maximum of 29 seconds.
- Lambda function has a two-phase commit implementation.
- DynamoDB is a serverless NoSQL database, but the R/W capacity unit can play in latency.
- The external API endpoint is out of the local control, and any unhealthy state must be considered.

To improve this design, we can achieve better scalability by redesigning it as follows (see *Figure* 5.8):

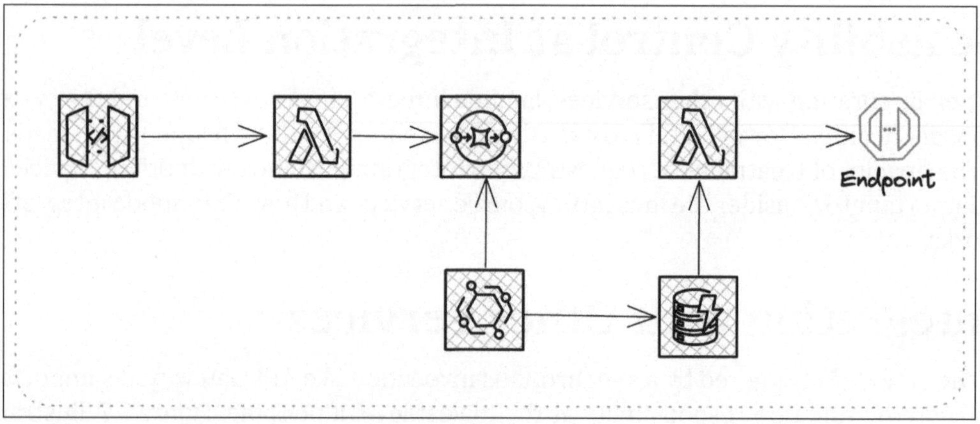

Figure 5.8: *Sync invocation integration controlled concurrency*

In this design, we simply use an async event-driven approach to decouple the potential point of failures from the service scalability and better control the scalability of the system:

- API Gateway response as soon as lambda returns a response.
- Lambda sends the command to the SQS queue after a light request validation.
- The message will be put into DDB using the EventBridge Pipe.
- The call to external API will be done using a lambda function triggered by the DynamoDB stream.

The integrations are controlled at ingestion with a lighter process and at distribution by Queue-based load balancing and also EventBridge pipes filtering and batching.

Filtering

Filtering is a crucial aspect of designing efficient and cost-effective serverless architectures, and it plays a significant role in enterprise integration patterns. AWS Lambda, as part of its event-driven architecture, offers event source mappings that allow you to filter events based on certain criteria.

Here are some practical recommendations and insights regarding filtering in AWS Lambda event source mappings:

- **Event Metadata Filtering:** AWS Lambda allows you to filter events based on metadata attributes, such as event source, event name, and event version. This is useful when you want to selectively process events from specific sources or with certain characteristics.

  For example, you might have different event sources producing events to the same Lambda function, and using metadata filtering can help ensure that the Lambda function processes only the relevant events.

- **Event Data Filtering:** Filtering based on event data involves inspecting the payload of the event. This can be particularly useful when you want to process events selectively based on the content of the data.
  For instance, if your events contain a specific attribute or key in the payload, you can set up a filter to trigger the Lambda function only when that condition is met.
- **Avoiding Unnecessary Compute Resources:** By using filtering, you can prevent lambda functions from being invoked for events that are not relevant to your use case. This helps in saving compute resources and reduces costs.
  Unnecessary invocations also contribute to longer execution times and potentially increased latencies, so effective filtering can enhance the overall efficiency of your serverless architecture.
- **Fine-Tuning Based on Use Case:** Consider the specific requirements of your use case when setting up filters. Some use cases may benefit from broad filters that capture a range of events, while others may require more granular filtering to target specific subsets of events.

In summary, leveraging AWS Lambda event source mapping filtering capabilities is a powerful technique for controlling the consumption of events, optimizing resource utilization, and enhancing the overall efficiency of your serverless architecture. It's a valuable pattern in enterprise integration for handling diverse event sources and ensuring that compute resources are utilized effectively.

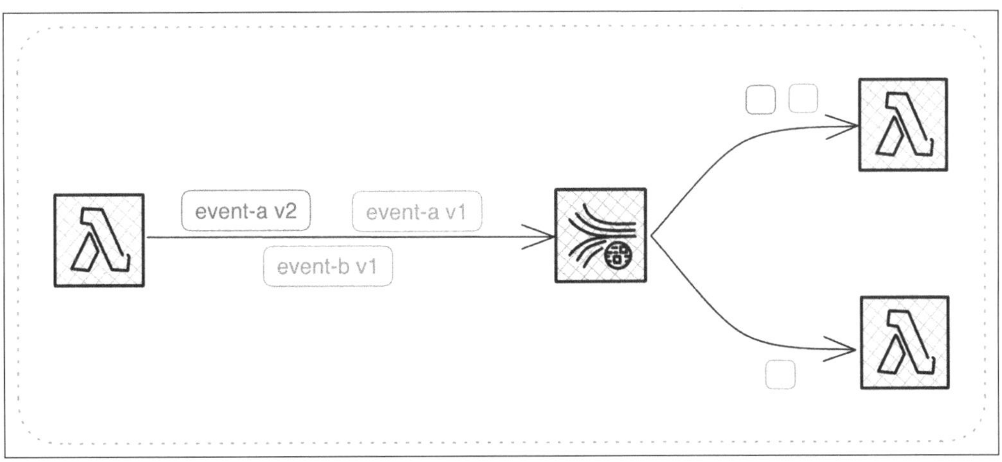

***Figure 5.9:** Event filtering*

Filtering covers mostly all services that integrate with ESM, such as Amazon DynamoDB, Kinesis Data Streams, SQS, MQ, and MSK; up to five filters are allowed.

```
filterCriteria: {
 filters: [{
     pattern: `{
```

```
      "dynamodb": {
        "NewImage": {
          "category": {
            "S": [ "LowPriority" ]
          }
        }
      }
    }`}]
}
```

Batching

Batching is a technique used to optimize the execution of functions by grouping multiple individual events into a single batch. This can be particularly beneficial as functions are invoked in response to events.

When there is a stream of events that could potentially trigger a function, rather than invoking the function for each individual event, you can collect and process them in batches. This helps in reducing the number of function invocations, which can be significant in terms of both performance and cost.

- **Cost Efficiency:** Function invocations often come with a cost, and by batching events, you can reduce the number of invocations, thus saving costs.
- **Reduced Latency:** Batching allows you to process multiple events in a single execution cycle, which can result in lower overall latency compared to processing each event individually.
- **Resource Utilization:** Batching can be more efficient in terms of resource utilization, as it allows you to process multiple events using the same execution environment.
- **Throttling and Limits:** Batching helps to overcome the limits on the number of function invocations or concurrent executions.

The decision to use batching depends on the specific use case, requirements, and characteristics of the system you are designing. It's often a trade-off between cost savings, latency, and resource utilization.

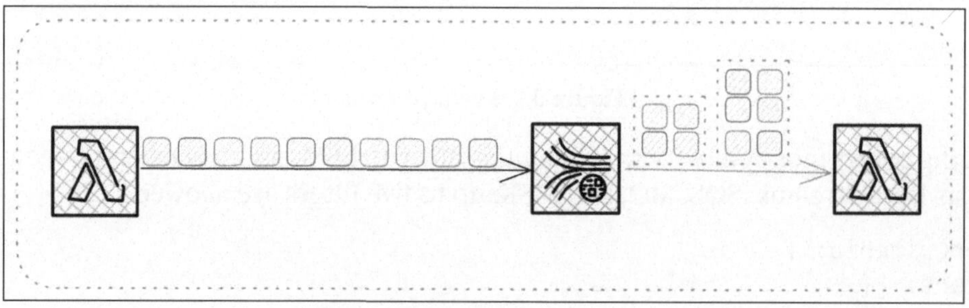

Figure 5.10: *Event Batching*

When using batch size configuration, lambda controls the presence of events to prepare a batch of events near the configured size, but this is always an approximate adjustment. The event source mapping batch time window configuration helps to define the maximum time that lambda service can delay invocation for having more chance to achieve the configured batchsize.

Concurrency Limit

Lambda event source mapping offers a concurrency limit configuration when integrating with SQS, this leads the event source mapping to take care of function concurrency. Previously, the reserved concurrency helped to not let the lambda go beyond a reserved number of executions, while this was a workaround to concurrency control, but for any request beyond that limit, the throttling metric was increased and this just polluted the monitoring.

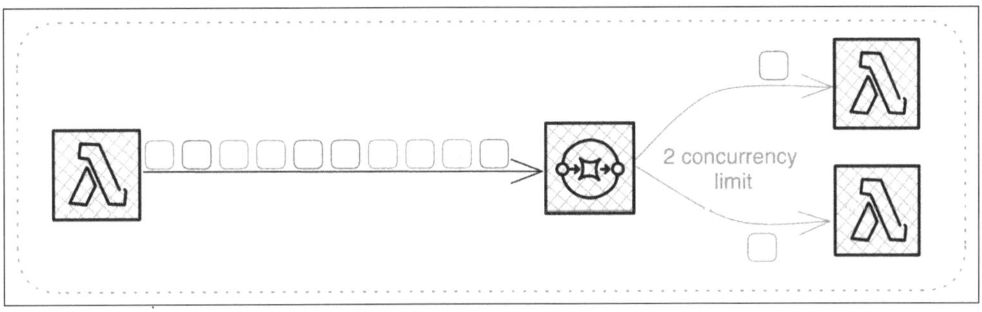

Figure 5.11: *Concurrency limit*

Recursive Invocation

Another concern to be aware of when designing event-driven architecture is the possibility of self-invoking or recursive invocations. This happens when lambda listens to an event and then performs actions that lead to the same event arriving again. *Figure* 5.12 demonstrates this situation:

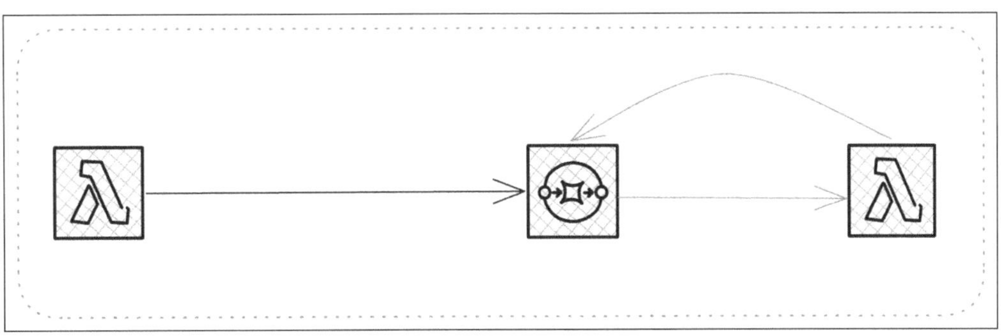

Figure 5.12: *Recursive invocation*

Lambda service offers recursive loop detection, which is by default active for all customers. Lambda service at the edge of 16 invocations for the same event will add an evaluation point to the recursive invocation metric to let customers be notified. The invocation of the same event beyond that limit will be dropped by the lambda service.

Being aware of unintentional recursive invocation is a practice in serverless design to eliminate the unintended function invocation to better protect the concurrency limits and avoid scalability bottlenecks.

Cold Start

A cold start happens when a new execution environment needs to be prepared and is the duration that the execution environment preparation needs. The cold start occurrence is a small and single-digit percentile of all invocations, but the rate of cold start depends on the request rate.

Having a function with a very low invocation rate often causes the cold start, as any already warmed execution environment may receive a shutdown hint due to the miss of requests. Contrary, any function getting a higher rate of request at any given time than the actual free warm execution environments will experience cold start.

Keeping the execution time short helps to have more warmed execution environments ready for reuse, and this can be useful for the periods of peak. Lambda service documentation indicates that, for on-demand concurrency, the **proactive initialization** managed by lambda service occasionally initiates execution environments.

> *For functions using on-demand concurrency, Lambda may occasionally initialize execution environments ahead of invocation requests. When this happens, you may also observe a time gap between your function's initialization and invocation phases. We recommend you to not take a dependency on this behavior.*
>
> *Source: https://docs.aws.amazon.com/lambda/latest/dg/lambda-runtime-environment.html*

Proactive Initialization

Lambda service pre-initializes the functions in different cases to improve the chance of having fewer cold start occurrences for the sake of reducing the impact of this initialization phase.

Pre-initialization can happen when lambda service can predicate the need for execution environments, and this is achieved by looking at the actual workload:

- Function updates lead to excluding the existing environments, so lambda pre-initializes the approximate amount of execution environment to prevent the subsequent invocation from encountering cold start.

- Shutdown of an existing execution environment is likely to happen.
- New function version is another situation that leads to pre-initialization.

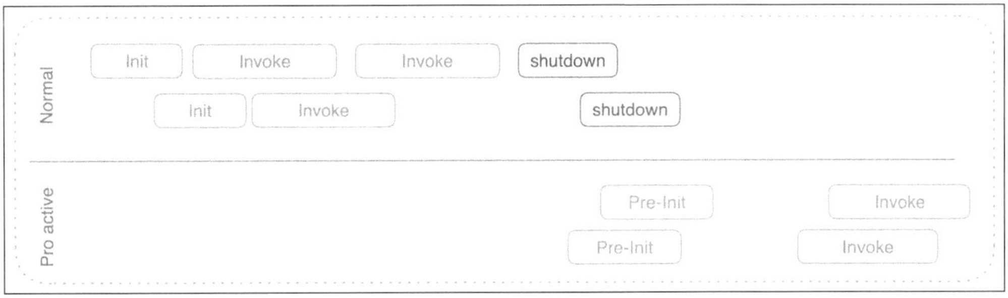

Figure 5.13: *Proactive initialization*

Warming Up

There is a wide range of proposed solutions on the net to keep lambda execution warmed up, but a deeper dive into the topic raises multiple questions:

- How many warm-ups are required for a production environment?
- When does the peak load happen?
- How is there a guarantee that the lambda service will assign the warm-up environment in Az1 and not a new one in Az2?

Having these questions in mind is enough motivation to stop warming up and instead focus in reducing the cold start impact on the software experience.

Cold Start Process

During cold start, the lambda service downloads the code package and prepares the execution environment. To optimize the cold start impact, understanding how any step impacts the cold start duration can be useful.

Downloading Code Package

The lambda service registers the code packages in an internal S3. This means that downloading a package will be on the network and via HTTPs protocol. This download can be harmful if the original package size exceeds a reasonable amount, so as a recommendation keeping the package size as small as possible is a practice to improve cold start.

In the TypeScript and Node.js world of development, there are multiple ways of improving the bundle size, such as minifying, tree shaking, using modules and not the whole libraries (**`moment.js`** is an example).

Another proposed approach is lazy loading the dependencies, but this needs to be tested and varies per dependency. An example of experience previously was the load of **`aws-sdk/client-kinesis`**, this reduced the cold start by 200 ms but increased the invocation time by 700 ms.

Tree shaking is a useful approach that works very well, but it does not actually work with the AWS CDK **`esbuild`** bundler.

If a function needs the **`aws-sdk`**, as the SDK is part of the runtime, those dependencies can be excluded by setting them as external.

```
// Create a DynamoDB table
const table = new dynamodb.Table(this, 'MyTable', {
      partitionKey: { name: 'id', type: dynamodb.AttributeType.STRING
},
});

// Create a Node.js Lambda function
const addTicketFunction = new NodejsFunction(this, 'AddTicketFunction',
{
 ...
 architecture: Architecture.ARM_64,
 runtime: Runtime.NODEJS_20_X,
 timeout: cdk.Duration.seconds(3),
 handler: 'handler',
 bundling: {
   minify: true,
   externalModules: [ '@aws-sdk/client-dynamodb' ]
 },
 environment: {
   TABLE_NAME: table.tableName,
 }
});

// Grant the Lambda function read/write permissions to the DynamoDB
table table.grantReadWriteData(addTicketFunction);
```

The above bundling configuration can be helpful, but it does not benefit from tree shaking (code trimming). The following snippet shows how to use the node modular approach and achieve tree shaking:

```
import { OutputFormat } from 'esbuild';

bundling: {
   minify: true,
   platform: 'node',
   format: OutputFormat.ESM,
   minify: true,
```

```
    sourceMap: true,
    sourcesContent: false,
    mainFields: ['module', 'main'],
    externalModules: [ '@aws-sdk/client-dynamodb' ]
  // metafile: true // this is used for bundle analysis and is not needed
for production
 }
```

Activate the metafile at the development phase to analyze the bundle and its dependencies; esbuild offers a free analyzer (https://esbuild.github.io/analyze/) that helps to visualize the bundle analysis.

The bundler generates a metafile named **`index.meta.json`** that can be imported to the **`esbuild`** analyzer tool and gives the results as demonstrated in *Figure* 5.14:

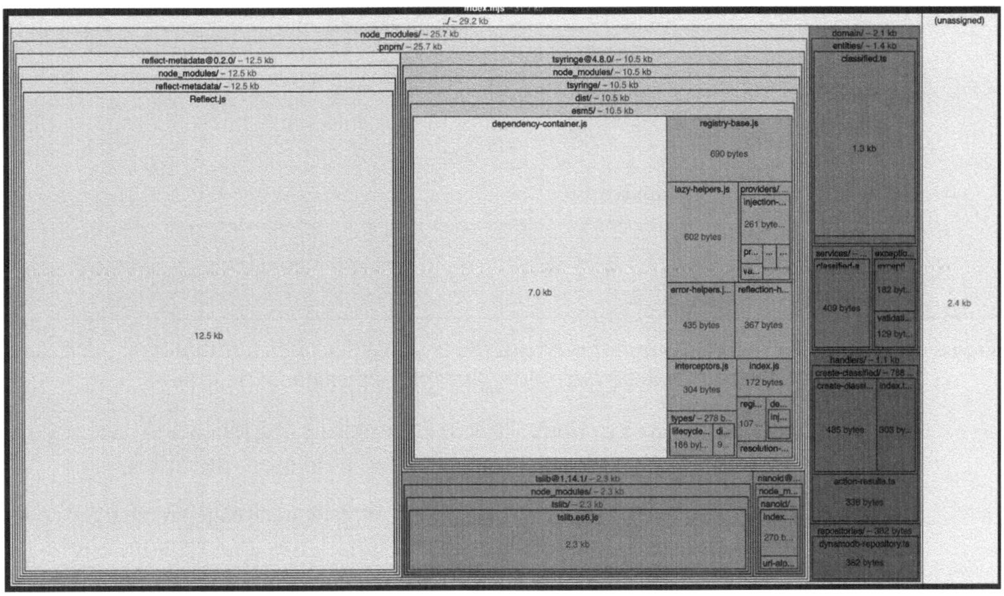

Figure 5.14: *esbuild bundle analyzer*

Execution Environment Preparation

The execution environment preparation, as explored earlier in this chapter, prepares the runtime, extensions, and function for the first-time environment invocation. This is a sequential pipeline with the next signals sent to each part.

This phase, as detailed earlier, consists of three separate steps as demonstrated in *Figure* 5.15:

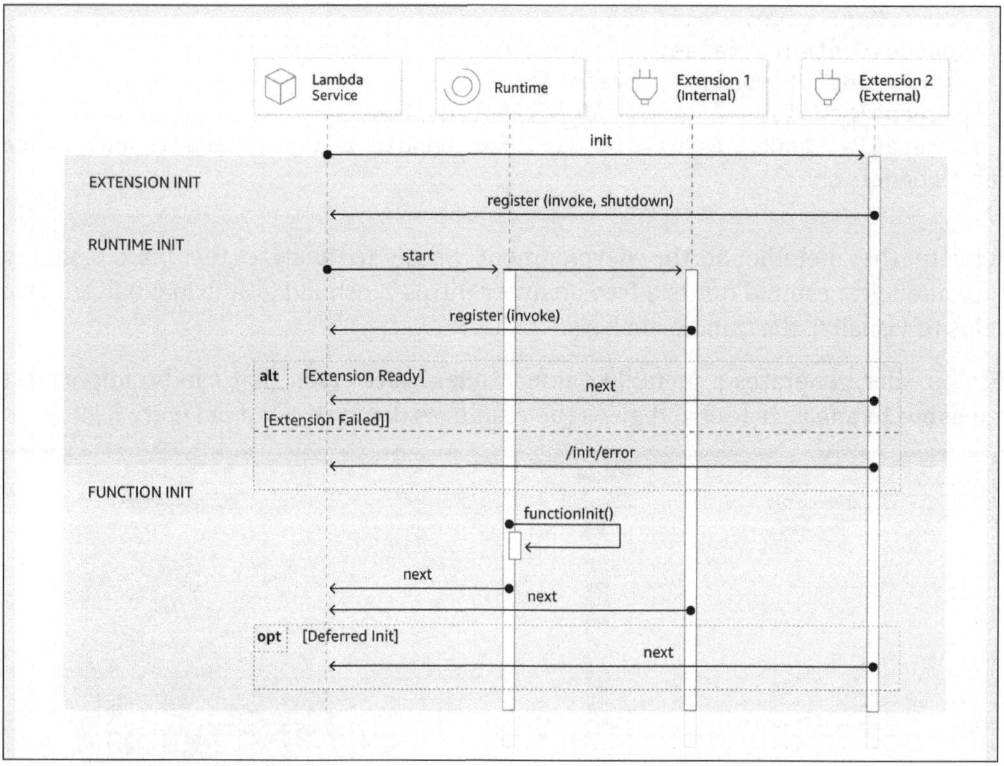

***Figure 5.15:** Lambda execution environment init (**Source:** AWS documentationhttps://docs.aws.amazon.com/lambda/latest/dg/runtimes-extensions-api.html)*

- **External extensions `init`:** Keeping the extensions initialization latency and error-free is a practice for secure and reduced cold start duration.
- **Runtime `init`:** The managed runtimes are tested and approved by AWS. It is more secure to use managed runtimes, but if for any reason, there is a need for a custom runtime, the bootstrap of runtime needs to be short and straightforward.
- **Function `init`:** The function **`init`** consists of running any initialization code outside of the handler function. This is also called static code; static code can run any code and actions that can be shared between invocations for a single execution environment. Usually this is used to fetch secrets from the secret manager, parameters from the system manager, and configurations from AWS Config or S3. These are useful but can add more latency and longer cold starts.

Lambda Power Tuning

Power tuning is an open-source solution to tune any single function per different axes, such as cost, performance, or both. The solution can be deployed easily using the available deploy template.

Ready-to-deploy application: https://serverlessrepo.aws.amazon.com/applications/arn:aws:serverlessrepo:us-east-1:451282441545:applications~aws-lambda-power-tuning

GitHub: https://github.com/alexcasalboni/aws-lambda-power-tuning

The power tuning can be used to measure different memory configurations for a function and visualize the cost and speed balance for any configuration. The power tuning solution creates a state machine, letting you execute multiple configurations for any single function. Starting a new state machine execution using the following payload will run the function under different memory configurations:

```
{
   "lambdaARN": "arn:aws:lambda:eu-west-1:1111111111:function:add-item
-function",
   "powerValues": [
     128,
     256,
     512,
     1024,
     2048,
     3008
   ],
   "num": 100,
   "payload": "{\"body\":{\"id\":1223333,\"name\":\"omid\"}",
   "parallelInvocation": true,
   "strategy": "balanced"
 }
```

Figure 5.14 shows the results for the item API (the code is available):

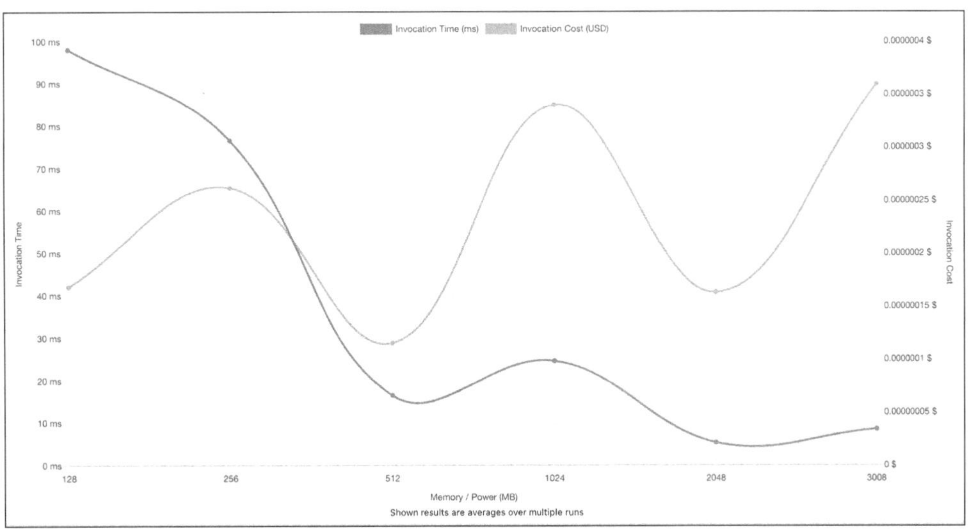

Figure 5.16: *Lambda power tuning*

Based on the results, the best balance of cost and speed will be between 2048 and 512. Choosing between two options can give different decisions based on the scenario; for the book example(add-item), the 512 is an ideal choice.

The power tuning has a compare option that lets you run two benchmarks and compare the results. This is useful when the code optimization is part of optimization, and this can simplify the comparison.

Choosing the Right Runtime

When working with lambda functions, one of the important parts of design is understanding how the execution environment behaves internally and externally. The external behavior will consist of service integrations, concurrency, and so on. The internal behavior is the process inside an execution environment. Previously, these details are explored in this book.

Figure 5.17 shows the MicroVM related to a function at a high level:

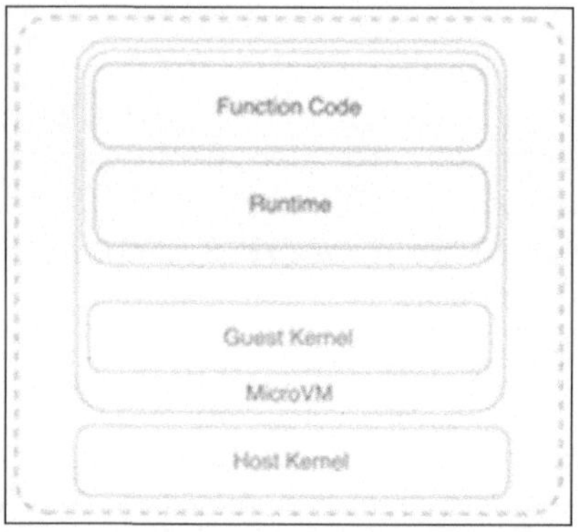

Figure 5.17: *Function MicroVM at high level*

The runtime being involved as part of the process guarantees the code translation and provides the best comprehensive instruments for a processor.

IL and JIT

Compilers serve the purpose of translating high-level languages into low-level languages for processors to comprehend. This process optimizes the code and enhances performance during runtime. In certain programming languages like C#, the compiler generates the Intermediate Language (IL) to optimize the runtime process and Just in Time (JIT) as a means of communication between the application and the processor during runtime. Although this method has proved to be effective, it requires a language-specific runtime to be available on the container at runtime.

To see this process deeply, sharplab.io (https://sharplab.io) will help to visualize the different levels of interpretation of IL and JIT from a high-level language syntax (for examples, visit https://sharplab.io/#v2:C4LghgzgtgNAJiA1AHwAICYCMBYAUKgZgAIMiBhIgbzyNpONQBYiBZACgEoqa6BfPXkA).

Ahead of Time

AOT, which stands for Ahead of Time, is a type of compilation process that helps to minimize the interpretation process at runtime. During the build phase, the AOT interprets the software code into a processor comprehensive language and creates a self-contained package. This package allows the software to run in any container without requiring a language-specific runtime to be available.

One of the great advantages of AOT is that it provides a way to interpret to a low-level language or for static languages to interpret to machine code. During the compilation, AOT applies the necessary optimizations that were traditionally done during JITing. However, as a disadvantage, the optimization cannot be done at 100% (though mostly they are) because some optimizations must be evaluated at runtime. In this kind of situation, runtime JITing shows its distinct advantages.

Compiled Languages

Compiled languages are the ideal choice if the software needs to eliminate the language interpretation at runtime to achieve a higher level of performance. However, at the same time, when working with critical workloads, it is important to benchmark and observe how those decisions behave at runtime.

Lambda Node.js Runtime

AWS Lambda provides managed runtimes for Node.js 18 and Node.js 20. Node has significant improvements in the latest versions, and these optimized runtimes cover a wide variety of workloads. However, at the same time, Node was originally not released for serverless functions and was initially related to the traditional Node application. It is evident that node actually works great in lambda, and higher level of performance can be achieved with some fine-tuning. Recently, a new lightweight runtime was released as an experimental runtime, which removes a lot of overhead of optimizations.

LLRT

Recently, AWS provided the LLRT runtime that brings real optimization and is very close to well-performing runtimes running in AWS Lambda functions. The LLRT comes with some sort of limitations or restricted capabilities by design, as mentioned in the following documentation: https://github.com/awslabs/llrt .

LLRT improves the cold start by hundreds of times compared to Node.js 20 runtime, as well as optimized invocation latency.

Comparing Node.js and LLRT

The LLRT can seem a great choice, but before deciding to try it, the following are important to consider:

- Cold starts has a low rate in most typical workloads.
- LLRT is a custom runtime, so the billing will be Init plus invocation duration.
- Node.js 20 has a close invocation duration to LLRT if not using SDK or heavy processing.
- LLRT shows a significant improvement when using AWS SDK.
- LLRT is experimental and not a choice for production workloads.

The code example, '**`C05/nodejs-llrt-runtime`**', provides an example to help create two separate lambda functions and provides a simple way of testing the performance behavior using the ***artillery*** library.

Conclusion

This chapter covered some detailed information about scalability and how the scalability of a system can be improved by improving the lambda concurrency as part of a serverless design.

In the past, cold start was one of the constraints when using lambda functions. However, with practices shared in this chapter and the efforts made by the lambda team set in recent years to improve and reduce the occurrence of cold start, this can become the smallest possible percentage in most workloads. Proactive initialization, since almost the beginning of 2023, was a big improvement in the occurrence of cold starts. The node community of the serverless ecosystem shares a lot about how the short-lived containers can benefit from different details of runtime, language-specific capacity, and development tools to improve bundle preparation.

The lambda extensions are great features of the lambda service that offload some out-of-the-box but required functionality in a separate and isolated process. Keeping in mind that the extensions need to be observed carefully, as they can introduce hidden functionality issues. Extensions will be explored in the **Lambda Instrumentation** chapter in detail, along with the use cases for which this lambda feature can be adopted.

CHAPTER 6
Instrumenting Lambda

Introduction

This chapter covers some AWS Lambda cross-cutting concerns. We delve into versioning, tracing, and how lambda service capabilities can be augmented. Some lambda process optimizations using layers will be discussed, followed by an exploration of the important role of lambda extensions and how they can help to add new capabilities to an execution environment in a transparent and non-blocking way.

The reader will achieve a detailed understanding of how software versioning has to be considered when using the lambda service, as well as how tracing helps for a higher visibility into the process at runtime.

Structure

In this chapter, we will discuss the following topics:

- Lambda Versioning
- Lambda Tracing
- Lambda Layers
- Log API Extension
- Telemetry API Extension

Versioning

Software versioning is the practice of assigning unique identifiers to different releases of software. These identifiers, typically represented as a series of incremental numbers, help reduce the software evolution impact and compatibility of the software.

Semantic versioning is an extension of numeric versioning aimed at conveying more meaning about the changes introduced in each release. Semantic versioning uses

`<major>.<minor>.<patch>` pattern. In SemVer, increments to the major version indicate backward-incompatible changes, increments to the minor version represent backward-compatible additions or enhancements, and increments to the patch version signify backward-compatible bug fixes.

AWS Lambda versioning and aliases provide mechanisms to manage different states of Lambda function in the same direction as software versioning, except for the semantic version format. This will help to have isolated releases that will be under validation or experimentation and also to control traffic routing during deployments or updates.

Lambda Version

Lambda Versions, in the context of AWS Lambda, refer to the ability to create and manage multiple versions of your Lambda functions. Each version represents a snapshot of your function's code and configuration at a specific point in time. Lambda versions are crucial for maintaining different iterations of your function and enabling you to roll back to previous versions if needed.

AWS Lambda creates a new version of the function when the function is created or updated. Each version gets a unique Amazon Resource Name (ARN), which includes a version number as `arn:aws:lambda:eu-west-1:123456789:function:CreateItem-Function:5`. A version is an immutable snapshot of the Lambda function code and configuration at a given point in time. Previous versions can be retained, allowing you to roll back to earlier versions if needed. The snapshot includes everything needed to execute the function, such as the code package, runtime environment, environment variables, and permissions.

A version configuration consists of Memory, Timeout, Runtime, and all related configurations to security, network, environment variables, and so on. A function can have an existing version with a runtime like Node.js and a new version with a Python runtime.

Aliases

An alias is a pointer to a specific version of a Lambda function. Aliases provide a way to decouple your applications from specific version numbers. You can create aliases such as `'live'`, `'experimental'`, `'v1'` `'version1'`, and so on, each pointing to a different version of your Lambda function.

When you invoke a Lambda function using an alias, AWS Lambda automatically routes the traffic to the version associated with that alias. Aliases allow you to implement features like blue-green deployments, canary releases, and A/B testing.

Aliases enable you to decouple the invocation code from specific versions of your function. This allows you to deploy new versions of your function without modifying the invoking applications or services. You can update the alias to point to a different version, allowing you to seamlessly switch traffic between different versions of your Lambda function.

Aliases provide stable references to your Lambda functions, even as new versions are published. This stability ensures that invoking applications always call the intended version of the function, regardless of changes to the underlying code.

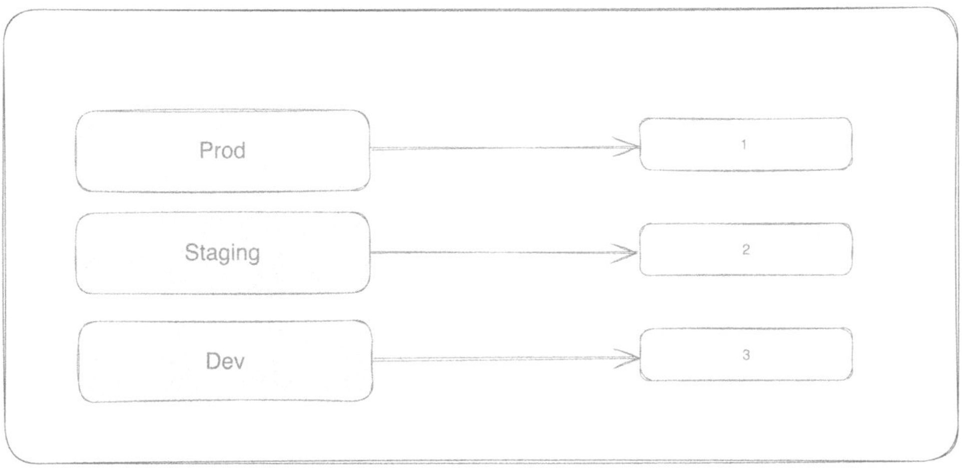

Figure 6.1: *Aliases and versions*

The lambda versioning practice is illustrated in *Figure* 6.2, following sequence of actions:

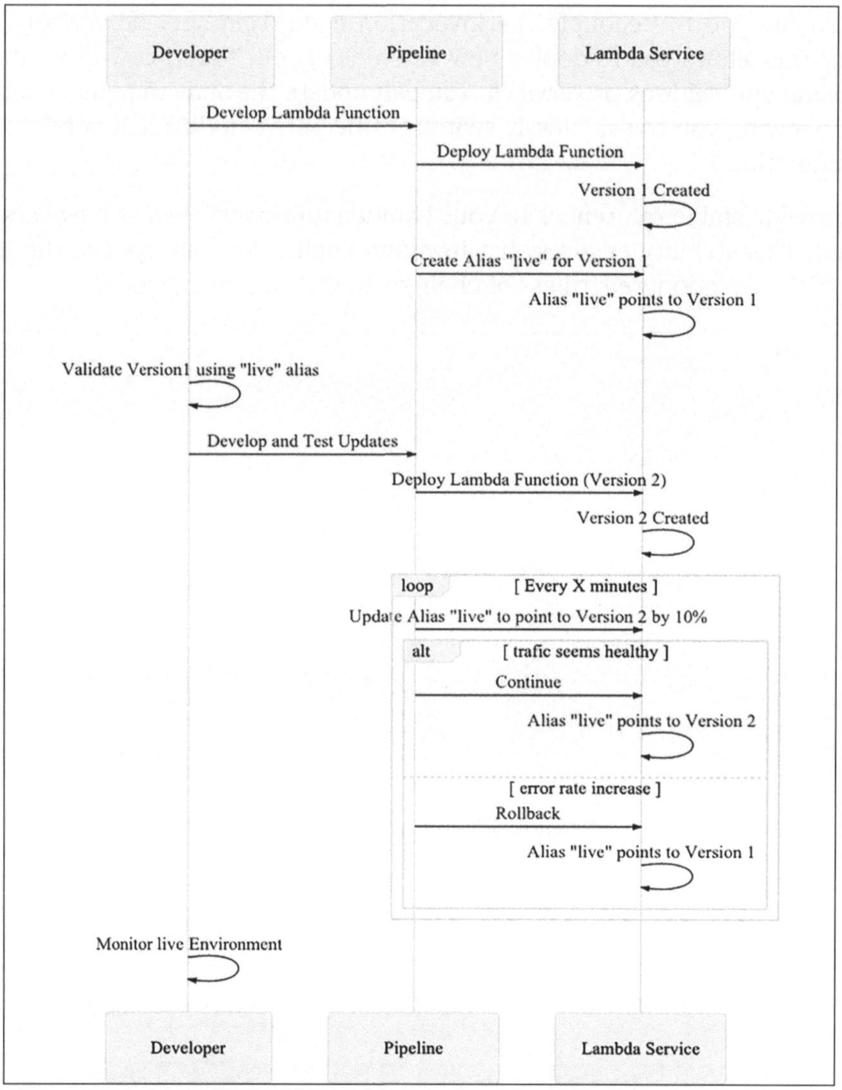

Figure 6.2: *Version and aliases operational sequence*

Creating Lambda Versions and Aliases

When deploying a new function using AWS CDK, the default behavior will create a function with no version and alias. To add a version using CDK, the lambda version construct can be used to generate a lambda version.

```
new Version(this, 'CreateItemFunctionVersion', {
  lambda: createItemFunction,
  removalPolicy: RemovalPolicy.DESTROY,
});
```

Deploying the stack will result in the creation of a new version. You can view the version by selecting the version and looking at the details.

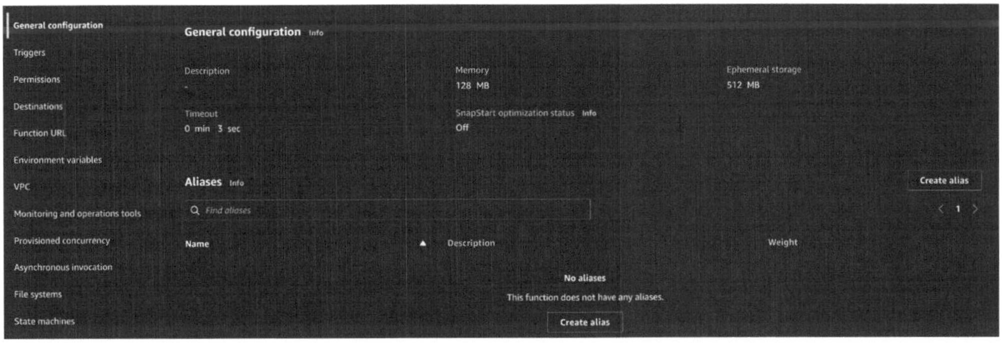

Figure 6.3: *Lambda version configuration*

The version contains a complete set of dedicated configurations, as follows:

- Memory
- Process Architecture
- Runtime
- Timeout
- Event Source Mapping
- Permissions
- Success and Failure destinations
- Environment variables
- Monitoring and Tracing Configuration
- Concurrency
- Network Configuration

Some configurations like function URLs are not attached to a version and are part of the whole function configuration.

Adding a new version in CDK while changing the timeout and memory size of the function will result in the creation of a new version with a new configuration while at the same time keeping the previous version intact.

Example source code can be found at **C06/lambda-versions/v1**

```
 const createItemFunction = new NodejsFunction(this, `CreateItemFunction`,
{
   ...
   memorySize: 256,
   timeout: Duration.seconds(15),
```

```
    ....
});
 new Version(this, 'CreateItemFunctionVersion2', {
   lambda: createItemFunction,
   removalPolicy: RemovalPolicy.DESTROY,
});
```

Deploying the stack results in a new version with a new configuration, as illustrated in *Figure 6.4*:

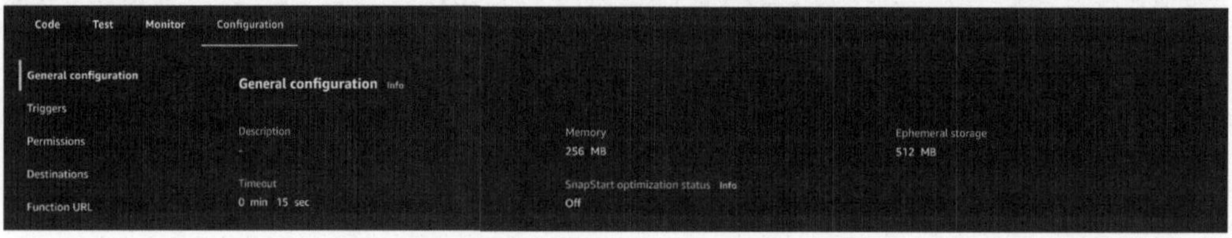

Figure 6.4: *Lambda version immutability*

In the following example, the function will be changed to use a new Runtime, and the Node.js runtime will be modified to Python:

Example source code can be found at **C06/lambda-versions/v2**

```
const createItemFunction = new Function(this, `CreateItemFunction`, {
   code: Code.fromAsset(resolve(__dirname, '../../src/python/handlers/
create-item')),
   handler: 'handler',
   runtime: Runtime.PYTHON_3_12,
   architecture: Architecture.ARM_64,
   logGroup: createItemFunctionLogGroup,
   memorySize: 256,
   timeout: Duration.seconds(15),
   role: functionRole,
});

new Version(this, 'CreateItemFunctionVersion3', {
     lambda: createItemFunction,
     removalPolicy: RemovalPolicy.DESTROY,
});
```

Deploying the stack creates a new version (version 3), and by looking at the version details and navigating to code and runtime details, the Python runtime and code are considered.

Figure 6.5: *Dedicated runtime per version*

The version 2 remains intact and has the previous runtime configuration:

Figure 6.6: *Version runtime immutability*

Overhead of Managing Too Many Versions

As software evolves, the need for adding new versions evolves. This can lead to having many versions in CDK code that can produce maintainability and readability problems. One way is to remove unused versions from CDK code and redeploy the stack; this way the old versions will be cleaned up.

Often the functions have a single version or two that are under traffic; if the function needs just a single or couple of versions, the CDK provides a simple and clean way of doing this.

```
const createItemFunction = new NodejsFunction(this, `CreateItemFunction`,
{
   ...
   currentVersionOptions: {
     removalPolicy: RemovalPolicy.DESTROY,
   }
 });
 createItemFunction.addAlias('live');
```

This code snippet defines a current version configuration and creates an alias and version. The current version options provide a simplified way of configuring the version as per the following table:

Name	Description
`codeSha256`	SHA256 of the version of the lambda source code
`maxEventAge`	The maximum age of a request that lambda sends to a function for processing
`onFailure`	The destination for failed invocations
`onSuccess`	The destination for successful invocations
`provisionedConcurrentExecutions`	Specifies a provisioned concurrency configuration for a function's version

removalPolicy	Whether to retain old versions of this function when a new version is created
retryAttempts	The maximum number of times to retry when the function returns an error

Table 6.1: *AWS CDK configuration options for versioning*

Weighted Aliases

Weighted aliases and versioning are useful in scenarios where we need to experiment the new versions like A/B testing or canary deployment.

Weighted traffic routing using lambda aliases can be performed with a minimum of two versions, as the versions can be created by the presence of a change; the first version needs to be deployed as a separate deployment.

```
const createItemFunction = new NodejsFunction(...);
const version1 = new Version(this, 'CreateItemFunctionVersion', {
 lambda: createItemFunction,
 removalPolicy: RemovalPolicy.DESTROY,
});
```

Deploying the stack will create a function version and, by default, all traffic is routed to this latest version. Creating a new version needs a change to function configuration like changing memory size. The following example applies a change to memory size and creates a new version and an alias with 30% of traffic routing the new version:

```
 const createItemFunction = new NodejsFunction(this, `CreateItemFunction`,
{
   ...
   memorySize: 128, // change 256 to 128
   ...
 });

 const version2 = new Version(this, 'CreateItemFunctionVersion2', {
   lambda: createItemFunction,
   removalPolicy: RemovalPolicy.DESTROY,
 });

 const aliasLive = new Alias(this, 'CreateItemFunctionAlias', {
   aliasName: 'live',
   version: version2,
   additionalVersions: [
     {
       version: version1,
       weight: 0.3
```

```
      }
    ]
 });
```

An alias helps to shift part of traffic to the new version for experimentation and get back to the original version or shift to the new version. Removing the `**additionalVersions**` parameter from the alias will shift the whole traffic to the new version.

Rolling Deployment

Weighted aliases offer value not only for version experimentation but also for deployment procedures. Through the deployment pipeline, automation facilitates monitoring and rollback to the prior version if the error rate exceed the predetermined threshold.

Leveraging AWS CodeDeploy enhances the deployment process in an automated manner, grounded in actual traffic patterns. CodeDeploy presents the following deployment configurations:

- **Linear Deployment**: This method gradually shifts traffic by an additional percentage every X minutes.
- **Canary Deployment**: With Canary Deployment, an initial portion of traffic undergoes redirection, with the remaining traffic shifted after validation.

The following code snippet illustrates an example deployment configuration for deploying a new version using CDK:

```
const application = new LambdaApplication(this, 'createItemFunctionApp',
{
 applicationName: 'createItemFunctionApp',
});

new LambdaDeploymentGroup(
 this,
 `CreateItem CodeDeploy Deployment Group`,
 {
   application,
   alias,
   alarms: [
     new Alarm(this, "DeploymentAlarm", {
       metric: alias.metricErrors(),
       threshold: 1,
       evaluationPeriods: 1,
     })
   ]
   deploymentConfig: LambdaDeploymentConfig.LINEAR_10PERCENT_EVERY_1MINUTE
```

```
  }
);
```

In this scenario, the traffic directed to the new version gradually increases by 10% every minute, while simultaneously monitoring the CloudWatch alarm. If the alarm detects even a single error during deployment, according to its configured settings, the rollout of the new version will be reverted.

Tracing

Tracing in distributed systems involves monitoring and analyzing the flow of requests as they propagate through various components of a system. It allows for understanding the end-to-end journey of a request, even as it traverses across multiple services, servers, and networks. By tracing requests, developers and operators can gain insights into performance bottlenecks, troubleshoot issues, and ensure system reliability.

Overall, tracing in distributed systems plays a crucial role in ensuring observability and understanding of complex interactions between different components, ultimately leading to better system reliability and performance.

Lambda Tracing

AWS Lambda offers a simple way of configuring tracing via AWS X-Ray. When tracing is active on a Lambda function, the lambda will capture the upstream requests and send them to X-Ray. The X-Ray represents the traces, as shown in *Figure* 6.7 (code example: **`C06/lambda-tracing/v1`**):

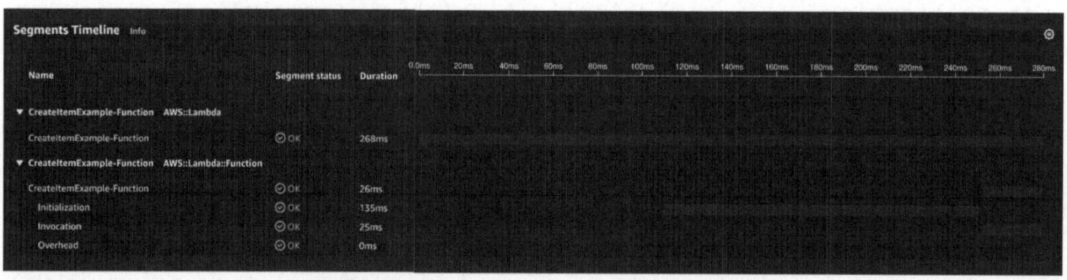

Figure 6.7: *Lambda function X-Ray spans*

AWS X-Ray segments timeline illustrates the request chain spots by correlating them into a segment. A segment represents a tracing context.

To find more, refer to X-Ray documentation: https://docs.aws.amazon.com/xray/latest/devguide/xray-api-segmentdocuments.html

As per *Figure* 6.7, the overall process is segmented into separate phases called subsegments. Initialization, invocation, and overhead are the visible subsegments represented above:

- **Initialization**: This `` `initialization` `` subsegment describes the **`Init`** phase of the Lambda function.
- **Invocation**: The `` `invocation` `` subsegment describes the invoke phase. This is the overall representation of the whole handler execution.
- **Overhead**: The `` `overhead` `` describes part of the execution trace where the runtime will be invoked to freeze the execution environment.

Chainable Tracing

The use of Lambda functions is not finite to the processing at the execution environment level, but a wide range of interactions with other services. Often, using AWS SDK is the way a Lambda function interacts with another service, such as writing to a DynamoDB table or sending a message to SQS.

AWS X-Ray helps to instrument the function and provides the necessary metadata that gives extra tracing information. The `` `aws-xray-sdk-core` `` is a **`Node.js`** library that helps instrument the **`sdk`** clients by adding extra metadata to the **`sdk`** client request.

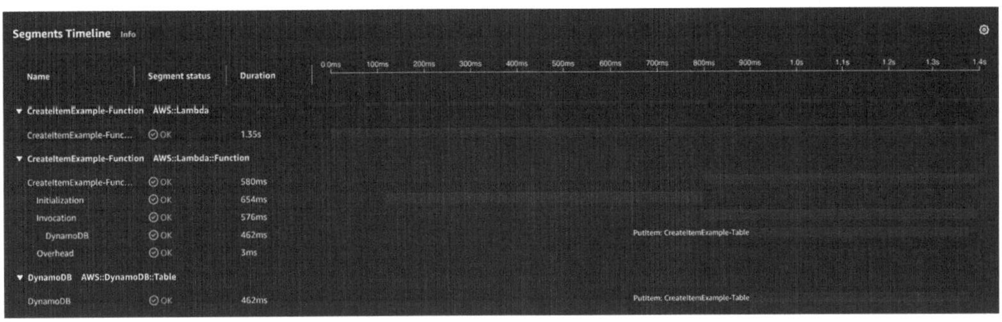

Figure 6.8: *Chainable Tracing*

This will add enough metadata to optimize the use of traces, such as the number of retries, **`operation`**, and **`request_id`** (code example: **`` `C06/lambda-tracing/v2` ``**).

In event-driven design, the process is not scoped to compute and database only, but a collaboration of Functions, Brokers, Change data capturing, and so on. The events transit between different components before reaching lambda. The lambda service also captures the incoming requests from other services that reach the function like SQS (code example: **`` `C06/lambda-tracing/v3` ``**).

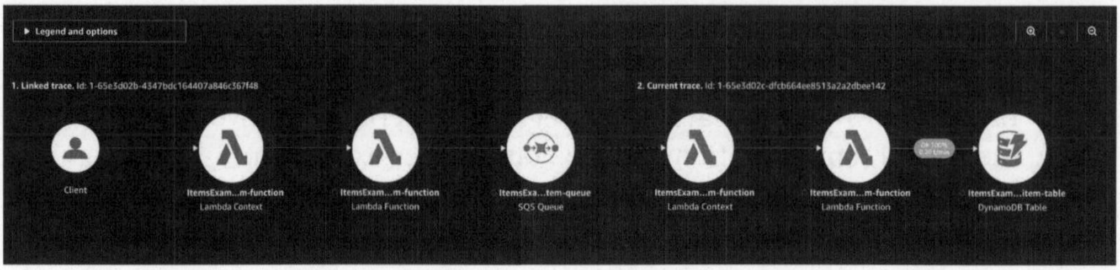

Figure 6.9: *Incoming requests traces*

The X-Ray traces are based on a Segmented Tree. It means a trace collection has many linked traces. Each trace is a collection of correlated segments, and subsegments represent the details of a segment. *Figure* 6.10 illustrates the X-Ray trace segmentation:

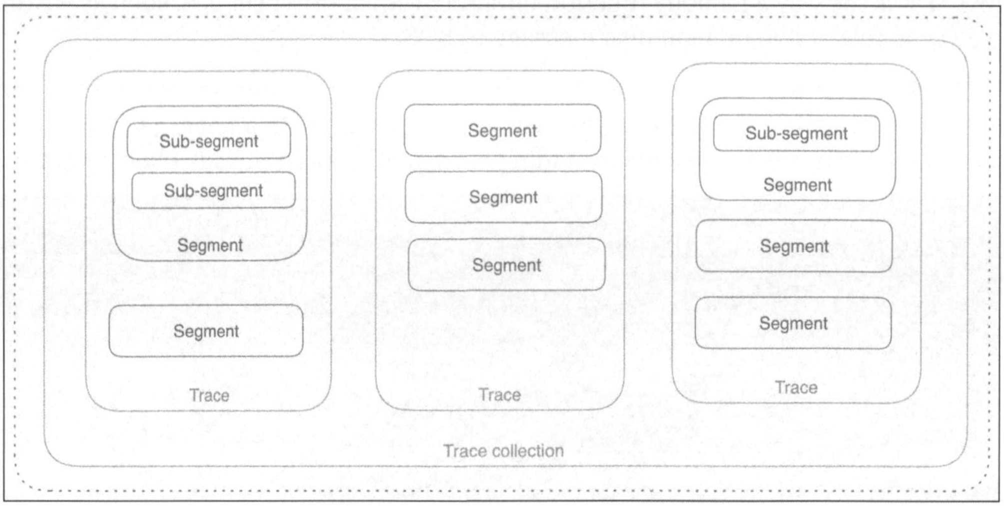

Figure 6.10: *Segmented tree tracing*

The traces are constructed as a tree data structure, having roots and expanding to the lower levels. This structure matches with the tracing usage as the higher level of interaction is detecting the top root status, further deep diving into the collection items, and finally reaching the subsegments.

Lambda Power Tools

Lambda Power Tools provide a collection of modules that help to better instrument the Lambda functions. Power Tools `` `@aws-lambda-powertools/tracer` `` module provides the functionality to capture, customize, and augment the default tracing explored earlier:

```
import { Tracer } from '@aws-lambda-powertools/tracer';
import { LambdaInterface } from '@aws-lambda-powertools/commons';
```

```
const tracer = new Tracer({ serviceName: 'serverlessAirline' });
const client = tracer.captureAWSv3Client(new SQSClient({ region:
process.env.AWS_REGION } ));

class Handler implements LambdaInterface {
 @tracer.captureLambdaHandler()
 public async handler(event: SNSEvent, context: Context): Promise<any>
{
   tracer.getSegment();
   await client.send(new SendMessageCommand({
     QueueUrl: process.env.QUEUE_NAME,
     MessageBody: JSON.stringify(JSON.parse(event.Records[0].Sns.
Message))
   }));

   const handlerSegment = tracer.getSegment()?.addNewSubsegment('###
handler');
   handlerSegment && tracer.setSegment(handlerSegment);

   tracer.putAnnotation('successfulBooking', true);
   handlerSegment?.close();
   handlerSegment && tracer.setSegment(handlerSegment?.parent);

   return {
     statusCode: 200,
     body: JSON.stringify('Hello from create item!'),
   };
 }
}

const handlerClass = new Handler();
export const handler = handlerClass.handler.bind(handlerClass);
```

The above handler shows how to instrument a handler using Power Tools. In this example, it is capturing the segment and adding subsegments (code example: `` `**C06/lambda-tracing/v4**` ``).

As shown in *Figure 6.11*, the SNS/SQS traces are linked in a single trace:

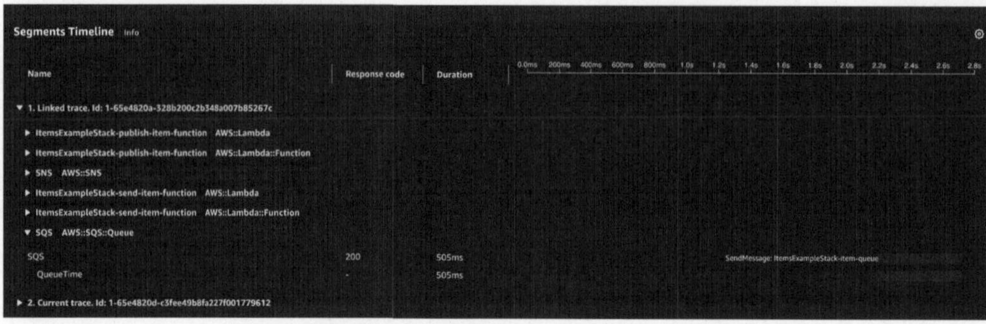

Figure 6.11: *Tracing using Power Tools*

Workflows in Handler

If the handler includes a sophisticated business workflow, it can be useful to trace the workflow by instrumenting the code for greater visibility at different steps. The following snippet demonstrates a simple workflow (code example: `**C06/lambda-tracing/v5**`):

```
const payload = JSON.parse(event.Records[0].Sns.Message);
await this.StepOne();
 if(payload.name === 'serverless') {
  await this.StepTwo();
} else {
  await this.StepThree();
}
await this.StepFour();

await client.send(new SendMessageCommand({
  QueueUrl: process.env.QUEUE_NAME,
  MessageBody: JSON.stringify(payload)
}));
```

Invoking this handler can be hard to trace, as any single step can have a degraded behavior at times, and detecting and doing analysis to find the degradation can be hard. This adds the overhead of debugging, reproducing production behavior, and collecting data.

Lambda Power Tools helps to instrument any single method involved in the process by adding `**captureMethod**` decorator:

```
@tracer.captureMethod()
async StepOne() {
  ....
}
```

Running the example, the X-Ray representation of trace segmentation will be detailed by workflow steps:

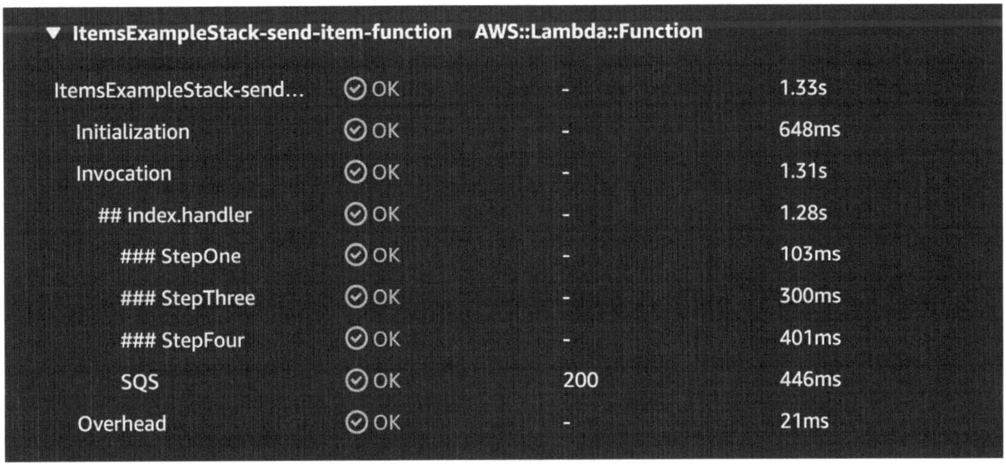

Figure 6.12: *Capturing methods*

Lambda Layers

As the name implies, Lambda Layers are a layer of abstraction that helps to have sophisticated Separation of Concerns (SoC). The layers can be powerful in some use cases, but they come with their proper pros and cons.

AWS documentation provides a list of reasons to show when to use lambda layers:

- Reduce the deployment size.
- Separate core logic from dependencies.
- Share dependencies between multiple functions.
- To use the Lambda Console code editor effectively.

The above reasoning elements are true, but in an opinionated way of looking at the exact necessity of each one, these are not necessarily true.

- With the growth of development tooling, there is no exact need to use AWS console lambda code editor, albeit a powerful and qualified tool in AWS Console.
- There is a wide range of tools that help to reduce package and deployment bundle size for typical applications, but in cases like when dealing with large libraries exceeding a normal size, the use of layers can be helpful.
- Separation of code from dependencies is an ideal logic proposition, but again in typical scenarios, there is no need to have complicated dependencies that can approve the use of layers. Any dependency presented in software code

is a library from public package managers like NPM or an internal package manager. Also, the libraries have evolved lately, and the modular approach is one way of reducing the impact of having a whole package as part of the function bundle.

- Sharing code across lambdas can be achieved by a package, and the package versioning is more standard and sophisticated than a layer versioning. Giving any software the ability to download and test any new shared code release seems more trustworthy than using layers.

Figure 6.13 illustrates the high-level view of layers in the context of Lambda functions:

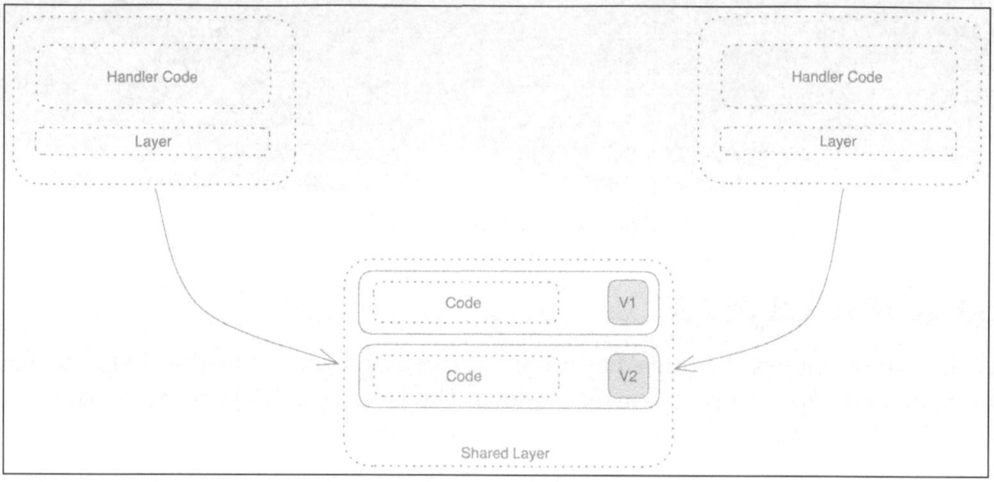

Figure 6.13: *Lambda Layers*

However, Lambda Layers offer more than just layering. The lambda service layers provide a way to extend the capabilities of runtime or add some cross-cutting concerns using extensions. Extensions are a great way of instrumenting a Lambda function due to their characteristics, such as asynchronous, isolated process, and post-execution.

Extensions

Lambda provides two kinds of extensions, internal and external, which differ in the capabilities they provide during the execution lifecycle. The internal extensions keep cohesion between the execution environment and extension by sharing the coupling between the function and the extension lifecycle, whereas the external extension provides a decoupled way of adding or augmenting capabilities to the Lambda function.

Extensions share the same memory and execution environment configs with the function. This is an important note to consider as any performance issue in an extension can impact the function execution.

Internal Extensions

Internal Extensions run in the same process as the execution environment and can act as a wrapper to customize runtime or instrumenting functions at the process level but within different threads. Internal extensions modify the Lambda runtime startup using wrappers or environment variables.

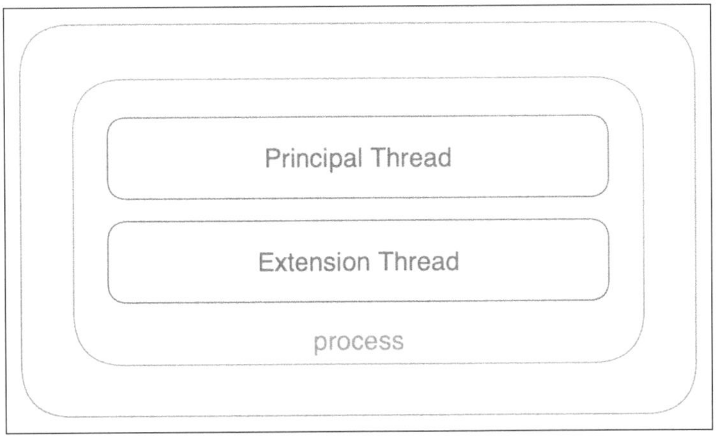

Figure 6.14: *Internal extensions process*

Environment variables can be used to pass extra parameters to the command line for changing runtime behavior. This is a simple and config-based way of customizing some runtime properties or specifications. The extension will be preloaded at the initialization phase. Lambda supports the following language-specific environment variables:

Java: **`JAVA_TOOL_OPTIONS`**

Node.js: **`NODE_OPTIONS`**

.Net: **`DOTNET_STARTUP_HOOKS`**

Wrapper scripts will be executed using the `**AWS_LAMBDA_EXEC_WRAPPER**` environment variable pointing to an executable binary or script, for example, `**opt/<folder>**`.

External Extensions

External Extensions are suitable for cross-cutting concerns and instrumenting the execution environment in an async and decoupled way. The external extensions run in separate processes and have no impact on the function execution.

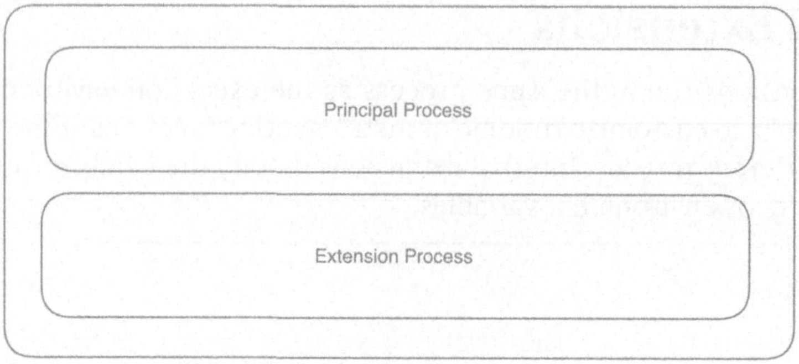

Figure 6.15: *External extensions process*

They are involved in all three phases of function execution: **`init`**, **`invoke`**, and **`shutdown`**. During initialization, the extension will be involved before function **`init`**, the invocation occurs in parallel and independent of the function invoke phase, and the extension invocation can continue posterior to function invocation termination (response to the caller). The shutdown phase will hint the extension Shutdown to let the extension release and terminate all non-terminated tasks.

The extension has a 2-second grace period to finish the shutdown process and respond to the received hint.

Lambda Telemetry API Extensions

Lambda provides a Telemetry API that helps to instrument the Lambda function by adding out-of-process tracing and observability capabilities. The lambda Telemetry API provides three categories of telemetry records: `**function**`, `**platform**`, and `**extension**`. An extension can subscribe to one or all records categories by sending a subscription request to the Telemetry API.

Figure 6.16 illustrates the extension registration process:

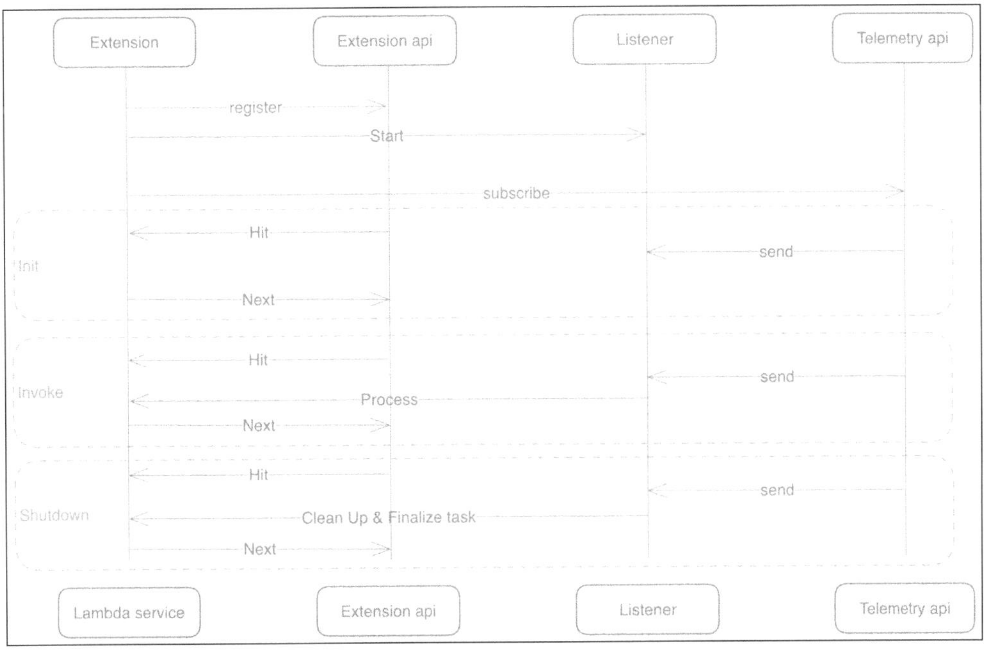

Figure 6.16: *Telemetry API extension sequence*

The extension will be first hit by the lambda service at the **`init`** phase, letting the extension be prepared for further process and task execution. The registration sequence will be as follows:

- **Extension API**: The extension first needs to register itself to the Lambda Extension API and receive an extension identifier. This identifier lets the extension communicate with lambda service idempotently.

```
const RUNTIME_EXTENSION_URL = `http://${process.env.AWS_LAMBDA_
RUNTIME_API}/2020-01-01/extension`;

const res = await fetch(`${RUNTIME_EXTENSION_URL}/register`, {
  method: 'POST',
  body: JSON.stringify({
    'events': [
      'INVOKE',
      'SHUTDOWN'
      ],
  }),
  headers: {
    'Content-Type': 'application/json',
    'Lambda-Extension-Name': basename(__dirname),
  }
});
```

The Extension API sends back the extension identifier as part of the response header under `**lambda-extension-identifier**` key.

- **Listener Server**: The listener can be any `**http**` or `**tcp**` based local server. It will be in communication under `**localhost**` with Telemetry API. The following snippet shows how this can be achieved in Node.js using the `**http**` module:

```
const LISTENER_HOST = 'sandbox';
const LISTENER_PORT = 4243;
const server = createServer((request, response) => {
   if (request.method === "POST") {
        let body = '';
        request.on("data", (data) => {
body += data;
});
        request.on("end", () => {
            try {
onLogReceived(JSON.parse(body));
      }
            catch (e) {
console.error('Failed to parse log data:', e);
    }

            response.writeHead(200, {});
            response.end("OK");
        });
   } else {
        console.error("unexpected request", request.method,
request.url);
        response.writeHead(404, {});
        response.end();
   }
});

server.listen(LISTENER_PORT, LISTENER_HOST);
return `http://${LISTENER_HOST}:${LISTENER_PORT}`;
```

The `**OnRecordReceived**` method is used to manipulate the received record. The listener host is `**sandbox**`, specifically on port `**4243**`.

- **Telemetry API**: The extension needs to call Telemetry API by sending a subscribe request providing `**extensionId**` and `**listenerUrl**`, as shown in the following snippet:

```
const subscriptionBody = {
   schemaVersion: "2022-07-01",
   destination: {
        protocol: "HTTP",
```

```
            URI: listenerUri,
        },
        types: ['function'],
        buffering: {
            timeoutMs: 100,
            maxBytes: 256 * 1024,
            maxItems: 1000
        }
    };

    const res = await fetch(`http://${process.env.AWS_LAMBDA_RUNTIME_
    API}/2022-07-01/telemetry`, {
     keepalive: true,
     method: 'PUT',
     body: JSON.stringify(subscriptionBody),
     headers: {
         'Content-Type': 'application/json',
         'Lambda-Extension-Identifier': extensionId,
     }
    });
```

The registration and subscribing to the Telemetry API will be achieved as demonstrated above. During the different phases of the execution lifecycle, the lambda service sends requests for different event types such as `**INIT**`, `**INVOKE**`, and `**SHUTDOWN**`. As part of extension implementation, the extension should consider the event type and process the task for that specific event type. The extension to understand the event type needs to interact with Extension API using the `**Next**` action as shown in the following code snippet:

```
const res = await fetch(`${RUNTIME_EXTENSION_URL}/event/next`, {
   method: 'GET',
   headers: {
       'Content-Type': 'application/json',
       'Lambda-Extension-Identifier': extensionId,
   },
   keepalive: true,
 });

 if (!res.ok) {
     console.error('[extensions-api:next] Failed receiving next event',
await res.text());
     return {};
 } else {
     return await res.json() as Record<string, any>;
 }
```

The **Next** call response will be an event containing an `**eventType**` attribute:

```
switch (event?.eventType) {
   case 'INVOKE':
       ...
       break;
   case 'SHUTDOWN':
       ...
       break;
   default:
       throw new Error('[Extension] unknown event: ' + JSON.
stringify(event));
}
```

The source code can be found at `**C06/external-extensions/telemetry-extension**`. Follow the Readme file to build and deploy the solution.

Lambda service works based on a predefined standard to integrate extensions into the execution process, and as part of this convention, the extension package scaffolding is important. Lambda copies layers with an extensions folder during the **Init** phase into the execution environment `**/opt**` path and intercepts each file `**/opt/extensions/**` directory as an executable bootstrap.

The extension bootstrap file will be as follows:

```
#!/bin/bash
OWN_FILENAME="$(basename $0)"
LAMBDA_EXTENSION_NAME="$OWN_FILENAME"
exec "/opt/${LAMBDA_EXTENSION_NAME}/index.js"
```

As the preceding example shows, the extension source Node.js bundle must be in a directory with the same name as the bootstrap filename.

```
-- extensions
     -- my-extension
-- my-extension
     -- index.js
```

Conclusion

This chapter covered detailed information about Lambda instrumenting, including how versions and aliases can be used and how they can improve the operational aspects of Lambda functions.

Distributed systems are hard, and without a well-defined observability, achieving a simple-to-maintain system can become time-consuming and requires a lot of effort. Tracing, as one of the primary pillars of observability in modern software, helps to obtain insights and simplify the problem-solving efforts in case of an inconsistent situation. Serverless design, which relies on the collaboration of small services, can be challenging without tracing as part of software instrumenting.

The lambda extensions are a way of offloading some out-of-process tasks and offloading some functionality in a separate and isolated process, keeping in mind that the extensions need to be observed carefully as they can introduce the hidden impacts.

The next chapter covers the Lambda resiliency topic and delves into the different integration types, as well as how to design a fault-tolerant and resilient solution.

CHAPTER 7
Resiliency and Design for Failure

Introduction

This chapter covers the resilience pillar and design for failure in serverless architectures when using AWS Lambda. The chapter covers the concept of errors and exceptional behaviors in software and delves into the different retry strategies, dead letter queues, and observing resiliency metrics. There is a particular focus on resiliency when using different invocation types, covering various service integrations such as Amazon SQS, Amazon Kinesis, Amazon SNS, Amazon Event Bridge, and API Gateway.

The reader will achieve a detailed understanding of how to manage software failures and error handling, as well as the key considerations to take into account when setting up a retry mechanism.

Structure

In this chapter, we will discuss the following topics:

- Lambda Errors and Exceptions
- Retry
- Dead Letter Queues
- Lambda Destinations
- Lambda Resilience Metrics

Lambda Errors and Exceptions

In distributed systems, errors come as part of any software and are inevitable. AWS Lambda detects errors during the execution of functions through various mechanisms. AWS Lambda being a highly available service that offers computational units distributed in multiple regions and availability zones can encounter the failures related to the customer responsibilities, such as application errors, misconfiguration, dependency failures, or service limits. While designing solutions using AWS Lambda, there are a variety of error types that need to be taken into consideration and dealt with:

- **Runtime Errors:** Lambda will detect runtime errors that occur during the execution of your function's code. These could be syntax errors, logical errors, or any other issues that cause the function to fail during execution. Lambda captures these errors and reports them in the function's execution logs.
- **Unhandled Exceptions**: If your function code throws an unhandled exception, Lambda will detect it and report it as an error. Unhandled exceptions could be due to various reasons such as incorrect input, resource unavailability, or programming errors.
- **Timeouts**: Lambda functions have a maximum execution time limit, which can be set by the user. If a function exceeds this limit, Lambda will terminate the execution and report a timeout error. Timeout errors often indicate that the function is taking too long to complete its task or is stuck in an infinite loop.
- **Out-of -Memory Errors**: If your lambda function consumes too much memory during execution, Lambda may terminate the function and report an out-of-memory error. This typically happens if your function is processing a large amount of data or if it has insufficient memory usage patterns.
- **Environment Errors**: Sometimes errors can occur due to issues with the execution environment itself, such as network connectivity problems, resource contention, or configuration errors. Lambda monitors the execution environment and detects such errors, which are typically reported as system errors or environment errors.
- **Invocation Errors**: Errors can also occur during the invocation of lambda functions, such as when incorrect input parameters are provided or when there are issues with the event source (for example, misconfigured triggers). Lambda captures these errors and reports them accordingly.

Lambda provides detailed logs for each function invocation, which include information about any errors or exceptions that occurred during execution and are integrated into CloudWatch for monitoring and alerting. Catched errors are represented as JSON documents.

The following snippet demonstrates a simple custom error:

```
class ItemNotFoundException extends Error {
 constructor(message: string) {
   super(message);
   this.name = "ItemNotFound";
   Error.captureStackTrace(this, this.constructor);
 }
}
```

If an error is thrown, the lambda-generated JSON document will be as follows:

```
{
 "errorType": "ItemNotFound",
 "errorMessage": "Item not found",
 "trace": [
  "ItemNotFound: Item not found",
  "    at Runtime.i [as handler] (/var/task/index.js:1:663)",
  "    at Runtime.handleOnceNonStreaming (file:///var/runtime/index.
mjs:1173:29)"
 ]
}
```

This `**errorType**` and `**errorMessage**` are the name and message properties of the error class. As shown above, the `**trace**` points to the error stack trace but has less interest for debugging purposes as it points to the minified JavaScript file. To improve the above error message when using TypeScript, AWS CDK handles **SourceMap** with less effort. Using SourceMap, information about the TypeScript code source will be included as part of the error log:

```
{
   "errorType": "ItemNotFound",
   "errorMessage": "Item not found",
   "name": "ItemNotFound",
   "stack": [
        "ItemNotFound: Item not found",
        "    at Runtime.i (/src/handlers/lambda-errors/index.ts:11:9)",
        "    at Runtime.handleOnceNonStreaming (file:///var/runtime/index.
mjs:1173:29)"
   ]
}
```

SourceMap Using AWS CDK

Adding the **SourceMap** for TypeScript code will be simple and straightforward. The following snippet demonstrates a CDK example:

```
new nodejs.NodejsFunction(this, 'LambdaErrorsFunction', {
 entry: resolve(`src/handlers/lambda-errors/index.ts`),
 ...
 bundling: {
   minify: true,
   sourceMap: true,
   sourceMapMode: SourceMapMode.INLINE,
   sourcesContent: false,
 },
 environment: {
```

```
    NODE_OPTIONS: '--enable-source-maps',
  }
});
```

The bundling section lets the `esbuild` bundler keep the map of the original source code as part of the bundle, and the **NODE_OPTIONS** environment variable helps to lead the Node.js process to point to the original source code by the best effort when dealing with stack traces. The Node.js documentation indicates that overriding **Error.prepareStackTrace** may prevent **--enable-source-maps**.

The following snippet shows how to handle and keep the `--enable-source-maps` functionality while overriding the `PrepareStackTrace`:

```
const originalPrepareStackTrace = Error.prepareStackTrace;
Error.prepareStackTrace = (error, trace) => {
      // Some logic around Error and stack trace
      return originalPrepareStackTrace(error, trace);
};
```

Lambda Errors

In Node.js, `stderr` and `stdout` are a way to asynchronously stream some data. AWS Lambda looks at `stderr` and `stdout` to collect the data and put them to CloudWatch log stream.

It is important to consider some differences between `Throwing Errors` and `Writing to stderr`. When throwing an error, the Node.js process catches the error from the event loop. If the error is not handled in software code, the process will be interrupted, and accordingly, the Lambda invocation will be interrupted. The `stderr` behaves differently and just puts a buffer of information into the stream asynchronously; `stderr` provides listeners that can be used to act behind received streams.

The following example will lead to a successful invocation but having the error logs in **cloudwatch**:

```
import { APIGatewayProxyEvent } from 'aws-lambda';

export const handler = async(event: APIGatewayProxyEvent) => {
 try {
   throw new ItemNotFoundException('Item not found');
 }
 catch (error) {
   const errorDetails = {
       name: error.name,
message: error.message,
stack: error.stack,
    };
```

```
    process.stderr.write(JSON.stringify(errorDetails));
  }
};
```

The result will be as follows in CloudWatch:

```
{
  "name": "ItemNotFoundException",
  "message": "Item not found",
  "stack": "ItemNotFoundException: Item not found\n at handler (/var/
task/index.js:8:11)\n
at processTicksAndRejections (internal/process/task_queues.js:93:5)"
}
```

As the above example demonstrates how **`stderr`** behaves, it's not a recommended way for observability requirements. In Node.js, the **`console`** object manages this properly and behind the scene writes to the corresponding stream.

Using console to log the thrown error will be presented as follows in CloudWatch:

```
export const handler = async(event: APIGatewayProxyEvent) => {
  try {
    throw new ItemNotFoundException('Item not found');
  }
  catch (error) {
    console.error(error);
  }
};


ERROR ItemNotFound: Item not found
    at Runtime.h (/src/handlers/lambda-errors/index.ts:12:11)
    at Runtime.handleOnceNonStreaming (file:///var/runtime/index.
mjs:1173:29)
```

Some external libraries and packages may write to **`stderr`**. It is possible to observe the **`stderr`** in lambda function code by overriding the **`stderr.write`** method:

```
export const handler = async(event: APIGatewayProxyEvent) => {
  process.stderr.write = (data) => {
    console.log(`Data received: ${data}`);
    return true;
  };
   try {
    throw new ItemNotFoundException();
  }
  catch (e) {
    process.stderr.write('ERROR');
  }
};
```

The `stderr` stream can be observed using the `on` method for child processes but not for parent processes.

Lambda Error Handling

While using Lambda Service, there are two categories of errors: Invocation and Function. The `Invocation Errors` are not considered as per function retry policy and are handled by AWS-provided tooling such as AWS CLI or SDK. These tools manage, by default, retries for errors, except bad requests. The `Function Errors` are errors thrown and happen after function invocation and will apply the configured retry policy.

Lambda execution environment will apply the retry policy if the process exits with an error signal. The lambda retry configuration will be applied per integration type being Async, Event source mapping, or client-based integrations.

Lambda Execution Environment

A function can be instrumented by extensions that can participate in lambda exceptional runtime behaviors. The extension initialization phase errors will lead to a restart of the execution environment. In the invocation phase for any related and shared exceptions like **OutOfMemory** or **Timeout**, the lambda will send the Runtime and all extensions a SHUTDOWN signal, letting them release the remaining work. These interrupting error records in Telemetry API are represented as `platform` records respecting a `SHUTDOWN` signal, including the **shutdownReason** for timeout or memory issue.

```
{
 "eventType": "SHUTDOWN",
 "shutdownReason": "reason for shutdown",
 "deadlineMs": "the time and date that the function times out in Unix
time milliseconds"
}
```

Retry

One common mitigation when dealing with transient errors in distributed systems is the retry mechanism. The retry is often considered a good way toward a successful design, but in real situations, an uncontrolled retry mechanism can bring the system down. Understanding when the failures happen in a distributed system can be an initial base for implementing an efficient retry mechanism.

- **Transient Errors**: These are the failures that happen for short periods due to availability, performance, or any resource-related unhealthy behavior. Reattempting can lead to success once the resource recovery is done.

- **Partial Failures**: A common scenario is when a percentage of requests fail due to node downtime, software errors, or network issues. Reattempting leads to overcoming inconsistencies and exceptional behaviors smoothly.

Challenges While Retrying

The retry mechanism, while a solution to handle the inconsistent behaviors in a system, can become challenging and may lead to overall failure in the whole system. The following list represents a list of challenges to consider when defining a retry strategy:

- **Back Pressure:** While a system experiences an inconsistent condition and the capability of responding to requests decreases, a retry can lead to amplifying the pressure and in some cases can bring a system to a full downtime. Applying an exponential backoff or a circuit breaker pattern can help control the back pressure.
- **Downstream Capacity**: An uncontrolled retry mechanism can lead to overloading the downstream, and controlling the retry helps to decrease the cost of downstream and inconvenient effects. The rate limiting and retrying can be helpful to give a chance of recovery to the unhealthy service.
- **Side Effects:** As a retry can lead to multiple reception of requests on the downstream side, it is important to design idempotency as part of software design to remove any potential side effects.
- **Retry Storm:** A retry storm is when many consumers send the requests at the same time and simultaneously reattempt the failed requests. Using some sort of **Jitting** with a randomized rate helps to distribute the load temporally to avoid a storm experience.

Figure 7.1 illustrates the unavailability problem in a distributed system:

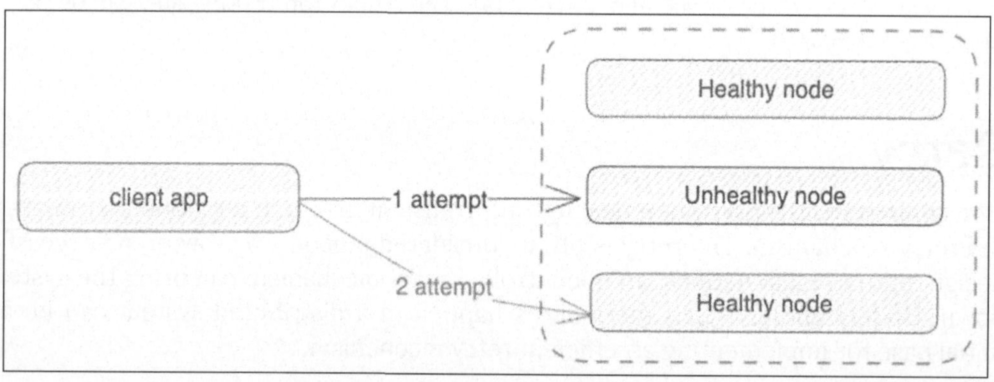

Figure 7.1: *Retries in distributed systems*

As shown in *Figure* 7.1, a retry can lead to a successful result behind a 1st failed attempt. An unhealthy node recovery process can take from some milliseconds to several minutes and designing highly available services can help in case of node failures, but in distributed systems, often multiple layers are involved to respond to a single request such as interacting with a database or other services, as illustrated in *Figure* 7.2:

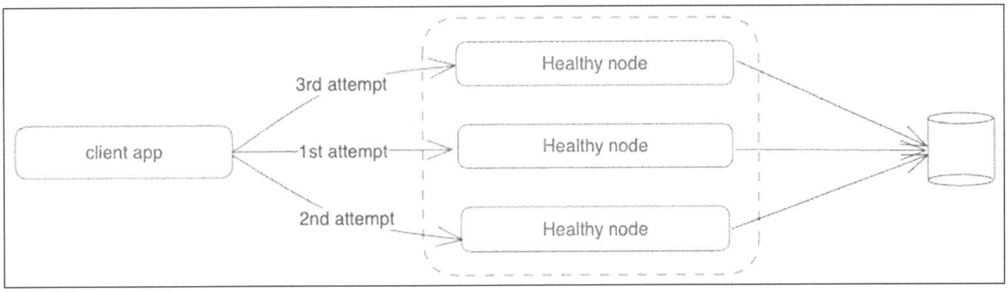

Figure 7.2: *Retries in layered distributed systems*

Figure 7.2 illustrates the situation that a caller retry process leads to two or three failed attempts, as well as this sequential retry will also bring the database instance down by introducing pressure on a partially unhealthy system. A better retry strategy is by considering the subsequence layer's health and providing some breathing time to increase the chance of fast recovery. *Figure* 7.3 illustrates an exponential backoff strategy:

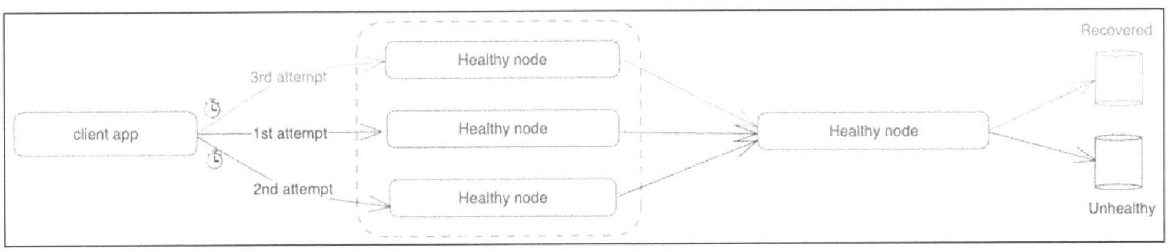

Figure 7.3: *Exponential backoff*

The figure demonstrates a four-layer communication failure with an exponential backoff strategy that gives the chance of getting recovered to the database instance.

Applying Retry with AWS Lambda

AWS Lambda, as the serverless compute service on AWS and with fine-tuned integration with other services, provides retry mechanisms for different integration types, such as synchronous, asynchronous, and polling integration. The retry strategy also can vary based on the source of invocation, whether it's a client or an AWS service. *Figure* 7.4 illustrates the different error occurrence layers when using lambda service:

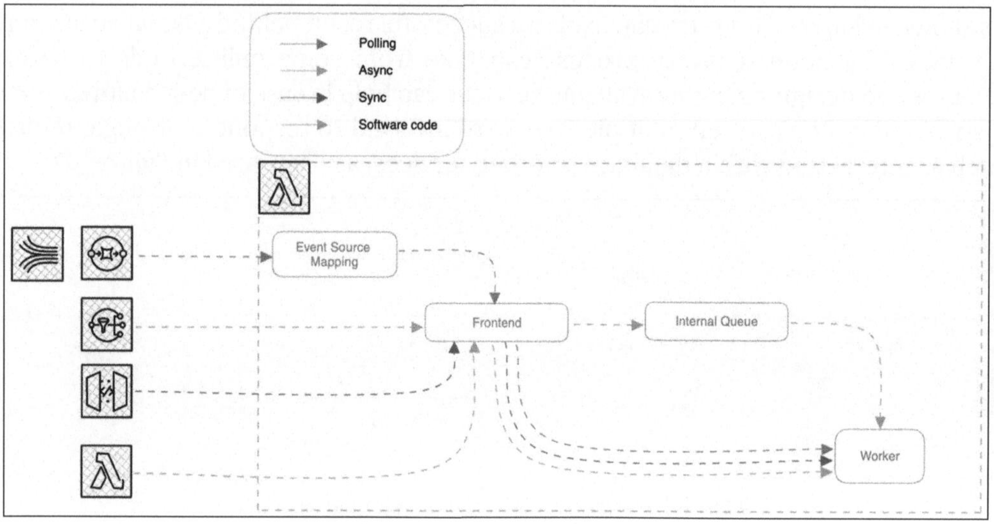

Figure 7.4: *Lambda invocation flow*

Lambda invocation can be synchronous, asynchronous, polling, or from software code. The applicable retry mechanism differs based on the invocation type.

- **Synchronous invocation**: When the caller uses a synchronous invocation, the retry strategy must be applied on the caller side. This means that the API Gateway requester or client must implement the logic to retry the failed requests.
- **Asynchronous invocation**: In asynchronous invocation, the caller is decoupled from the worker and the retry can be managed at the function level. Lambda provides an async invocation confirmation that applies when a function fails in async invocation. By default, functions have an async invocation configuration with 6 hours of buffering and two retries after the first invocation on failure. The retries use an exponential backoff strategy, with delays of 1 and 2 minutes for each retry, respectively.
- **Polling invocation**: The polling invocation, being applied at the Event Source Mapping (ESM) and caller level, gives more flexibility to manage the retries. ESM provides a mechanism of backoff strategy at the integration level by letting the failed invocations be retried. The event source mapping does the retries behind any function failure from the source service. For streams, the retry mechanism considers the records until the record expiration reaches, the maximum age exceeds, or the maximum retry is reached. For SQS invocations, lambda will reduce the concurrency level during the retry; lambda tries till the max attempts are reached.
- **Software code invocation**: When the lambda function is invoked by a software code, the retry mechanism differs by the fact that the invocation was done by AWS SDK or from any other request libraries. In case of using a library

other than the AWS SDK, the requester must apply the corresponding retry mechanism and backoff strategy. However, when using AWS SDK, the retries are managed exponentially for service errors such as throttling, timeout, and so on. For function code-level errors, though, the retries need to be implemented.

Batch Items Bisections

The Bisect works for DynamoDB streams and Kinesis using **`BisectBatchOnFubctionFailure`** parameter of event source mapping. The event source mapping will manage the failures due to a single record and reduce the risk of repeated failures by dividing the batch consequently to give more chance to extract the poison pill from the batch of records.

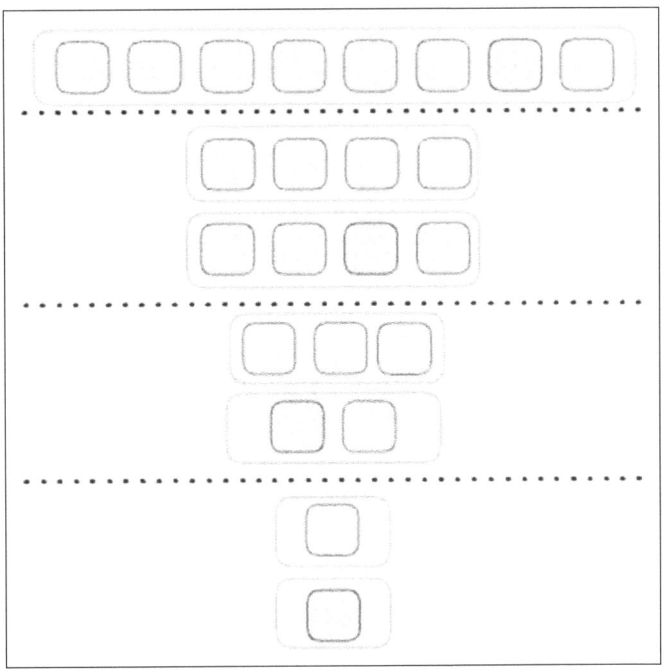

Figure 7.5: *Bisect on failure*

As a result, using bisect, there will be a risk of reprocessing the records, which can lead to a corrupted state on the consumer side.

Partial Batch Failure

The failures can happen when the event source mapping for poll-based invocation has a batching configuration. If any single record in a batch fails, this leads to the whole batch being retried. This can lead to a potential poison pill situation where a single record will introduce the whole batch being considered as failed. Using partial batch response, the event source mapping will keep track of the failed items and help to avoid reprocessing of successful events.

For Amazon SQS event source mapping, the **batchItemFailures** will make visible only the failed messages after visibility timeout reaches its end, which will make only the failed messages available for further invocations.

For DynamoDB Streams and Kinesis, partial batch failure will let the event source mapping change the track of the sequence number. The difference between Streams and SQS is that, for streams, the event source mapping will resend all records after the first failed records, which is theoretically acceptable as a stream is a batch of related and ordered records. As a recommendation, when writing code to process batch of related records, parallelism should be avoided. This recommendation also applies when implementing partial batch failures.

To implement partial batch response, the function handler must return in a predefined format as the following snippet:

```
{
 "batchItemFailures": [
        {
            "itemIdentifier": "<FAILED_ITEM_IDENTIFIER>"
        }
    ]
}
```

Dead Letter Queues (DLQ)

One of the risks in distributed systems is the loss of information, which can happen at any time or at any communication layer. Lambda provides a way of removing the data loss by applying a simple way to use a dead letter queue as a storage for failed requests. The way a dead letter queue can be applied and operates varies based on the invocation type.

If the invocation is an asynchronous invocation, the lambda **OnFailure** destination helps to move the failed events to a destination dead letter queue of type Amazon SNS or Amazon SQS. For polling invocation, the `**OnFailure**` destination can be configured for DynamoDb Streams, Amazon Kinesis, and Amazon MSK (Amazon Managed Streaming for Apache Kafka). For Amazon SQS event source mapping, the dead letter queue will be applied at the Queue level, as the lambda service keeps the source Queue informed by the success or failure of an event processing after retry attempts.

Dead Letter Queue for Polling Invocations

Configuring a DLQ for polling invocations can be applied at event source mapping configuration or source service configuration. The integration of the SQS service needs a DLQ to be configured at the SQS level, as illustrated in *Figure 7.7*:

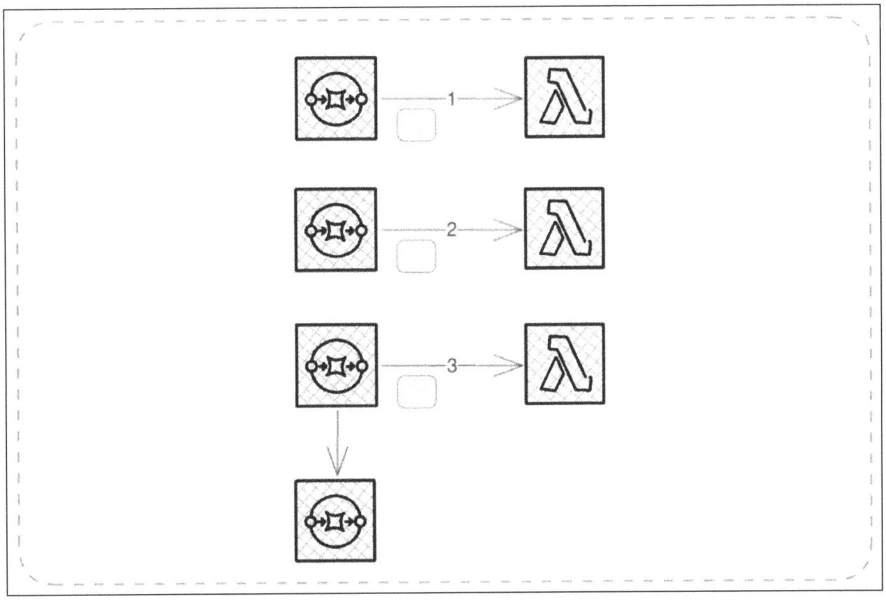

Figure 7.6: *SQS retry and dead letter queue*

For DynamoDb Streams and Kinesis integrations, the DLQ will be applied using Lambda Destinations. The destination can be applied in AWS CDK as Function `OnFailure` or Event Source Mapping `OnFailure` parameter; both approaches are illustrated in the following snippet of CDK:

```
import { NodejsFunction } from 'aws-cdk-lib/aws-lambda-nodejs';
import { Queue } from 'aws-cdk-lib/aws-sqs';
import { SqsDlq } from 'aws-cdk-lib/aws-lambda';
import { KinesisEventSource, StartingPosition } from 'aws-cdk-lib/
aws-lambda-event-sources';

// OnFailure using NodejsFunction construct:

new NodejsFunction(this, 'lambda-function', {
     ...
    onFailure: new SqsDlq(new Queue(this, 'lambda-function-dlq', {})),
    ...
});

// OnFailure using EventSourceMapping:

lambdaFunction.addEventSource(new KinesisEventSource(kinesisDataStream,
{
    startingPosition: StartingPosition.LATEST,
```

```
    enabled: true,
    onFailure: new SqsDlq(new Queue(this, 'lambda-function-dlq', {})),
    retryAttempts: 3
}));
```

Using both approaches will result in the same behavior and add an `**OnFailure**` lambda destination:

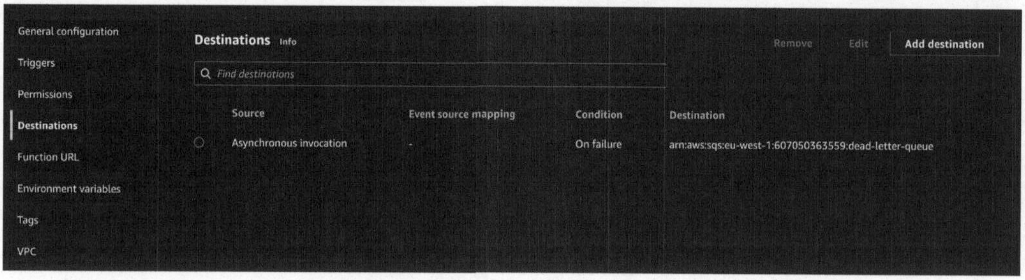

Figure 7.7: *Lambda destination for polling*

Dead Letter Queue for Asynchronous Invocations

For services that invoke the lambda asynchronously, the dead letter queue can be set up using Lambda Asynchronous Invocation configuration. The following AWS CDK snippet showcases how this can be applied:

```
new NodejsFunction(this, 'lambda-function', {
 ...
 deadLetterQueue: new Queue(this, 'lambda-function-dlq', {})
 ...
});
```

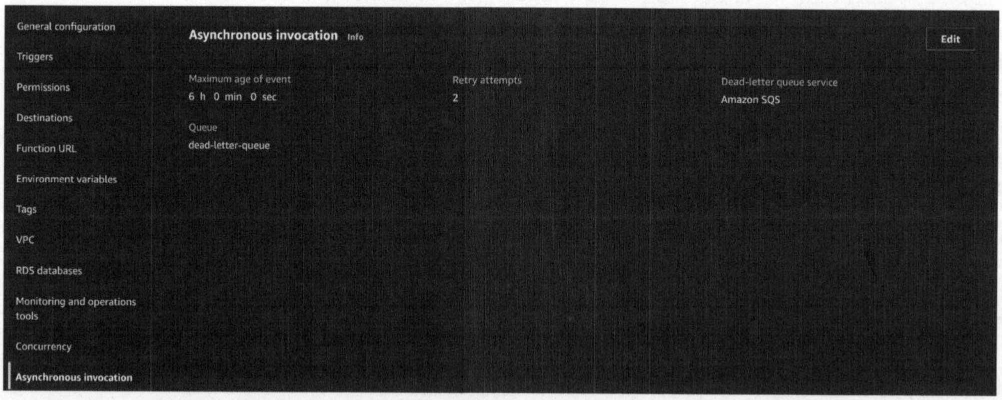

Figure 7.8: *Lambda asynchronous invocation SQS dead letter queue*

An SNS dead letter queue can also be applied using Asynchronous Invocation:

```
new NodejsFunction(this, 'lambda-function', {
     ...
     deadLetterTopic: new Topic(this, 'lambda-function-dlq', {})
     ...
});
```

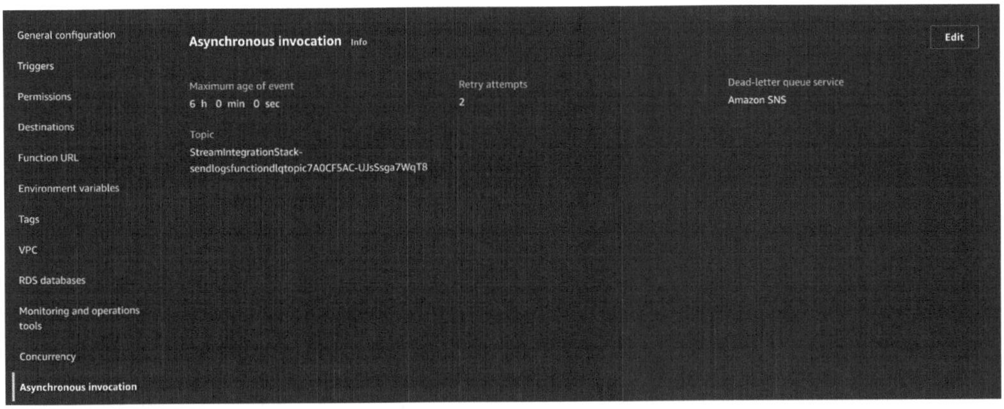

Figure 7.9: *Lambda asynchronous invocation SNS dead letter queue*

Lambda Destinations

Lambda destinations are a mechanism for applying the next steps of event processing in an event-driven fashion. Destinations can be applied in two situations, Success and Failure, to send the succeeded and failed events to the second queue or topic.

The Lambda destination can be applied for two kinds of invocations: Asynchronous or Polling. If applied for failures, any failed event after all configured retry attempts will be sent to the destination.

- **Asynchronous Invocation**: Lambda destination can be configured at function-level configuration and will be applied for all asynchronous invocations. The following snippet shows how to configure destinations using AWS CDK:

```
const lambdaFunction = new NodejsFunction(this, 'Asynchronous
InvocationFunction', {
     ...
     onFailure: new SqsDestination(new Queue(this, 'OnFailure-
Queue', {}))
     ...
});
```

The lambda handler receives the SNS event and directly throws an error. This failure leads to a retrying process, as per the default Lambda Asynchronous Invocation configuration:

```
export const handler = async(event: SNSEvent) => {
    throw new ItemNotFoundException();
};
```

Looking at lambda execution logs in CloudWatch, the exponential strategy can be shown by looking at platform report logs:

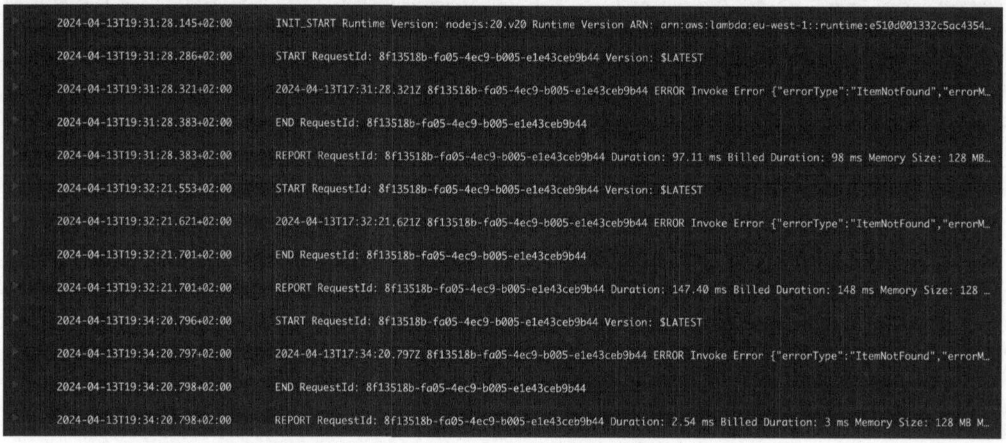

Figure 7.10: *Asynchronous invocation retry*

- **Polling Invocation:** When using DynamoDb/Kinesis streams, the destination can be applied at event source mapping. This way the lambda will avoid interacting with the stream for the shard iterator and will send the records directly to the failure destination after reaching the maximum retry attempts. The event source mapping can be applied using AWS CDK, as demonstrated in the following snippet:

```
import { KinesisEventSource, StartingPosition } from 'aws-cdk-lib/aws-lambda-event-sources';
import { SqsDlq } from 'aws-cdk-lib/aws-lambda';

lambdaFunction.addEventSource(new KinesisEventSource(kisnesis-Stream, {
        onFailure: new SqsDlq(deadLetterQueue),
         startingPosition: StartingPosition.TRIM_HORIZON,
   }));
```

It is important to consider the importance of retry attempts when using streams. By default, in case of failures, lambda will attempt the failed records until they reach the record expiration, which has a minimum of 24 hours (default) for streams. Using this above configuration results in retries lasting up to the stream retention period.

It is a best practice to configure a retry policy and also define the maximum age of records. The following configuration uses the **`MaxRecordAge`** configuration for event source mapping to help reduce the increase in shard iteration age; for demonstration, the batch size is configured by 1:

```
import { SqsDestination } from 'aws-cdk-lib/aws-lambda-destinations';

const deadLetterQueue = new Queue(this, 'DeadLetterQueue');

   lambdaFunction.addEventSource(new KinesisEventSource(kisnesisStream,
{
          onFailure: new SqsDestination(deadLetterQueue),
          startingPosition: StartingPosition.TRIM_HORIZON,
          batchSize: 1,
          maxRecordAge: cdk.Duration.minutes(1),
   }));
```

Setting the iteration age to 1 minute, the Lambda Poller will discard any failed records after 1 minute. With this configuration, when the lambda will retry, the records will be considered expired and will not be retried. *Figure* 7.11 shows that **`GetRecords`** was done for a single record sent to the Kinesis. This example ran an array of 118 records to the stream, and the **`GetRecords`** metric shows 118 calls:

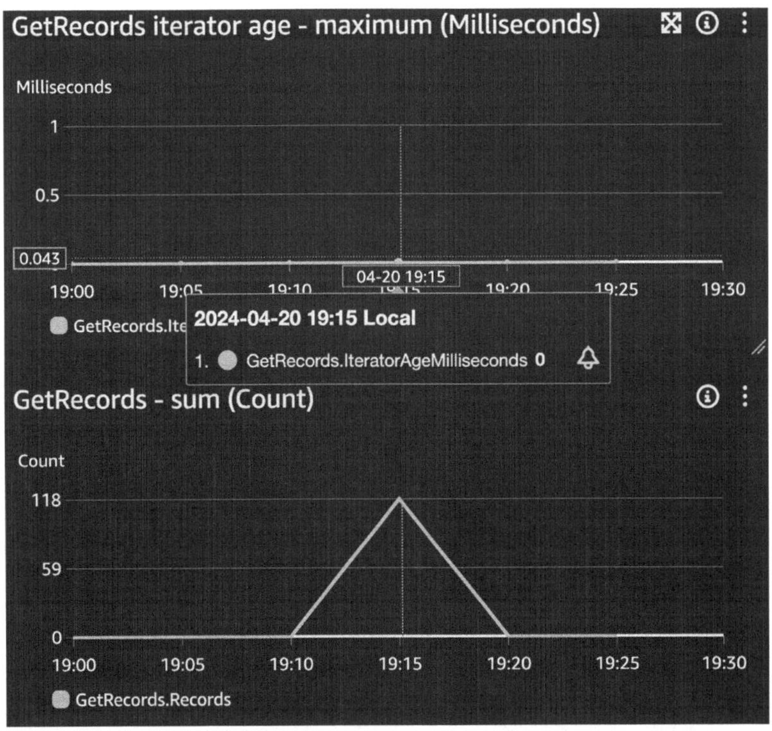

Figure 7.11: *Stream polling with max record age*

This configuration helps to get rid of any poison pill record, but at the same time, it leads to the loss of untreated records with the same age or close to the poison record. *Figure* 7.12 shows the invocation of a single record for 1 minute over 9 attempts. The mentioned record, alongside all other 117 records, was discarded after reaching the maximum record age limit and was presented in DLQ.

#	@timestamp	Records.0.kinesis.sequenceNumber	Records.0.kinesis.data
▶ 1	2024-04-20T19:17:10.0…	49651297481456749091612839373180173370384875376504471554	refvalue1key2value2key3value
▶ 2	2024-04-20T19:16:47.1…	49651297481456749091612839373180173370384875376504471554	refvalue1key2value2key3value
▶ 3	2024-04-20T19:16:31.3…	49651297481456749091612839373180173370384875376504471554	refvalue1key2value2key3value
▶ 4	2024-04-20T19:16:26.1…	49651297481456749091612839373180173370384875376504471554	refvalue1key2value2key3value
▶ 5	2024-04-20T19:16:23.0…	49651297481456749091612839373180173370384875376504471554	refvalue1key2value2key3value
▶ 6	2024-04-20T19:16:21.2…	49651297481456749091612839373180173370384875376504471554	refvalue1key2value2key3value
▶ 7	2024-04-20T19:16:20.5…	49651297481456749091612839373180173370384875376504471554	refvalue1key2value2key3value
▶ 8	2024-04-20T19:16:20.1…	49651297481456749091612839373180173370384875376504471554	refvalue1key2value2key3value
▶ 9	2024-04-20T19:16:19.8…	49651297481456749091612839373180173370384875376504471554	refvalue1key2value2key3value

Figure 7.12: *Max age reaches for close records*

To solve the above problem, the event source mapping can be configured with a defined number of retry attempts, allowing lambda to retry a limited number of times before placing the failed record in DLQ.

```
lambdaFunction.addEventSource(new KinesisEventSource(kisnesis-
Stream, {
 onFailure: new SqsDestination(deadLetterQueue),
 startingPosition: StartingPosition.TRIM_HORIZON,
 batchSize: 1,
 retryAttempts: 3,
 maxRecordAge: cdk.Duration.hours(1)
}));
```

This time the Lambda function will process all 118 records, but will only retry each failed record up to 3 times.

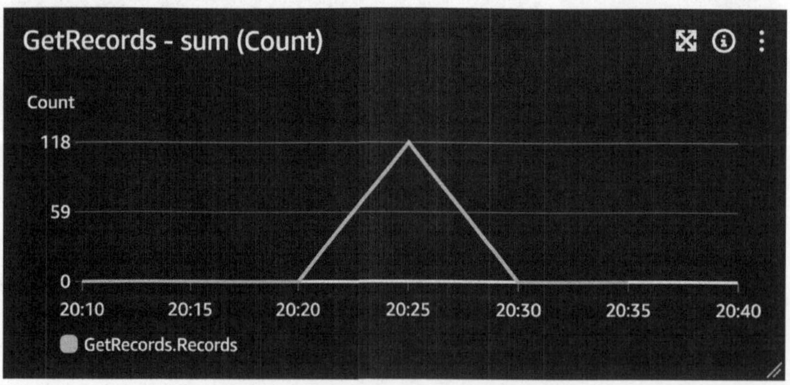

Figure 7.13: *Stream polling with configured retry attempts*

Using the max record age parameter helps to avoid introducing large backlogs. A reasonable `maxRecordAge` helps to avoid blocking the more recent records behind an inconvenient situation related to older records. In these cases, an effective operational approach is to keep those older records in a dead letter queue and treat them for a second time.

Lambda Resilience Metrics

As lambda integrates with a wide range of services based on the integration, the metrics to observe will vary. However, as part of resiliency when using AWS Lambda, it is crucial to look at the following metrics:

- **Concurrency**: The concurrency metric helps to understand the way a function behaves at a given time. This metric will be useful and will be a means of analysis in conjunction with the throttling metric.
- **Error Rate**: The rate of errors versus success can be a means to detect anomalies in function behavior.
- **Throttles**: This metric shows that your level of concurrency needs to reach the limit and no new execution environment can be initiated. The limit can be per function or per account.
- **Async Event Age**: This metric helps to observe the delay between event reception and queuing the event and the time that the function is invoked. An increase shows a processing issue that leads to the incapacity of function to treat the events fast enough.
- **Iterator Age**: This metric shows the time gap between the record original reception time in the source (for example, DynamoDB/Kinesis Stream) and the time the event source mapping invokes the function for that record. An increase shows a lack of processing power or a problem that prevents the records from being treated fast enough.

Conclusion

This chapter walked us through resilience and design for failure, which are among the most important pillars when designing serverless distributed systems. It highlighted key considerations when using AWS Lambda alongside the AWS serverless ecosystem and how to apply the concept of resilience software when using different integration patterns. Considering the note of '*Everything Fails all the Time*', the chapter covered various design and implementation details, including monitoring, error handling, retries, dead letter queue, and batch and streaming failure management.

The next chapter will focus on Lambda-Less Design while reducing the custom code needs through the use of AWS-managed services. The goal will be to introduce how low/no code software can be designed on AWS using managed service.

CHAPTER 8
Lambda-Less Design

Introduction

The chapter walks through the necessary use of lambda service and showcases scenarios where the use of direct integrations is more beneficial in terms of agility, maintainability, and quality. Knowing when the use of lambda service is beneficial is an important argument when integrating with the AWS ecosystem.

The chapter focuses on the definition of imperative and declarative transition and demonstrates, using concrete examples, how to implement a lambda-less design using direct integrations without adding complexity to the software.

We will illustrate the use of API Gateway direct integration, Step Functions optimized/ SDK service integration, and EventBridge Pipes with examples and important details to consider.

Structure

In this chapter, we will discuss the following topics:

- Lambda Role in Serverless
- Defining Integration Boundaries
- API Gateway Direct Integration
- Step Functions Service Integration
- EventBridge Pipes Integration

Lambda Role in Serverless

The software development approach is evolving, and the adoption of patterns like serverless has always been a step toward achieving higher levels of velocity, agility, and quality. However, in the serverless adoption journey, the learning curve, mindset, and complexity are some time-consuming concepts to tackle. Despite this, using lambda service as a core of software in the early adoption of serverless seems normal.

Before delving into 'Is *lambda a necessary part of design?*', it is fair enough to look at the problems that lambda functions solve. *Figure* 8.1 demonstrates a typical serverless solution:

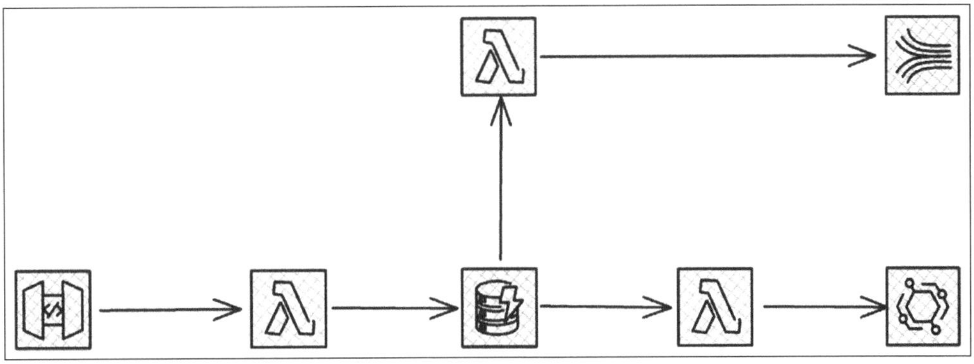

Figure 8.1: *Typical serverless design*

As demonstrated, lambda has a principal role in this design and handles the compute needs. The following list briefs the responsibilities of each function:

- Validating the request and saving an entity in a DynamoDB table.
- Receiving the DynamoDB stream record and sending an event in the EventBridge bus.
- Receiving the DynamoDB stream record and sending records to the Kinesis Data Stream.

Looking at the preceding list, the only crucial part is request validation. This is evident that often in serverless and event-driven designs, a significant number of functions do just transition of objects without doing a real processing.

Imperative Transition

In event-driven design, a transition can be called imperative when that transition is related to a software logical decision and applies some sort of enrichment or processing. In this case, the choice of compute services will be to manage the software decision complexity, giving the processing power and transition flow flexibility. This approach was mandatory when the software was communicating over some synchronous standard protocols. The event producer decides how and where the events are sent.

The following example demonstrates a piece of software code that applies the imperative transition based on logical decisions:

```
type Command = { type: string; timestamp: number; details: any;};
type EventType = 'normal' | 'vip' | 'gold';
type BaseEvent = { id: string; type: EventType; timestamp: number;
promotRate: number; };
```

```
type NormalEvent = BaseEvent & { type: "normal" };
type VipEvent = BaseEvent & { type: 'vip'; accumulatedPoints: number;
endOfValidation: number; };
type GoldEvent = BaseEvent & { type: 'gold'; body: string; accumulated-
Points: number; };

interface IService {
 process: (command: Command) => Promise<BaseEvent>;
}
interface IEventPublisher {
 publish: (event: BaseEvent) => Promise<void>;
}

const normalService: IService;
const vipService: IService;
const goldService: IService;
const eventPublisher: IEventPublisher;

export const handler = async (event: SQSEvent) => {
 console.log('Received event:', JSON.stringify(event, null, 2));
 for (const record of event.Records) {
   let BaseEvent: BaseEvent;
   const command = JSON.parse(record.body) as Command;

   switch (command.type) {
     case 'normal':
       BaseEvent = await normalService.process(command);
       break;
     case 'vip':
       BaseEvent = await vipService.process(command);
       break;
     case 'gold':
       BaseEvent = await goldService.process(command);
       break;
     default:
       throw new Error(`Unknown event type: ${command.type}`);
   }

   await eventPublisher.publish(event);
 }
}
```

Declarative Transition

A declarative transition is when a simple, human-readable, and easy-to-set-up processing can be achieved without writing code. These are often some kind of declarations and YAML or JSON configurations. Declarative setup is easier and simpler to maintain and evolve, as it can be read by any visualizer and interpreted in a standard and simple way. However, it may not be the best fit when dealing with sophisticated and business-oriented software decisions. In these situations, a move toward the declarative transition will increase the complexity and bring technical debt.

The following example demonstrates a declarative transition approach. This example produces the same results with a difference that the processing is done beforehand and the processing results are persisted in a **`stateStore`**:

```
type Command = { type: string; timestamp: number; details: any;};
type EventType = 'normal' | 'vip' | 'gold';
type BaseEvent = { id: string; type: EventType; timestamp: number;
promotRate: number; };

interface IService {
 getState: (command: Command) => Promise<BaseEvent>;
}

interface IEventPublisher { publish: (event: BaseEvent, topicName:
string) => Promise<void>; }

const stateService: IService;
const eventPublisher: IEventPublisher;

export const handler = async (event: SQSEvent) => {
 console.log('Received event:', JSON.stringify(event, null, 2));
 for (const record of event.Records) {
   let event: BaseEvent;
   const command = JSON.parse(record.body) as Command;

   eventState = await stateService.getState(command);

   let topicName: string;
   if (eventState.type === 'normal')
     topicName = 'normal-topic';
   else if (eventState.type === 'vip')
     topicName = 'vip-topic';
   else if (eventState.type === 'gold')
     topicName = 'gold-topic';
   else
     throw new Error('Invalid event type');

   await eventPublisher.publish(eventState, topicName);
 }
}
```

Declarative Transition No Code Approach

Looking at the above example representing the declarative transition, the TypeScript code brings no value and can be done using any no/low code approach. On AWS, we can apply a no-code approach for this example using choreography or orchestration.

The choreography approach can be applied using a Filter and Pipes pattern, as illustrated in *Figure 8.2*:

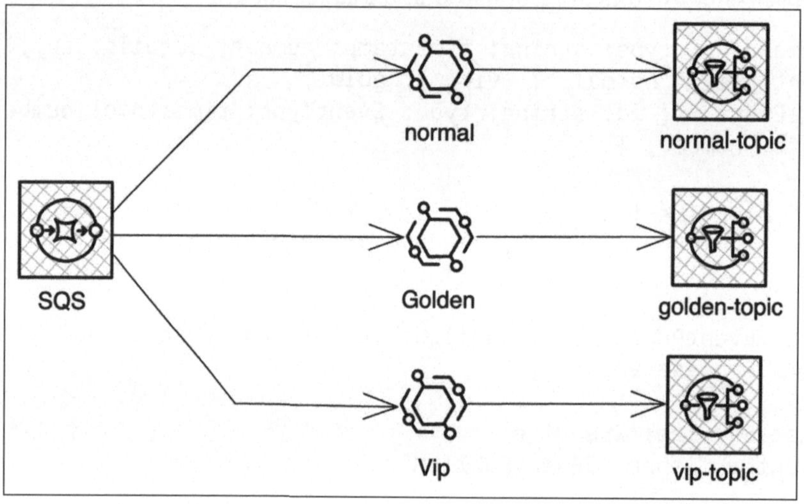

Figure 8.2: *Declarative transition using choreography*

The choreography approach is ideal when there is no overall state shared between the distributed events. It means the event's transition failure, success, or latency, being normal, golden, or VIP, has no impact on the other types of business results. Knowing when the processing layers are fully isolated or not is an important element when deciding if choreography is the best fit or not.

In some cases, the unique transitions don't introduce a state coupling, but the overall result needs a correlated state of multiple transitions. In this case, the orchestration can be a better choice, as illustrated in *Figure 8.3*:

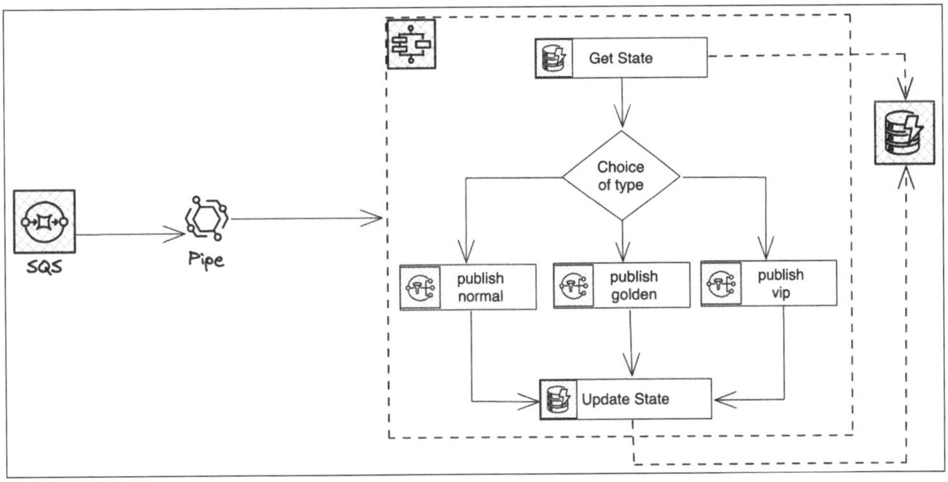

Figure 8.3: *Declarative transition using orchestration*

Defining Integration Boundaries

Applying No/Low Code in design requires a good understanding of the software and how the requirements must be applied. The first step toward these decisions is to define the boundaries at those integration levels. One efficient approach is to look inside any gray box encapsulating some complexities and consider how those complexities can be simplified for application using other No/Low code approaches.

Figure 8.4 demonstrates a design where a command reaching the service will be processed and an event will be distributed:

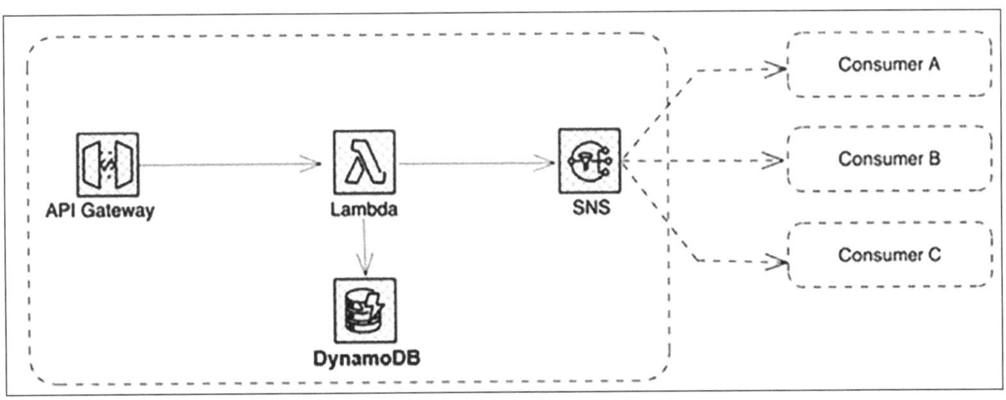

Figure 8.4: *Apply boundaries definition*

First, we need to look at lambda and the responsibilities it has:

- Lambda validates the request
- A verification based on data in the DynamoDB table

- Updating or inserting data with new Status in **DynamoDB**
- Publishing an event representing the change

The Considerations to take into account while applying integration:

- What service requester needs is an identifiable response or just the success of reception?
- How to guarantee the transactional concurrency?
- How to avoid a two-phase commit?

As a result, in the best case, if the requester is only interested about the success, the final solution will be as illustrated in *Figure* 8.5:

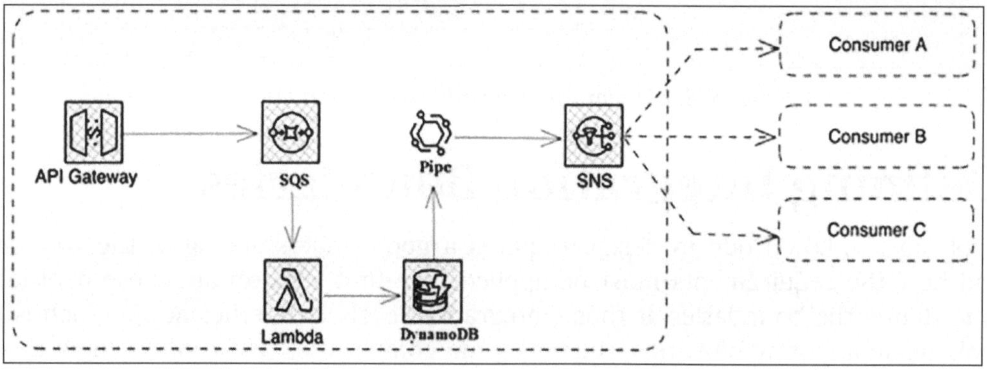

***Figure* 8.5:** *Simplifying boundaries and integration definitions*

The design has applied multiple levels of direct service integration. First, API Gateway direct integration with SQS. The lambda validates and writes the final state in DynamoDB. The EventBridge pipe integrates with DynamoDB Streams and publishes events to the SNS topic.

Direct Integration Considerations

When deciding to use direct integration, it is worth looking at the runtime requirements and how an overall process needs to be treated. These are sort of detailed elements that can be critical for any significant reason, including operational, performance, cost, or resiliency.

The following list includes some considerations that are often discussed:

- Batching
- Parallelism
- Error Handling
- Ordering
- Consistency

Batching

Batching often is applied to avoid having a stale state and also serves as a technique to reduce the costs of compute resources. Batching can be applied when using EventBridge pipes when the source service supports the batching. Also, Step Functions support batching to control concurrency when using the Map state.

Parallelism

Parallelism was often achieved using compute resources like Lambda to improve the overall processing performance or fetching data, This is achievable using the Step Function using Standard Map to have a low-level concurrency or distributed map to achieve a higher level of parallelism.

Error Handling

Both Step Functions and EventBridge pipes have the error handling and retry mechanism and can redirect the untreatable events to a DLQ. For API Gateway, the responsibility of retry and error handling will be the responsibility of the requester.

Ordering

When ordering is an important consideration, the use of EventBridge pipes brings a level of insurance if the source service supports the ordering, such as Kinesis or DynamoDB Streams. The pipes treat the events or batch of events in the order they arrive if the source service tracks the order of events.

Consistency

Consistency, being a constraint, is always eventually maintained in distributed systems, but strong consistency can be also achieved when using Step Functions by applying the state control and rollback in case of potential failures in the workflow. EventBridge pipes can also guarantee consistency by treating events as explained in the ordering section, but that consistency is only achievable as per the isolation level or partitioning that the source service applies.

Direct Service Integrations

Direct service integration helps to use a configuration-first approach to streamline two services without custom code. This approach will help reduce the cost of computing, development, and maintenance. When using lambda to transit data, events, and streams between services, usually, the software code uses the AWS SDK or some sort of packages that help achieve the goal of integration. However, even though these are versioned and well-documented libraries, the End of Life (EOL) can be applicable at any time. Here, the constraint is not runtime problems but rather the effort of migration and keeping track of potential upgrades.

When using direct service integrations, AWS applies the required effort of implementation and testing, providing customers with a managed integration feature to let them streamline their integration requirements. The effort of writing code for integration can also be measured by the knowledge that any single team must invest to achieve per service, which is not always required for all scenarios.

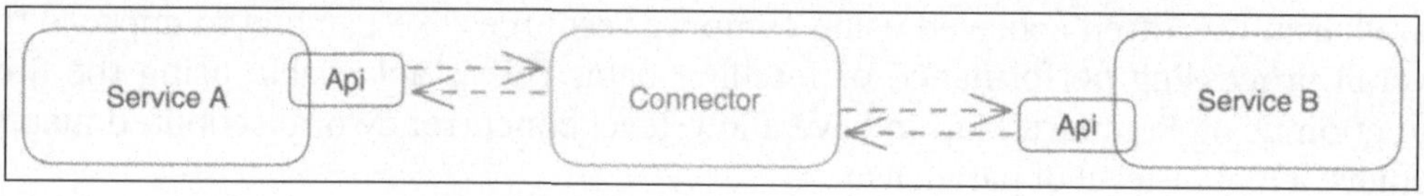

Figure 8.6: *High-level service integration*

The connector knows all source and target service APIs and provides some declarative mechanisms to configure the overall integration. These configurations are often Retry Attempts, Failure behavior, Filtering, Batching, Ordering, Wait Time, and more. As the number of eventual source services increases, applying these integrations using lambda can become frustrating and needs a lot of integration testing to approve the quality of software code. Another important consideration with integrations is latency; the direct integration has a reduced latency of 2-digit milliseconds compared to code-based integration.

Direct Integration Under the Hood

Direct integration in serverless architectures on AWS typically involves one AWS service directly invoking another service's API or triggering events without the need for an intermediary service. Here is how it works under the hood:

- **Service Communication**: Let's say two AWS services, Service A and Service B, need to communicate directly. Service A needs to call an API endpoint or trigger an event in Service B.
- **IAM Roles and Policies**: Each AWS service operates within the context of an IAM (Identity and Access Management) role with specific permissions. To enable direct integration, you need to define IAM roles and policies that allow the calling service (Service A) to invoke actions in the target service (Service B).
- **IAM Permissions**: You configure IAM policies to grant the necessary permissions to Service A. These permissions typically include actions such as `` `InvokeFunction` `` for AWS Lambda functions or `` `PutItem` `` for Amazon DynamoDB tables. These policies specify the resources that Service A can access in Service B.

- **Authentication and Authorization**: Depending on the security requirements, you might need to implement authentication and authorization mechanisms to ensure that only authorized requests are allowed to invoke the target service. This could involve using AWS IAM roles, API Gateway API keys, or custom authentication mechanisms.
- **Invocation**: Once the IAM roles and permissions are configured, Service A can directly invoke Service B by making API requests (for example, HTTP requests for RESTful APIs) or triggering events (for example, invoking lambda functions asynchronously or putting messages into an Amazon SQS queue).
- **Error Handling and Retry Mechanisms**: Implement error handling and retry mechanisms to handle failures gracefully. This might involve configuring exponential backoff and retry strategies to handle transient errors or implementing dead letter queues for asynchronous invocations.
- **Monitoring and Logging**: Implement monitoring and logging to track the performance and health of the direct integration. AWS services like CloudWatch can be used to monitor metrics, set alarms, and collect logs for debugging and analysis.
- **Scaling and Performance**: Direct integration allows for efficient communication between services, often resulting in low latency and high throughput. However, it's essential to monitor performance metrics and scale resources appropriately to handle varying workloads.

Direct and Indirect Integrations

Defining integration boundaries involves determining whether to directly integrate services or not based on the application's requirements, scalability needs, and cost considerations.

Some considerations to help make the best decision are as follows:

- **Understanding Requirements**: Start by understanding the requirements. What services does it need to interact with? What data needs to be exchanged between these services?
- **Evaluate Integration Options and Analyze Trade-offs**: AWS offers various integration options, including direct service integration and using intermediary services like AWS Lambda. Evaluate options based on factors such as performance, latency, scalability, ease of maintenance, cost, complexity, and maintenance overhead.
- **Prototype and Test**: Prototype different integration approaches and test them to evaluate their performance, scalability, and cost-effectiveness under realistic conditions.
- **Monitor and Iterate**: Continuously monitor your application's performance

and cost metrics after deployment. Iterate your integration strategy based on real-world usage patterns and feedback.

- **Document Decisions**: Direct integrations being a nice and clean approach can lead to adoption without considering trade-offs. Documenting your integration decisions, rationale, and any trade-offs can ensure clarity of that decision, help other future decisions, and be useful as a reference.
- **Consider Direct Service Integration**: Direct service integration involves allowing one AWS service to directly invoke another service's API or trigger events. This can be suitable for tightly coupled services where low latency and high throughput are crucial. Evaluate the following when considering direct integration:
    - **Latency**: Direct integration can minimize latency as there are no intermediary services involved.
    - **Cost**: Direct integration might be cost-effective for small-scale applications with predictable workloads.
    - **Complexity**: It might simplify your architecture and reduce complexity by eliminating the need for intermediary services.
- **Assess Indirect Integration**: Indirect integration involves using intermediary services, such as Amazon API Gateway, AWS Lambda, or Amazon SQS, to decouple services and handle communication. Consider the following when assessing indirect integration:
    - **Scalability**: Indirect integration can improve scalability by decoupling services and allowing them to scale independently.
    - **Flexibility**: It offers flexibility to add authentication, authorization, caching, and transformation logic.
    - **Cost Optimization**: Indirect integration might be more cost-effective for large-scale applications with varying workloads, as it allows you to optimize resource usage and scale based on demand.

API Gateway Direct Integration

API Gateway provides direct integration with other AWS services, such as SQS, DynamoDB, and so on. This mechanism removes the need to use lambda functions for transmitting data that does not include any business logic.

Direct integrations bring the following advantages:

- Removing unnecessary computing resources, such as lambda, reduces the cost of maintenance.
- Using direct integrations reduces the number of network hops, which in turn reduces overall latency.

- Direct integrations are tested and validated by AWS, so this removes the need for testing.
- Keeping SDK and API versions up to date needs effort and vigilance when using lambda functions, but using direct integration, this is handed over to AWS, simplifying the software.

Integration with DynamoDB

The following figure shows a typical serverless ingestion API:

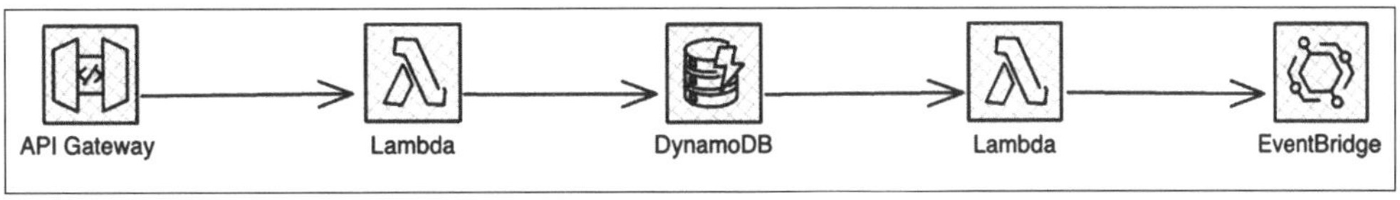

Figure 8.7: *API Gateway serverless API using lambda*

If there is no business logic in the lambda functions, the design can be done using direct integrations, as represented in *Figure* 8.8. The change will improve the latency and also remove the need to maintain code.

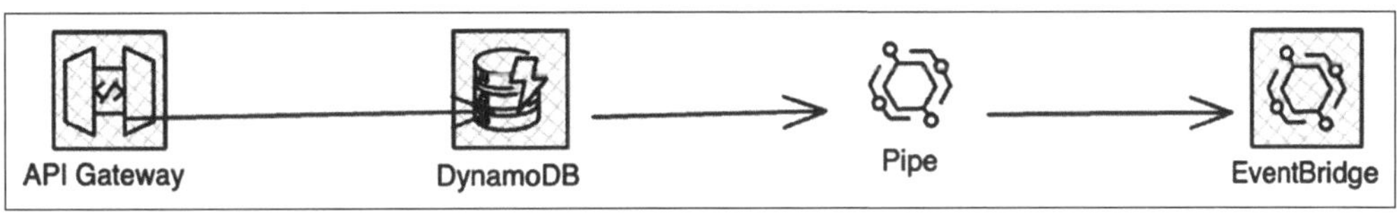

Figure 8.8: *API Gateway serverless API direct integration*

The direct integration with DynamoDB can be implemented using AWS CDK `**AwsIntegration**` construct as follows:

```
props?.table.grantWriteData(props.integrationRole);

const response = {
 statusCode: '200',
 responseTemplates: {
   'application/json': `{
     "requestId": "$context.requestId"
   }`,
 },
}
const errorResponse = {
  statusCode: "500",
  selectionPattern: "5\\d{2}", // Match 5xx responses
  responseTemplates: {
      'application/json': `{
      "status": "error",
      "message": "An error occurred."
```

```
    }`,
  },
}
const options = {
 credentialsRole: props.integrationRole,
 integrationResponses: [ response, errorResponse ],
 requestTemplates: {
 'application/json': `{
   "Item": {
     "PK": {
        "S": "$context.requestId"
     },
     "SK": {
        "S": "$input.path('$.Id')"
     },
     "Name": {
        "S": "$input.path('$.Name')"
     }
   },
   "TableName": "${props?.table.tableName}"
   }`
 },
} satisfies IntegrationOptions;

this.integration = new AwsIntegration({
 action: 'PutItem',
 options: options,
 service: 'dynamodb',
});
```

Deploying the provided example in `**C08/apigatway-ddb-direct-integration**`, the DynamoDB direct integration uses the **application/json** content type, and the request payload has to be passed in JSON format. The integration needs service and action names to map the integration to the corresponding service and action, DynamoDB and PutItem.

AWS documentation provides details and has a dedicated API reference section for all services:

```
curl --location '<API_GATWAY_STAGE_ENDPOINT>/ddb' \
--header 'Content-Type: application/json' \
--data '{
   "Name": "Omid",
   "Id": "986bc4cb-b621-4db8-b2ca-f201b7e3c5b3"
}' -o /dev/null -s -w 'Total: %{time_total}s\n'
```

The request latency of 70-100 milliseconds is much lower compared to a Node.js lambda function acting as a proxy behind the API Gateway.

API Gateway also integrates with other AWS services, such as Step Functions, SQS, SNS, Kinesis, and EventBridge.

Integration with SQS

The SQS direct integration and the configuration is simpler than integrating with DynamoDB or kinesis, as the template mapping can be done by transmitting the request body as SQS message body. The only difference compared to DynamoDB integration is the consistent latency; SQS occasionally introduces higher latencies around 300 milliseconds, but often the latency is consistent as 50-90 milliseconds.

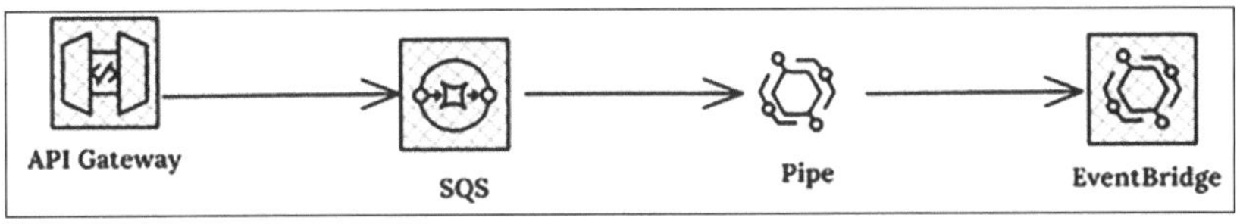

***Figure 8.9**: API Gateway direct integration with SQS*

The integration using CDK can be done as shown in the following code snippet:

```
props?.queue.grantSendMessages(props.integrationRole);

const response = {
     statusCode: "200",
     responseTemplates: {
            'application/json': `{
                   "requestId": "$context.requestId"
            }`,
       },
}  satisfies  IntegrationResponse;

const integrationOptions  = {
     credentialsRole: props.integrationRole,
     passthroughBehavior: PassthroughBehavior.NEVER,
     requestParameters: {"integration.request.header.Content-Type":
"'application/x-www-form-urlencoded'"},
     requestTemplates: { "application/json": `Action=SendMessage&
MessageBody=$util.urlEncode($input.body)` },
     integrationResponses: [response],
} satisfies IntegrationOptions;

this.integration = new AwsIntegration({
     service: "sqs",
     path: `${Stack.of(this).account}/${props.queue.queueName}`,
     integrationHttpMethod: "POST",
     options: integrationOptions,
});
```

The SQS API queue identifier here passed a path parameter in the form of **<AccountID>/<QueueName>**. The request template is much simpler as it provides a simple mapping between the request body and message body of SQS, **`Action=SendMessage&MessageBody=$util.urlEncode($input.body)`**. It is important to note that the content type used for SQS integration is **`x-www-form-urlencoded`**. In this example, the AWS query protocol is used, but the Amazon SQS API also supports JSON integration using the AWS JSON protocol (the content type must be **`application/x-amz-json-1.0`**).

Integration with SNS

Amazon SNS also integrates with API Gateway using direct integration. Again using the AWS CDK **`AwsIntegration`** construct simplifies configuring the integration. The following snippet demonstrates the usage. Amazon SNS also provided a consistent latency of 50-90 milliseconds, with a higher latency during tests around 125 milliseconds that will occur occasionally.

```
props?.topic.grantPublish(props.integrationRole);

const response = {
    statusCode: "200",
    responseTemplates: {
       'application/json': `{
             "requestId": "$context.requestId"
       }`
     }
} satisfies IntegrationResponse;

const integrationOptions = {
     credentialsRole: props.integrationRole,
     passthroughBehavior: PassthroughBehavior.NEVER,
     integrationResponses: [response],
     requestParameters: { 'integration.request.header.Content-Type':
x_www_form_urlencoded },
     requestTemplates: { 'application/json': `TopicArn=$util.url
Encode(\'${props?.topic.topicArn}\')&&Message=$util.urlEncode($input.
body)` },
} satisfies IntegrationOptions;

this.integration = new AwsIntegration({
     service: 'sns',
     action: 'Publish',
     integrationHttpMethod: 'POST',
     options: integrationOptions
});
```

The Topic will be identified using encoded **TopicArn** as part of the request template. The request template is simple such as was demonstrated for SQS and provides a mapping between request body and message body such as **TopicArn=$util.urlEncode(\'${props?.topic.topicArn}\')&&Message=$util.urlEncode($input.body)**. Amazon SNS supports only AWS query protocol, so the **x-www-form-urlencoded** content type will be used.

Integration with EventBridge

EventBridge being a core event-driven service in the AWS ecosystem also integrates directly with the API Gateway and provides a simple integration and a consistent latency of less than 100 milliseconds, The EventBridge integration can be initiated as demonstrated in the following snippet:

```
props.eventBus.grantPutEventsTo(props.integrationRole);

const response = {
    statusCode: '200',
    responseTemplates: {
      'application/json': JSON.stringify({
          id: "$input.path('$.Entries[0].EventId')",
      }),
    },
} satisfies IntegrationResponse;

const options = {
    credentialsRole: props.integrationRole,
    passthroughBehavior: PassthroughBehavior.NEVER,
    integrationResponses: [response],
    requestTemplates: {
      'application/json': `
          #set($context.requestOverride.header.X-Amz-Target
="AWSEvents.PutEvents")
          #set($context.requestOverride.header.Content-Type
="application/x-amz-json-1.1")
      ${JSON.stringify({
        Entries: [
          {
            DetailType: 'putEvent',
            Detail: "$util.escapeJavaScript($input.json('$'))",
            Source: 'async-eventbridge-api',
            EventBusName: props.eventBus.eventBusArn,
          },
        ],
      })}
    `,
```

```
  },
} satisfies IntegrationOptions;

this.integration = new AwsIntegration({
   service: 'events',
   action: 'PutEvents',
   integrationHttpMethod: 'POST',
   options: options
});
```

Some services need some headers, and EventBridge is one of them. It asks to give the operation as part of headers. Using the request template mapping, the headers can be set as done in the example using `` `#set($context.requestOverride.header.X-Amz-Target ="AWSEvents.PutEvents")` ``. The two headers, `` `X-Amz-Target` `` and `` `Content-Type` ``, are required for a successful integration; if not provided, no event will be sent to the EventBridge bus.

Integration with StepFunctions

In scenarios, it can be useful to start Step Functions execution to run an orchestrated workflow via an HTTP request. API Gateway direct integration helps achieve this by simple integration, as demonstrated in the following snippet:

```
props.statemachine.grantStartExecution(props.integrationRole);

const response = {
   statusCode: "200",
   responseTemplates: {
     'application/json': `{
       "requestId": "$context.requestId"
     }`
   }
 } satisfies IntegrationResponse;

const options = {
   credentialsRole: props.integrationRole,
   integrationResponses: [response ],
   requestTemplates: {
       "application/json": `{
           "input": "{}", "stateMachineArn": "${props.statemachine.
stateMachineArn}"
       }`,
   },
} satisfies IntegrationOptions;

this.integration = new AwsIntegration({
   service: "states",
```

```
    action: "StartExecution",
    integrationHttpMethod: "POST",
    options: options
});
```

The Step Functions integration latency varies between 100 and 200 milliseconds, but occasionally, more than 200 milliseconds latencies can be encountered. In this example, the state machine has a single lightweight pass step.

API Gateway Request and Response Template Mapping

API Gateway template mapping uses the Velocity Template Language (VTL) syntax to manipulate the whole HTTP request by using or overriding different parts such as Headers, Query String, Path and body, and HTTP status codes. The documentation provides enough details about the possibilities and details of each part. The Velocity Template Language (VTL) reference can be the first reference to discover how VTL works.

VTL and template mapping being a powerful feature need to be used with caution. To avoid producing maintainability in APIs, avoiding to include the business logic and business-oriented decisions is a best practice. When dealing with these kinds of logic, Lambda Service is a better choice.

Step Functions Direct Integration

AWS Step Functions provides a smooth and simple way of interacting with other AWS services, with less complexity for request mapping compared to API Gateway. AWS Step Functions supports different types of integration, such as Service Integration (using SDK) or Optimized Integration (using Tasks).

Optimized Integration

Optimized integrations provide an efficient way of integrating with a range of AWS services, such as SQS, SNS, APIGateway, Bedrock, Lambda, and more. The integration pattern supported can vary per service. AWS Step Functions support three integration patterns: Request/Response, sync, and callback.

Request/Response Pattern

Request/Response integration pattern provides a basic integration by requesting the AWS service and waiting for a response before following the rest of the workflow. This is the default and is supported for all services covered by the optimized integration type. The request-response integration is ideal when the workflow needs immediate results to process the rest of the workflow.

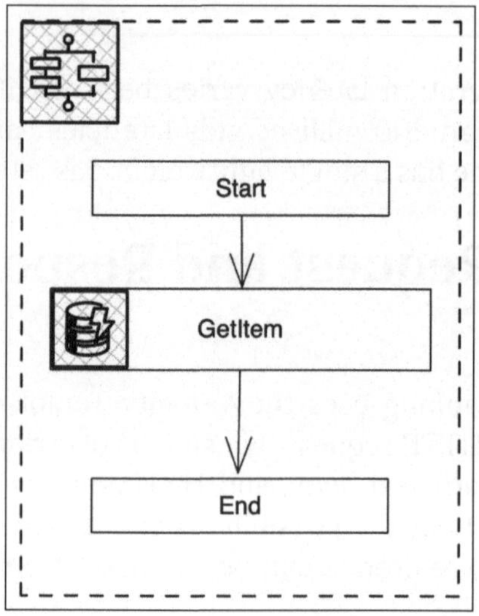

Figure 8.10: *Step Functions optimized integration with DynamoDB*

The following snippet shows a simple optimized integration to get an Item from DynamoDB. It uses the `Id` in state machine input and gets an item from DynamoDB. The integration also provides lower latency than using the AWS Lambda service, as demonstrated later.

```
const stateDefinition = new DynamoGetItem(this, 'Get Item', {
        table: props.Table,
        key: { 'PK': DynamoAttributeValue.fromString(JsonPath.
stringAt('$.Id')) },
});
const stateMachine = new StateMachine(this, 'ItemStateMachine', {
        stateMachineName: 'item-state-machine',
        definitionBody: DefinitionBody.fromChainable(stateDefinition)
});
```

Running the execution by providing the following input will introduce a 2-digit millisecond latency:

```
{
    "Id": "<ARBITARY_ID>"
}
```

As shown in *Figure* 8.11, the **getItem** latency is 72 milliseconds (**00:00:00.110 - 00:00:00.182**):

ID	Type	Step	Resource	Started After	Timestamp
▶ 1	ExecutionStarted			0	May 31, 2024, 20:12:52.429 (UTC+02:00)
▶ 2	TaskStateEntered	Get Item		00:00:00.036	May 31, 2024, 20:12:52.465 (UTC+02:00)
▶ 3	TaskScheduled	Get Item	dynamodb:getItem	00:00:00.036	May 31, 2024, 20:12:52.465 (UTC+02:00)
▶ 4	TaskStarted	Get Item	dynamodb:getItem	00:00:00.110	May 31, 2024, 20:12:52.539 (UTC+02:00)
▶ 5	TaskSucceeded	Get Item	dynamodb:getItem	00:00:00.182	May 31, 2024, 20:12:52.611 (UTC+02:00)
▶ 6	TaskStateExited	Get Item		00:00:00.227	May 31, 2024, 20:12:52.656 (UTC+02:00)
▶ 7	ExecutionSucceeded			00:00:00.270	May 31, 2024, 20:12:52.699 (UTC+02:00)

Figure 8.11: *DynamoDB optimized integration execution results*

Sync Pattern

Sync integration pattern is the second pattern supported by AWS Step Functions that is useful in scenarios when the workflow needs to wait for long-running jobs, such as AWS Batch, where the workflow will keep track of job results before moving on to the next step.

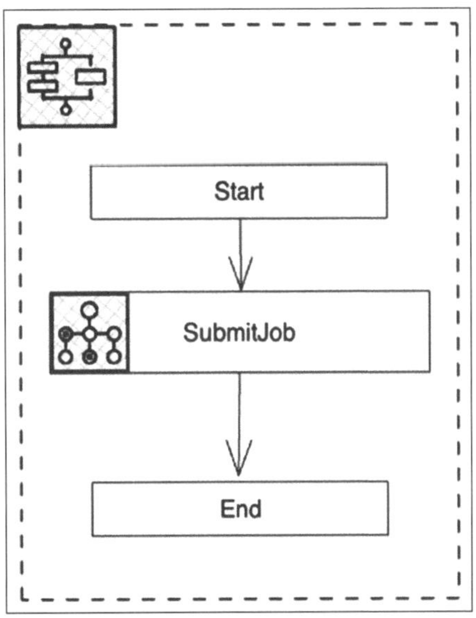

Figure 8.12: *Step Functions optimized integration with AWS Batch Job*

The following example illustrates an integration with AWS Batch Job using a sync pattern:

```
const stateDefinition =  new BatchSubmitJob(this, 'Submit Batch Job', {
      jobDefinitionArn: props.JobDefinition.jobDefinitionArn,
      jobName: JsonPath.stringAt('$.Id'),
      jobQueueArn: props.JobQueue.jobQueueArn,
});

const stateMachine = new StateMachine(this, 'ItemStateMachine', {
```

```
    stateMachineName: 'item-state-machine',
    definitionBody: DefinitionBody.fromChainable(stateDefinition)
});
```

The Project example creates a simple AWS Batch Job using AWS CDK. The environment is configured in a Public VPC subnet just for ease of demonstration and provides a public IP address to the job.

```
const vpc = new Vpc(this, "vpc-sfn-integration", {
     ipAddresses: IpAddresses.cidr("10.0.0.0/24"),
     natGateways: 0,
     subnetConfiguration: [
       { name: "public-subnet", subnetType: SubnetType.PUBLIC},
     ],
   });

   const computeEnvironment = new FargateComputeEnvironment(this,
'ComputeEnv', {
        vpc,
        vpcSubnets: { subnets: vpc.selectSubnets({ subnetType: Subnet-
Type.PUBLIC }).subnets },
        platformVersion: FargatePlatformVersion.LATEST,
   });

   this.JobQueue = new JobQueue(this, 'JobQueue', {
        priority: 1,
        computeEnvironments: [ { computeEnvironment, order: 1 } ],
   });

   this.JobDefinition = new EcsJobDefinition(this, 'MyJob', {
        container: new EcsFargateContainerDefinition(this, 'Container', {
         image: ContainerImage.fromAsset("src"),
         memory: Size.mebibytes(512),
         cpu: Cpu.millis(256),
         assignPublicIp: true,
     }),
   });
```

Starting a new execution will result in the Fargate Batch Job and will be Succeeded if the Job execution is successful.

ID	Type	Step	Resource	Started After	Timestamp
▶ 1	ExecutionStarted			0	Jun 1, 2024, 16:45:16.501 (UTC+02:00)
▶ 2	TaskStateEntered	Submit Batch Job		00:00:00.034	Jun 1, 2024, 16:45:16.535 (UTC+02:00)
▶ 3	TaskScheduled	Submit Batch Job		00:00:00.034	Jun 1, 2024, 16:45:16.535 (UTC+02:00)
▶ 4	TaskStarted	Submit Batch Job		00:00:00.090	Jun 1, 2024, 16:45:16.591 (UTC+02:00)
▶ 5	TaskSubmitted	Submit Batch Job	Batch job	00:00:00.210	Jun 1, 2024, 16:45:16.711 (UTC+02:00)
▶ 6	TaskSucceeded	Submit Batch Job	Batch job	00:00:43.712	Jun 1, 2024, 16:46:00.213 (UTC+02:00)
▶ 7	TaskStateExited	Submit Batch Job		00:00:43.736	Jun 1, 2024, 16:46:00.237 (UTC+02:00)
▶ 8	ExecutionSucceeded			00:00:43.779	Jun 1, 2024, 16:46:00.280 (UTC+02:00)

Figure 8.13: *AWS Batch Job optimized integration execution results*

Callback Pattern

In scenarios requiring deferred action, the callback pattern offers an efficient method for managing workflow execution without unpredictable wait times or lengthy iterative checks. This pattern pauses the workflow, waiting for a provided token to be received before resuming. The task can be discontinued based on a configured `**timeout**` or `**heartbeat**`. Using `**SendTaskSuccess**` and `**SendTaskFailure**`, the processing results can be communicated back to the State Machine.

Timeouts help prevent stale executions; for example, if a state machine pauses for a maximum of 1 hour, 1 day, or 1 month, it will time out after that period. However, sometimes a timeout alone isn't sufficient. In such cases, a long-running event processor can periodically inform the execution, helping the state machine decide to wait longer for a response and ensuring the process doesn't get stuck. This is where the Heartbeat comes in. Using heartbeat, the state machine periodically checks if any signal is received from the processor. If no signal is received, the task will time out. The heartbeat signal can be sent to the state machine using `**SendTaskHeartbeatCommand**`.

Figure 8.14 demonstrates how token-based callback integration works:

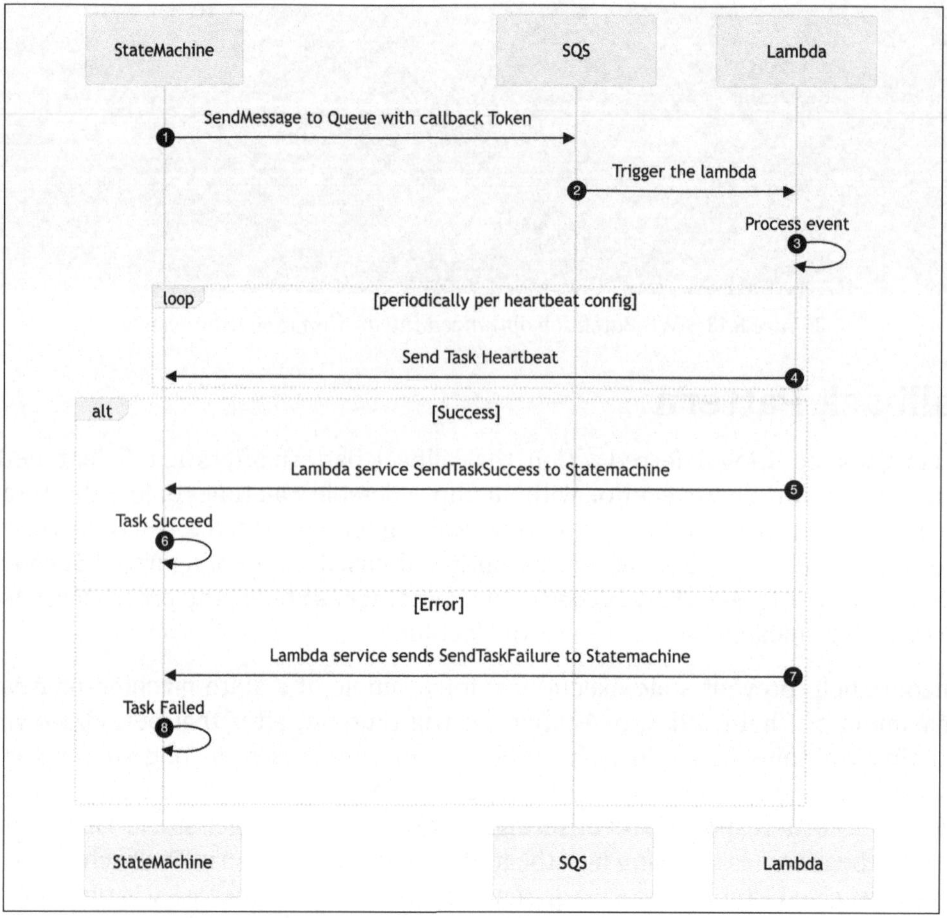

Figure 8.14: *Callback optimized integration sequence diagram*

The callback pattern is supported by API Gateway, SQS, SNS, Lambda, and EventBridge. The integration with AWS CDK is straightforward, as shown in the following code snippet:

```
const stateDefinition =  new SqsSendMessage(this, 'Send Message', {
      queue: props.Queue,
      integrationPattern: IntegrationPattern.WAIT_FOR_TASK_TOKEN,
      taskTimeout: Timeout.minutes(5),
      heartbeatTimeout: Timeout.seconds(15),
      messageBody: TaskInput.fromObject({
        'data': JsonPath.stringAt('$'),
        'token': JsonPath.taskToken,
      }),
      resultPath: '$',
});
```

```
const stateMachine = new StateMachine(this, 'ItemStateMachine', {
      stateMachineName: 'item-state-machine',
      definition: DefinitionBody.fromChainable(stateDefinition)
});
```

The integration will timeout in 5 minutes or if no signal is received by heartbeat for 15 seconds. The processor (lambda service) will inform the processing results using AWS SDK, as shown in the following code snippet:

```
const client = new SFNClient({ region: process.env.AWS_REGION });
export const handler = async (event: SQSEvent) => {
     try {
        const payload = JSON.parse(event.Records[0].body);
        await client.send(new SendTaskSuccessCommand({
          taskToken: payload.token,
          output: JSON.stringify({
            processResult: 'SomeThing done asynchronously!',
            messageId: event.Records[0].messageId
          })
        }))
      } catch (exception) {
          await client.send(new SendTaskFailureCommand({
               taskToken: payload?.token,
               error: exception.message,
               cause: exception.stack
        }));
      }
};
```

If a heartbeat signal is required, this can be achieved with the following snippet of code. Here, **stateMachine** sends the configured heartbeat timeout in the sent event. The producer will apply the signals before the heartbeat reaches. In this example, we track the termination of the principal process:

```
let isFinished = false;
treatEvent(payload).then(() => isFinished = true);
if( payload?.data?.heartBeat ) {
     let i = 0;
      while (!isFinished) {
        await client.send(new SendTaskHeartbeatCommand({
          taskToken: payload.token,
        }))
        console.log(`Heartbeat sent ${i} for ${payload.token}`);
        const sleepTime = Math.max(payload.data.heartBeat - 500, 0);
        await sleep(sleepTime);
        console.log(`Process ${i++} Slept for ${sleepTime} ms`);
      }
}
```

The **TreatEvent** calls a sleep function just to simulate long-running process:

```
const treatEvent = async (payload: Payload) => await sleep(60000);
const sleep = (ms: number) => new Promise((resolve) => setTimeout
(resolve, ms));
```

The StateMachine will stay on pause while the Task Success or Failure response will be received.

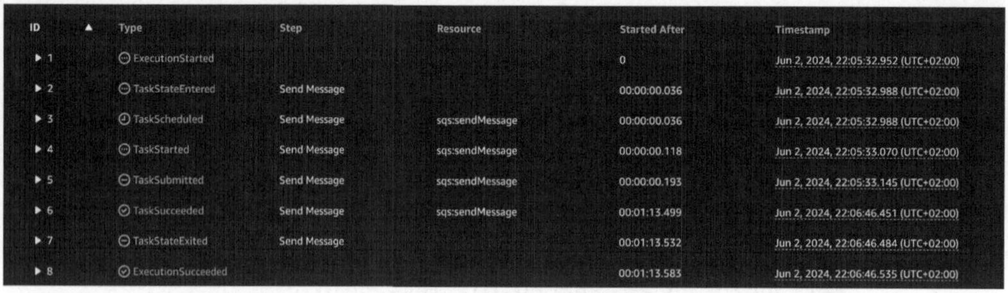

ID	Type	Step	Resource	Started After	Timestamp
1	ExecutionStarted			0	Jun 2, 2024, 22:05:32.952 (UTC+02:00)
2	TaskStateEntered	Send Message		00:00:00.036	Jun 2, 2024, 22:05:32.988 (UTC+02:00)
3	TaskScheduled	Send Message	sqs:sendMessage	00:00:00.036	Jun 2, 2024, 22:05:32.988 (UTC+02:00)
4	TaskStarted	Send Message	sqs:sendMessage	00:00:00.118	Jun 2, 2024, 22:05:33.070 (UTC+02:00)
5	TaskSubmitted	Send Message	sqs:sendMessage	00:00:00.193	Jun 2, 2024, 22:05:33.145 (UTC+02:00)
6	TaskSucceeded	Send Message	sqs:sendMessage	00:01:13.499	Jun 2, 2024, 22:06:46.451 (UTC+02:00)
7	TaskStateExited	Send Message		00:01:13.532	Jun 2, 2024, 22:06:46.484 (UTC+02:00)
8	ExecutionSucceeded			00:01:13.583	Jun 2, 2024, 22:06:46.535 (UTC+02:00)

Figure 8.15: *SQS Callback optimized integration execution results*

SDK Integration

SDK service integrations are a way of integrating with almost over 200 AWS services. The SDK integration passes all provided parameters to the corresponding service API and follows the target service API parameter references. The QDK integration covers the same patterns for request/response, sync, and callback as optimized integrations.

The SDK target service must be provided for any workflow task using resource parameters as **`arn:aws:states:::aws-sdk:sqs:sendMessage.waitForTaskToken`**. The following snippet demonstrates how SDK integration can be implemented using AWS CDK:

```
const stateDefinition = new CustomState(this, 'Send Message', {
   stateJson: {
      Resource: 'arn:aws:states:::aws-sdk:sqs:sendMessage.waitForTask
Token',
      Type: "Task",
      TimeoutSeconds: Duration.minutes(5).toSeconds(),
      HeartbeatSeconds: Duration.seconds(15).toSeconds(),
      Parameters: {
         "MessageBody.$": JsonPath.stringAt('$'),
         "MessageAttributes": {
            "taskToken": {
                 "DataType": "String",
                 "StringValue.$": JsonPath.taskToken,
            }
         },
```

```
        QueueUrl: props.Queue.queueUrl,
      }
    },
});
```

The example applies a **heartBeat** and timeout. When using SDK integration, the target service needs to have the possibility to pass parameters, as done in this example using SQS message attributes.

The lambda function behind the SQS will look at the message attribute provided, as follows:

```
export const handler = async (event: SQSEvent) => {
    const payload = JSON.parse(event.Records[0].body) as Payload;
    const taskToken = event.Records[0].messageAttributes["taskToken"].
stringValue;
  ...
}
```

EventBridge Pipes Integration

When designing event-driven systems, often the requirement can be designed using choreography. In a choreography design, the processing node and consumer nodes can be communicated by following a simple and straightforward communication pattern, as illustrated in *Figure* 8.16:

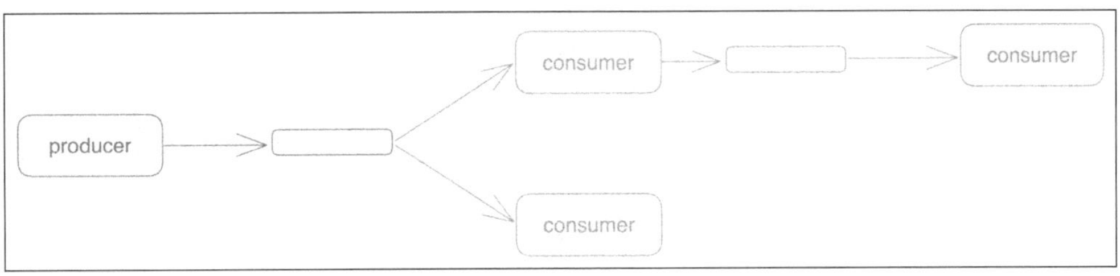

Figure 8.16: *Choreography event-driven system*

As shown in *Figure* 8.16, each consumer needs to set up an integration to receive the produced event, followed by a processing to apply required business logic, and finally distribute a new event for interested consumers.

EventBridge pipes help to configure a no-code integration while also providing filtering/transformation and enrichment steps to respond to a wider range of software requirements. Supported services for EventBridge pipes are Amazon SQS, Amazon MSK, Amazon MQ, Amazon Kinesis/DynamoDB Data Streams, and Apache Kafka Streams.

The following example demonstrates the EventBridge pipe integration and transformation capabilities using AWS CDK. The example receives a message from an SQS queue, sends it to the EventBridge bus as the target, and also transforms the message payload:

```
new CfnPipe(this, 'Pipe', {
 source: queue.queueArn!,
 target: eventBus.eventBusArn,
 targetParameters: {
     eventBridgeEventBusParameters: {
         detailType: 'MessageReceived',
         source: 'com.serverless.c08'
     },
     inputTemplate: `
         {
             "Id": "$.body.Id",
             "Name": "$.body.Name"
         }
     `,
 },
 ...
})
```

The preceding example brings the possibility to apply simple integration and transformation without the need to write code. Sometimes the integration needs a higher level of complexity, such as when there is a need for validation transformation or enriching the received message based on some logic. EventBridge pipe provides the enrichment phase that lets execution of the enrichment process before sending the event to the target.

EventBridge pipe enrichment supports API destination, Amazon API Gateway, Lambda Function, and Step Functions state machine. The enrichment trigger needs to give the required permission to pipe role to trigger the enrichment service, such as Step Functions `` `StartExecution` `` or Lambda `` `InvokeFunction` ``.

EventBridge pipe sends the part of the event that seems to be meaningful for enrichment service; for example, if the pipe receives messages from SQS, then the received payload for enrichment will be the array of records.

```
[
  {
     "messageId":"309df4dc-245c-4efd-b571-cfac09551633",
     "receiptHandle":"AQEBVziWjf3eD+qQhzKbqZom7NVcp71dgm…",
     "body":"{\"Id\":\"c08\",\"Name\":\"c08.pipes.example\" }",
     "attributes":{
        "ApproximateReceiveCount":"7",
        "SentTimestamp":"1717863013142",
        "SenderId":"607050363559",
        "ApproximateFirstReceiveTimestamp":"1717863013148"
     },
```

```
      "messageAttributes":{

      },
      "md5OfBody":"a822b85c595831a25eda2488d9708342",
      "eventSource":"aws:sqs",
      "eventSourceARN":"arn:aws:sqs:eu-west-1:...:AppStack-Queue…",
      "awsRegion":"eu-west-1"
   }
]
```

The enrichment phase must return a collection that the EventBridge pipe will use for the target invocation phase. The target input transformation must be applied considering the enrichment result and not the original received event from the source. A function handler will receive the array of `**SQSRecord**` and must return any array of results. The enrichment can abort some events based on business logic by excluding the related result in the lambda returned response.

The handler can be as simple as the following code snippet:

```
import { SQSRecord } from 'aws-lambda';

type Payload = {
 id: string;
 name: string;
}

const treatRecord = async (payload: Payload) => {
 ...
}
export const handler = async (event: SQSRecord[]) => {
 return event.map((record) => {
   const payload = JSON.parse(record.body) as Payload;
   const result = await treatRecord(payload);

   return result;
 })
};
```

The enrichment can be activated by using AWS CDK as follows. The following CDK code also shows how to use Pipes logging with event data included; this is a great way of debugging:

```
new CfnPipe(this, 'Pipe', {
   ...
   enrichment: enrichmentFunction.functionArn,
   logConfiguration: {
       level: 'TRACE',
       cloudwatchLogsLogGroupArn: loggroup.logGroupArn,
```

```
        includeExecutionData: ["ALL"],

    }
})
```

Conclusion

Recently, designing software with no/low code has become popular in the industry. The goal of this chapter was to demonstrate how the AWS ecosystem can help design software with minimum required code, allowing for more focus on business requirements and less on integration and infrastructure. A variety of useful services that integrate natively with lambda service were introduced, such as API Gateway for designing APIs, Step Functions for designing orchestrated workflows, EventBridge Pipes for setting up communication between different services.

The next chapter will walk through edge computing and demonstrate the different ways of serving content at the edge using Lambda Edge and CloudFunctions. In addition, the chapter will present the advantages of edge computing and delve into the principal considerations for making the best decision and choosing the best candidate among others for processing at the edge.

CHAPTER 9
Edge Computing

Introduction

This chapter provides a detailed overview of serverless computing at edge using Amazon CloudFront, discussing the applicable designs for different cases and the advantages of each. It delves into the benefits of edge to leverage the performance, security, and computing and deep dives into some challenges brought by these solutions, as well as briefing how to avoid these challenges without exceeding the cost, complexity, and performance barriers.

Structure

In this chapter, we will discuss the following topics:

- Edge Overview
- Amazon CloudFront
- Caching at Edge
- Computing at Edge
- Security at Edge

Edge Overview

An edge is a geolocated point of presence (PoP) situated in a specific zonal region, isolated from other PoPs. Each edge consists of a Content Delivery Network (CDN), Amazon Route 53 (Domain Name Service), and a Global Accelerator (Network Optimizer).

Amazon offers over 410 PoPs, including edge locations and regional caches. These edge locations are connected to AWS regions through Amazon's high-throughput fiber network, enhancing connectivity and accelerating dynamic content delivery.

In theory, an edge can serve multiple use cases, including edge computing, caching, security, and geolocated distribution. *Figure* 9.1 illustrates a typical edge configuration:

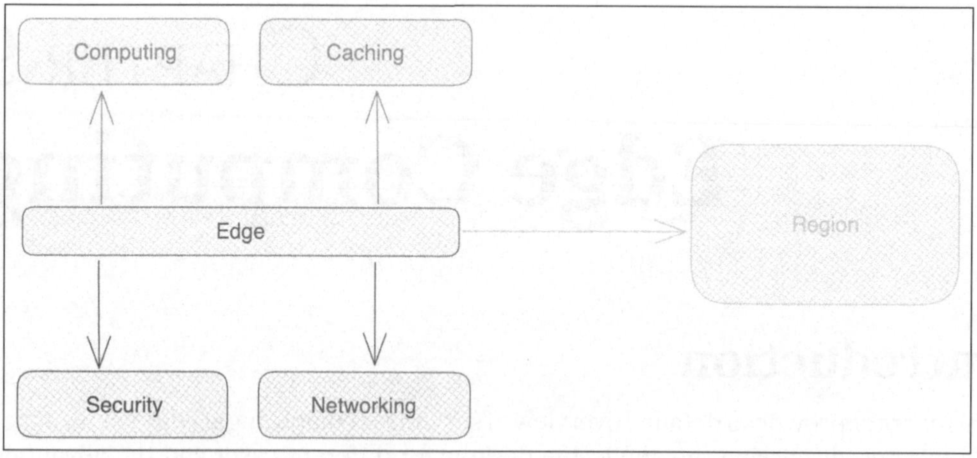

Figure 9.1: *An edge location*

However, the advantage will become significantly important when used as a means to increase the power of regional services in terms of performance, operability, reliability, and security.

- **Performance**: Using edge for performance is a popular solution by putting the service entry point closer to the consumers as edges provide distributed geolocalized PoPs. This means that the user consuming a service from Asia will be routed to the closer PoP based on its location, and the same applies to a user from the USA. This will reduce the latency.
- **Operability**: Edge can increase operational needs by providing computing at the edge or using caching mechanism to enhance the overall user experience when regional services are not required to deal with those requirements. Some scenarios include keeping data cached or applying some cross-cutting computing needs at the edge.
- **Reliability**: By meeting certain requirements at the edge, the service can remain operational even if the regional service experiences degradation or if network disruptions affect origin connectivity.
- **Security**: Applying security measures at the edge adds an extra layer of protection by handling verification and compliance away from the origin. This reduces the risk of data exposure and DDoS attacks at the core of the service by establishing barriers at the edge.

Amazon CloudFront Edges

While CloudFront offers the core functionalities of a Content Delivery Network, it offers extra computational and security features that will enhance the use of CloudFront and extend its adoption for the public internet. When a user requests data or an object from your application, the request travels from the client to the AWS servers and then back to the user. Using CloudFront applies the leverage of edge networking locations to efficiently distribute your content.

CloudFront Points of Presence (POPs) are strategically located within the AWS network, facilitating direct peering with Internet Service Provider (ISP) networks. With a global footprint spanning over 100 cities across more than 50 countries, CloudFront boasts a robust network of 600+ POPs worldwide. With the goal of optimizing the viewer experience, CloudFront released a new type of PoPs this year, where the embedded Points of Presence are located within ISPs and mobile network operators (MNO). Deploying embedded POPs within their networks allows ISPs to efficiently deliver cacheable content without needing to scale the peering links connecting CloudFront to their infrastructure. CloudFront Global Edge Network provides the Regional Edge Caches (RECs) that will act as an intermediate node between PoPs and origin software.

Figure 9.2 demonstrates how the viewer requests are transited through the AWS network:

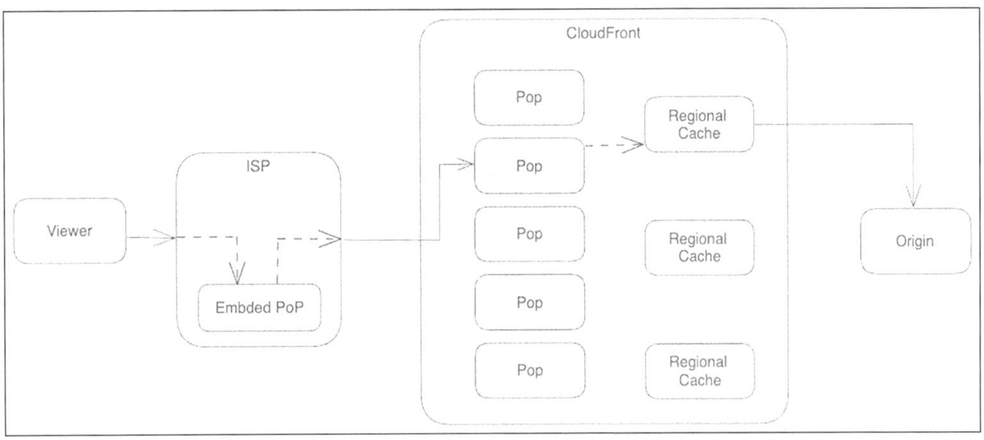

Figure 9.2: *Viewer request transition*

Point of Presence

Each Point of Presence (also known as edge location) underlying infrastructure is located within the AWS global network, and each PoP also has a dedicated cache. CloudFront's PoPs guarantee to serve content to the viewer with the lowest latency; the selection of the best suitable PoP is done by the Domain Name Server (DNS). If the requested content is present in the cache, the content will be returned; otherwise, the request will be routed to the origin server, and the response will be sent to the viewer. Additionally, CloudFront feeds the cache with the received response. Each PoP has an individual cache that serves as a means of rapid content delivery, allowing CloudFront to evacuate some content to give space for more frequently requested content.

Regional Edge Cache

A Regional Edge Cache (REC) is located between PoP and the origin server and is deployed globally. The RECs cache has more capacity than PoP's individual cache and keeps content longer in the regional cache closer to the origin. This helps to reduce the need to target the origin server if the content is available. In case of a miss of content in a PoP's individual cache, the regional edge cache will be asked for content availability. Upon returning the content to the viewer, it will put the content to PoP's individual cache.

Request Collapsing

Amazon CloudFront applies a pause mechanism to optimize the origin request forwarding and avoid sending requests to the origin unnecessarily by pausing the simultaneous requests for the same object when a request for the same object is forwarded to origin at the same time. The distribution will use the same response returned from the origin for all other simultaneous paused requests.

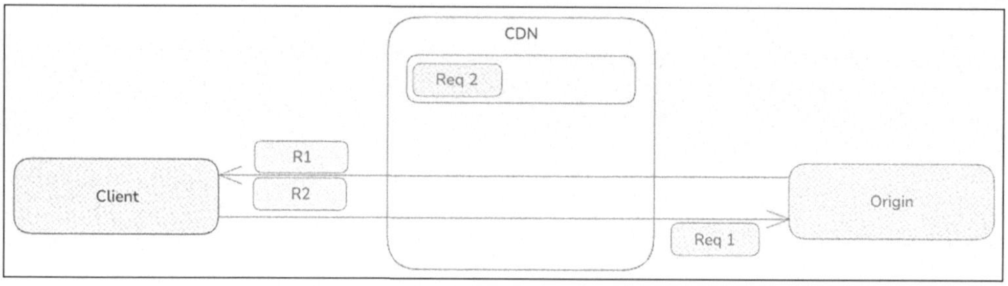

Figure 9.3: *Request collapsing*

Origin Shield

As Amazon CloudFront cache is distributed in many edge locations, the challenge is the lack of a trusted cache node. CloudFront helps to reduce the load on origin servers, but the distributed nature of edge locations affects the rate of cache miss and forwarding requests to the origin, while incoming requests evenly reach different edge locations. It is important to look at the real metrics and define the exact need; for example, if an application has 95% requests coming from a single country, such as UK, and 5% from others, such as the USA, Asia, Africa, this actually does not justify the evidence of having a problem. However, if the scenario includes requests that are evenly from different locations, this means that for the same object, the origin server will be reached four times to respond to the UK, USA, Africa, and Asia.

Origin Shield provides a regional caching layer close to the origin and behaves as a proxy between RECs and Origin. This helps to achieve a higher cache consistency, better performance, and reduce the cost by offloading the origin servers.

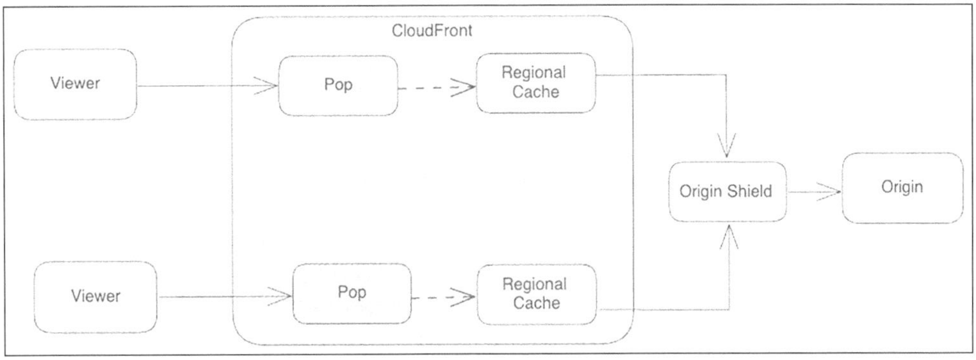

Figure 9.4: *Origin shield*

Origin and Distribution Specification

CloudFront Specification represents the configuration that leads a request to a specific origin. The specification verification happens when no content is available in PoP or regional edge cache. CloudFront has different constraints for cache verification:

- CloudFront does not proxy the POST, PUT, OPTIONS, DELETE, and PATCH methods through REC.
- CloudFront does not proxy the dynamic content through REC.

Origins and Behaviors

Configuring a CloudFront distribution to interact with an origin can be applied by adding an origin and configuring the required behavior for a specific request using that origin. A distribution has a default behavior, which is the default routing if no specification will be found for the incoming request. Since Amazon CloudFront distributions are public, the origin must be publicly resolvable. This means that if a distribution has an origin like API Gateway, Application Load Balancer, and so on, those must be internet-facing; either consulting those endpoints directly is restricted such as by disabling the API Gateway default endpoint.

The following snippet shows the creation of a distribution with a default origin:

```
this.Distribution = new Distribution(this, 'CloudFrontDistribution', {
      enabled: true,
      defaultRootObject: 'index.html',
      priceClass: PriceClass.PRICE_CLASS_100,
      minimumProtocolVersion: SecurityPolicyProtocol.TLS_V1_2_2021,
      errorResponses: [
```

```
        {
            httpStatus: 404,
            responseHttpStatus: 200,
            ttl: Duration.seconds(0),
            responsePagePath: '/'
        },{
            httpStatus: 403,
            responseHttpStatus: 200,
            ttl: Duration.seconds(0),
            responsePagePath: '/'
        },
    ],
    defaultBehavior: {
        allowedMethods: AllowedMethods.ALLOW_GET_HEAD,
        origin: new S3Origin(props.FrontSiteBucket),
        viewerProtocolPolicy: ViewerProtocolPolicy.REDIRECT_TO_HTTPS,
        cachePolicy: CachePolicy.CACHING_OPTIMIZED,
         compress: true,
    }
});
```

Caching

Caching is the most known functionality offered by Amazon CloudFront. A caching serves as a layer of temporary storage near the users to improve the performance and user experience. CloudFront serves the cached data in the local PoP cache but keeps a longer copy of the cache in REC. This helps to achieve better performance in the PoP but has the possibility to respond to a wider range of requirements by serving the REC. This caching will help reduce the request rate reaching the origin and avoid overwhelming the origin resources while forwarding requests to the origin when needed.

Amazon CloudFront initially follows a Cache-Through pattern where the cache behaves as a facade in front of every read-and-write request and updates the cache storage following the origin response. However, there is no replication and synchronization between edge locations.

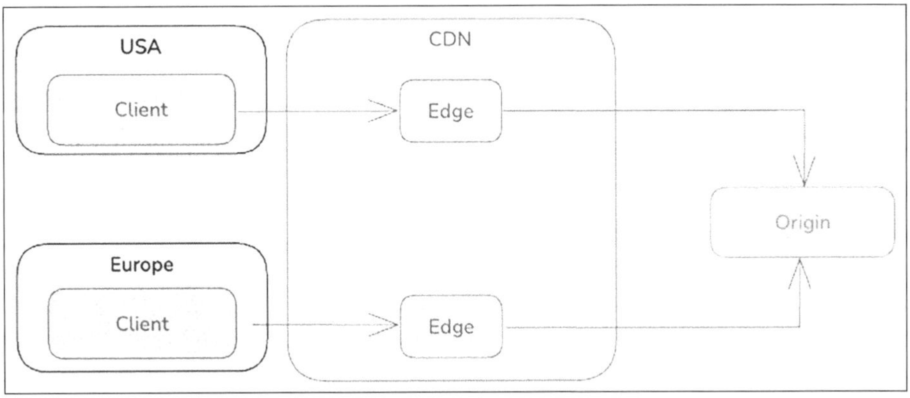

Figure 9.5: *Cache through pattern*

Cache Consistency

The principal challenge with this design, being Amazon CloudFront or any other solution in the marketplace, is cache consistency, as CloudFront follows an eventually consistent approach. There are always trade-offs to consider and bring the design into a more convenient way.

Amazon CloudFront offers three levels of Pricing Class (Price Class ALL, 200, 100), which impacts the number of edge locations. To achieve the best consistency, the design can reduce the number of locations by setting the appropriate Pricing Class. For example, if the solution runs only in Europe, then the best choice will be Pricing Class 100, which gives locations in the United States, Mexico, Canada, Europe, Turkey, and Israel. This is a trade-off between performance and consistency. While the number of locations reduces the consistency gap, pricing will be lowered, but at the same time, some users will experience somewhat higher latency.

Cache Key

A cache key is the cache identifier generated by CloudFront, including all configured details in a cache policy document. This can include QueryString, Headers, and Cookies alongside the initial behavior path parameter. When CloudFront sends a response back to the user, the underlying response includes the X-Cache header, indicating if CloudFront found the resource in the cache or not. This is presented by a value of 'Miss From CloudFront' or 'Hit From CloudFront'.

Cache Policy

A Cache Policy represents a cache configuration set containing different attributes such as min/max and default TTL (Time to live), as well as cache key parameters like QueryStrings, Headers, and cookies.

Query String

When developing APIs over HTTP, one of the means for transiting data is the use of QueryString parameters. CloudFront can be configured to consider query string parameters as part of the cache key and to forward query strings to your origin and whether to cache content based on some or all of them. This flexibility can be useful in scenarios such as multilingual websites, where different versions of the same page are accessed via a language parameter. By configuring CloudFront accordingly, each language version can be cached separately based on the language parameter value. CloudFront will still cache content, even if the origin server returns identical content for all parameter values.

The order of parameters must be respected, or CloudFront considers the two different orders as two different keys. Also, the cache keys are case sensitive, so for a single parameter having uppercase value and also lowercase in requests, those will be considered as two different cache keys.

Headers

CloudFront allows you to configure whether headers are forwarded to your origin and whether separate versions of an object are cached based on the header values in viewer requests. This capability enables serving different content versions depending on headers such as use-agent, location, and host. CloudFront treats headers as case-sensitive.

To cache objects based on specific header values, you need to set cache behavior settings for your distribution using different options: Forward All, a selected set of headers, or default headers only. The default headers are CloudFront's standard set of headers, including some set of known standard headers: **`CloudFront-Is-Desktop-Viewer`, `CloudFront-Viewer-*`**, and so on. When configuring headers, it is recommended to apply them to achieve a higher cache hit ratio. CloudFront does not allow configuring Connection, Host, Proxy-Authorization, TE (Transfer-Encoding), and Upgrade headers and Cookie header for S3 origin type.

As an example, header-based caching will be serving different versions of a resource based on viewer country using CloudFront-Viewer-Country header.

CloudFront returns all headers from the origin to the viewer, with some exceptions. For details on these exceptions, refer to CloudFront documentation for Amazon S3 and custom origins. CloudFront will replace or modify some headers returned from the origin server, such as Set-Cookie, Trailer, Transfer-Encoding (value will be set to **`'chunked'`**), upgrade via in addition to origin-type specific headers, S3 origin will manipulate **`X-Amz-Id-2`**, **`X-AMZ-Request-Id`**, while a custom origin will manipulate the header.

Cookies

Amazon CloudFront has the option to use cookies as part of the caching strategy, but this is not the default behavior. When choosing cookies as part of caching, it is important to understand the change a cookie will bring to the caching mechanism, and see how this change can be beneficial.

Defining cookies can be useful for personalized caching or dynamic caching, such as a cache per country or user information, but as a recommendation, it is better to bring the predictable cache elements, like country or user ID, if needed as part of path, query string, or headers. The reason for this recommendation is how the cookie forwarding will impact the request collapsing.

AWS documentation indicates that if you configure the cookie forwarding, the request collapsing will be impacted and there will be an increase in origin request forwarding. This may not be a problem at some scale but can bring a significant performance and cost increase at a higher scale.

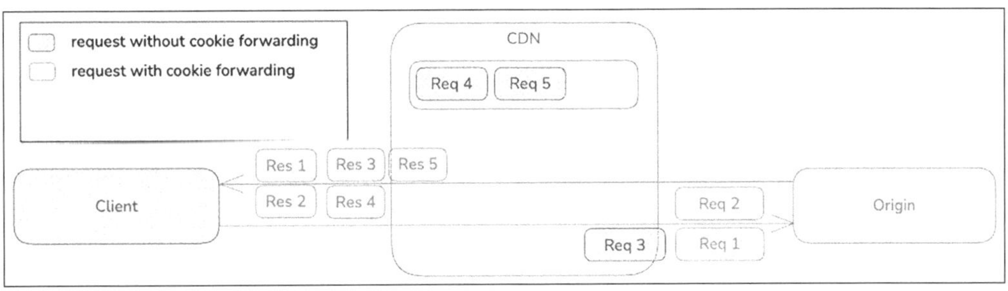

***Figure* 9.6**: *Request collapsing while forwarding cookies*

When CloudFront is set to forward cookies to the origin, the Set-Cookie header received from the origin's response will be cached and included in CloudFront's response to the viewer. There is no possibility to prevent this header from being forwarded to the origin, but by setting the Cache-Control header in the origin side with a value of Cache-Control: no-cache="Set-Cookie", the header can be prevented from being cached.

Monitoring and Metrics

Amazon CloudFront provides standard logging and metrics to simplify the monitoring of Distribution and gives the means to observe how the origin and viewer are impacted in near real-time. CloudFront gives the possibility to activate the logging with a destination of type S3 bucket. This will provide the logs in the configured bucket, each log file is a GNU zip file (`.gz` extension) containing a chunk of logs at a given time.

Each standard log field contains useful information that simplifies monitoring. The following list includes some important fields found in a standard log:

- **`date`**
- **`time`**
- **`x-edge-location`**: This is the edge location identifier such as CDG50-P3
- **`sc-bytes`**: The number of response bytes returned to the viewer
- **`c-ip`**: The viewer IPv4 or IPv6 address
- **`cs-method`**: The request HTTP verb
- **`cs(Host)`**
- **`cs-URI-stem`**: The request path part without query parameters
- **`sc-status`**: The response HTTP status code
- **`cs(Referer)`**
- **`cs(User-Agent)`**
- **`cs-URI-query`**: The request `QueryString`
- **`cs (Cookie)`**: The cookies Header
- **`x-edge-result-type`**: `Hit`, `Miss`, `LimitExceeded`, `CapacityExceeded`, `Error`, `Redirect`
- **`x-edge-request-id`**
- **`x-host-header`**
- **`cs-protocol`**: The request protocol such as HTTPS, HTTP, WS, or WSS

The standard metrics CloudFront provides are limited to Request Count, Data Transfer, and Error Rate. CloudFront provides the Internet Monitor, this feature creates a CloudWatch dashboard in which the metrics are based on traffic and geolocalized traffic with an automated analysis done by CloudWatch.

Defining the Layer of Caching in a Design

Before enabling caching, it is recommended as a best practice to look at the different layers that interact together to achieve a final result. In this section, we will walk through a Micro-Frontend approach where smaller distributed services provide results for a website. This example gives a more comprehensive approach to understand the definition of caching layers.

The following design is a simplified and high-level micro-frontend design. This design demonstrates a static website fetching two micro-frontends: Bookmarks and Product Catalog.

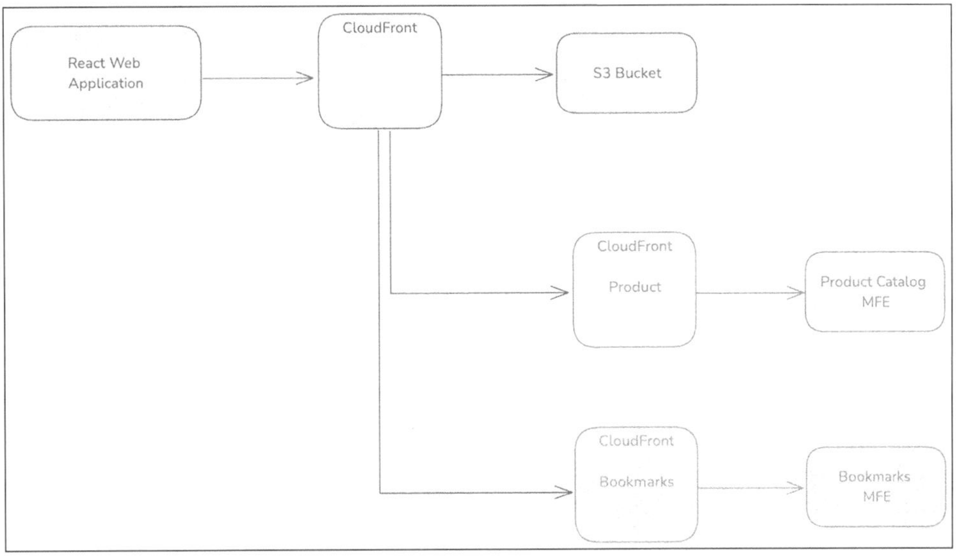

Figure 9.7: *Micro-frontend high-level design*

To provide a comprehensive answer to the caching questions based on the provided high-level architecture diagram, let's break down the requirements for each component:

Web Application:

- ***What is the distribution caching configuration?***

  Caching strategy for the React Web Application shall be configured to cache static assets such as HTML, CSS, JavaScript, and images stored in the S3 bucket. This ensures fast delivery of static content. Using separate cache behaviors for different types of content, such as '`/static/*`' for `CSS/JS/images` and `/*` for the main application. Additionally, enable a long TTL (Time to Live) for static content.

- ***What parts of the request must be forwarded to the dynamic origin?***

  Forward essential headers like Authorization, Accept-Language, and User-Agent to handle authenticated requests, localization, and device-specific rendering. If the web application relies on them for user sessions, forwarding authentication and session cookies will be required. All query string parameters must be forwarded to ensure that dynamic content and personalized responses are correctly fetched from the origin.

Bookmark:

- ***Is there a need to apply personalized caching?***

  While the Bookmarks micro-frontend (MFE) provides personalized bookmark lists per user, CloudFront must be configured to cache based on user-specific headers or cookies. User-specific headers like Authorization or User-ID and cache responses are uniquely based on these values to ensure each user receives their personalized content.

Product:

- ***How to manage caching per different catalog filtering parameters?***

  Per filtering requirement, Dynamic Content Caching shall be configured to forward query strings related to catalog filters. Setting up distribution to cache responses based on query string parameters will ensure that different filter combinations are cached separately, enhancing performance for repeated requests with similar filters.

General Recommendations: Starting from the lower level downstream helps in accurately defining domain-specific caching requirements:

- **Product and Bookmark MFEs**: Manage caching strategies for these MFEs by forwarding appropriate headers, cookies, and query strings to ensure both personalized content and dynamic filtering are correctly handled.
- **Headers and Cookies Management**: Carefully choose which headers and cookies to forward to avoid overloading the origin and to maintain efficient caching strategies. Also, avoid cookie forwarding if not needed as this will impact the request collapsing and put more load on the origin.
- **S3 Bucket and Static Content**: Ensure that static assets served from the S3 Bucket are cached with long TTLs to improve performance and reduce the load on the origin.

By focusing on the downstream components first, you can make more informed decisions about what needs to be cached at each layer, ensuring optimal performance and a seamless user experience.

Cache-Control by the Origin Server

The origin can control the cache using HTTP cache headers like Cache-Control and Expires. These headers override the default TTL of the CloudFront cache behavior. Resource caching can be controlled at two layers: Distribution and Browser. The Browser looks at max-age, while the Distribution considers the s-max-age or max-age, respectively.

If the origin server returns a '**`Cache-Control: max-age=1800`**', the browser will cache the resource for 30 minutes, but the distribution will take it into account per behavior cache Min/Max TTL configuration.

If the max-age is between the min TTL and Max TTL, it will be effectively considered as a cache value; otherwise, the Min TTL is configured if it is bigger than the max-age, and the Max TTL if it is lesser than the max-age.

To distinguish the browser and distribution cache control, the origin can return the cache control header such as '**`Cache-Control: max-age=1800; s-max-age:3600`**' that leads to having a browser cache based on max-age and distribution cache based on s-max-age.

Also, the Expires header can be used, so the browser will always respect that header. However, CloudFront takes it into account with the same constraints for max-age and s-max-age.

The origin can control the cache by indicating to the distribution or browser not to cache contents using Cache-Control: with a value of no-cache, no-store, and/or private. This way if there is no Min TTL configured, Distribution will respect the header; otherwise, this header will not be effective, but the browser will take it into account.

Applying the Caching Using CDK

First, the Bookmarks service has the requirement to identify the user. To take advantage of CloudFront caching and achieve a better performance, the Distribution must have a cache policy. As the service needs to receive multiple parameters such as **`userID`** (primarily), the cache can be configured considering the **`userID`**.

For the sake of simplicity in this part, the **`userID`** is passed via query string.

```
this.Distribution = new Distribution(this, 'BookmarkDistribution', {
      ...
      defaultBehavior: {
          origin: new
FunctionUrlOrigin(props.DefaultOriginListBookmarksFunctionUrl),
          allowedMethods: AllowedMethods.ALLOW_ALL,
          cachedMethods: AllowedMethods.ALLOW_GET_HEAD_OPTIONS,
          cachePolicy: new CachePolicy(this, 'BookmarksCachePolicy', {
                  headerBehavior: CacheHeaderBehavior.none(),
                  cookieBehavior: CacheCookieBehavior.none(),
                  queryStringBehavior: CacheQueryStringBehavior.
                  allowList(
                          'userid',
                          'ref',
                          'name'
```

```
                ),
                defaultTtl: Duration.hours(1),
                minTtl: Duration.hours(0),
                maxTtl: Duration.hours(24),
        }),
        viewerProtocolPolicy: ViewerProtocolPolicy.REDIRECT_TO_HTTPS,
        originRequestPolicy: OriginRequestPolicy.ALL_VIEWER_EXCEPT_
        HOST_HEADER,
    }
}
```

Even the default value for **'headerBehavior'** and **'cookieBehavior'** is 'none', for demonstration purposes, these are explicitly assigned in the above example. It is recommended to well define the responsibilities of each layer in a distributed design; in this example, the bookmarks micro-frontend owns the caching and has the responsibility to manage the bookmarks lifecycle. This decision brings more flexibility into the design and simplifies future evolutions.

The Products Service has a behavior with the same general configuration, except for the list of query parameters in the cache policy.

```
queryStringBehavior: CacheQueryStringBehavior.allowList(
   'seller',
   'ref',
   'name'
)
```

Looking at the website, it will use a routing approach to construct a page template. The website stack is aware of the different MFEs included on the home page but has no responsibility for the lifecycle of the underlying services. The website distribution will deactivate the caching and forward all parameters to origins. This way, the origins will take care of caching and logic based on parameters, if needed, while the website only consumes the results. The following snippet shows the dynamic content configuration in CDK that is used for behaviors attached to the bookmarks and products origins:

```
const dynamicContentCachePolicy = new CachePolicy(this, 'DynamicContent-
CachePolicy', {
        headerBehavior: CacheHeaderBehavior.none(),
        cookieBehavior: CacheCookieBehavior.none(),
        queryStringBehavior: CacheQueryStringBehavior.none(),
        defaultTtl: Duration.seconds(0),
        minTtl: Duration.seconds(0),
});

const dynamicContentOriginRequestPolicy = new OriginRequestPolicy(this,
'DynamicContentOriginRequestPolicy', {
        queryStringBehavior: OriginRequestQueryStringBehavior.all(),
        headerBehavior: OriginRequestHeaderBehavior.none(),
```

```
        cookieBehavior: OriginRequestCookieBehavior.none()
});

this.Distribution.addBehavior('bookmarks/*', new HttpOrigin(props.Book-
markServiceDomainName), {
        allowedMethods: AllowedMethods.ALLOW_ALL,
        cachePolicy: dynamicContentCachePolicy,
        viewerProtocolPolicy: ViewerProtocolPolicy.REDIRECT_TO_HTTPS,
        originRequestPolicy: dynamicContentOriginRequestPolicy
});

this.Distribution.addBehavior('products/*', new HttpOrigin(props.Prod-
uctServiceDomainName), {
        allowedMethods: AllowedMethods.ALLOW_ALL,
        cachePolicy: dynamicContentCachePolicy,
        viewerProtocolPolicy: ViewerProtocolPolicy.REDIRECT_TO_HTTPS,
        originRequestPolicy: dynamicContentOriginRequestPolicy
});
```

Also, the website distribution has a default behavior targeting the static website S3 bucket:

```
defaultBehavior:  {
        allowedMethods: AllowedMethods.ALLOW_GET_HEAD,
        origin: new S3BucketOrigin.withOriginAccessControl(
props.FrontSiteBucket
         ),
        cachedMethods: AllowedMethods.ALLOW_GET_HEAD,
        cachePolicy: new CachePolicy(this, 'WebSiteCachePolicy', {
                headerBehavior: CacheHeaderBehavior.none(),
                cookieBehavior: CacheCookieBehavior.none(),
                queryStringBehavior: CacheHeaderBehavior.none(),
                defaultTtl: Duration.hours(1),
                minTtl: Duration.hours(0),
                maxTtl: Duration.hours(24),
        }),
        viewerProtocolPolicy: ViewerProtocolPolicy.REDIRECT_TO_HTTPS,
}
```

The default TTL indicates the duration for keeping objects in the cache. The Min TTL and Max TTL will only be effective if the origin server controls the cache using response headers.

Computing

In some scenarios, the interest of applying some validation, process, or transformation at an early stage and outside the network or region where the services run will be a crucial requirement. Using CloudFront, an edge function can be executed for some computing needs at an early stage, closer to end users. These functions serve as a means to treat requests and responses. Amazon CloudFront offers two types of functions: Lambda Edge and CloudFront Function. Each one can be adopted based on requirements, as these are slightly different in terms of characteristics and the programming language runtime engine.

CloudFront Request Response Life Cycle

When a viewer request reaches the PoP, there are multiple stages before and after the CloudFront caching system. The viewer request and response happen in front of the caching layer, but the origin request and responses happen behind the origin side.

The following figure demonstrates the request and response lifecycle of CloudFront:

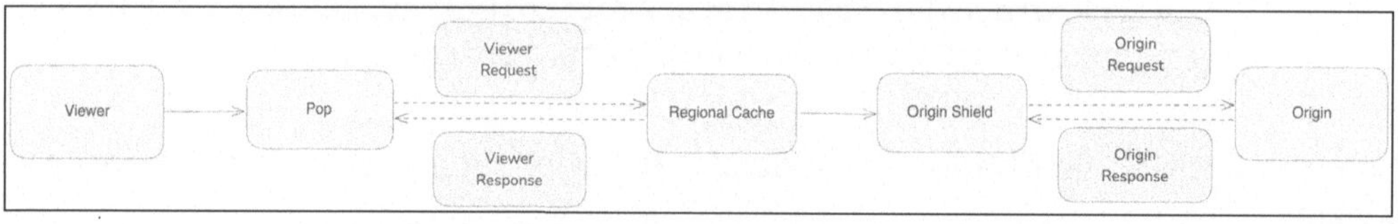

Figure 9.8: *Request and response lifecycle*

As demonstrated, the viewer request trigger will be before reaching the cache, while the origin request will be triggered after cache verification. AWS has no concrete mention if the trigger happens before the Origin Shield or after. However, since Lambda Edge is executed regionally and, as per Origin Shield documentation, the trigger happens in the region where the shield has the availability at a given time, even if it is not the principal region configured; the assumption is that this happens after Origin Shield.

Choosing between viewer and origin triggers can vary per requirements and the level of necessity to have caching before or after that treatment. If the origin trigger is required, the only choice will be Lambda Edge as CloudFront functions only support the viewer triggers.

CloudFront Function and Lambda Edge Differences

Lambda Edge is an extension of AWS Lambda, but CloudFunctions are lightweight computing functions within the CloudFront service. The following table shows per-axis differences:

	Lambda Edge	**CloudFront Function**
Programming Language	Node.js/Python	JavaScript (`JS_1`, `JS_2`)

Duration	Viewer 5s/Origin 30s	Sub-milliseconds (<1 millisecond)
Memory	Up to 10 GB	2 Mb
Network/File System	Yes	No
Throughput	10 000/s	10 000 000/s
Triggers	Viewer/Origin	Viewer
Access to Request Body	Yes	No

Table 9.1: *Lambda Edge vs. CloudFront Function*

Adding Redirection

To better demonstrate how the viewer/origin request can be used, this section will introduce a new functionality to the Micro-Frontend example. The requirement is that for the period of Black Friday, specific requests should be redirected to the **OnSold** catalog of products. *Figure* 9.9 illustrates the design:

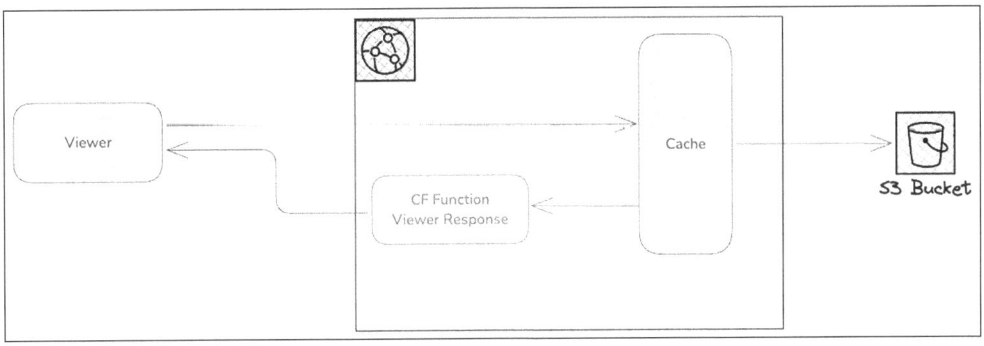

Figure 9.9: *Viewer response redirection*

When the viewer requests an object in S3, CloudFront fetches that object from the origin if it is not present in the cache. The function will be triggered before sending a response to the viewer. The function looks at the object metadata and redirects to the URL if the specific metadata is present.

The function code is as simple as the following snippet:

```
function handler(event) {
 const { response } = event;
 const headers = response.headers;
 const header = 'x-amz-meta-location';


 if (
   event.request.method === 'GET' &&
   response.statusCode === 200
```

```
  ) {
    if (headers[header] && headers[header].value) {
      headers.location = { value: headers[header].value };
      return {
        statusCode: 302,
        statusDescription: 'Found',
        headers,
      };
    }
  }
 return response;
}
```

In this example, specific products, such as a product with a reference of **`Ref_2`** under the path '**`/product/ref_2`**', will be redirected to the landing page with the **`OnSold`** category filter applied (this can be any other web app page) '**`/?category=ON_SOLD`**'.

The registered file must have a user-defined metadata, '**`x-amz-meta-location`**', which can be easily done with CDK. In real use cases, this upload can be done using other means, such as an API, an admin app, and so on.

```
new BucketDeployment(this, 'RedirectionDeployment', {
   sources: [ Source.asset(join(process.cwd(), '/front-app/src/
redirection-files')) ],
   metadata: {
       'location': `https://${distribution.Distribution.distribution
DomainName}/H?category=ON_SOLD`,
   },
   destinationBucket: frontStack.Bucket,
   prune: false,
});
```

Accessing Other AWS Resources

In scenarios when accessing other AWS services is required, like fetching data from a database such as DynamoDB or any interaction that requires reaching the network, CloudFront Function cannot be the choice; instead, a Lambda Edge can be used.

Origin-Related Computing

If the process to be applied is related to the origin, an origin request function will be a better choice. This helps to avoid unnecessary computing for the requests reaching the cache.

Available Information in Function

Some restrictions exist related to information in the trigger event source received by an edge function:

- **Unavailable Headers**: The `Connection`, `Keep-alive`, `x-edge-*`, and so on; headers are not present.
- Some headers cannot be modified and are read-only:
    - Viewer Requests: `Content-Length`, `Via`
    - Viewer Response: `Via`, `Warning`, and for Lambda Edge only: `Transfer-Encoding`, `Content-Length`, `Content-Encoding`
    - Origin Request: `Via`, `Transfer-Encoding`, `Content-Length`, and so on
    - Origin Response: `Transfer-Encoding`, `Via`
- The query strings are available with the following constraints:
    - **Viewer/Origin Request**: All query strings are available and can be modified or created.
    - **Origin Request/Response**: Only if the behavior is configured to Forward All QueryString, the query strings will be available.
    - **Viewer/Origin Response**: Only read but no modification allowed.

When An Edge Function is Not Triggered

For Viewer Response, the edge function will not be triggered if the origin response status code is 400 or higher.

CloudFront Compression Impacts

When a CloudFront has gzip compression active, the viewer response will not receive the Content-Length header; instead, the Transfer-Encoding will be received with the '*chunked*' value.

Security

Security being the most important pillar in design decisions is always a concern with public-facing layers. CloudFront, being a public service by nature, imposes a public layer in front of the internal enterprise ecosystem, and due to the level of criticality, CloudFront provides some level of security-related integrations:

- **Security at Transit**: CloudFront offers TLS to achieve security at transit and apply protection against MITM attacks while providing confidentiality and integrity of data. CloudFront offers TLS 1.1, 1.2, and 1.3 (recommended TLS

1.3), as well as the field-level encryption can be applied to guarantee sensitive information encryption and confidentiality using an asymmetric encryption.

- **Security at Rest**: All data stored in edge locations (PoP), Regional Edge Cache, and all related storages are encrypted by default. Also, the code and configurations related to edge function are encrypted at rest.
- **Signed URLs/Signed Cookies**: By using signed URLs/cookies, CloudFront offers a higher level of security to restrict access and restrict the content to a limited audience. These are often the short valid URLs consulted by an authenticated user.
- **Web Application Firewall ACLs**: Web ACLs are a collection of rules with conditions that provide limited access to resources and content at the edge.

Conclusion

The chapter focused on specific details of edge-level computing, caching, and security, providing concrete use cases to help readers better comprehend the concept of edge computing. Readers will gain an understanding of designing and implementing real software requirements at the edge using CloudFront, understanding how to achieve caching and better performance, controlling caching per origin server requirements, applying the cross-cutting concerns and computing requirements using edge function. Also, they will obtain an overview of possibilities to design secure public services.

The next chapter will focus on serverless design patterns and practices with concrete examples that show real scenarios and use cases in the software industry.

CHAPTER 10
Patterns and Practices

Introduction

This chapter provides some patterns and practices while designing new business requirements using a serverless ecosystem and focus on the value that the event-driven design brings to those architectural patterns.

Some patterns are already discussed in detail in previous chapters but aim to provide a concrete scenario and use case.

Structure

In this chapter, we will discuss the following topics:

- Scalable Serverless Computing
- High-Performance Computing
- Interactive Distributed Communication
- Generative AI Using Serverless
- Governance

Scalable Serverless Computing

The previous chapters were a deep exploration of the AWS serverless ecosystem and how the AWS Lambda as a computing service can collaborate to apply the business requirements. Also, as part of delving into the serverless and integrations, different ways of removing unnecessary custom code and replacing the integration lambdas with native integration solutions such as EventBridge pipes were explored.

Starting a new business has always been a challenging process that involves the TCO (Total Cost of Ownership), ROI (Time to Market), and TTM (Time to Market) analysis. Also, considering the capacity of scaling is also a challenging topic. A startup will introduce an idea and that idea can be achieved using different technologies, including the serverless as a principal choice.

A simple market at an early stage can achieve a rapid Time to Market by adopting serverless ecosystem and the use of AWS Lambda as a computing service, as demonstrated in *Figure 10.1*:

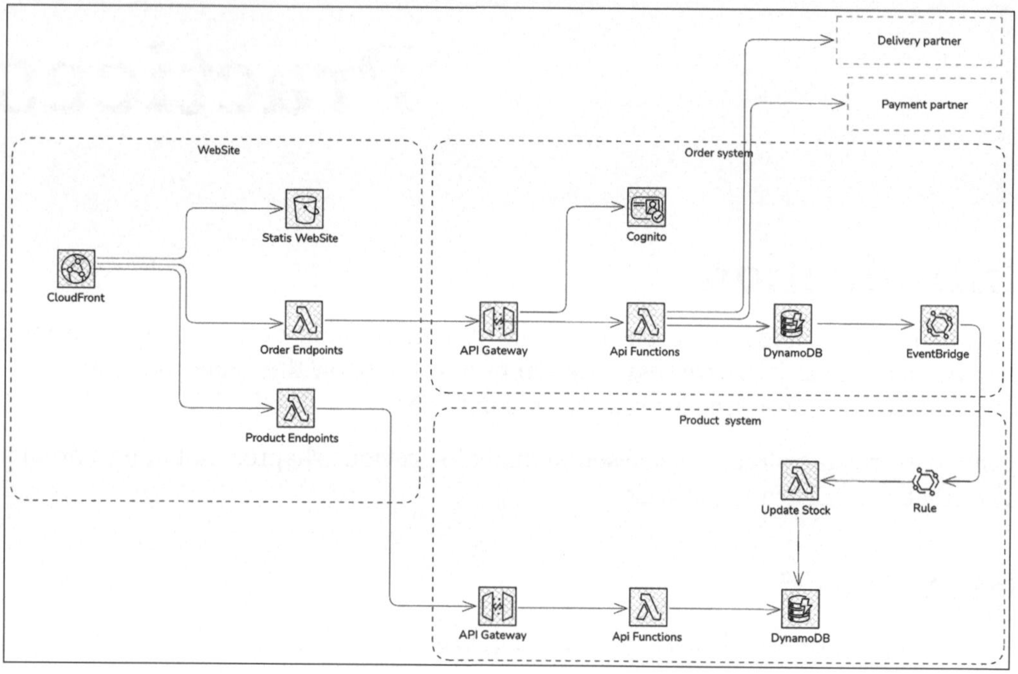

Figure 10.1: *Startup early stage design*

Now, as the business grows by achieving more online products, more orders, and consequently more payments and deliveries, the question arises, '*At which level of scale can we keep our users satisfied?*', '*How does the system behave with more load?*', '*How can the cost be controlled?*'. Answering these questions needs insights and an adaptable design.

Achieving a highly scalable system needs considering different pillars, such as Performance, Resilience, Operation, and Cost, while balancing trade-offs to make it easier to apply the correct design. A business in the first stage of scaling can consider cost control as an important option, as revenue may not increase at the same pace and it also needs to keep cost aligned with the other pillars. However, at some higher scale, and based on how long the company has been present in the market, it can accept higher costs and apply performance over other pillars.

The design presented in *Figure 10.1* already has some bottlenecks at scale. The order system is highly coupled to the payment and delivery partners, which are two external systems. This means that any inconsistency on the partner side will impact directly the users and the overall business process. We can achieve this SPOF (Single Point of Failure) easily using an event-driven approach, considering that an order can logically be treated asynchronously, but with some small process changes.

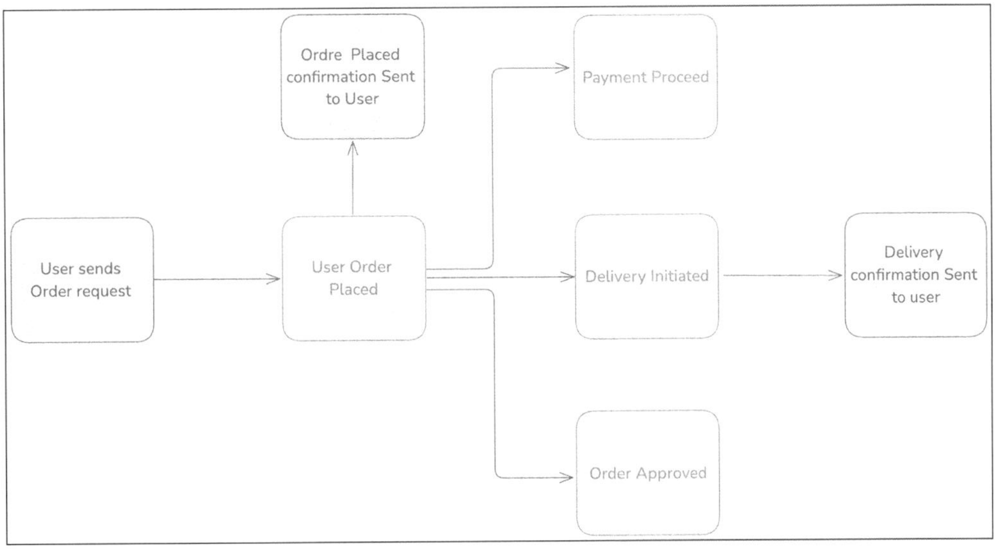

Figure 10.2: *Order business process*

The changes in order to process apply a higher level of emails, which introduces the costs. However, at the same time, the design reduces costs and effort for the actual computing resources (*Figure* 10.2 demonstrates a new proposal for the order system.):

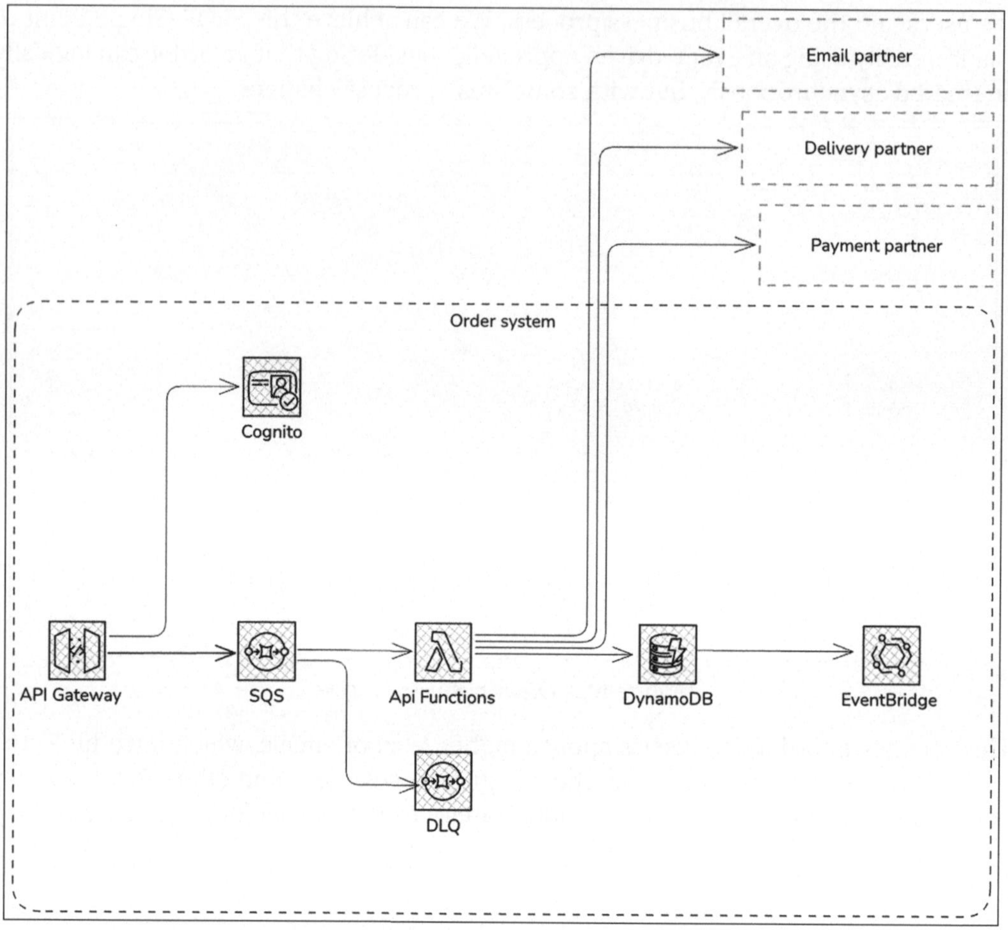

Figure 10.3: *Order system async design*

This design allows offloading and balances the rate of order processing using an SQS queue and also guarantees the processing and resiliency by adding a Dead Letter Queue and retry mechanism. However, now, the lambda function has a new dependency: email provider.

When designing asynchronous systems, one of the most important points is how to achieve idempotency. If the confirmation is sent and the payment fails, a retry will resend the confirmation, and in the worst case, when the delivery fails, the retry will recall the payment partner. It is important to isolate all transactions or commitments in a way that the overall design can guarantee operational concerns. *Figure* 10.4 demonstrates how to apply transactional isolation:

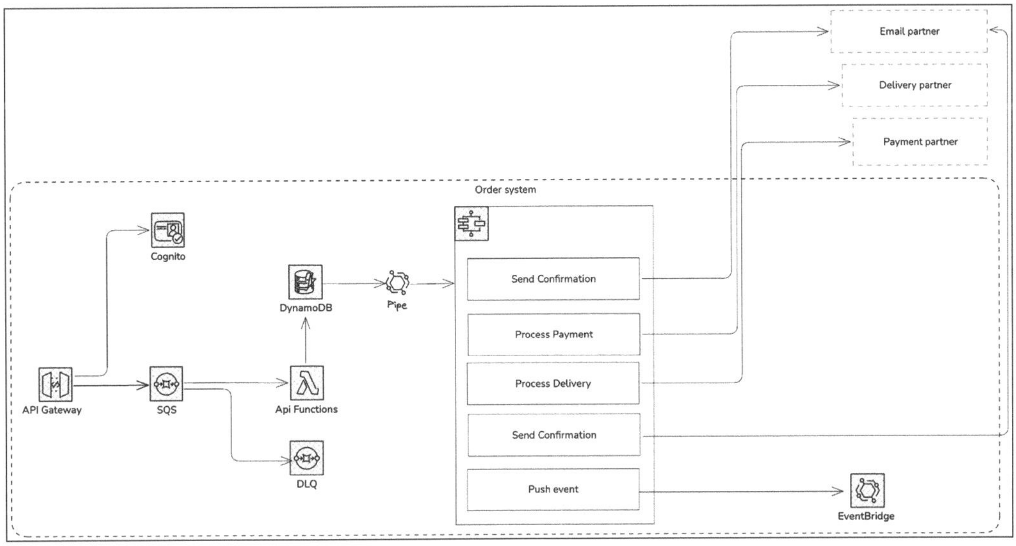

Figure 10.4: *Orchestrated order processing*

When applying orchestration, keeping a consistent state for the whole workflow is an important consideration. If for any reason any step fails, all workflow stages must be rolled back to the previous state. Some patterns like saga help to overcome this challenge by tracking the stages and redoing the commitment of previous stages.

This can be easily done for a payment or delivery by simply calling those services to request a cancellation. However, what about an email? An email cannot be rolled back. To avoid resending emails in case of retry, we can keep track of the state and decide if any email has been sent already or not. When a rollback is required for an email, a better approach is to send an email indicating the reason for the unsuccessful process.

High-Performance Computing (HPC)

In *Chapter 1, Introduction to Serverless Computing*, the HPC was explored at a deep level. However, achieving high-performance computing requires some considerations, such as Parallelism and Speed. An HPC workload may require a CPU to run a workload with a higher number of tasks rapidly, or may require a GPU processor to achieve higher concurrency and parallelism accuracy levels. The CPU and GPU have some conceptual differences. *Figure* 10.5 demonstrates these architectural differences at a core level:

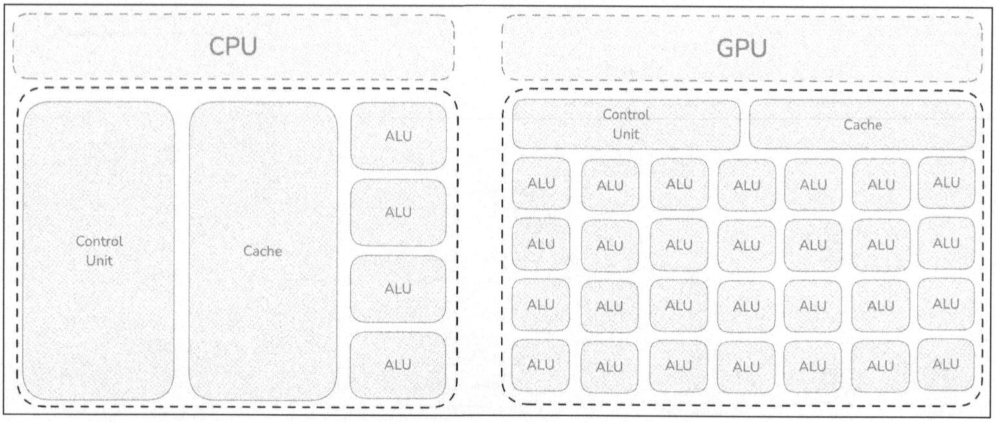

Figure 10.5: *CPU vs. GPU*

- **Central Processing Unit**: A CPU aims to achieve higher processing speed and reduce latency by splitting the overall capacity into isolated units or Core. A core represents two logical processors that can run tasks in parallel. However, a CPU at a high level executes the processes serially and applies prioritization to schedule and reschedule tasks.
- **Graphics Processing Unit**: A GPU can provide many streaming multiprocessor (SM), which can have many Cores. The GPU Warp schedulers allow running a batch of many cores, giving the possibility to achieve higher-performing processes. The Batches allow achieving higher throughput, while the cores for higher parallelism.

A typical scenario for HPC workloads is ML, Model Training, batch processing, and so on. However, how the design will be influenced depends on the process and requirements. For example, if a model training requires permanent restraining and will be executed multiple times per day, the principal consideration will be the duration and how to keep the execution time small, but at the same time, the cost can be an option to look at. A model training can achieve faster and more cost-effective solutions using GPC, while another can achieve the same advantages with CPU.

Designing Batch Processing

Often in software, the need for executing recurrent processes aims to schedule jobs that run for a duration of time or behind a change in the system that leads to trigger that process execution. On AWS, these kinds of processing can be achieved using AWS Batch Jobs or ECS tasks (*Figure* 10.6 demonstrates a simple scheduled job processing.):

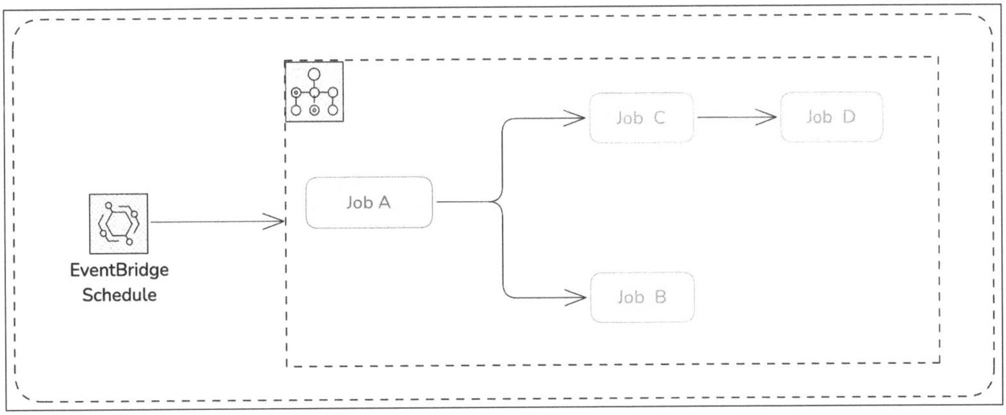

Figure 10.6: *Scheduled batch job processing*

A job can be executed on an EC2, or Fargate instance, and also can benefit from on-demand or SPOT instances. In some scenarios, a job must be triggered per changes, (*Figure* 10.7 illustrates a file processing job for large files with related items that must be processed and considered while keeping track of the overall file state, such as the number of lines or items and characteristics of each category of items.):

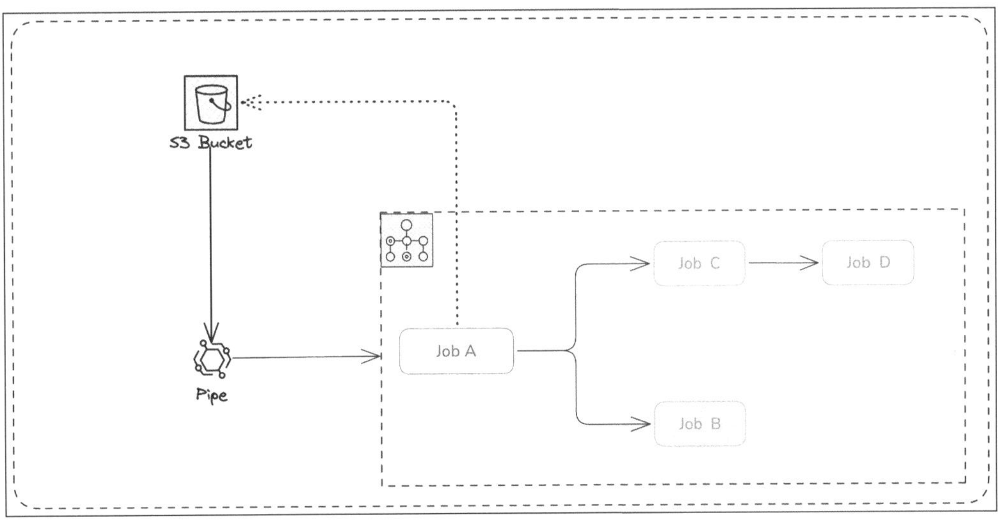

Figure 10.7: *Triggering batch jobs*

In this design, a large file is uploaded on S3 and contains all items related to a customer. Items are a mix of normal and VIP categories. A customer can have all X normal items and Y VIP for free, while the rest will be tagged as Pending until the customer pays the facture.

Designing with Step Functions Distributed Maps

As HPC provides higher parallelization and throughput by concept, another option will be to use the **`StepFunctions`** Distributed Maps. Distributed maps parallelize the treatment of a batch of items in isolated logical contexts called child workflow executions that are orchestrated and controlled using Map Run resource. The distributed maps can be configured to fetch data from an S3 bucket as a datasource, but also the data can be passed as the item collections from previous steps (*Figure* 10.8 illustrates how distributed maps work at high-level design.):

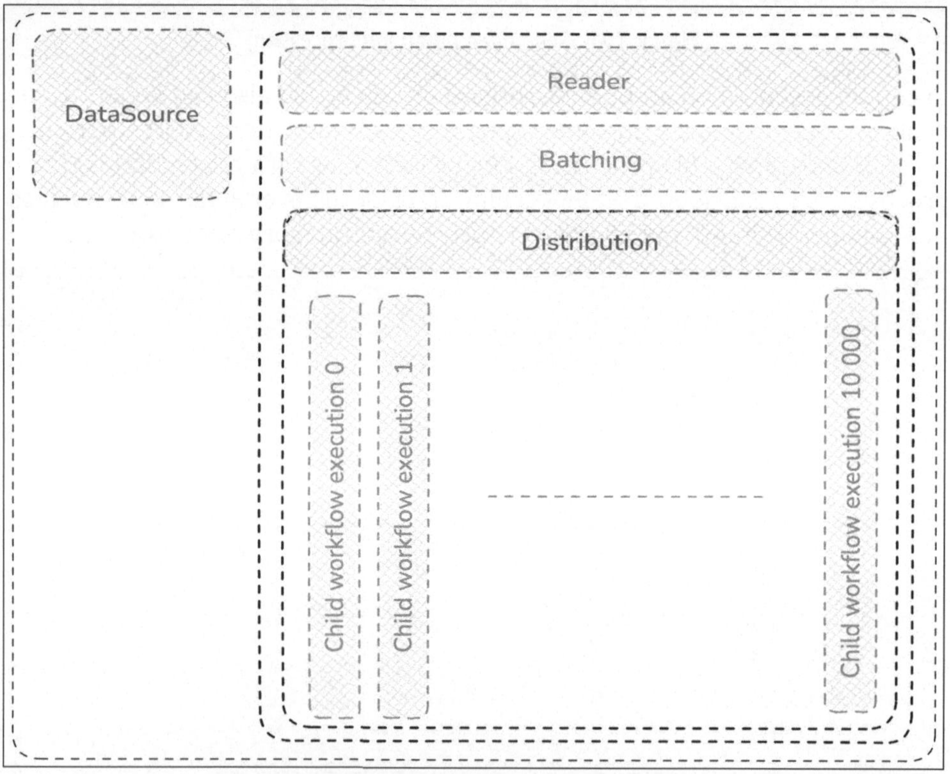

Figure 10.8: *Step functions distributed map*

In use cases with significantly large assets, the processing can be significantly improved using Distributed Map and Inline Maps to process large S3 files and increase the parallelization. The following figure demonstrates how distributed maps can be used:

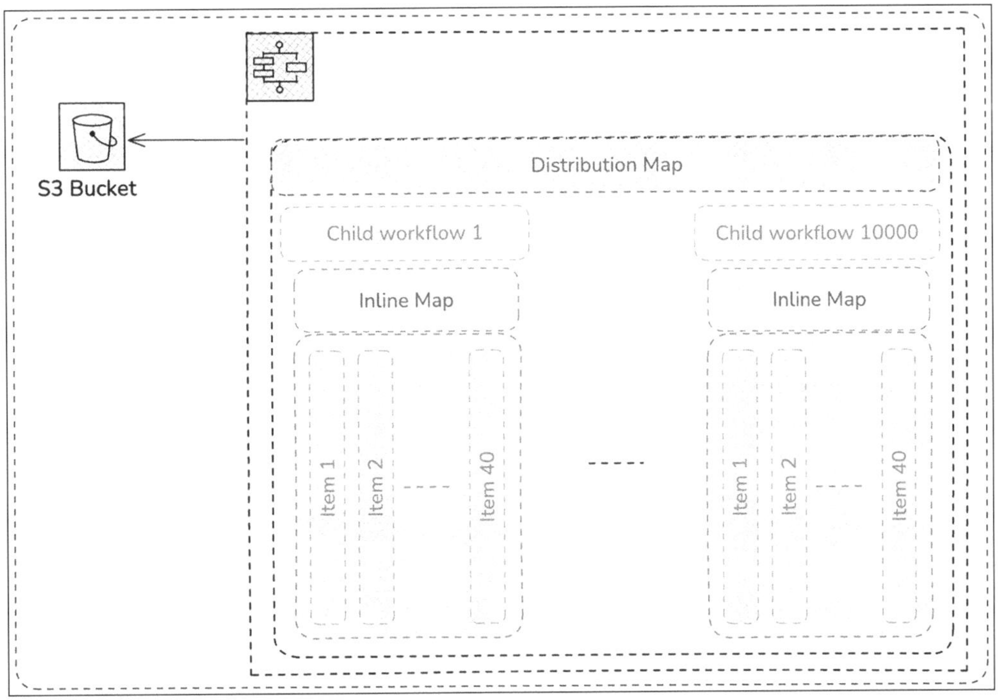

Figure 10.9: *Distributed map with nested inline map*

The design uses a distributed map to achieve a higher level of parallelism and uses the inline map for any child workflow to treat items one by one. The distributed map can take time to generate the child-run task. This time-consuming process can become significantly obvious and can lead to cost increase and overall process latency. A solution is to reduce the number of parent distributed maps instead of letting it achieve a maximum number of 10,000 parallel or concurrent run tasks. Instead, use the nested distributed map inside each generated parent to parallelize the time distribution evenly.

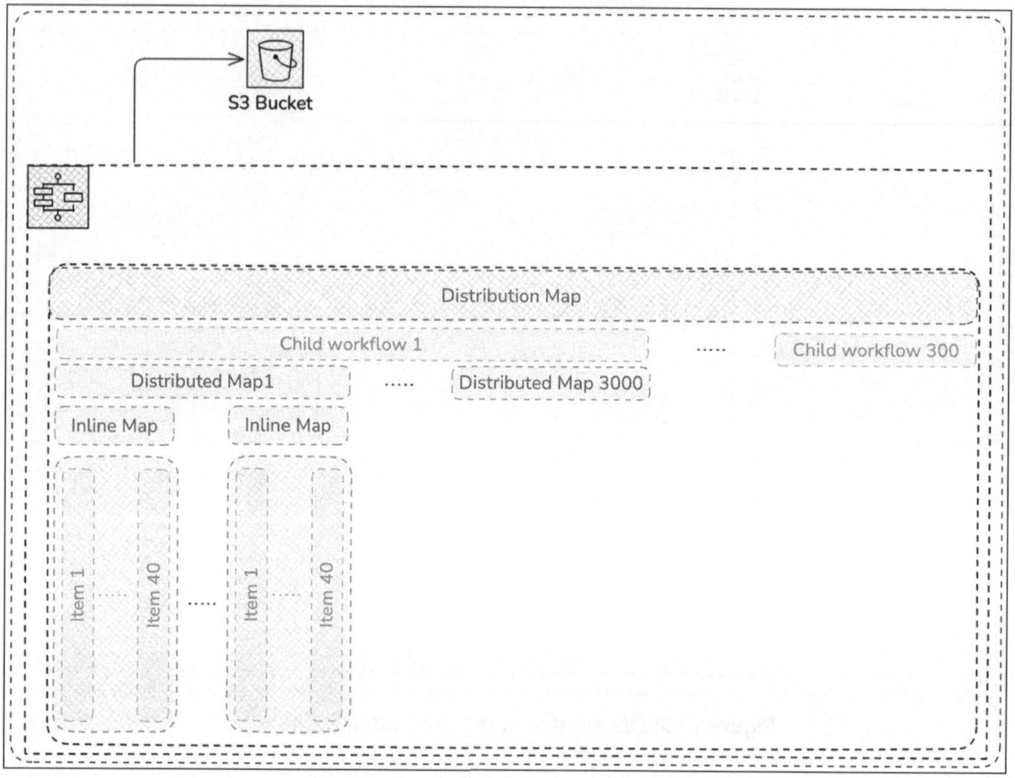

Figure 10.10: *Nested distributed maps*

Designing ML Model Training

AWS offers a variety of services to help run machine learning processes in a managed way. Some services such as EMR, Redshift, and Sagemaker inference have serverless options. Training a model is one of the most known challenges these days in ML teams (*Figure 10.11* demonstrates a typical machine learning solution to train a model.):

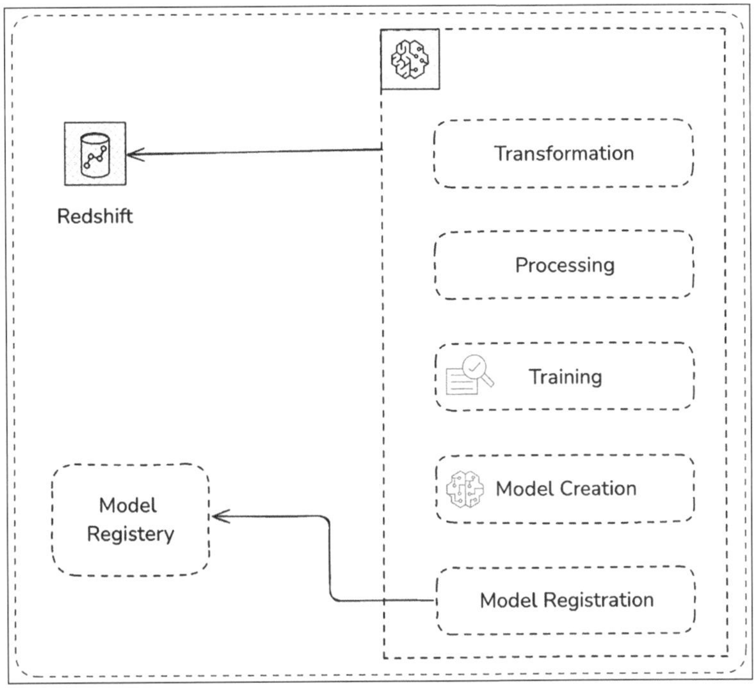

Figure 10.11: *Sagemaker pipeline*

In this design, Redshift as a datasource allows users to have up to petabytes of data and achieve high-performing queries for large datasets. The Transform step allows the transformation of incoming data and applies cleanup and synthesizes the data to achieve better data quality. The training step will train the data and give them a data point or score. Finally, a model will be created and registered in the Model Registry. This model will be used in the inference pipeline to predict a value for incoming data.

As the training process relies on data and data quality, a model may be required to retrain the model recurrently as data and data lifecycle evolve. The quality of data cannot be identified by humans and must be automated. Detecting whether data needs to be retrained can be done using a scheduled trigger, as shown in *Figure 10.12*:

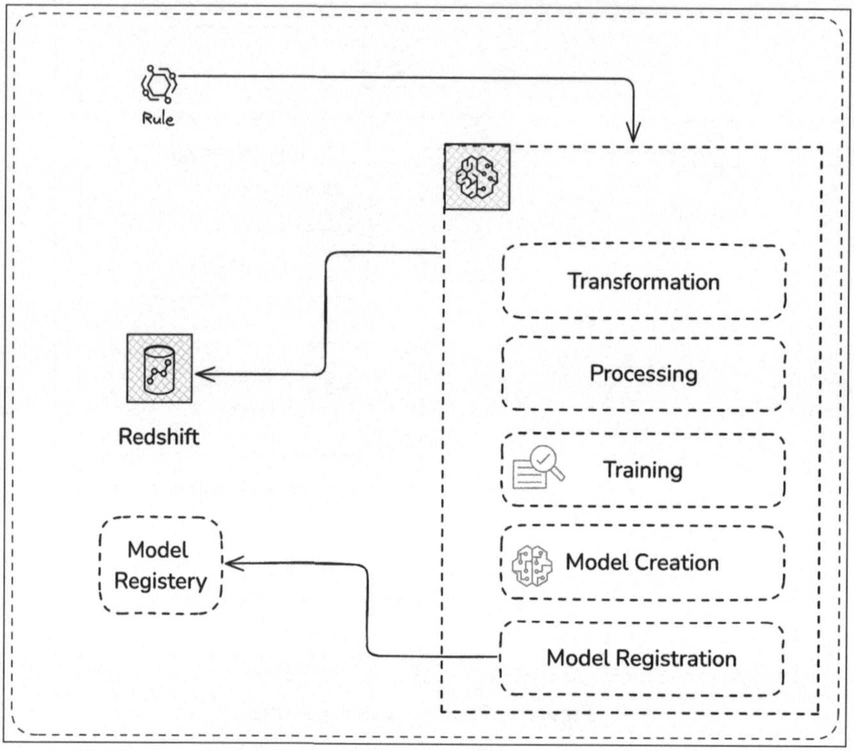

Figure 10.12: *Scheduling pipeline*

However, defining the best scheduling time for a model is not a reliable option, as retraining may or may not evolve the model. To tackle this challenge, there are various options. This is important because a model helps to apply predictions, but there will be no concrete solution to verify if retraining is required or not. Nonetheless, these options can help to improve the model quality and remove useless retraining. One option will be to trigger the training behind significant changes that assure the model retraining effectiveness, such as listening to a stream of model-dependent entity changes and deciding if the changes will result in any new asset.

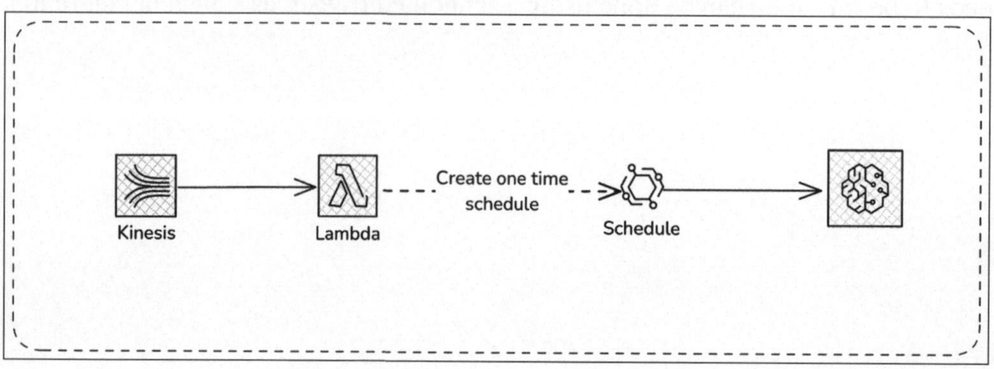

Figure 10.13: *One-time schedule trigger*

Another option will be to identify whether the prediction quality is aligned with the real-time verification in the inference process:

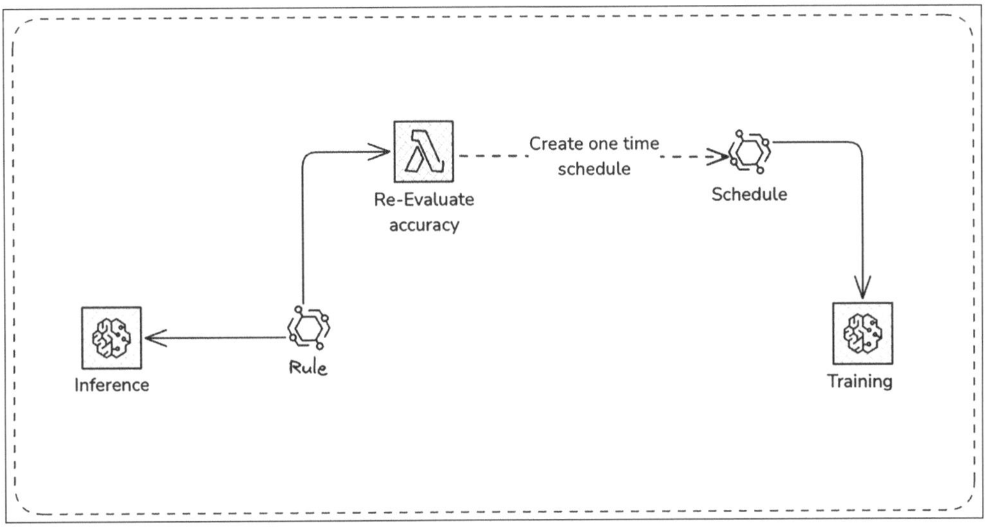

Figure 10.14: *Re-evaluating in inference*

It is important to consider the duration of a training process and avoid overlapping training, for example, if any new schedule is created, all consequence verification must be abandoned. *Figure 10.14* can be evolved to schedule a training trigger while verifying the state of the latest schedule before rescheduling.

Interactive Distributed Communication

One of the most important requirements in distributed systems is duplex communication, which means a system needs a response after requesting a process. The results are important as a response is a means to keep consistency across boundaries. In traditional distributed systems, often a process takes time and may be long enough that will impact the responsiveness in the consumer side or calling system. In event-driven design, as communication relies on asynchronous channels to achieve a higher level of responsiveness, consistency across boundaries becomes a principal challenge. How can a system keep track of process results after requesting? To answer the question, having a clear perspective of the overall system and landscape is important. The landscape helps to identify the coupling and decoupling at different levels of design being system, context, software, and deployment container (C4 model).

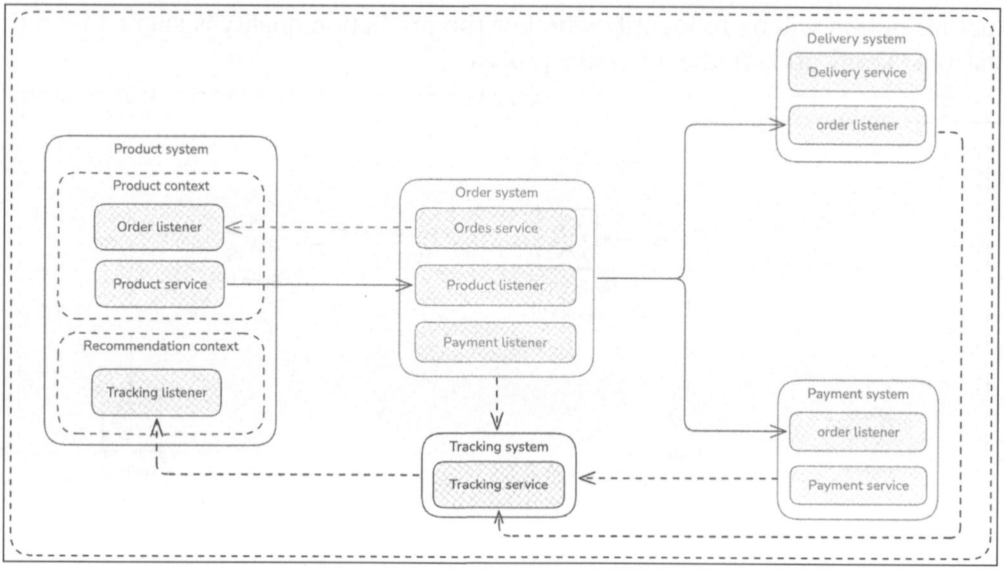

Figure 10.15: *Overall system landscape*

Figure 10.15 demonstrates a landscape representing the system, context, software, and deployable containers. The importance of looking at these kinds of sketches is the vision and clarity that will be achieved. In an event-driven architecture, the important elements to identify are Communication entities (commands, events, queries, and so on), Datastore (states), interactiveness (flow), and complexity (alignment). Looking at these details gives the ability to avoid unintentional complexity and coupling.

Figure 10.16 shows the order system's relation with payment:

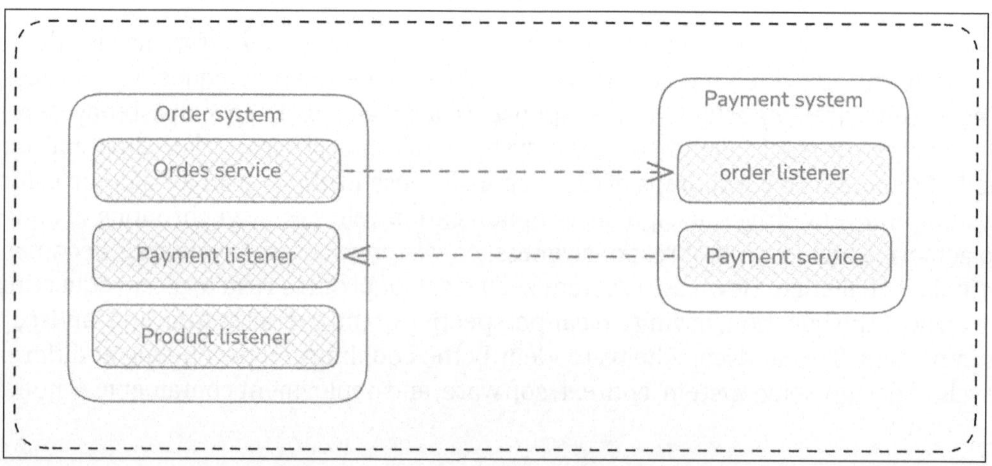

Figure 10.16: *Order and payment system integration*

The Order service represents an independent container providing messages consumed by the payment system. The order system, as an enabler context, will need to keep track of payment results to provide process result consistency. Focusing on the duplex communication between two contexts, it is important to note the separation of service and listeners in different runtime threads and deployment assets. This helps to achieve the full decoupling during both runtime and build-time phases.

The key question to answer is about states: should the payment needs to store all orders and orders all payments? In this context, the two systems can collaborate without requiring data and state duplication, as they provide a unique result that must be achieved collaboratively. However, when looking at the Order and Product system, they represent two distinct and independent contexts in terms of processes, but at the same time, a business coupling is required to achieve consistency (*Figure 10.17* demonstrates a different dimension of order and product communication.):

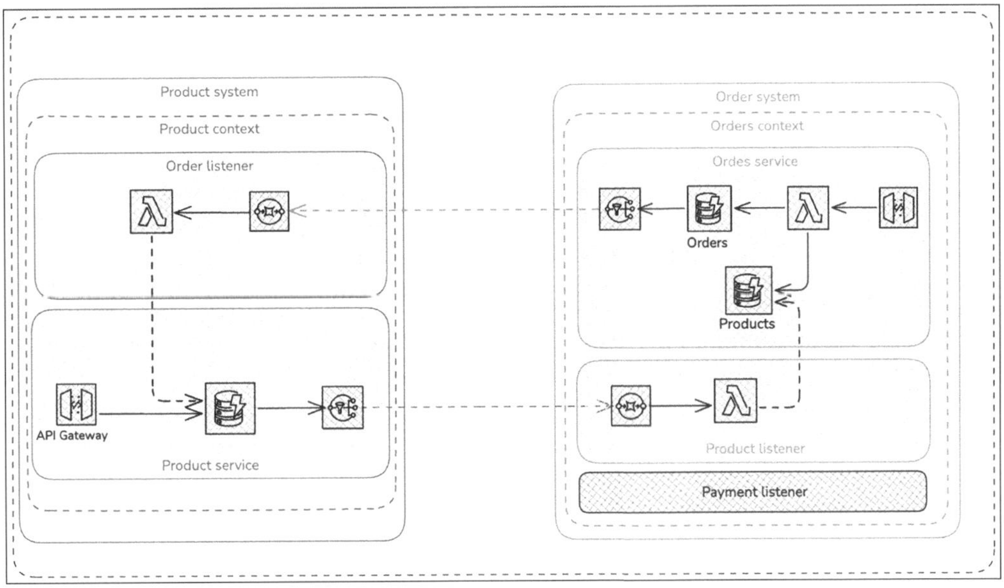

Figure 10.17: *Order and product system integration*

The Product service manages the lifecycle of products and provides an interface to the consumers to send new products, update existing ones, or delete them, as well as a collection of management endpoints. The order system, on the other hand, also provides an interface to let consumers interact with orders. From the separation of consumer-facing layers, there are two distinct sorts of consumers who interact with these systems. As part of order reception, it is beneficial for the order system to confirm the availability of a product by chaining and crossing the network calls, while providing an eventually consistent verification at an early stage and letting the consumer be informed about any lack of product in stock. This result can also be processed asynchronously between the order and product system, but it will add another layer of complexity by adding the requirement for mobile or email notifications to inform the consumers about any process decision.

Generative AI Using Serverless

As generative AI takes its peak, companies look for new ways of innovating using generative AI. In this era, there are requirements that can use market-trained models, but often more sophisticated requirements need to integrate the business data and let data and market models integrate to achieve more concrete business-oriented results.

A typical generic use case can be achieved using a simple design using AWS Bedrock, as shown in *Figure 10.18*:

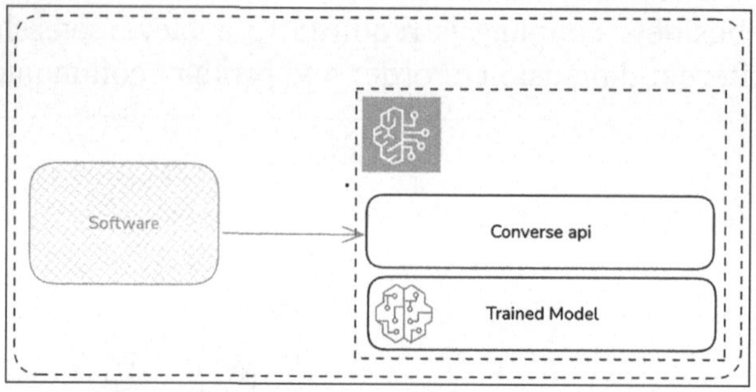

Figure 10.18: *Amazon Bedrock integration*

Converse API provides a model-agnostic interface, helping the integration of any model without changing the software code, while Bedrock will manage the parameter mapping for each model. An example will be using the Titan model to identify the fraudulent messages in a conversation. *Figure 10.19* illustrates this design:

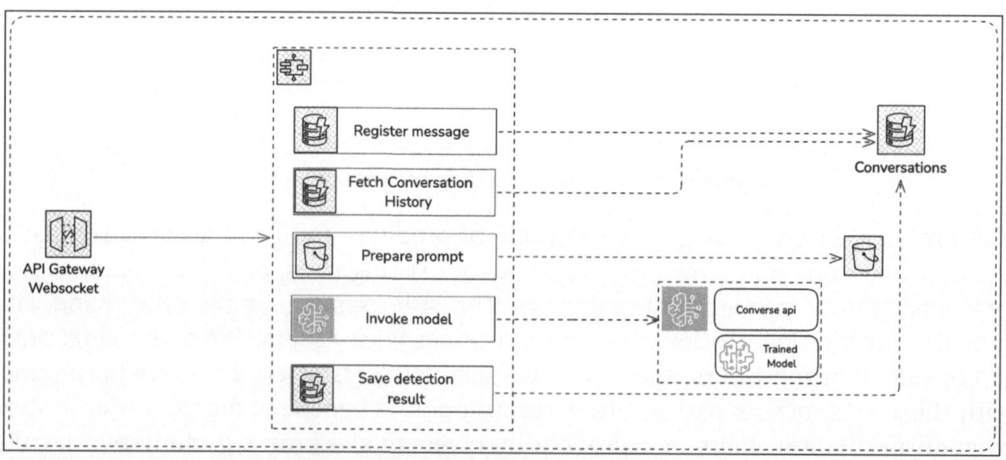

Figure 10.19: *Fraudulent message detection*

This design introduces some significant challenges in terms of reliability and performance. First, the integration between the API Gateway and step function is synchronous, resulting in useless wait and latency that impacts the responsiveness on the consumer side. Second, as some models are not available in the region where that software is deployed, this can add some level of latency. For this particular scenario, the design can be evolved by adopting an asynchronous and event-driven oriented approach.

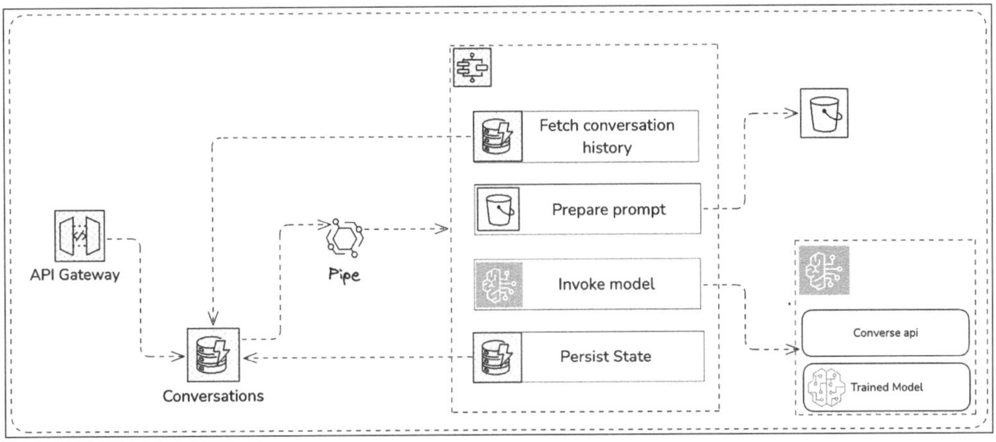

Figure 10.20: *Async fraudulent message detection*

Augmenting the business process while taking advantage of Gen AI needs to provide the business data side of the available market model. This brings the possibility to design RAG (Retrieval-Augmented Generation) using Amazon Bedrock knowledge base, a managed feature allowing to attach a vector datasource and providing the results considering the business data. *Figure 10.21* demonstrates how to design a search (product lookup service) to augment the capabilities of Bedrock and provide some conversational search mechanisms. The data store is fed by an event-driven approach using S3 and event triggers, allowing a lambda function to ask the knowledge base to start syncing data with the OpenSearch service vectorial collection.

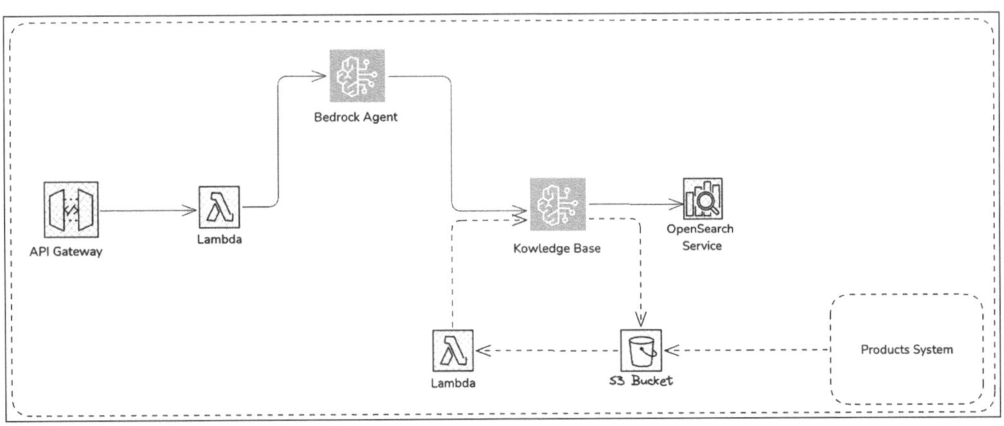

Figure 10.21: *Bedrock knowledge base with vectorial datasource*

While this design answers the requirements, there may be cases where the business requirements need to call multiple APIs and aggregate the results. To avoid adding useless complexity, the design can adopt Bedrock agent actions. Bedrock agent action provides the capability for looking at an OpenAPI specification and calling the API after preparing the API request. *Figure 10.22* illustrates this approach:

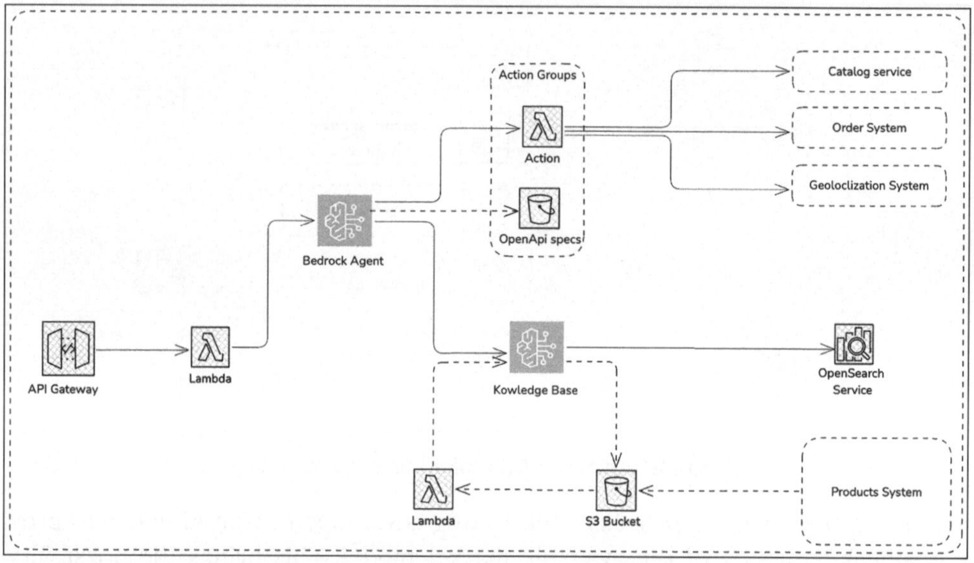

Figure 10.22: *Bedrock agents actions groups*

This design lets augment the product search process by adopting other services that can help to enrich or refine those result sets.

Governance

An important part of software development is considering how the software can be maintained, operated, and consumed. As requirements evolve and new consumers start consuming the software, adopting the governance as part of the software development phase, and at an early stage, will be an advantage and assurance in the long term. While adopting an event-driven approach, the systems' communication will be applied using messages, be it command, event, or query. As per need, two software will communicate over different protocols, and the only means toward a well-governed software will be in adopting standards. Some highly adopted and well-known standards can be named explicitly such as AsyncAPI, Cloudevents, and Distributed Tracing.

AsyncAPI

AsyncAPI is a specification for event-driven system documentation. It relies on fundamental topics of event-driven design, such as Server (communication interface by a defined protocol - HTTPS, WSS, MQTT, and so on), Channel (broker as a means of event-based communication), Messages (events, commands, or queries), Operations (a behavioral action that result from the presence of a message).

A simple specification example is as follows, where the service provides a process around order management in an e-commerce:

```
asyncapi: 3.0.0
info:
 title: Order Service
 version: 1.0.0
defaultContentType: application/json
servers:
 orders-sns:
   host: sns.eu-west-1.amazonaws.com
   protocol: https
 orders-sqs:
   host: sqs.eu-west-1.amazonaws.com
   protocol: https
channels:
 ordersTopic:
   address: 'orders.events'
   title: Orders Topic
   servers:
     - $ref: '#/servers/orders-sns'
 ordersQueue:
   address: 'orders.commands'
   title: Orders Queue
   servers:
     - $ref: '#/servers/orders-sqs'
operations:
 onOrderPlaced:
   action: receive
   channel:
     $ref: '#/channels/ordersQueue'
   messages:
     classifiedEvent:
       $ref: '#/components/messages/OrderPlaced'
 onOrderConfirmed:
   action: send
   channel:
     $ref: '#/channels/ordersTopic'
   messages:
     classifiedEvent:
       $ref: '#/components/messages/OrderConfirmed'
components:
 messages:
   OrderPlaced:
```

```
    title: Order Placed event
    payload:
      type: object
      $ref: "#/components/schemas/OrderPlacedEnvelope"
  OrderConfirmed:
    title: Order Confirmed event
    payload:
      type: object
      $ref: "#/components/schemas/OrderConfirmedEnvelope"
schemas:
  OrderPlacedEnvelope:
    type: object
    required:
      - orderId
      - placedAt
      - time
      - type
    properties:
      type:
        type: string
      id:
        type: string
      placedAt:
        type: string
      time:
        type: string
      user:
        type: object
        required:
          - email
        properties:
          email:
            type: string
          name:
            type: string
          id:
            type: string
  OrderConfirmedEnvelope:
    type: object
    required:
      - orderId
      - time
      - type
    properties:
      type:
        type: string
      orderId:
```

```
        type: string
      time:
        type: string
```

This specification represents a simple service receiving the order placement commands from an SQS queue and sending order's confirmation events via an SNS topic. The specification provided the command and event schema.

Having a specification on its own does not bring any advantage, except providing documentation support, but a specification will be advantageous if it is used for contract generation, validation, discovery, and backward compatibility checks.

Contract Generation

Using a specification, contract testing becomes easy. This is an excellent way to achieve a test-driven approach. All software products, whether consumer or producer, will generate the code contracts using specifications. AsyncAPI provides enough tools for a variety of requirements, and as part of them, the **`@asyncapi/modelina`** allows code contract generation for a variety of programming languages:

```
import { TypeScriptGenerator } from '@asyncapi/modelina';
import { Parser, fromFile } from '@asyncapi/parser'
import { writeFileSync } from 'node:fs';
import { AsyncAPIDocumentInterface } from '@asyncapi/parser';

const parser = new Parser();

const output = './contracts';
const schemaPath = process.argv[2];

export async function generate(
 document: AsyncAPIDocumentInterface,
 generator: TypeScriptGenerator
) {
 try {
   const models = await generator.generate(document?.json() || {});
   let content = models.map(m => m.result.slice(0)).join('\n\n')

   mkdirSync(output, { recursive: true });

     writeFileSync(
`${output}/${document?.info?.title}-${document?.info?.version}.ts`,
content);

 } catch (err) { console.error(err); }
}
```

```
const parse = async (specPath: string): AsyncAPIDocumentInterface  => {
 const parseOutput = specPath.startsWith("http") ?
   await fromURL(parser, specPath): await fromFile(parser, specPath);

 return parsedOutput.parse().document;
}

const generator = new TypeScriptGenerator({  modelType: 'interface' });
const document = await parse(schemaPath);
generate(document, generator);
```

The preceding snippet generates the TypeScript code contracts from specification and saves the results in a defined output. This is the ideal way of defining a service contract when the producer is the owner of the service and the consumers look at the specification as the single source of trust.

Validation

Validation is a crucial part of event-driven design. Some of the challenges of event-driven architecture were discussed previously, and one of the most important challenges was inverting dependency direction and consequently the inverting flow direction. This is one important note in EDA that leads to double validation of messages on the producer and consumer side. It is important to validate the messages before sending and before consuming. EDA removes the failure and unintentional behavioral failures by inverting dependency direction; however, without care, this will introduce hidden failures and stale data.

The validation of specification can be done using some packages like AJV, as shown in the following snippet. The validator validates the AsyncAPI specification; a specification document must be fetched and parsed using any parser like **`@asyncapi/parser`**, and the validator will validate an event against that schema:

```
import Ajv from "ajv";
import addFormats from "ajv-formats";
import { Parser, fromUrl, fromFile, AsyncAPIDocumentInterface } from "@
asyncapi/parser";

const ajvOptions = { allErrors: true };

class SchemaValidator {
   validate = async (event: any, document: AsyncAPIDocumentInterface) =>
{
         return this.AjvValidate(
event, document.json(),
event.dataSchema?.split('#')[0],
event.dataSchema);
   }
```

```
    private AjvValidate(obj: any, schema: any, key: any, ref: any) {
        const ajv = new Ajv(ajvOptions);
        addFormats(ajv);

        ajv.addVocabulary([
            'asyncapi', 'info', 'servers', 'channels','components',
            'x-parser-api-version', 'x-parser-spec-parsed',
            'x-parser-schema-id', 'x-parser-circular',
            'x-parser-message-parsed', 'x-parser-original-traits',
            'x-parser-original-schema-format','x-parser-message-name',
            'x-parser-original-payload' ]);

        ajv.addSchema(schema, key);
        const valid = ajv.validate({ $ref: ref }, obj);
        if (!valid) {
            const errorMessage = JSON.stringify(ajv.errors);
            throw new Error(errorMessage);
        }
        return valid;
    }
}

const eventExample= {};
const specSchema = { ... };
const validator = new SchemaValidator();
await validator.validate(eventExample, specSchema);
```

Discovery

Often the teams use the specifications to consume the events. The event consumption is not a complex process, but the consumption must be done carefully. The producer distributes the events, but as part of the building phase, the changes can be applied, and occasionally, some schema changes can be done. It is important to discover the new changes applied and notify those changes. EventBridge registry and discovery is a managed feature that provides the discovery of events and detects changes in near real-time. It allows triggering a lambda function to run custom processes and verification, and if required, sending a notification to the enterprise communication channel (*Figure* 10.23 illustrates this design.):

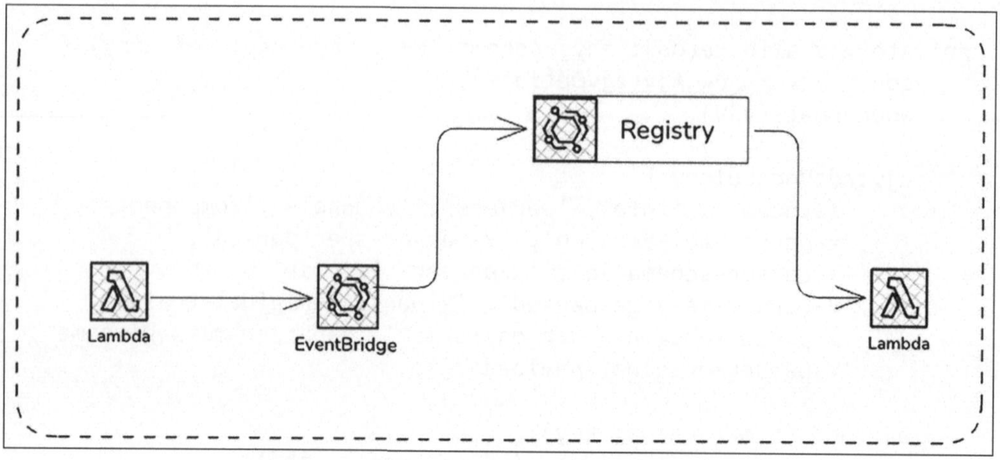

Figure 10.23: *EventBridge schema discovery*

Backward Compatibility

As part of governance, providing a simple way for comparing two schemas and identifying compatibility may be an interesting topic for almost every company. While relying on standards, the chance of achieving solutions in the community rises. Regarding AsyncAPI specification, the **`@asyncapi/diff`** is a package that helps to compare two schemas and provides an output indicating breaking, non-breaking, or unclassified status for any single attribute in a schema.

```
import { diff } from "@asyncapi/diff";
const output = diff(oldDocument, newDocument, {});
```

CloudEvents

The CloudEvents, as the single official specification for event-driven architecture, brings a standard into the event-driven systems and provides a simplified way to guarantee the quality and extensibility of communication. The specification introduces a pragmatic event model, allowing to standardize the communication and collaboration.

CloudEvents specification describes an event as a data record expressing an occurrence and its context, which are routed from an event producer (the source) to interested event consumers. The routing can be performed based on information contained in the event, but an event will not identify a specific routing destination. Events will contain two types of information: the Event Data representing the Occurrence and Context metadata providing contextual information about the Occurrence.

CloudEvents support the following data types: *Boolean*, *Integer*, *String*, *Binary*, *URI*, and *Timestamp*, with the only exception being ***data*** attributes, which are identified using the **`datacontenttype`** attribute.

CloudEvents specification proposes a standard event model as follows:

- **`id`:** A unique identifier to identify an event in the boundaries of `` `source` ``. The ID may have a UUID, nanoid, or ULID. If the possibility of ordering and sorting lexicographically is a requirement, ULID will be the best choice. The id attribute is an excellent choice for idempotency purposes, as it provides uniqueness in the context of the source attribute.
- **`source`:** The unique identifier of the context or boundaries in which a change resulted in the production of an event. This value can be varied if this is a SaaS product, an internal service, or a public service.
- **`type`:** The type of event to identify what the event intention is. A good choice of defining event type will be to include some organizational or context terms in event type such as **`orders.placed`**, or for multi-brand services such as **`appel.orders.placed`**.

In addition to the above-required attributes, the optional attributes are tagged as optional because their presence depends on the category of the event and other factors.

- **`datacontenttype`:** It defines the content format of event data payload. This can be a content type, such as **`application/json`**. This attribute brings value if there are other types of content.
- **`dataschema`:** The URI to the corresponding schema of the event. The URL must hit the schema of that event for that specific event version. This attribute is useful for analysis and automation.
- **`subject`:** The subject is helpful for filtering when a consumer requires events related to a specific subject. A subject can be a **`customer id`**, **`product id`**, **`product category`**, and more. The importance is that its existence must help to simplify events filter on the consumer side without looking at the complex event data structure.
- **`time`:** Timestamp of when the occurrence happened.
- **`data`:** The payload of events representing all service and business-specific contracts. The data format must correspond to the **`datacontenttype`** to avoid any unintentional parsing errors on the consumer side.

The following event example represents an order confirmation message:

```
{
 "id": "01HSTR34JDRWMZP8NEJ3VJF3PP",
 "source": "eu.ecommerce.orders.service",
 "type": "order.placed",
 "time": "2024-05-01T13:35:00.000",
 "datacontenttype": "application/json",
 "dataversion": "1.0.0",
```

```
  "data": {
    "placeAt": "2024-05-01T13:30:23.765",
    "orderId": "01HSTQR6968PQ133Q16VZ3CPNG",
    "basketId": "ea08e079-d542-4c67-9a58-1d8c8cc03b8e",
    "userId": "aiESIex6a77FVtlYUm59Y",
    "products": [
      { "id": "DZxuXuB37cHt7C6VHP5w5", "quantity": 3 },
      { "id": "x7riCxC53QbsU1JTO3dyt", "quantity": 1 }
    ]
  }
}
```

The **CloudEvents** specification introduces the extensions, which provide a way to extend the events as per needs. All extension attributes are optional and are on top of the basic formats and cannot be presented as structured such as JSON. For example, the sequence extension provides two attributes, **sequence** and **sequencetype**, and these can be presented in an event as follows:

```
{
  "id": "01HSTR34JDRWMZP8NEJ3VJF3PP",
  "source": "eu.ecommerce.orders.service",
  "type": "order.placed",
  "time": "2024-05-01T13:35:00.000",
  "datacontenttype": "application/json",
  "dataversion": "1.0.0",
  "sequence": "1",
  "sequencetype": "Integer",
  "data": { ... }
}
```

Tracing

To achieve tracing as part of the standardization process, distributed tracing can be used as a simple, high-level tracing standard that is protocol-agnostic. The advantage of representing distributed tracing as part of event-based communication is that observability and tracing tools can easily interpret these attributes and correlate them with other observability entities such as logs or metrics. CloudEvents introduces a tracing extension, representing two attributes, **traceparent** and **tracestate**, which can be presented in an event at the root level.

The trace attributes can be easily extracted using **OpenTelemetry** propagator, **W3CTraceContextPropagator**, by simply calling the propagator extract method at the early stage of event reception and using the extracted context to start a trace span for the lambda handler.

@opentelemetry/core package provides **W3CTraceContextPropagator**, which can be used when setting up the Node OTEL SDK:

```
import { propagation, context } from '@opentelemetry/api';
import { W3CTraceContextPropagator, W3CBaggagePropagator, CompositeProp-
agator } from '@opentelemetry/core';

export const propagator = new CompositePropagator(
 {
   propagators: [
     new W3CTraceContextPropagator(),
     new W3CBaggagePropagator()]
 }
);

propagation.setGlobalPropagator(propagator);
```

The propagator will fetch the **traceparent**, which will be automatically extracted. After setting up, the propagator can be used to extract the trace information from the event as follows:

```
 const extractedContext = propagation.extract(
context.active(),
event,
new EventCustomMapGetter('traceparent'));

class EventCustomMapGetter {
  constructor(privateKey) {
       this.privateKey = privateKey;
  }

  get(carrier, key) {
       return carrier[this.privateKey];
  }

  keys(carrier) {
       return Object.keys(carrier);
  }
}
```

Conclusion

In this chapter, several patterns were explored in the serverless era for a variety of requirements, such as computational needs, business scalability, communication patterns, GenAI adoption, and governance.

Some practices were explained alongside examples to provide hints and practice guidelines for the reader, allowing the right approach based on internal strategy and consideration.

There is no silver bullet in design practice, and every practice or pattern is susceptible to changes depending on the context. This is why the examples in this book follows a general approach while also trying to show how to challenge and consider different trade-offs in the architecture decision-making process.

Index

A

B

C

F

G

H

I

L

R

S